New Horizons in Sociological Theory and Research

The frontiers of sociology at the beginning of
the twenty-first century

Edited by
LUIGI TOMASI
University of Trento, Italy

Ashgate

Aldershot • Burlington USA • Singapore • Sydney

Published by
Ashgate Publishing Limited
Gower House
Croft Road
Aldershot
Hampshire GU11 3HR
England

Ashgate Publishing Company
131 Main Street
Burlington, VT 05401-5600 USA

Ashgate website: http://www.ashgate.com

British Library Cataloguing in Publication Data
New horizons in sociological theory and research : the
    frontiers of sociology at the beginning of the twenty-first
    century
    1.Sociology
    I.Tomasi, Luigi
    301'.01

Library of Congress Control Number: 00-111409

ISBN 0 7546 2053 0

Printed and bound in Great Britain by MPG Books Ltd, Bodmin, Cornwall

Contents

PART II: THE NEW REALITIES OF TODAY: COSMOPOLITAN SOCIETY, GLOBALIZATION, ETHNICITY, NATIONALITY, IMMIGRATION

PART III: THE NEW FRONTIERS OF SOCIOLOGY

Sociology for the twenty-first century: necessary reconceptualizations

LUIGI TOMASI

Introduction

When at the beginning of 1999 I began preparation of this book by contacting eminent sociologists – some of them my friends – and enquiring whether they would contribute an essay, I received immediate support for a project that has now reached its successful conclusion.

I remember writing as follows in my letter to those who later became the book's authors:

> (t)he main intention is to describe the central task of sociology for the third millennium, to provide a profound and innovative interpretation of the changes now taking place world-wide. The second purpose of the book is to reflect on the complex structure and organization of sociological inquiry, revitalizing the discipline and beginning new and systematic analysis of theoretical and methodological problems essential for the survival of sociology.[1]

I decided to produce this book for two reasons. Firstly, I was prompted to do so by the criticisms and doubts that beset sociology and grow increasingly insistent and widespread. As Raymond Boudon points out in the book's opening essay,

> we cannot evade the issue of the criteria with which a theory may be defined 'scientific' in an age when scepticism as to sociology's ability to produce genuine knowledge affects even sociologists themselves (p. 48).

Sociology, it is frequently claimed, will grow increasingly unable to make a valid contribution to a proper understanding of society unless it undertakes profound renewal of its epistemological and methodological apparatus.

My second reason for producing this book is that I wanted, perhaps with a certain presumption, to draw up an agenda for sociology in the third

---

1   I refer to my letter sent to friends and colleagues on 10 March 1999.

millennium. The essays that follow are a rejoinder to the criticisms levelled against sociology: they mark out specific avenues of inquiry, and they conduct profoundly original theoretical and interpretative analysis. Topics can be extrapolated from them that are both *perennial* (because they are the constants of sociological analysis) and *pioneering* (because they concern issues proper to what Ulrich Beck calls 'the second age of modernity').

Pioneering inquiry is such because it examines the new features of contemporary society and the new forms of behaviour displayed by both individual and collective actors. Accordingly, there is *routine* type of sociological inquiry and constantly *innovative* sociological inquiry. When the latter flags, the discipline atrophies.

This book advocates innovation: the purpose of sociology is not to do sociology for sociology's sake, nor to develop theory merely to serve theory. Weber (1969) is still correct in his contention that sociology must seek to *understand* (*verstehen*) society. As Zdzisłav Krasnodębski succinctly puts it in his essay:

> (s)ociologists seldom let themselves be surprised by reality. Too seldom do they leave university and go to the 'real world' (p. 216).

It was the assumption that sociologists must 'go to the real world' that determined the birth itself of sociology; yet too often in the recent past this assumption has been pushed into the background. There are numerous reasons why this has been so, but the principal one is that sociological practice has grown often obsolete because it is devoid of the scientific features discussed by Boudon in the opening chapter.

I shall seek in this introductory essay to give a systematic yet brief account of the new frontiers of sociology by discussing, sometimes not without criticism, the various themes developed by the essays collected in this work.

Of course, my discussion cannot claim to be exhaustive; even less can it claim to cover all the numerous sectors of a discipline so complex as sociology. It is one interpretation among the many recently published (De Nardis, 1998; Abu-Lughod, 1999; *Contemporary Sociology*, vol. 29, no. 1, 2000; *American Sociological Review*, vol. 65, no.1, 2000; *The British Journal of Sociology*, vol. 51 no. 1, 2000), but it takes a different and independent slant. I shall refer to these publications as and when my discussion requires it.

In the fourth part of the introduction I shall point out a number of themes that the essays in this book do not deal with, or only treat in passing, but which I believe to be further areas for sociological inquiry. They concern issues which, in a context of globalization, are of major importance for the analysis of society. Which is, of course, the prime purpose of sociology.

1. Theory and research: new horizons

The first part of the book deals with the new horizons of sociology from the point of view of theory and research. It begins with a question that has accompanied sociology since its beginnings: that of its scientificity. This recurrent issue is addressed by Raymond Boudon in the chapter 'Sociology between scientism and aestheticism, or can sociology be positivist today?'.

Boudon's thesis, which he has already set out in his book *Le sens de valeurs* (1999: 349-85), is given further clarification here, and in view of its great topicality it very appropriately opens the book.

In answering the question 'Must we be so pessimistic about the past and the future of sociology?', Boudon opts, *sine conditio*, and setting Marxism and rationalism aside, for positivism, because

> it raises a question of essential importance for any discipline that claims to be scientific, that of the criteria with which to distinguish a scientific theory from one that is not, and with regard to scientific theories between those that are valid and those that are not (p. 48).

After acknowledging that positivism has made a valuable contribution by yielding 'a number of crucial intuitions', Boudon expounds the differing positivisms of Auguste Comte and Emile Durkheim, emphasising both the contrasts between the two thinkers' positions and their joint contribution to analysis of scientificity and non-scientificity in sociology.

Boudon's careful reading of Carnap's and Friedman's positivism, and of Popper's thought, prompts him to draw a distinction between 'hard' positivism ('Durkheim adhered to this distinctive programme') and its 'moderate' or 'soft' counterpart

> which maintains ... (the assertion of science as a higher form of knowledge), but proposes a completely different definition of scientificity insofar as it accepts (contrary to Carnap but in accordance with Popper or Friedman) the introduction of non-observable elements into a scientific theory and discussion of the acceptability of these unobservables (contrary to Popper and Friedman) (p. 52).

In so far as Popper and Friedman are 'a link between hard and soft positivism', Boudon contends that the latter enables us to give better account of the fact that a theory may be judged valid or invalid in the natural sciences, in the social sciences and in sociology in particular (p. 52).

As Boudon proceeds with his thorough discussion of the scientificity of science, he gives full credit to Popper's criteria. Nonetheless, he maintains that 'criteria define a necessary but not sufficient condition for scientificity and scientific validity' and therefore concludes that Popper's theory is inadequate. Boudon consequently accepts neither the positivism of Carnap and Friedman nor the 'critical rationalism' of Popper. Instead he argues for a 'moderate' or 'soft' positivism, which he sums up in three points:

a) (t)here are theories of a scientific nature and theories of a non-scientific nature;
b) (a) scientific theory must be amenable to evaluation in terms of its congruence with reality. Ideally, it should be constituted in such a way that it does not include incongruences with reality;
c) (t)hose of its elements and propositions which cannot be subjected to the congruence test must be considered acceptable, in the sense that they may be cited in explanation of other phenomena. The more numerous these phenomena, the more solid the guarantees that they offer to 'unobservables' (p. 57).

I take this to be the crux of Boudon's essay (although other important elements should not to be overlooked, notably its digression on 'American religiosity'), the part that is most innovative and with the closest bearing on sociology in the twenty-first century. The discussion of the scientificity and non-scientificity of a theory is all the more opportune in that it is an issue that the sociology of today, if it wishes to be a true science for tomorrow, cannot afford to ignore.

The question is certainly not a new one, for it was already posed at the beginnings of sociology. One thinks, for example, of the work by Albion Small in the United States and more generally that of the Chicago School of Sociology, the primary purpose of which was to construct a science – namely sociology – for the interpretation of society (Tomasi, 1998).

The distinctiveness of Boudon's analysis and the logic of its argument is of yet further importance. Given the rarity of such analyses, it opens a window onto what is now, and presumably will also be in the future, a new frontier for sociology: the issue of its scientificity and its ability to *reinvent itself.*

Can sociology continue to call itself scientific? What will be the value of classical sociology in the future? In what way might it be superseded and for what reasons? Clear answers to these questions are forthcoming from Michel Wieviorka's chapter 'Post-classical sociology, or the twilight of sociology?', which opens with the lapidary statement that 'Classical sociology is behind us'.

By means of careful historical reconstruction, Wieviorka traces the evolution of classical sociology from the age of Talcott Parsons until today. His survey culminates with the question: 'Is the destructuring of classical sociology more than simply a manifestation of the crisis of modernity as it was superseded by the onset of a post-modern era?'.

In his discussion of the birth of post-modernity, Wieviorka, with markedly critical intent, takes pains to emphasise the non-originality (they 'did not really invent new categories') of those theoreticians of the post-modern who

> stressed the urgent need to analyse a historic change characterized mainly by a split with everything articulated by modernity, or with what could still be envisaged as associated with it (p. 74).

This prompts the observation that

> post-modernism ... theorized the shift from the modern project to impose reason over tradition to a challenge raised against rationality itself. The result was images of a shattered modernity or, in the expression widely used today, of "multiple modernities" (ibid.).

The new context generated by post-modernity has spelt an end to a precise 'idea of society'. Here Wieviorka discerns a broad discrepancy between contemporary and classical sociology:

> classical sociology was interested in societies for which one could postulate or envisage a degree of correspondence among values, norms and roles, and in which the institutions played a central role. Its tendency towards evolutionism gave rise to the idea that every sub-set in society was defined by its place in modernization as a whole, in the universal process of progress. This correspondence increasingly seems to be artificial, and it is gainsaid by the facts, while the idea that there is 'one best way' towards progress or stages in economic growth appears to be pure ideology (p. 75).

With particular regard to my own research, I would point out that numerous themes now current – some of which are mentioned in this book – were addressed both theoretically and methodologically by the sociology of the late nineteenth and early twentieth centuries: suffice it to mention racism, which is an issue that Wieviorka knows very well (Wieviorka, 1991). Some of these themes belonged to the classical sociology of the time: numerous examples can be cited, but the matter becomes of importance if it is related to the debate on the scientificity of sociology and connected to the birth and growth of sociological theories.

Without lingering too long on the great themes analysed by the founding fathers of sociology, themes of even greater significance in the ongoing social change of today – *religion* (Weber, 1920), *suicide* (Durkheim, 1897), and the *positivism of sociology* (Comte, 1830-42) – I would mention three further areas of inquiry now on world sociology's agenda but which *have already been so* in the past: *immigration* (Park, 1928: 881-93), *sex and gender* (Thomas, 1898, 1899), and *social differences and social disorder in cities* (Smith and White, 1929).

The classical sociology of the late 1800s and early 1900s made a theoretical and interpretative contribution to the solution of these problems (as well as many others) that those who set out to understand similar problems today cannot ignore. Research and explanations often coincided with the foundation itself of sociology: perhaps we can apply here what Münch has written about Germany, whose

> classical period...was the time when the founding fathers set the framework of sociolog(ical) theory (Münch, 1994, 1:X).

What is the sense, for example, of studying sex and gender without taking account of the work of the above-mentioned William I. Thomas? What significance could attach to a study on immigration in Europe which failed to consider the findings of the Chicago School of Sociology? (Bulmer, 1984). How could any scientific study be made of integration without reference to the Chicago School's theory of assimilation and marginal man? (Park, 1913: 66-83). Pertinent in this regard is the following observation by Saskia Sassen:

> (i)t is perhaps one of the ironies at this century's end that some of the old questions of the early Chicago School of Urban Sociology should re-emerge as promising and strategic to understand certain critical issues today, notably the importance of recovering place and undertaking ethnographies at a time when dominant forces such as globalization and telecommunications seem to signal that place and the details of the local no longer matter. Yet the old categories of analysis are not enough (Sassen, 2000:144).

Why this digression? Because I believe that classical sociology and its findings should not be forgotten. Instead they should be flanked by the categories which the new social context necessarily imposes; rather than being consigned to oblivion, they should be *used* for new purposes. The problems of *yesterday* (immigration, racism, violence, and so on) are those of *today*, and in seeking to solve them the contributions of classical sociology cannot and must not be neglected. By this I mean that the classical period – which I define as the late 1800s and early 1900s – is still a period to which we should look for the solution of current problems. But this does not prevent me from agreeing with Immanuel Wallerstein (2000:1) that:

> (t)he golden era of sociology as a discipline was probably 1945-1965, when its scientific tasks seemed clear, its future guaranteed, and its intellectual leaders sure of themselves.

A further aspect scrutinized by Wieviorka in his essay is globalization, with regard to which he is highly critical of that 'lazy form of sociology' which neglects

> every institutional and political mediation between the system of globalization and those subjected to it, and underestimates the capacity for action of all the actors between the global elites and those who in one way or another undergo the effects or the consequences of their strategies (p. 77).

This prompts Wieviorka's forceful assertion that

> sociology will not advance if it restricts itself to a conception of globalization as a general principle for explanation of contemporary social problems (ibid.).

Here he conducts a critique which is given further development by Steven Grosby later in the book.

If on the one hand

> the advance of globalization provides sociology with the occasion to move upstream from classical sociology while resisting the ravages of post-modernism (p. 78),

on the other Wieviorka emphasises the need to re-examine the notions of society, nation and state, and to abjure classical sociology because

> it is no longer possible to postulate the systematic unity of society, nation and state, either as the sole reality for sociological analysis or as the only dimension that is possible or desirable (ibid.).

One of Wieviorka's most insightful remarks is that globalization invites the sociologist to address an array of problems and sub-problems by moving

> from the general, the global, the universal, to the singular, the local, and the individual him/herself – to the 'subject' (p. 79).

After reviewing various interpretations put forward in the past, amongst others by the Palo Alto school, Wieviorka comes to the nub of his analysis: the attribution of greater importance to the *subject*:

> (s)ociologists are now rediscovering the subject. Indeed, the main thesis propounded in this essay is that by focusing on the subject, sociological analysis will be much better equipped to enter the twenty-first century (p. 81).

This emphasis on the subject is undoubtedly the most innovative aspect of Wieviorka's chapter. He argues that the subject must *return* to the focus of sociological analysis, becoming *once again* the agent of his/her life. Which is, I believe, a powerful warning against a type of sociology, sometimes abstract, produced in the recent past and still common today; a sociology which with the passage of time has proved itself devoid of interpretative impact.

Wieviorka's analysis of these matters is profound, and he advances an articulated definition of the subject:

> in each individual, the subject is the capacity to struggle against the domination of instrumental reason... the capacity to withstand subordination to the community... the assertion of personal liberty... *But* the subject is also the ability to choose, to participate, to consume, to be a rational individual... (p. 82).

This emphasis on the subject is not only a matter of methodological reflection; it is also a critique brought against the consequences of global society and an invitation extended to the subject to *reappropriate* his/her decisions. Wieviorka's focus on the subject necessarily entails analysis of the diverse and sometimes harmful effects of globalization. The close discussion of the development process conducted in the final part of the essay further clarifies Wieviorka's highly apposite analysis.

Another important aspect discussed by Wieviorka concerns the institutions of the family and the school, as well as various movements, which should be studied 'from the point of view of the subject'. In this regard, sociology has too long restricted itself to *recording* the crisis of these agencies rather than *proposing* their new function for the subject. Evident here is criticism of a sociology that has only *interpreted* problems with new categories without proposing innovative policies. However, it should be pointed out that recent approaches to themes such as the *family* (Waite, 2000) or the *divorce culture* (Whitehead, 1998) propose interpretations that, I submit, differ from those of the past.

The final point covered by Wieviorka's essay is the ethical duty of sociologists:

the professional sociologist is an expert, a specialist; s/he possesses knowledge and expertise that identifies him/her with rationality and which s/he will use not in ideological political debates (p. 91).

This is of crucial importance for sociology, which not infrequently in the past has interpreted society more under the pressure of political interest than through the objective analysis of data. There are numerous examples of such behaviour, and Europe cannot claim to be an exception: who could forget the ideological interpretations propounded in the 1960s and 1970s? Krasnodębski's essay on Eastern Europe later in the book is very clear on the matter. If sociology is today on the defensive, and if as claimed it is not yet a full-fledged science, this is largely because it has been unable to resist the blandishments of the *sirens*, or of the *Prince of the moment*.

Wieviorka's reference to the profession of sociologist once again raises the important question of whether a sociologist can be a *professional* (Gollin, 1990). There is no disputing that sociology today occupies an important place among the social sciences. The public perceive it as able to furnish interpretations of – sometimes even solutions for – social problems, but it has not always performed this task honestly. As said, perhaps too often it has served instrumental purposes, and this conduct has not completely disappeared since the fall of the Berlin Wall.

Instrumental sociology is today at the service not so much of ideologies (Lemert, 1991), given their current decline, as of particular political factions which exploit the discipline for their own ends. Sociology's objectivity thus collapses, and so too does its interpretative validity.

Wieviorka's persuasive and stimulating arguments, together with his trenchant criticisms, are intended to bring the status of sociology up to date; a status that must be renewed through attention paid to the subject as it reclaims the central role that it occupied at the beginnings of sociology.

In the third chapter of the book, entitled 'The challenge of multiple modernities', Samuel Eisenstadt applies his customary methodical analysis to the great diversity of modernity, even in societies apparently similar in their economic features:

developments in the contemporary era ... have emphasised the great diversity of modern societies, even of ones similar in terms of economic development, like the major industrial capitalist societies (p. 99-100).

Eisenstadt's analysis of modernity makes specific reference to civilizations and their pluralism, given that close re-examination or reappraisal of the assumptions of studies on modernization may yield understanding of some of the problems facing sociology today (p. 100).

He focuses on what he calls 'the cultural programme of modernity', which with the passage of time has wrought major and fundamental changes in social life, or in what we might call the manner in which people live in society, bringing with it

the autonomy of man... 'his' emancipation from the fetters of traditional political and cultural authority, and on the continuous expansion of the realm of personal and institutional freedom, of human activity, creativity and autonomy (p. 102).

Eisenstadt considers this independence of man to be crucial in explanation of the plurality of orientations in modern society. It is, so to speak, the interpretative key to contemporary society, as well as being the very foundation of modernity.

The characteristics of modernity laid the bases for the modern political order, for collective identities and for new boundaries while the old order underwent profound modification:

(t)he core of the political programme of modernity was the breakdown of the traditional legitimation of the political order; with the concomitant opening up of different possibilities for construction of that order and contestation of the ways in which it was constructed (p. 103).

For Eisenstadt, the multiple programmes of modernity have generated strong convergences among contemporary needs:

but it is not only in the societies of Asia or Latin America that developments have occurred which go beyond the initial model of Western society. At the same time, in Western societies themselves new discourses have developed which have greatly transformed the initial model of modernity, undermining the original vision of modern and industrial society with its hegemonic and homogenizing vision (p. 110).

Equally stimulating is Eisenstadt's discussion of 'collective identities', the second theme treated in his chapter. Analysis of collective identities, or better of *new collective identities*, is of crucial importance for sociology, a contention borne out by developments in south-east Asia, and Cambodia in particular.[2]

---

2   Cambodia provides the clearest example for Eisenstadt's thesis. The country's national collective identity erased by the Pol Pot regime and then by the Vietnamese invasion is now being laboriously reconstructed.

The emergence of 'new types of collective identity' – a phenomenon, together with that of community, closely studied by Edward Shils (1996) – opens up new horizons for sociological analysis and requires the creation of new interpretative categories. It induces Eisenstadt to talk later in his essay of the fundamental relationship between 'elites' and 'collective identities', pointing out that

> continual changes in the composition of the elite gave rise to important changes in the constitution of collective identities (p. 119).

The theme of collective identities is of such especial significance today because globalization not only alter lifestyles but constantly generates new ones, and with ambivalent features. Collective identities take shape more rapidly than they did in the past, and they are also shorter-lived: consider the identities of young people, which arise and proliferate in forms of behaviour that constantly differ from those of the past as well as being transnational in nature (Tomasi, 2000a).

New identity or the reconstruction of identity – of both an individual and a society – stem both from the renewed importance of ethnicity, as Beck affirms when he talks of the 'ethnic globalization paradox', and from increasingly insistent territorial claims by ethnic movements in Eastern Europe (former Yugoslavia) but also in Africa (Burundi) and the Pacific (Fiji). The ethnic revolts that traverse the benighted continent of Africa, and those which keep a part of Europe in a constant state of conflict, testify to the role of ethnicity in the construction and reconstruction of collective identities. How has sociology responded to these problems in the past and what remedies does it propose today?

Once again the criticism applies: all too often sociology has done nothing more than record events, without developing theories capable of suggesting even a generic solution. The various flashpoints of ethnic conflict around the globe are still little studied, indeed they are often ignored, by sociological inquiry.

The ethnic movements discussed in the contemporary context by Eisenstadt's essay are of signal importance for sociological analysis. One might also add, without claiming powers of prophecy, that ethnicity and the conflicts that it provokes will be the subject of analysis and exploration by sociological theory in the future.

These various aspects link with the third theme addressed by Eisenstadt: that of the 'dramatic' transformation of the 'nation-state' consequent on 'the recent intensification of the forces of globalization', a process which has deprived the nation-state of much of its former power. This is a topic also discussed by Steven Grosby in this book, and elsewhere by Talis Tisenkopfs, which constitutes further proof of its importance.

Sociology's role and approach in the study of modern societies is also explored in Nico Stehr and Volker Meja's essay on 'Modern societies as knowledge societies'. Here the argument is that 'advanced modern society' is a 'knowledge society' characterized 'by the penetration of all of its spheres by scientific and technical knowledge'.

A prime feature pointed out by Stehr and Meja is the striking difference between contemporary society and that of the past:

> in present-day society knowledge has clearly become much more fundamental and even strategic for all spheres of life, greatly modifying and in some cases replacing factors that until recently had been constitutive of social action (p. 128).

Defining 'knowledge as capacity for action', the authors argue that

> it is dependent on (or embedded within) the context of specific social, economic and intellectual conditions (p. 129).

They then go on to examine 'the material realization and implementation of knowledge', 'the knowledge and the transformation of the economy', given that 'the emergence of knowledge societies signals first and foremost a radical transformation in the *structure of the economy*'. This transformation has been brought about by the economy of industrial society, where

> *knowledge* is emerging as the leading dimension in the productive process, the primary condition for its expansion and for change in the limits to economic growth in the developed world (p. 131).

Of particular significance is the passage in Stehr and Meja's essay which discusses pluralism and emphasises the rise of different forms of organization and also of thought:

> the emergence of knowledge societies does not mean that societies are becoming uniform social and intellectual entities. Knowledge as a capacity for action encourages the co-existence and interdependence of historically distinct forms of social organization and thought (p. 134).

Stehr and Meja accurately pinpoint the central component of knowledge societies in what they call the 'objectified knowledge' that consists of the highly differentiated stock of intellectually appropriated nature and society that constitutes society's cultural resource (ibid.)

what is generally termed 'modernization' or 'rationalization'. Although knowledge has always played a central role in 'human history', today it

is assuming a greater significance than ever before. Advanced industrial societies in particular may increasingly be regarded as "knowledge societies" (p. 137).

For evidence of this, the authors write, one need only look at the increased numbers of experts in contemporary societies and the major investments made in them.

Stehr and Meja's treatment prompts me to formulate, as is my duty, the criticism that they insufficiently emphasise the differences among knowledge societies. The contemporary world comprises a plurality of such societies – as Stehr and Meya rightly point out – not just one. Moreover, there is a North of the world with *strong* knowledge societies and a South of the world with knowledge societies which, given my first-hand experience of those regions, I would unhesitatingly call *weak*. Should these latter, the *weak knowledge societies*, be the object of sociological analysis in the twenty-first century? I believe that they should. Indeed, the knowledge differential may be one of the reasons for the wide gap between the North and South of the world, a question to which I shall return below in that it is undeniably a horizon, and a challenge, for the sociology of the twenty-first century.

Having outlined analyses that have indubitably augmented our sociological knowledge, I now turn to the final essay in this part of the book: Pierpaolo Donati's analysis of 'Freedom versus control in post-modern society: a relational approach'.

Donati begins his essay by drawing a distinction between 'lib theories', which interpret society 'from the side of freedom and as a function of freedom', and 'lab theories', which instead interpret society 'from the side of control and as a function of social control'. He then conducts detailed analysis of the transition from the modern to the post-modern, his thesis being that

the passage from modern to post-modern society is distinguished by the need to adopt a *relational approach* to the freedom/control distinction which is *post-lib* and *post-lab,* post-individualistic, post-holistic (p.149-50).

Donati is brought to this conclusion by the fact that

the crisis of the dialectic between freedom and control suggests that we are entering a post-modern era which will induce substantial changes in the most general assumptions of sociological theory (p. 149).

To resolve this crisis he proposes an alternative approach which is both distinctive and original.

Donati develops his theory in several stages:

> *lib* and *lab* theories are not true opposites. Instead, they are largely *complementary* (p. 150); freedom contradicts itself; social control loses its legitimacy (p. 153); the *lib/lab* code contradicts empirical evidence and subjective experiences of daily life (p. 155).

In discussion of Talcott Parsons' thought, after emphasising its theoretical positivism, Donati highlights those of its features which have now been superseded:

> Parsons' theory still assumes that: (i) freedom and control work within a certain symbolical framework of values, and (ii) they augment each other by respecting the famous cybernetic hierarchy. But both of these conditions have collapsed today (p. 157).

He then discusses the three alternatives that have arisen since Parsons ('anti-modern, neo-modern, post-modern') and declares:

> my thesis is that many of today's attempts to examine the relationship between freedom and control end up by merely taking note of implosions, irrationalities and distortions, rather than seeing positive aspects (p. 161).

Donati then turns to analysis of the 'communications paradigm'. This fails to convince him, for

> the paradigm of society as communication lends itself better than the previous one (*lib/lab*) to grasping the new social aspects. But I also believe that the communications paradigm does not offer an adequate view of freedom and control as social relations (p. 165).

Donati concludes by advocating what he has long called 'the relational approach', which seeks to provide a sociological representation of society consonant with the physiognomy that the latter has acquired over time (Donati, 1991).

The core of Donati's theory is its assumption that the social relation is the 'prime presupposition of sociology'. The purpose is to promote an awareness of society able to cope with the risks and challenges that increase inasmuch as artificial complexity brings with it a structural deficit in both reflexive capacity and orientation.

> Society is (and is becoming) post-modern if and to the extent that it takes the originative and original nature of social relations seriously (p. 167).

Donati's essay introduces the second part of the book, which is concerned more with macro-social issues and conducts reflection on social phenomena that affect society on a planetary level.

2. The new realities of today: cosmopolitan society, globalization, ethnicity, nationality, immigration

This part of the book deals with themes of paramount importance for the sociology of the twenty-first century. Discussed are issues that are constantly recurrent in the sociological literature, ones to which the authors devote considerable space, and on which they conduct analysis of signal interest.

They are issues, indeed, of such importance that sociology's responses to them will very probably determine its future as a discipline and a science. If sociology is able to interpret phenomena of such magnitude, it will consolidate its international status and gain recognition and respect in an age, that of the Internet, so very different from the period in which it was born.

The chapter that opens this part of the book – 'The cosmopolitan society and its enemies' – has been written by one of the foremost exponents of contemporary sociology: Ulrich Beck, whose 'deserved fame', as Zygmunt Bauman rightly points out, rests 'on the term *Risikogesellschaft*' (Bauman, 2000: 150). Beck's essay clarifies what to my mind is the most recurrent concept in the sociological literature: *globalization*.

> Globalization does not exist or happen as such; it is not a linear process, but a reflexive and dialectic one in which the global and the local (or the universal and the particular) do not exist as cultural polarities but are combined and mutually implicating principles (p. 182).

Globalization, argues Beck – who has also written a celebrated book on the subject (Beck, 1997) – imposes major conceptual and methodological changes on sociology. It firstly entails that social processes cannot be interpreted in the light of the nation-state because this is no longer their container; and secondly that sociology

> need(s) ...to explore and understand the emerging worlds of transnational flows, networks, socioscapes, life-forms, identities, classes and power structures. A sociology that remains happily glued to its own society and times will not have much to contribute (p. 183).

Thus, the first important aspect pointed out by Beck is that we are now moving towards a 'cosmopolitan sociology', or in other words towards a way of doing sociology that takes account of events at the world-wide level. But Beck emphasises a further aspect, this too of great significance:

> one of the most important consequences of the globalization discourse is the recovery of the concept of 'place' (...) The national must be rediscovered as the *internalized global*. (...) (The concept of globalization includes the) cosmopolitization of nation-state societies (p. 184).

The importance that Beck attributes to the local is evident.

A key part of Beck's analysis is its insistence on the need for new sociological categories, because

> normal sociology categories are becoming *zombie* categories, empty terms in the Kantian sense. Zombie categories are the living-dead categories, which blind sociology to the rapidly changing realities inside the nation-state containers and outside as well'. (...) We need descriptions and descriptive categories for economic flows and social networks of people and groups who live transnationally. (For this reason, Beck proposes) a sociology which must start all over again and redefine its basic research units, its categories, and its frame of reference (p. 185-6).

In this regard, Beck distinguishes between a 'nation-state sociology' and a 'cosmopolitan sociology': the former being 'based on a container theory of society', while the latter 'tries to redefine the sociological frame of reference under conditions of globalization, and so on'.

In his discussion of 'world culture', Beck – the author of a well-known study on the 'global market risk' in contemporary society – states that this world culture is

> the confrontation with fundamental differences everywhere and the necessity to live (with) these contradictory certainties somehow – often with violent outbursts (p. 189).

An important question raised by Beck concerns the content of what he calls 'cosmopolitan culture'. What precisely does this term mean? No advanced theoretical-methodological proposal has yet been put forward for a thorough interpretation of the phenomenon. Consequently, Beck's question goes unanswered and urges new interpretations of what is meant by 'world culture'. Later in the book Krasnodębski discusses the 'uniformity of sociology', a concept which seemingly comes close to that of 'world culture', as does that of 'global sociology' proposed by Goran Therborn (2000: 50).[3]

To this question one may perhaps add another: What is meant by a *cosmopolitan culture for the South of the world*? Does it not perhaps mean *Western culture*? Here, too, interpretation requires the devising of new categories.

A further issue of importance concerns the *enemies* of cosmopolization. Beck first calls attention to the 'ethnic globalization paradox' whereby in precisely a period of unity one witnesses the resurgence of ethnicity.

> In every corner of the world, ethnic identities are being refurbished and recast. What is so frightening about this ethnic resurgence is that all the different protest movements against globalization, willingly or unwillingly, seemingly enforce an ethnic and tribal reaction to the ambivalences and uncertainties of a post-national second age of modernity (p. 195).

The second enemy identified by Beck is 'globalism'.

> (G)lobalism, the free market ideology, is a powerful enemy of a cosmopolitan society. And there is the even greater danger that an alliance will arise between post-modern nationalism and global capitalism (a Haider capitalism in Europe and elsewhere) (p. 197).

The third and final phenomenon emphasised by Beck is the onset of what he calls 'New Democratic Authoritarianism': the process by which the state enforces its domains by violence and manipulation of the media. And this gives rise to what Beck calls the paradox of 'democratic authoritarianism'.

In conclusion, the analysis set out by Beck in his essay is a powerful call for the construction of a new type of sociology. It offers a set of crucial insights, both theoretical and methodological, for which reason its inclusion in this book is of great benefit to the reader.

While Beck addresses and develops a key theme by examining the sociological categories, the chapter by Zdzisław Krasnodębski, 'Sociology after the revolution in Eastern Europe: can it survive?', raises further questions concerning the role of sociology today, as well as conducting a critique of the sociology of the past.

---

3   Therborn offers various definitions of global sociology in his essay. The most incisive of them appears on p. 50: 'A global sociology means a sociology that takes globality and human social life on the planet Earth as serious issues'.

Starting from the acute observation that 'the transition to a new epoch happened, not at the turn of the year but eleven years previously in 1989 and in 1990', Krasnodębski emphasises that 'today's sociologists give different interpretations to many processes which were already visible in the past'.

The Polish sociologist argues that sociology claimed in the past to have the answer to all problems and harboured grand aspirations which combined

> two ideas at the same time: being a science of society and, paving the way for a new, better society (p. 205).

Krasnodębski is censorious, however, when he points out that 'sociology long remained silent on the dark sides of modernity', a fact on which sociology should reflect at length. Yet it is precisely with this critical reflection on the past that the new horizons for sociology unfold:

> (t)he opening of a new horizon for sociology demands on critical reflection on its own past (p. 206).

Critical retrospection is of paramount importance: one need only consider the Nazi era and Marxism to see that sociology has not always been 'on the side of democracy'. How routine it used to be to declare oneself a Marxist. Why do certain sociologists no longer do so? This is a matter on which sociology should ponder carefully.

Krasnodębski's powerful critique of sociology's Marxist past offers an occasion to observe how certain sociologists have bent sociology to service of the *Prince of the moment*, to employ the term used earlier. Of relevance here is Louis Horowitz's assertion, perhaps somewhat exaggerated, in his book *The Decomposition of Sociology*:

> sociology is now an ideology (or at least a set of ideologies) instead of what it had been in an earlier time, a *study* of ideology (...) Sociology has become a series of demands for correct politics rather than a set of studies of social culture (1993: 16-17).

Krasnodębski is no less critical in his treatment of a sociology unable to predict the fall of communism, perhaps the most significant event of the last century. He points out that

> Western sociologists missed one of the important historical events of our era, the decline of communism, which put an and to the twentieth century, (while) it was East European sociologists who joined the opposition movement (p. 208).

Krasnodębski thus brings a serious charge against the discipline, although he somewhat mitigates it later in his essay. A final observation by Krasnodębski concerns the uniformity of sociology:

> in my view it is not diversity that is a danger to sociology; dangerous is uniformity, which still exists despite the discipline's seemingly limitless diversity (p. 214).

He maintains that sociology must become more pluralistic (a conviction also expressed by Edward Tiryakian later in the book) and more positivist: it must concern itself more closely with the 'real world'; it must 'look more carefully instead of thinking too quickly'.

Perhaps implicit here is a call for a return to the methods (obviously updated) of the Chicago School of Sociology. I would add that the large body of literature on the latter published in recent years (Harvey, 1987; Bulmer, 1984; Alan Fine, 1995; Smith, 1988; Platt, 1996; Tomasi, 1998, 2000b; Abbott, 1999) is clear testimony to interest in the 'old methods of the sociological masters' discussed by Krasnodębski. My contention, however, may be called into question by Krasnodębski's judgement on classical sociology:

> (t)he classics of sociology are losing their influence and seem to be less popular than even before. Even sociologists like Karl Marx, Emile Durkheim, or Max Weber seem to be too Eurocentric or parochial. Perhaps Georg Simmel is the only exception (p. 212).

In short, Krasnodebski opportunely points up the limitations of sociology in the former Soviet empire and the features that it should assume in the twenty-first century. His call for more research in the 'real world' is an extremely useful recommendation for a renewed approach to society which bears in mind the past shortcomings of sociology.

Innumerable insights are offered by Talis Tisenkopfs in his essay on 'Globalization and peripheral identity'. Many of the themes addressed by this sociologist have been, or will be, discussed in other chapters.

In describing both the positive and negative aspects of globalization, Tisenkopfs defines it as

> a process that links people, organizations, markets, technologies, finances, information and governance together in one common interactive network stretching beyond the borders of national states (p. 223).

And a little later, citing Friedman, he writes that

(t)he discourse of globalization is based on the contraposition of the cold war system against the order of an open world (p. 223).

However, this assertion may be over-hasty, in that the connection that Tisenkopfs discerns between the cold war and globalization is the result not only of the contraposition that he mentions but also of a process that began much earlier and which resembles the one now apparent in North Korea.[4]

Basing his analysis on his own country of Latvia, Tisenkopfs evidences the difficulties faced by this and other countries in achieving the development that should allegedly spring from globalization.

Latvia and the other countries of the Baltic region and Central and Eastern Europe are undertaking an even more difficult mission to achieve rapid development and to maintain cultural identities in a world where frontiers are disappearing and competition grows increasingly fraught (p. 224).

Tisenkopf's observation highlights the difficulties that beset numerous countries in this period of transition – mainly but not only political – in adjusting to what was termed *world culture* earlier in this introduction. The difficulties consist in reconciling these countries' cultural specificity with the process that increasingly tends to standardize cultures world-wide. Here Tisenkopfs rightly doubts Latvia's ability to preserve its identity and its traditional values, or in other words, to sustain its current level of social cohesion.

The process of modernization, with its four characteristic features identified by Tisenkopfs as 'new markets, new technologies, new agents, new norms', has indubitably established a new relationship between centre and periphery, and in doing so has decided the winners and the losers.

Globalization may exacerbate backwardness and inequality for those individuals, nations and territories that do not have access to the new markets and technologies (p. 229).

Though persuasive, this view requires a certain amount of clarification. Firstly, equal and generalized development comes about *progressively* and *gradually*. Secondly, the reason that certain groups are marginalized, or even excluded, is largely *political* in nature, and responsibility for their marginalization or exclusion is to be laid at the door of elites. Thirdly, one

---

4   I refer to the meeting between the presidents of the two Koreas, Kim Dae Jung and Kim Jong II, at Pyongyang on 13 June 2000 and to the situation of severe shortages in the North, which resembles that of the Soviet empire immediately prior to the fall of the Berlin Wall.

should not neglect the democratic *maturity* or *immaturity* of the country in question.

Tisenkopfs emphasises in particular the impact of globalization on the individual in the populations of peripheral nations.

> The populations of peripheral countries experience stress, as their taste and consumer desires are dictated by global and usually Western standards ... (T)he inability to maintain this level of consumption creates stress and leads to corruption ... (T)he basic human condition is transforming under the pressure of globalization (p. 236).

These findings by a sociologist from the East such as Tisenkopfs evidence the contraposition between centre and periphery very clearly. The periphery, in present circumstances, is forced to rely on the centre, which is the West; or better, as Tisenkopfs puts it, it is forced to obey the latter's dictates. However, this situation may also arise within the West, where the gap between those countries able to exploit the benefits of globalization and those that are not is constantly widening. The case of Russia, as Silverman and Yanowitch (1997) have shown, is exemplary.

Today one is rarely able to talk of social classes, probably because in the past the expression carried ideological connotations; but one talks increasingly more of the rich and the poor, or of the *new rich* and the *new poor*: terminology which applies not only to the countries of Eastern Europe but also, as Pinches has recently well argued (1999), to those of Asia.

Also persuasive is Tisenkopfs's concluding statement, although it does not apply exclusively to peripheral countries:

> (u)nfortunately, differences between losers and winners have a tendency to become structurally embedded as the signs of inequality become more closely tied to specific social groups, such as rural residents, pensioners, single mothers, families with many children, the disabled, those in pre-pensionable age looking for work and those who lack the will, the skills, or the resources to find alternative employment in a competitive environment (p. 239).

The chapter by Steven Grosby on 'Mind and collective consciousness' develops the profoundly original thesis that

> (o)ne task facing sociology in the twenty-first century is to revive critically those earlier traditions of sociological analysis that refused to abjure the complexity of life as it is actually lived out of a misguided fidelity to the artificial simplism of a theoretical schema (p. 258).

Grosby starts by questioning what he calls the 'cultural uniformity' that has allegedly resulted from globalization. He supports his thesis by pointing out that

> the impartial observer cannot fail to recognize significant and ubiquitous counter-developments. Ethnic and national attachments, for example, have not yet been undermined by cross-national "interests" arising from participation in the international market, including, significantly, those areas of the world where an international market for goods and services is most developed, that is, in the industrially and technologically advanced Occident; for example, the devolution of Scotland from the United Kingdom, and such movements of secession as that of Quebec from Canada and Euzkadi from Spain (ibid.).

Grosby is critical of those who maintain that differences have become irrelevant, arguing that

> (s)uch a contradictory situation – where relatively rational and rationalizing tendencies co-exist with tendencies that are parochial – is not in fact new; rather, it seems historically to be the norm (p. 259).

Whence derives his censure of certain sociologists:

> it nevertheless appears that the rush among many sociologists to embrace 'globalization' as an analytic rubric descriptive of the Occident at the beginning of the twenty-first century may be overly hasty and simplistic (ibid.).

That 'may' suggests that although the general trend is indubitably towards globalization, a number of specifications are in order. This acute observation is substantiated by both *cultural pluralism* – which still persists, although as we saw in the previous chapter by Tisenkopfs, we cannot say for how long – and by the *ethnic claims* that have proliferated in the past ten years.

Here we may usefully draw on an essay by Ulrich Beck, 'The Cosmopolitan Perspective: Sociology of the Second Age of Modernity', in which he asks, while discussing national identities:

> (w)hat is the relationship of the number and kind of national identities to citizenship identity? Does cosmopolitanism cancel national identity? Or is there something like a "cosmopolitan nation" and what does that mean? (2000: 97).

I believe that Beck's question poses a challenge for the sociology 'of the second age of modernity', as the German sociologist terms it. A tentative answer may be inferred from John Rex's studies on ethic relations, and especially from his 'concept of multi-cultural societies' (1986: 119-35).

Grosby is also critical of that certain brand of sociology which propounds a dichotomous interpretation of the passage from *Gemeischaft* to *Gesellschaft*.

> (T)he distinction between the historically earlier and religiously infused *Gemeinschaft* and the later and putatively secularized *Gesellschaft* should be rejected as antiquated, as a relic of a previous theoretical perspective that has been rendered invalid by subsequent historical developments (p. 260).

This assertion Grosby justifies as follows:

> (T)he most manifest of these developments, evident at the beginning of the twenty-first century, are two. The first is the persistence of religious attachments – a persistence described increasingly by some as 'fundamentalism' ... The second development is the persistence of ethnicity and nationality not only in Asia and Africa, but also in the Occident – a persistence that indicates the resilience, however susceptible to transformation, of the attachment to the primordial objects that bear the significance of vitality: territory and varying structures of kinship (ibid.).

Here Grosby takes certain interpretations to task and takes the permanence of nationality, ethnicity and religion as the central pillar for his argument. To be sure, with specific regard to religion, we are very far from the advent of a *world religion*, but we nevertheless witness, and with increasing frequency, the strengthening of the bond between identity and religion, the spread of a *religious pluralism*, and the constant birth of *new religious movements* (Dawson, 1996, 1998).

Today, perhaps more than ever before, we observe the persistence and indeed resurgence of religion in the various parts of the world. Even in those countries where religion has been viciously repressed, it is now re-emerging. Indeed, it is now prominently displayed on national emblems: a case in point being Cambodia's in which, despite the ferocious regime of Pol Pot, religion is at the centre of the nation's three-word motto: 'Nation, Religion, King'.[5]

Grosby sets out his critique of sociology in the following terms:

> the prevailing theoretical apparatus remains a simplistic one that too often views human action today as being entirely within the category of *Gesellschaft*, and, as such, homogeneous (ibid.).

---

5   On 21 September 1993, the Cambodia constitutional assembly adopted the Constitution promulgated by the head of state three days later. Article 4 runs as follows in the French translation: 'La devise du Royaume est: La Nation, la Religion, la Roi'.

This position

> rejects an understanding of human action and association as uniform in favour of a recognition of a plurality of incommensurable orientations and associations (p. 261).

Thus we have the persistence of 'symbolic complexes that are constitutive of ethnicity, nationality, and religion'.

These acute observations are intended to draw attention to the object of sociology, which Grosby identifies uncompromisingly as follows:

> (t)he subject matter of sociology ... is preoccupied with the consequences of the existence of the human mind' (p. 261) (or, as he then puts it) the pluralistic orientation of the mind (p. 273).

The chapter by Grosby affords insights of great theoretical interest and it sheds extremely useful light on contemporary society. Unfortunately, however, space precludes its further discussion.

The final chapter of this part of the book – 'Beyond national and post-national models: transnational spaces and immigrant integration' written by Thomas Faist – deals thoroughly, and not without some complexity, with one of the most dramatically important issues of the century. Faist states his thesis thus:

> this analysis presents the various patterns of transnational ties entertained by immigrants in transnational spaces, and reviews their implications for concepts of integration in immigration countries. To the canonical models of assimilation, ethnic pluralism and post-modernism, it adds a new and thus apocryphal concept of border-crossing expansion of social space (p. 278).

Faist analyses aspects that have been much discussed in the past, but he does so from a fresh perspective: he flanks the models of 'assimilation', 'ethnic pluralism' and 'post-modernism' with the 'concept of border-crossing expansion of social space', arguing that

> the reality of these transnational exchanges and the growing legal tolerance of multiple membership indicates that migration and return migration are not definite, irrevocable and irreversible decisions. Transnational lives in themselves may become a strategy of survival and betterment (ibid.).

In his complex and comprehensive treatment, of which I can only give an outline here, Faist develops a variety of concepts, but most notably that of 'transnational spaces'. These differ from clearly demarcated state territories. 'Space' here denotes the cultural, economic and political practices of individual and collective actors within territories or places. Thus, the term 'space' does not only pertain to physical characteristics, as in a more traditional geographical orientation, but also comprises the ties among actors in pluri-local places, whereas 'place' refers to one specific location (p. 281).

Faist naturally takes cognisance of the theories of assimilation and ethnic pluralism, to which he connects his model of the 'border-crossing of social space'.

The proposition is that neither nationally-bounded container models such as assimilation and ethnic pluralism, nor limitless ideas of post-nationalism and post-modernism capture all facets of immigrant integration in today's world (p. 289).
Account should be taken of the following three seminal changes in international migration: ongoing international migration flows, albeit guided by restrictive policies on the side of immigration countries; an ongoing communications and transport revolution; and diversifying economic opportunities for immigrants (p. 290).

The assimilation process, which Faist defines as

the melting of immigrants and their offspring into the majority core of the immigration country in all spheres of public and private life (p. 291),

is perhaps the most pressing of contemporary problems. Today, in fact, the tendency is not to be assimilated, or rather to be assimilated with difference, which means becoming part of the nation but preserving one's cultural characteristics or specificities, and not solely religious ones.

Faist's chapter furnishes further useful insights (the models of 'ethnic pluralism', 'dual citizenship', 'transnational communities', and 'acculturation') with which to interpret, and with increasing profundity, the phenomenon of emigration: a phenomenon which, as said at the beginning of this introduction, is one of the most significant of the present epoch, and whose analysis is undoubtedly of prime importance for the sociology of tomorrow.

Having outlined the main issues and aspects examined in the second part of this book, we may now move to the third, which discusses the agenda for sociology in the twenty-first century.

3. The new frontiers of sociology

This, the third part of the book deals specifically with the new frontiers of sociology. Edward Tiryakian opens his chapter on 'Some challenges for sociology in the new era' as follows:

> (t)he present juncture is indeed a critical period for sociology, fundamentally because we are entering a new era; not so much a new chronological era as a new era in the human condition, one which for sociology as a discipline, and for sociological theory as the centre of the 'sociological imagination' demands a rigorous stock-taking and reappraisal of its conceptual framework and boundaries (p. 316).

Tiryakian's profound theoretical essay makes a major contribution to marking out sociology's new frontiers. Sociology, he maintains, is a science which will prove of great relevance in the future as it orients itself towards the new: towards what one might call the 'avant-garde'.

Tiryakian discerns this new era in movements that traverse the traditional boundaries of the nation-state amid profound technological change and globalization. He adds that

> the new era envisaged here is also characterized by vast new *mappings* of the world, from the depths of the ocean to the celestial heights opened up by the Hubble telescope as a window on a near-infinity of galaxies which increase the possibility that life exists elsewhere; and perhaps of even greater potential significance for sociology (p. 317).

Tiryakian descries new possibilities for sociology in so far as

> democratization and economic development, singly if not together, tend to favour new centres of sociology, in different regions of the world with different experiences of modernization in the past half century (ibid.).

This view – which he largely shares with Eisenstadt – prompts him to assert that a 'remapping of sociology' is necessary. The new era is also one

> in which systematic knowledge is implemented in the technological adaptations of this knowledge to alter basic features of our biosphere (ibid.).

After discussing the theories advanced by Donald Levine and Martin Albrow, whose contribution to analysis of the 'global age' he deftly summarizes, Tiryakian turns his attention to issues such as the 'nation-state' or 'global citizenship', dwelling on the current pluralism of sociology.

(T)he discipline in all its proliferation and in terms of its political temper has evolved too much for a single voice today to provide an authoritative assessment in the manner of Talcott Parsons some forty years ago (p. 318).

As he describes the most important events of the twentieth century, Tiryakian highlights those of a political-social nature, and in particular the collapse of the Soviet empire – an event that 'Sovietologists' failed to foresee – ethnic nationalism, and religious fundamentalism. At this juncture, he acutely points out that

it is more likely that the coming decades of the new century hold more large-scale surprises in store, some undoubtedly pleasant, some nasty, in some regions and some countries, than that there will be smooth continuity in the globalization process (p. 328).

Tiryakian believes that technology will continue to advance in the new era. As he aptly points out:

(t)echnological change (which of course is not a single entity) should be viewed as an independent or intervening variable in the translation and transfiguration of "nature" to the human condition (p. 329).

Finally, as in Wieviorka's essay – and like Therborn (2000: 46) – Tiryakian emphasises the importance of a sociological approach to biology: '(g)enetic therapy, transgenic implants, genetic counselling, genetic mapping are related features of the emergent transformation of the human condition in the new era'.

In the following chapter in this part of the book, 'Toward a science of global marginality', Anthony J. Blasi argues that

(t)he principal empirical trend that I suspect will set the agenda for a social science in the twenty-first century is the detachment of systems of marginality from their former geographical bases (...) I suspect that in the coming century the sociology of education will need to focus on a division between an informal transnational system and many formal local systems (p. 339-41).

An important issue addressed by Blasi's chapter is oppression, for which he provides a complete and ramified definition.

Oppression is the stratagem of depriving people with an objective interest in jeopardizing the position of elites of the resources with which to exert power. To be denied the resources of power is to be debilitated, to be made weaker (p. 342).

Physical or social oppression may be opaque in form; it 'becomes *opaque* when culturally prescribed motives for retaining existent elite statuses come to be institutionalized separately from the culturally prescribed motives for changing them'.

In this regard, Blasi writes, traditional oppression was a political practice whilst today the pattern of traditional oppression has come to an end in most places of the world.

> A sociology of the new marginality would examine the negotiation of boundaries between the various institutional orders...the aggregations of resources that make some institutions macro, the separate recruitment of people into the macro and micro organizations, the recruitment into upward mobility tracks and non-upward mobility tracks within macro organizations, the socialization of new participants in macro versus micro organizations, and the formation of newly politicized interest groups within the macro/micro structure (p. 345).

Here Blasi examines the new marginalities and the role that sociology should perform in analysing them.

Blasi also discusses the marginality of the family in the twentieth century on the premise that it

> has lost its ability to provide its members with a small community as the economic roles have been removed from family farms and family businesses and located within work places away from the home (p. 346).

His insistence on the marginality of the family may be somewhat over-stated, however, given that recent surveys of young people have shown that the family – obviously defined in different terms from those used in the past – is still one of their principal value-referents.

The third essay in this part of the book, 'New horizons in religious evolution' by Yves Lambert, conducts a panoramic survey of contemporary religious phenomena. Central to Lambert's treatment is his view of modernity as a new 'axial period':

> the hypothesis of modernity as a new axial turn prompts consideration of very long-term effects, those of civilizations, and enables comparative study and an interpretation which accounts not only for religious decline but also for revivals, mutations and inventions (p. 353).

The principal concern of Lambert's article is to examine the effects of modernity on religion, and most notably 'the primacy given to reason', 'science', 'individual consciousness and freedom', 'the emergence of the masses on the historical stage', 'the development of capitalism', 'functional differentiation and globalization'. All these phenomena have impacted on religion, with effects that Lambert describes with clarity and precision, backed by detailed documentation and, where possible, empirical research. Lambert identifies

> four typical religious effects for each feature of modernity: decline, adaptation or re-interpretation, conservation and innovation (p. 363).

He then specifies the religious outcomes produced by modernity as

> the *disassociation between sin and one's fate after death, de-hierarchization, de-dualization, bringing nearer the human and the divine,* the *pluralistic, relativistic, ubiquitary forms of faith* (p. 375-77).

Lambert also discusses the

> *self-spirituality* where the desire for freedom is combined with empiricism in a pluralistic environment (p. 375).

In this instance, although I fully agree with Lambert, I would prefer the definition of contemporary religion as a *supermarket*,[6] (Tomasi, 2000c) because it emphasises the practice of picking and choosing among religions for the elements most suited to personal needs. This a less categorical concept than those of *self-religion or self-spirituality,* which are perhaps more applicable to the founders of a religion, of a sect, or of one of the many religious movements that abound today. The aim of Lambert's essay is less to draw conclusions than to prompt further research by sociologists of religion. It is an analysis that problematizes more than it resolves; a study from which the sociology of religion may start in its further exploration and inquiry. One of its most distinctive features, moreover, is that it does not deal with Catholicism alone, but unlike much sociology of Western religion, extends its compass to other religions as well. I shall return to this topic later.

The chapter written by Dirk Kaesler, 'Sociology in the twenty-first century: a discipline at the crossroads between senility and regeneration', resumes the argument on the purposes of sociology. Of the five questions posed and addressed by Kaesler in his article, the fourth is perhaps of especial importance:

> (w)hat might be the agenda for sociological intellectuals in the twenty-first century? (p. 383).

---

6   The reference is to my study based on interviews with young people aged 18-30.

Kaesler's analysis is essentially concerned with sociology's role in the conduct of intellectual inquiry. Starting in the relatively distant past with discussion of Comte, Quételet, Tönnies and Weber, Kaesler goes on to explain what was, and still is, the project of sociology. This Kaesler sums up as follows:

> (s)ociology is still the intellectual enterprise by which one can learn about human beings and about society without direct practical and professional application outside the reproduction of academic sociology itself. And the ultimate aim of such learning is to help human beings understand themselves as members of societies and comprehend the working of societies and their history, to help them cope with society and not only remain prey to social pressures or so-called historical laws (p. 388).

Also of great interest, and resuming the topic of the first part of the book, is Kaesler's discussion of the crisis of sociology:

> (i) believe that one crucial reason for the atmosphere of discontent is the fact that the sociological quest for a 'good society' has been almost totally banned from the scientific agenda of academic sociology. This, I argue, has led to something akin to an intellectual paralysis of sociology. The original belief in science – in former times almost grotesquely strong – has changed into complete subjectivity and the well-known mentality of 'anything goes' (p. 388-89).

Kaesler reasserts the 'moral mission' of sociology with impassioned conviction, declaring that of paramount importance

> is putting an end to the paradigmatic separation wrought by the infamous micro- and macro-version of sociological theories, as well as to the split between quantitative and qualitative methods in social research (p. 389).

In this regard I would observe that though the former objective is still feasible, the latter – also discussed by Horowitz (1993: 9) – is probably impracticable, given that the dichotomy between quantitative and qualitative methods is by now irremediable.

However, Kaesler's central concern is

> the necessity for sociology as a discipline to participate in attempts to find therapies of moral orientation for human beings who have not only lost their orientation but are desperately looking for it (p. 390).

And again:

> (t)he challenge facing sociology is to help and participate in the construction of new forms of value-consensus in a contemporary world of such complexity and differentiation (p. 391).

Kaesler thus re-plots the subject matter of sociology and the role of history in the discipline, affirming its currency and importance with both enthusiasm and cogency. His treatment brings to mind a remark made by R. W. Connell in his article 'Why is Classical Theory Classical?':

> What we need instead of "classical theory" is better history – sociological history – and an inclusive way of doing theory (1997: 1546).

The final chapter in the book, 'The idea of alternative discourses', has been written by Syed Farid Alatas. It is a chapter apparently different from the others but which discusses an important issue: the colonialism of science, and with specific reference to Asia. Alatas defines 'alternative discourses' as

> a descriptive and collective term referring to that set of discourses that emerged in opposition to what was understood to be mainstream, Euroamerican social science (p. 400).

And again:

> (a)lternative discourses are also, implicitly or explicitly, concerned with the analysis of the problems presented by the structure of the world system of social science, in which the dominant discourse of the core social science powers of the United States, Great Britain and France result in conformity, imitation and lack of originality in the periphery (p. 400-1).

A little later Alatas gives further specification to his definition:

> the aims and objectives of alternative discourses are not to be understood simply in negative terms, in terms of delinking from metropolitan, neocolonialist control. They are also to be understood in a more positive way, in terms of the contribution of non-Western systems of thought to theories and ideas (p. 401).

Alatas bases his treatment on the premise that Asia's intellectual culture must change because it is too deeply imbued with Western culture, and on the conviction that

> the project of alternative discourses in Asian sociology is equivalent to the task of creating relevant sociology (p. 406).

The merit of this chapter is that it poses the problem of the interpretation – in this case of Asia, although the problem concerns other parts of the world's South as well – by the West: a long-standing issue that has generated not a few problems of comprehension.

A possible remedy may lie in the 'new centres of sociology' which, as Tiryakian pointed out in his essay, are now arising almost everywhere in the world as a result of different experiences of modernization. And this raises the problem of theories – or better the validity of theories – developed in the West to account for realities which are culturally very distant from it.

The issue raised by Alatas should spur sociology to develop *new indigenous* theories – which recalls the 'multiplication of indigenous sociologies' discussed by Wieviorka – and to problematize the *importing* of Western sociology. The point has a great deal in common with the notion of 'postcolonial discourse' set out by Linda Tuhiwai Smith in her book *Decolonizing Methodologies: Research and Indigenous Peoples* (1999), and with the call by Su-Hoon Lee in *Sociology in East Asia and Its Struggle for Creativity* (1998) for 'indigenous sociological methods' based on local history and traditions.

I would add that analyses such as that conducted by Alatas are relatively rare in sociology, a fact which demonstrates the extent to which the discipline as a whole is still highly *Westernized*. There is no doubt, however, that the process of globalization so thoroughly discussed in this book will throw up *local* (international) problems to which the discipline will have to provide equally *local* answers (ones, that is, which concern a specific geographical area).

4. Further new horizons

As stated at the outset, this book and the present introduction lay no claim to being exhaustive or to providing an all-inclusive treatment of the issues that will confront sociology in the future. Rather, the purpose is to focus on *some* of these issues, the ones that I believe to be today most urgent.

Various other sociologists – all of whom I obviously cannot list here, although I must at least mention Janet L. Abu-Lughod editor of the already-mentioned *Sociology for the Twenty-first Century. Continuities and Cutting Edges* (1999) – have recently marked out further avenues for sociological research. Andrew Abbott, for example, in his densely-argued essay 'Reflections on the Future of Sociology' maintains that 'there are two aspects of sociology: social structural and intellectual' (Abbott, 2000: 296). With reference to the former aspect he states that

> the main structural event of the near future for U.S. sociology will be the contact with the newly robust sociologies of Europe, with their heavy funding, their

quasi-experimental analytic object, their powerful social data bases, and their relative freedom from the hard work of teaching that is the foreground of daily experience for most American sociologists (ibid.: 298).

With regard to the latter, Abbott argues that

> the first intellectual challenge for the sociological future flows from the technological transformations of the last two decades (ibid.: 298-9); a second basic intellectual challenge arises from the sheer passage of time, (while the third is) to rebuild general social theory. Sociology needs a big new theoretical idea (ibid.: 299).

Although Abbott's reflections fail to convince as far as the former, structural aspect is concerned, given that American sociology's *tradition* and *consolidated market* put its organizational capacity beyond question, they can be fully endorsed regarding the need for a new theory, as the essays in this book have shown.

Equally interesting is the analysis by R.W. Connell, who argues in 'Sociology and World Market Society' that

> (t)he future of sociology, if it is to escape marginalization and slow decline, is to be reconstituted as a democratic science – as the self-knowledge of global society. This necessarily means new media, new forms of research, and above all, new participants. The greatest obstacle to the advancement of sociology is sociology's professionalism. Every organizational move that limits participation in sociological work, that constitutes sociology as a closed unit or a self-contained culture, is against sociology's long-term interests (Connell, 2000: 294).

Other approaches by sociologists are more concrete, so to speak, but no less important. One prevailing notion is that of 'reducing inequalities', which Jacqueline Johnson, Sharon Rush and Joe Feagin explain in their article 'Doing Anti-Racism: Toward an Egalitarian American Society' (2000: 95-120). Although these authors are specifically concerned with reducing racism in the United States, the more general purpose of their article is 'to create a society where respect for humanity, rather than racial hierarchy, is the social foundation' (ibid.: 96).

Making further significant contributions to current theory are the studies by Amitai Etzioni, 'Creating Good Communities and Good Societies' (2000: 188-95), Pepper Schwartz, 'Creating Sexual Pleasure and Sexual Justice in the Twenty-first Century' (2000: 213-19) and Peter Evans, 'Fighting Marginalization with Transnational Networks: Counter-Hegemonic Globalization' (2000: 230-41). These authors highlight issues that the sociology of the next century cannot ignore; issues, for that matter, already the subject of sociological debate. Particularly noteworthy, given their great topicality, are the articles by Anthony Oberschall, 'Preventing Genocide' (2000: 1-13) and Frederick H. Buttel, 'Ending Hunger in Developing Countries' (2000:13-27). The former article, with its striking title, draws sociology's attention to the prevention of genocide and forcefully poses the problem of *ethnic conflicts*:

> (t)he twenty-first century is about to start with a huge backlog of unresolved, severe ethnic conflicts (2000: 1).

The latter focuses on the equally dramatic problem of continuing hunger in the developing countries, while a related topic is the *new slavery* well described by Kevin Bales in his recent book *Disposable People: New Slavery in the Global Economy* (1999).

I doubt that anyone would dispute that these are problems on sociology's agenda for the twenty-first century; indeed they are integral to that agenda, together with others already mentioned. And this, by different routes, brings us to the crux of all problems: *underdevelopment* in the world, a theme frequently mentioned in this introduction, an issue of paramount importance, and a concrete problem still awaiting solution.

As I move towards the conclusion of this introduction, the theme of underdevelopment introduces two further aspects bound to be of crucial importance in the coming century: religion and young people. The four questions – *development, underdevelopment, religion* and *young people* – will, I believe, mix and sometimes merge on the agenda of twenty-first-century sociology.

Much has been written and *theorized* about development, and also about underdevelopment. On the strictly sociological side, theory has concentrated on the process of modernization, seeking to relate the difficulties of what used to be called the Third World countries to the process of modernization typical of the developed countries – those, that is, of the West (Peet, 1999).

The sociology produced on these matters has been essentially a *Western sociology*. In the 1960s, analysis of the development/underdevelopment relationship connected it closely to the independence of nations, in both Africa and America.

This was indeed a new interpretative approach, but the theory that sprang from it was largely *immediate* in its character. That is to say, it was concerned with *how* to bridge the gap between North and South rather than with understanding *why* the problems existed. This, therefore, was not a Weberian sociology of *verstehen* but predominantly a sociology of Marxist, or distorted Marxist, inspiration.

The ongoing tragedy of underdevelopment in the world stems from an array of problems that go well beyond colonization and extend their roots into local *cultures* and *elites*. It is, I believe, precisely the phenomenon of *culture* that provides the key to proper understanding of underdevelopment. My conviction is borne out by the findings of Ronald Inglehart and Wayne E. Baker in their essay 'Modernization, Cultural Change, and the Persistence of Traditional Values':

> (e)conomic development is associated with major changes in prevailing values and beliefs. The worldviews of rich societies differ markedly from those of poor societies. This does not necessarily imply cultural convergence, but it does predict the general direction of cultural change and (in so far as the process is based on intergenerational population replacement) even gives some idea of the rate at which such change is likely to occur (Inglehart and Baker, 2000: 50).

More important than ever before at the beginning of the twenty-first century is the *indigenization* of development theory. Western categories are inadequate: they are, to use Beck's expression, 'zombie categories'.

A sociological theory of development must devise an approach able to promote at least minimal development. It must start with the fundamental elements of local culture, especially in rural areas, and ensure that it does not foster or reproduce a two-speed development. A sociology of this kind must also seek to articulate a theory which seeks to *resolve* problems, rather than producing *arid surveys* of those same problems.[7]

In view of all its implications for the lives of people and groups, this approach cannot be uncoupled from the new frontiers of the sociology of religion.

The classical era of religion – the period leading up to the 1920s – is the one that has been most written about, and it comprised the lives of the founding fathers of sociology: Comte, Durkheim and Weber.

The debate on Max Weber's and Emile Durkheim's theories on religion has been, and in certain respects continues to be, a constant feature of the sociology of religion. It has undoubtedly been a productive debate, in that it has greatly encouraged the growth of the discipline, but at the same time it has been *sterile* in that it has stunted analysis of religious phenomena.

The historical period in which Weber developed his sociology of religion

---

7 Innumerable attempts have been made to redefine or rethink development. None of them has produced satisfactory results.

was profoundly imbued with modernity. Weber lived at a time when feudal Europe had been superseded, and in which European consciousness was undergoing profound evolution. Another type of person came to the fore, a person forcefully shaped by the *city* and by the *contract*: the person described by Georg Simmel.

Max Weber was influenced by religion as it is *practised*. This he had witnessed at first hand during his travels through America in 1904 and it had, I submit, a decisive impact on his *Die protestantischen Sekten und der Geist des Kapitalismus* first published in 1904 - 1905. His analysis was intended to construe an important phenomenon of the time, the 'spirit of capitalism', or better the difference between the spirit of modern and ancient capitalism – as also evidenced by some of his previous writings.

In his introduction to the Italian edition of Weber's *Sociology of Religion* (1982), Pietro Rossi writes that

> Weber was not interested in – or at least he had not yet addressed – the problem of the origin of modern capitalism considered in terms of its overall structure and functioning. He was concerned with a more specific question, that of the origin of the spirit of modern capitalism, and this brought him to the more general question of the relationships between economy and religion. Secondly, unlike Brentano who later identified the origin of capitalism with the monetary economy, Weber did not discern the beginnings of modern capitalism or of its 'spirit' in medieval Europe. Instead, he identified them in the moment when the Protestant Reformation split away from medieval religiosity (M. Weber [1920] 1982: vol. I, XVI).[8]

Rossi maintains, therefore, that Weber's prime intention was to study ongoing change in society, and that it was this endeavour that brought him to religion. It was, in other words, Weber's desire to explain the capitalist economy that induced him to analyse the *universal religions*:

> the study of the relationship between the Protestant ethic and the capitalist spirit amounts to comparative analysis of the universal religions from the point of view of their economic ethics (M. Weber [1920] 1982: vol. I, XXII).[9]

Herein lies the core of Weber's sociology: the analysis of religion signifies historical-comparative analysis conducted in order to elucidate the Protestant ethic and the spirit of capitalism 'as produced by the development of the modern West'.

For too long the sociology of religion did no more than furnish statistics

---

8   Translated from the Italian.
9   Ibid.

on the church memberships and their religious vitality (Le Bras, 1955), thereby hampering the study of more far-reaching religious phenomena. For twenty-odd years sociological studies confined themselves to surveys on the percentages of people who prayed, who believed, who observed their church's precepts. Such analysis may have yielded information of use to individual churches, but it did little to increase knowledge of religion as such. And it was very different from Weber's conception of the discipline.[10]

From the 1960s onwards, the leading analysts of religious phenomena were mainly North-American sociologists (Berger, 1967), though not exclusively so (Luckmann, 1963). This was an important period for two reasons. Firstly because the sociology of religion was enhanced, from both the theoretical and empirical points of view, by its abandonment of the purely historical and sociographical approach. Secondly because it extended its compass beyond solely institutional or ecclesial religion.

In the meantime, however, there had been growing debate on *secularization*, a term that would long condition the sociology of religion and the study of religious phenomena. Secularization attracted most interest in Europe, where its study proceeded *pari passu* with the evolution of European society: a society in transition, and increasingly affluent as it left the rural world and moved towards the *industrial* and *urban* system.

The evolution of society had a profound impact on a sociology of religion which at times seemed entirely preoccupied with the decline in *religious practice*.

A great deal was known in that period about religious institutions, mainly Christian, but very little about the other great religions. The crisis of the sacred was announced in Europe, but insufficient study was made of the situation in other continents.

Only recently have religious phenomena been analysed from other standpoints. Theories have appeared which, although still distant from those of the classical period, evince a new need to interpret religion and to develop new paradigms (Warner, 1993: 1044-93). This awareness has gradually gained ground among sociologists, some of whom are beginning to realize that the theory of secularization has its shortcomings, although prior to the 1990s little was done to confute it. Of signal relevance here is another passage from Inglehart and Baker's already-mentioned essay.

> The secularization thesis is oversimplified. Our evidence suggests that it applies mainly to the industrialization phase - the shift from agrarian society to industrial

---

10   By this I mean that interest waned in sociology of religion *à la* Weber.

society that was completed some time ago in most advanced industrial societies. This shift was linked with major declines in the role of the church, which led Marx and others to assume that, in the long run, religious beliefs would die out. The shift from agrarian to urban industrial society reduces the importance of organized religion, but this is counterbalanced by growing concerns for the meaning and purpose of life. Religious beliefs persist, and spiritual concerns, broadly defined, are becoming more widespread in advanced industrial societies (Inglehart and Baker, 2000: 49).

The discussion thus far suggests that the time has come for the sociology of religion to analyse the sacred from other perspectives. This is because in the contemporary context of rapid globalization the approach to religious phenomena must diversify if it wishes to be *truthful*.

The analysis of religion must necessarily concern itself with the problem represented by the countries of the South of the world. Here the relationship between *development* and *religion* is of fundamental importance if we are to understand the reasons for those countries' *non-development*; the reasons, that is, for the existence of a North and a South.

As said, there was in the past a certain tendency in the West to interpret non-European or non-American realities using Western categories but overlooking a particular and crucial element: the *culture*, and therefore also the religion or religions, of those countries.

I have lost count of how many times I have travelled to the countries of the world's South and witnessed their abject misery at first hand. And on each occasion I have asked myself the same questions: What are the causes of so much poverty? Why is the South still the South and the North still the North? After working in Cambodia for several years, I have come to realize that traditions may, even today, not only hamper development but also give rise to perennial *underdevelopment* for the majority and *hyperdevelopment* for a minority. What will be the impact of globalization on this situation?

It is of crucial importance to rethink the methodological and theoretical approach to development so that one of its fundamental components becomes analysis of religion and its multiple manifestations (Dawson, 1996, 1998).

The new frontier of the sociology of religion must necessarily embrace world themes, and in this it will be aided by the process of globalization. By analysis of 'world themes' I mean a study of the great religions which examines their inner structure and their impact on society. The sociology of religion still, I believe, restricts itself too narrowly to analysis of Christianity.

The approach to religion in the twenty-first century must achieve greater objectivity; otherwise there is a danger that it will develop theories inapplicable to religious experience in continents other than Europe and

North America. Significant changes, therefore, can be glimpsed on the horizon.

I turn finally to young people. In the space of a few lines, I certainly cannot convey the complex topic of youth culture, about which so much has been written. I must at least emphasise, however, that much closer attention must be paid to this section of the population than in the twentieth century. Research should be more proactive, in the sense that it should not restrict itself to analysis of young people as a social class but also put forward concrete proposals for their orientation in society. The century that has just ended was marked by the almost total failure of sociology to understand the behaviour of young people. Not only was the discipline unable to foresee the student protest movement of the mid-1960s, it was unable to learn from that protest.

On strictly theoretical analyses have been conducted on these matters. Still the most outstanding, more than forty years after its publication, is Eisenstadt's *From Generation to Generation: Age Groups and Social Structure* (1956) which, amongst other things, carefully analysed the problems of young people. Among more recent studies I would mention the book setting out the results of multi-year research by an international team (of which I had the honour of being a member) led by Roland J. Campiche: *Cultures jeunes et religions en Europe* (Campiche, 1977).

It is true that the final fifteen years of the last century saw a burgeoning of empirical and theoretical research which gave rise to a specific sector of inquiry: the *sociology of youth culture*. But this is in reality a *poor* sector given that it is largely ignored by the rest of the sociological community.

Sociology lacks any true commitment to analysis of young people, of the *young subject* as Wieviorka would put it, and this deficiency is due to the poverty of theory, as well as to the scant attention that society has invariably paid to young people.

How can one explain this neglect of such an important section of the population, the one that will constitute the central component of society in the future? What accounts for this general lack of interest? May not the reason be that there is no tradition of research into youth culture? But if so, what are we to say about the myriad *new sociologies* that constantly enrich the sociological lexicon with terms such as gay, lesbian and transvestite sociologies? (Kuklich, 1998; Bailey, 1999). Do these have a consolidated theoretical underpinning?

Accordingly, should not the sociology of the twenty-first century devote itself more closely to young people? Should not one of its main purposes be exploration of their constantly evolving life-worlds? Will sociology lose credibility if it devotes time and effort to helping young people find their bearings in society by promoting effectively *new* youth policies?

Conclusions

Reconceptualizing is the key term of this introduction. But what does the word mean? The answer is twofold: first, as I have repeatedly stressed, it means questioning categories which may be valid but are no longer pertinent to contemporary society, or devising new ones; second it means that sociologists must be open to new theoretical and empirical approaches.

The essays in this book clearly mark out the route that sociology should follow in the century to come. At the same time they bolster the sociologist's *confidence*, they reinforce his or her sense of *professionalism*, they convey *enthusiasm* for research, and they inject *fresh ideas* into the profession.

At issue, therefore, is not the crisis of sociology but its *relaunching* predicated on the conviction that sociology can grow *increasingly more* a science, that globalization *urgently* entails change in theory and in practice, that the new technologies are a *springboard* to new sociological horizons. To this relaunching, I am certain, this book will make a significant contribution.

Bibliography

Abbott, A. (1999), *Department & Discipline. Chicago Sociology at One Hundred*, University of Chicago Press, Chicago.

Abbott, A. (2000), 'Reflection on the Future of Sociology', *Contemporary Sociology*, vol. 29, no. 2, pp. 296-300.

Abu-Lughod, J.L. (ed) (1999), *Sociology for the Twenty-first Century. Continuities and Cutting Edges,* University of Chicago Press, Chicago.

Alan Fine, G. (ed) (1995), *A Second Chicago School? The Development of a Postwar American Sociology*, University of Chicago Press, Chicago.

Bailey, R.W. (ed) (1999), *Gay Politics, Urban Politics: Identity and Economics in the Urban Setting*, Columbia University Press, New York.

Bales, K. (1999), *Disposable People: New Slavery in the Global Economy*, University of California Press, Berkeley.

Bauman, Z. ([1999] 2000), *La solitudine del cittadino globale*, Feltrinelli, Milano.

Beck, U. (1986), *Risikogesellschaft. Auf dem Weg in eine andere Moderne*, Suhrkamp, Frankfurt am Main.

Beck, U. (1997), *Was ist Globalisierung? Irrtumer des Globalismus-Antworten auf Globalisierung*, Suhrkamp, Frankfurt am Main.

Beck, U. (2000), 'The Cosmopolitan Perspective: Sociology of the Second Age of Modernity', *The British Journal of Sociology*, vol. 51, no. 1, pp. 79-105.

Berger, P.L. (1967), *The Sacred Canopy. Elements of a Sociological Theory on Religion*, Doubleday, New York.

Boudon, R. (1999), *Le sens de valeurs*, Puf, Paris.

Bulmer, M. (1984), *The Chicago School of Sociology: Institutionalisation, Diversity, and the Rise of Sociological Research*, University of Chicago Press, Chicago.

Buttel, H.F. (2000), 'Ending Hunger in Developing Countries', *Contemporary Sociology*, vol. 29, no. 1, pp. 13-27.

Campiche, J.R. (sous la direction de) (1977), *Cultures et religions en Europe*, Cerf, Paris.

Comte, A. (1930-42), *Cours de philosophie positive*, Alcan, Paris.

Connell, R.W. (1997), 'Why is Classical Theory Classical?', *American Journal of Sociology*, vol. 102, no. 6, pp. 1511-57.

Connell, R.W. (2000), 'Sociology and World Market Sociology', *Contemporary Sociology*, vol. 29, no. 2, pp. 291-6.

Dawson L.L., (ed) (1996), *Cults in Context. Readings in the Study of New Religious Movements*, Canadian Scholars' Press, Toronto.

Dawson L.L. (1998), 'The Cultural Significance of New Religious Movements and Globalization: A Theoretical Prolegomenon', *Journal for the Scientific Study of Religion*, vol. 37, no. 4, pp. 580-95.

De Nardis, P. (a cura di) (1998), *Le nuove frontiere della sociologia*, Carocci, Roma.

Donati, P.P. (1991), *Teoria relazionale della società*, Angeli, Milano.

Durkheim, E. (1897), *Le Suicide: étude de sociologie*, Alcan, Paris.

Eisenstadt, S.N. (1956), *From Generation to Generation: Age Groups and Social Structure*, Free Press of Glencoe, Glencoe.

Etzioni, A. (2000), 'Creating Good Communities and Good Societies', *Contemporary Sociology*, vol. 29, no.1, pp. 213-9.

Evans, P. (2000), 'Fighting Marginalization with Transitional Networks: Counter Hegemonic Globalisation', *Contemporary Sociology*, vol. 29, no. 1, pp. 230-41.

Gollin, A.E. (1990), 'Whither the Profession of Sociology', *The American Sociologist*, vol. 21, no. 4, pp. 316-20.

Harvey, L. (1987), *Myths of the Chicago School of Sociology*, Avebury, Aldershot.

Horowitz, I.L. (1993), *The Decomposition of Sociology*, Oxford University Press, Oxford.

Inglehart, R. and Baker, W.E. (2000), 'Modernization, Cultural Change, and the Persistence of Traditional Values', *American Sociological Review*, vol. 65, no. 1, pp. 19-51.

Johnson, J., Rush, S. and Feagin, J.C. (2000), 'Doing Antiracism and Making a Nonracist Society', *Contemporary Sociology*, vol. 29, no. 1, pp. 95-110.

Kahn, J.S. (1998), *Southest Asian Identities: Culture and the Politics of Representation in Indonesia, Malaysia, Singapore and Thailand*, St. Martin's Press, New York.

Kulick, D. (1998), *Travesti: Sex Gender, and Culture among Brazilian Transgendered Prostitutes*, University of Chicago Press, Chicago.

Lambert, Y. (1999), 'Religion in Modernity as a New Axial Age: Secularization or New Religious Forms?', *Sociology of Religion*, vol. 60, no. 3, pp. 301-31.

Le Bras, G.(1955), *Études de Sociologie religieuse*, Puf, Paris.

Lee Su-H. (ed) (1998), *Sociology in East Asia and its Struggle For Creativity*, International Sociological Association, Madrid.

Lemert, Ch. (1991), 'The End of Ideology', *Sociological Theory*, vol. 9, no. 2, pp. 164-72.

Luckmann, Th. (1963), *Das Problem der Religions in der modernen Gesellschaft*, Rombach, Freiburg.

Münch, R. (1994), *Sociological Theory*, vol. 1, *From the 1850s to the 1920s*, Nelson-Hall Chicago.

Oberschall, A. (2000), 'Preventing Genocide', *Contemporary Sociology*, vol. 29, no. 1, pp. 1-13.

Park, R.E. (1913), 'Racial Assimilation in Secondary Groups with Particular Reference to Negro', *American Sociological Society*, no. 8, pp. 66-83.

Park, R.E. (1928), 'Human Migration and the Marginal Man', *American Journal of Sociology*, vol. 33, no. 6, pp. 881-93.

Peet, R. (1999), *Theories of Development*, The Guilford Press, New York.

Pinches, M. (ed) (1999), *Culture and Privilege in Capitalist Asia*, Routledge, London.

Platt, J. (1996), *A History of Sociological Research Methods in America 1920-1960*, Cambridge University Press, Cambridge.

Rex, J. (1986), *Race and Ethnicity*, Open University Press, Buckingham.

Sassen, S. (2000), 'New Frontiers Facing Urban Sociology at the Millennium', *The British Journal of Sociology*, vol. 51, no. 1, pp. 143-59.

Schwartz, P. (2000), 'Creating Sexual Pleasure and Sexual Justice in the Twenty-first Century', *Contemporary Sociology*, vol. 29, no. 1, pp. 213-9.

Shils, E. (1996), 'The Culture of Local Community' in L. Tomasi (ed), *The Local Community. A Sociological Interpretation of European Localism*, Angeli, Milano, 1996, pp. 15-55.

Silverman, B. and Yanowitch, M. (1997), *New Rich, New Poor, New Russia: Winners and Losers on the Russian Road to Capitlism*, M.E. Shape, New York.

Smith, D. (1988), *The Chicago School. A Liberal Critique of Capitalism*, Macmillan, London.

Smith, T.V. and Withe, L.D. (1929), *Chicago: An Experiment in Social Science Research*, University of Chicago Press, Chicago.

Therborn, G. (2000), 'At the Birth of Second Century Sociology: Times of Reflexivity, Spaces of Identity, and Nodes of Knowledge', *The British Journal of Sociology*, vol. 51, no. 1, pp. 37-57.

Thomas, W.I. (1898), 'On a Difference in the Metabolism of the Sexes', *American Journal of Sociology*, vol. 3, no. 1, pp. 31-63.

Thomas, W.I. (1899), 'Sex in Primitive Industry', *American Journal of Sociology*, vol. 4, no. 4, pp. 474-88.

Tomasi, L. (ed) (1998), *The Tradition of the Chicago School of Sociology*, Ashgate, Aldershot.

Tomasi, L. (a cura di) (2000a), *La cultura dei giovani europei alle soglie del 2000. Religioni, valori, politica e consumi*, Angeli, Milano (2nd edition).

Tomasi, L. (2000b), *La Scuola sociologica di Chicago. La teoria implicita*, Angeli, Milano (2nd edition).

Tomasi, L. (2000c), 'Young Adult Experience in Italy: Towards a Religious and Moral Supermarket?', in J. Fulton, A. M. Abela, I. Borowik, T. Dowling, P. Long Marler and L. Tomasi, *Young Catholics at the New Millennium*, University College Dubin Press, Dublin, pp. 90-111.

Tuhiwai Smith, L. (1999), *Decolonizing Methodologies: Research and Indigenous Peoples*, Zed Books, New York.

Waite, L. (2000), 'The Family as a Social Organization: Key Ideas for the Twenty-first Century', *Contemporary Sociology*, vol. 29, no. 3, pp. 463-9.

Wallerstein, I. (2000), 'From Sociology to Historical Social Science: Prospects and Obstacles', *The British Journal of Sociology*, vol. 51, no. 1, pp. 25-35.

Warner, R.S. (1993), 'Work in Progress toward a New Paradigm for the

Sociological Study of Religion in the United States', *American Journal of Sociology*, vol. 98, no. 5, pp. 1044-93.

Weber, M. (1904-1905), 'Die protestantische Sekten un der Geist des Kapitalismus' in *Archiv für Sozialwissenschaft und Sozialpolitik*, J.C.B. Mohr, Tübingen, vol. XX-XXI.

Weber, M. (1920), *Gesammelte Aufsätze zur Religionssoziologie*, J.C.B. Mohr, Tübingen.

Weber, M. ([1920] 1982), *Sociologia della religione*, Edizioni di Comunità, Milano, vol. 1 e 2.

Weber, M. ([1921-1922] 1969), 'On the Concepts of Sociology and the "Meaning" of Social Conduct', on H.P. Secher (ed), *Basic Concepts in Sociology by Max Weber*, Citadel Press, New York.

Whitehead, B.D. (1998), *The Divorce Culture: Rethinking Our Commitments to Marriage and Family*, Vintage, New York.

Wieviorka, M. (1991), *L'espace du racisme*, Editions de Seuil, Paris.

PART I:
THEORY AND RESEARCH:
NEW HORIZONS

1 Sociology between scientism and aestheticism, or can sociology be positivist today?[1]

RAYMOND BOUDON

Introduction

Durkheim and Weber did not share the same conception of sociology, but they harboured no doubts that it should pursue no other goal than that of a science: the goal, that is, of creating knowledge.

A careful reading of the comments formulated on sociology by philosophers of the social sciences, by historians of sociology, and by sociologists themselves yields the impression that, on the contrary, sociology has never been able to create authentic knowledge, that its goals have been both multiple and indeterminate, and that in all cases it has been forced to abandon the scientific ambitions of its great founders. In an article published in the prestigious weekly *Die Zeit*, the commentator went so far as to argue that sociology will not survive unless it officially renounces every scientific ambition.[2]

Must we be so pessimistic about the past and the future of sociology? Is it necessary to forgo the 'positivist' goals of the classical sociologists? Whence derives the scepticism of so many sociologists on this issue? These are the questions upon which I shall reflect in what follows.

However, before attempting to answer these questions, clarification is required of what is meant by 'science'. The notion, of course, is a complex one, and yet few commentators have sought to define it before asserting the capacity or incapacity of sociology to be a scientific discipline like the others.

---

1 This essay is largely based on my article in Cuin, C.H. (1997), *Durkheim d'un siècle à l'autre*, Puf, Paris, pp. 265-88.
2 Bell (1995), Berger (1994), Busino (1993), Lepenies (1990), Turner and Turner (1990) and many others doubt the capacity of the social sciences to create authentic knowledge. Some consider the social sciences to be suited by their nature to essay-writing, others claim that they have fallen under the influence of 'post-modernist' nihilism. The success of Lepenies's book is due to its merits, but also to the fact that it has expressed the mood of many sociologists by taking the scientific claims of the pioneers of sociology and suggesting that sociology has never managed to be a science. Since nor is sociology an art, it is at most a minor branch of literature specialized in socio-political non-fiction, and its success derives from the fact that it satisfies a strong demand. See Chazel (1993).

1. Positivism or positivisms?

For Durkheim, like many contemporary sociologists, a discipline that claims to be scientific must pursue a positivist programme. Yet 'positivism' is a set of complex ideas. Like every influential intellectual movement, it encompasses a wide range of positions, in the same manner as empiricism does, for instance, or marxism or rationalism.

Despite this diversity, like marxism or rationalism, positivism conveys a number of crucial intuitions. Above all, it raises a question of essential importance for any discipline that claims to be scientific, that of the criteria with which to distinguish a scientific theory from one that is not, and with regard to scientific theories between those that are valid and those that are not. Durkheim raised this 'demarcation' issue in *Les Règles*, where he insisted that sociology should set itself the goal of being a science. This presupposes that a demarcation line can be drawn between scientific and non-scientific. Although it is not certain that this assumption is valid, we cannot evade the issue of the criteria with which a theory may be defined 'scientific', in an age when scepticism as to sociology's ability to produce genuine knowledge affects even sociologists themselves.

Comte's positivism envisaged science as a superior form of knowledge. But it cannot be reduced to this principle alone, for Comte also contended that the notion of 'cause' should be replaced by that of 'law' and that science is made up of a finite set of interrelated or distinct disciplines arranged in a complex hierarchy. It follows from these principles, for example, that psychology and economics cannot claim the status of sciences (in that they do not belong among the fundamental disciplines), or that sociology must employ the methods of disciplines lower down in the hierarchy of sciences, like biology or physics or chemistry, while at the same time treating societies as entities with a higher level of complexity than that of organisms.

Durkheim took several of his master's lessons on board. He wholly endorsed Comte's classification of the sciences, as well as his idea that the ontological discontinuity among the orders of phenomena entails a methodological discontinuity among the scientific disciplines that study them (Durkheim, 1972: 106). One condition for sociology to acquire scientific status is, according to Durkheim, that it should respect this discontinuity. It is consequently necessary to exclude psychology from sociological explanation, and to prohibit the interpretation of social facts by means of anything other than social facts. Not to do so would be as unacceptable as claiming that 'biological phenomena can be analytically explained by means of inorganic phenomena' (Durkheim, 1972: 102): an idea that Durkheim deemed so obviously mistaken that he used it to sustain by analogy his maxim that social facts should be explained through social facts. However, the idea that underpins modern biology – that the organic can be explained on the basis of the inorganic – was unacceptable to Durkheim because it breached the principle that 'a whole is not identical with the sum of its parts' (Durkheim, 1972: 102). From the continuity/discontinuity relation between sociology and biology, he drew the idea that societies must be considered as wholes, although these wholes are more complex in nature than living organisms. Durkheim condemned economics and psychology for other reasons as well, and again in the light of Comte's theory: economics, he argued, is the product of an arbitrary division among phenomena; by interesting itself in non-observable phenomena, psychology breaches an essential principle of positivism, namely that the scientist must abide by the facts alone.

The academic character of Durkheim's style contrasts with Comte's prophetic style; it was Durkheim's determination to base his analysis on systematically collected data that distinguished him from Comte; indeed, he declared his disagreement with him on a number of significant points. For example, he rejected Comte's conception of sociological laws, writing (Durkheim, 1972: 125) that he had a 'particular conception of sociological laws'. Comte sought laws of historical evolution instead of looking for conditional laws of the kind 'if A then B'. According to Durkheim, 'sociological explanation consists solely in establishing causality relationships' (Durkheim, 1972: 124).

As a new 'fusion' of the theory of science which contained, amongst other things, elements of Comte's positivism, Durkheim's positivism was therefore much more complex, and in any case more heterogeneous, than that of Claude Bernard, for example. As latterly for Hempel (1965), so for Bernard science was defined by an objective – that of explanation – which in its turn was defined as the subsuming of phenomena under laws. One gains the impression that Durkheim's aim in *Le Suicide* was to establish laws in sociology that were similar in their form to Boyle's Law or Mariotte's Law because they joined variables with a functional form (so that suicide rates are tied to 'anomie' and to 'egoism' by a U-curve). But, although evoking Hempel, he had a restricted conception of causality that modern positivists would reject, in particular when he maintained that the same cause always corresponds to the same effect: 'Thus, to return to the examples cited above, if suicide depends on more than one cause, this is because there are in reality different types of suicide' (Durkheim, 1972: 127).

Another version of positivism, the one developed by Carnap, is much more radical than Bernard's. This version contends that, at least in principle, an authentic scientific theory must be amenable to translation into a form that contains only empirical statements – that is, statements which can be immediately verified by observation. There is, of course, a linking thread between Viennese positivism and the early positivism of Comte: for both Carnap and Comte, scientific thought has greater reliability than other forms of thought, and it owes this superiority to the attention paid to the elimination of hidden causes, so that sociology eschews mention of 'human nature', which is a 'metaphysical' notion, according to Comte. In general, this determination to adhere as closely as possible to the observable is a principle that appears in diverse forms in the majority of the variants of positivism.

Carnap's positivism has been strongly criticised, but his extremist conception of science is to be found in all the movements of influential ideas (more often denoted by other names). Mach's 'empirio-criticism' in physics, Malinowski's 'functionalism', 'behaviourism', whose influence on psychology is well known, Milton Friedman's 'positivism' in economics: all these can be considered to be transformations of Carnap's 'positivism' in that they all identify the notion of scientificity with at least the potential elimination of non-observable phenomena from scientific discourse. Behaviourist psychologists argue that psychological theory in its entirety can be reduced to statements about relations between stimuli and responses, given that both are observable. Malinowski contended that anthropology should restrict itself to studying the relations among observable social entities and to proving, for example, that some social institutions are inter-related while others are mutually exclusive. The same principles are to be found in Murdock. Lévi-Strauss took up the idea and radicalized it: his structuralism maintained that the anthropologist should study the regularities in observable phenomena and in general seek to identify the 'structures' that support them. Friedman has defended the idea in a more flexible manner, arguing, for example, that economic actors pursue non-observable interests or preferences. But he treats these latter as 'black boxes' which should not be opened, or in other words, as axioms that may not be discussed in themselves. He merely asks whether the consequences that they produce in observable phenomena – that is, whether the 'predictions' that they permit us to formulate about reality – are confirmed or refuted by reality. Here the non-observable is admitted but it is excluded from discussion.

Popper, as we know, was highly critical of his predecessor and fellow-countryman Rudolf Carnap, but he may not have distanced himself from Carnap to the extent that he claimed. Popper invariably protested when he was called a 'positivist', and he vigorously opposed his 'critical rationalism' to positivism. Yet he shared a fundamental 'empiricism' with Carnap. Both of them regarded the congruence between scientific theory and observed reality to be the sole criterion of scientificity, and for both of them a good theory was one that was congruent with the real. Popper undoubtedly denied that a theory can be reduced, even in principle, to statements with the status of protocols of observation. Yet he was uninterested in any discussion of the non-empirical components of scientific theories. What counted for Popper was solely the fact that a theory could be compared against reality and considered to be congruent or otherwise with it. A valid theory was one which was endorsed by the real, or which at least did not appear to be incompatible with it. The fact that Friedman has called his position 'positivist' while it is actually Popperian, indirectly demonstrates the kinship between 'positivism' and 'critical rationalism'. For Friedman, it is of little importance to know whether the non-empirically verifiable propositions introduced into an economic theory are realistic or not. It is for this reason that the Friedmanian economist (like the sociologist who follows him) believes that s/he can legitimately interpret all behaviour on the basis of the utilitarian axiomatic of rational choice theory and reject criticisms expressed in the name of realism. According to the Friedmanian positivist, an axiomatic cannot in fact be discussed in itself. All that matters is knowing whether it produces results that successfully pass the Popperian test of congruence with reality.

These remarks may suffice to show the diversity of the ideas that have been grouped under the heading of positivism. This historical complexity notwithstanding, it is possible to discern a number of features shared by the main versions of positivism. These common features are the following:
1. the assertion of science as a higher form of knowledge;
2. definition of scientificity on the criterion of the elimination of the unobservable (with the two variants described: absolute elimination on principle, or elimination from discussion);
3. definition of the purpose of science as the study of the relations among observable phenomena.

Although not always to the letter, Durkheim adhered to this distinctive programme of what one might call 'hard positivism'; a programme to which he added a number of supplementary principles derived from Comte. It is evident that 'egoism' and 'anomie' are not unobservable phenomena, but rather, in Lazarsfeld's sense, variables which are indirectly measurable by means of 'indicators'.

One may counterpose 'hard' positivism with a 'moderate' or 'soft' positivism which maintains the first of the above principles but proposes a completely different definition of scientificity insofar as it accepts (contrary to Carnap but in accordance with Popper or Friedman) the introduction of non-observable elements into a scientific theory and discussion of the acceptability of these unobservables (contrary to Popper and Friedman).

Unobservables – that is, non-observable elements and the non-verifiable propositions of a theory – constitute an issue of central importance in the debate on the criteria of scientificity. Admitting unobservables is not to claim entitlement to introduce any whatever explanatory theory; this is the preoccupation of the positivist. To the extent that they admit that the axioms of a theory may be discussed in terms of their observable consequences, Popper and Friedman form a link between 'hard' and 'soft' positivism. An unobservable may therefore be indirectly judged positively or negatively according to whether its introduction gives rise to acceptable theories (that is, congruent with reality). We shall see, however, that it is necessary to go further than Popper and Friedman, and that it is not enough to discuss unobservables solely in terms of their empirical consequences.

2. 'Hard' positivism versus 'soft' positivism

What I propose to call 'soft positivism' takes from the core intuitions of positivism the idea that a scientific explanation is different from other types of explanation and that it is more reliable. But it refuses to judge a theory – as Carnap, but also Friedman and Popper wanted – solely on the basis of empirical criteria, and in particular the criterion of congruence with reality.

This 'soft' positivism enables us to give better account of the fact that a theory may be judged valid or invalid in the natural sciences, in the social sciences and in sociology in particular.

According to this 'soft' positivism implicit in the theories of Huygens or Tocqueville to be considered below, a good explanatory theory may be defined as follows. Let us suppose that we wish to explain a phenomenon.[3] To do so we must develop a theory T, or in other words, a set of propositions of which 'f' is the consequence. We thus observe the fact 'f', namely that Jews are over-represented among American professors of bacteriology and under-represented compared with Protestants or Catholics among professors of music or languages.[4] Why? The answer to the question (which cannot be

---

3   On this see also Boudon 1994a.
4   This example is developed in Boudon 1990.

developed fully here) consists in reconstructing a set of propositions of which one consequence is 'f': in the circumstances considered 'Jews are over-represented among American professors of bacteriology and under-represented compared with Protestants or Catholics among professors of music or languages'.

The difficulty resides in the fact that an infinity of theories may have proposition 'f' as their consequence and may therefore be taken to be explanations of the fact 'f'. Thus, one explanation might be that President Lincoln decreed that 'f', and the people of the United States have always obeyed his injunction. Of course, this explanation is immediately discredited because the two propositions are blatantly false: in other words, it can be shown that they are incompatible with reality. There exist, therefore, means with which to eliminate certain items from the great quantity of potential explanatory theories. One of these means, the one that I have just used, is verification that the propositions of the theory which can be compared against reality are compatible with it. In this case, the two propositions are contradicted by reality, and consequently the theory can be rejected.

It is this type of operation of comparison against reality which defines what Popper calls 'critical rationalism', or the theory of science that he himself expounded.

Why is this theory of science important? Because it establishes a *necessary* condition for a theory to be deemed scientifically acceptable. When a theory contains at least one proposition incompatible with reliable observations it cannot be accepted, at least in principle.

However, it is necessary to moderate this proposition in the light of observations which today are canonical: when a theory is compatible with an entire set of facts, but not with one particular fact, this does not entail its rejection. As the so-called 'Duhem-Quine' thesis states, when a fact is incompatible with a theory, one never knows beforehand what it is in the theory that is responsible for this incompatibility. It may be the core of the theory, but it may equally be a minor element of it. An astronomical theory may have almost certain validity and nevertheless yield false predictions concerning the behaviour of a planet, because the course of the latter is altered by as yet unidentified cosmic dust. Even if the astronomer does not possess the technical means with which to verify the presence of this dust, until proof to the contrary is forthcoming s/he will continue to accept the idea that his/her theory is valid, deciding that it is sufficient to add an auxiliary hypothesis (the existence of cosmic dust) in order to render it wholly compatible with the set of facts observed.

But these observations in no way discredit the fact that the criterion of a theory's congruence with reality as observed is an absolute criterion of the scientificity of a theory. In other words, it is impossible to treat as definitively acceptable a theory which displays an irresolvable incompatibility with certain observed facts. So strong is this principle that Popper elevates it to the status of *the* criterion of scientificity: a theory is scientific when it can be compared against reality without this giving rise to consequences or propositions that are definitively incompatible with reality. The theory outline above 'President Lincoln…' is 'falsifiable' and therefore scientific according to Popper, and definitively unacceptable because it contains a proposition that is definitively incompatible with reality.[5]

The importance of Popper's theory derives from the fact that it identifies a necessary condition which every theory must satisfy: namely that the theory must not display definitive incompatibility with reality. The weakness in Popper's theory is that it takes a necessary condition to be sufficient.

Let us examine an exemplary case, that of Huygens' theory of the pendulum. This theory is valid because it is falsifiable (it makes precise predictions about the behaviour of a certain pendulum in a particular place and with particular characteristics) and not falsified (it correctly predicts the behaviour of all pendulums observed in all latitudes).

But Huygens' theory is not only valid because it satisfies the conditions posited by Popper.

Let us imagine two theories alternative to Huygens':

President Lincoln decided that all pendulums must behave in accordance with the rules defined by Huygens' theory.

The great invisible Sage who lives on the summit of Montmartre has decided that all pendulums must behave in accordance with the rules defined by Huygens' theory.

The former theory adds an undesirable empirical proposition to Huygens' theory. It can be immediately discarded: it is empirical but evidently incompatible with the observed facts. However influential President Lincoln may have been, no-one has ever reported that he had power over natural phenomena. Moreover, pendulums followed Huygens' laws well before Lincoln was born. What is more, the theory is entirely irrelevant because the facts that it explains are exactly those that Huygens' theory clarifies. The verdict is therefore irrevocable, but it is not exclusively grounded on empirical considerations. It is also based on the fact that the

---

5   Note that 'The train leaves at 8.47' is a 'falsifiable' proposition. Yet it can hardly be considered scientific.

proposition 'President Lincoln … Huygens' theory' is *useless*: it is a non-empirical assertion which has nothing to do with the criterion of congruence between theory and reality.

Also the second theory has the air of a joke, but it is more difficult to reject. Since the great Sage who inhabits the summit of Montmartre is invisible and intangible, it is impossible to determine whether or not he actually exists. The extent of his powers cannot be established. But, it will be said, does not the introduction of an unobservable element such as this render the theory unscientific? Did not Popper argue that a theory cannot contain non-falsifiable elements? The answer is evidently 'no'. Popper rightly argued that a scientific theory must be confutable by observation, but not that all of its propositions should be thus confutable. Had he argued in this manner, he would have been forced to consider Huygens' theory of the pendulum as an example of a non-scientific theory. Indeed, Huygens tells us that in order to predict the movement of a pendulum, one must envisage its movement as resulting from a set of forces. Thus one force pulls it towards the centre of the earth, another counteracts the former and pulls it towards the point from which the rod swings. The movement of the pendulum is the result of forces which combine according to the rules of the parallelogram of forces. But who has ever seen a 'force', a 'force which pulls objects towards the centre of the earth', a 'parallelogram of forces', or again 'a force which pulls objects towards the extremity of the wires to which they are fixed'? These entities are neither more nor less visible than the great Sage who lives on the hill of Montmartre.

It is for this reason that Popper does not claim that unobservables must be eliminated from a scientific theory. He merely states that the theory which contains them must yield consequences amenable to comparison against reality. Hence, theory 2 ('The great Sage…') contains unobservables but it is 'falsifiable' or, put better, 'confutable'.[6] However, no-one would regard it as scientific.

This proof by absurdity suggests that Popper's theory is inadequate. For a scientific theory to be acceptable, it is necessary for the propositions containing unobservable elements, and in general its non empirically verifiable components, to be acceptable in themselves. Otherwise, there is no means available to account for the difference between Huygens' theory and the theory that introduces the great Sage living on the heights of Montmartre. Yet one has the inescapable sensation that the former is acceptable while the latter is not. Because both of them predict reality in exactly the same way, they

---

6   Popper uses 'falsifiable' in English when 'confutable' would be more appropriate.

cannot be distinguished on the basis of Popperian criteria. It is therefore necessary to be able to assess unobservable elements. Given that by definition one cannot apply the criterion of congruence with reality to these elements, they must be assessed on the basis of other criteria.

Why is the 'force that pulls objects towards the centre of the earth' acceptable when the 'great Sage' is not? The answer is obvious. Though unobservable, 'the force that pulls objects towards the centre of the earth', and more generally the notion of 'force', are acceptable because they enable explanation of all types of phenomena in a satisfactory manner. One may therefore admit the existence of this 'invisible', of this 'unobservable', although one cannot demonstrate or feel any 'force' – in other words, even if it is not a sensible phenomenon but an intellectual construct, and even if we do not know exactly which elementary phenomena comprise the notion of 'force'. It will be noted, however, that reality is readily granted to this intellectual construct. In other words, there is no serious doubt as to the existence of forces.

It follows that Popper's criteria define a necessary but not sufficient condition for scientificity and scientific validity. The unobservable elements introduced into a theory cannot be treated as a 'black box'. Consequently, one cannot accept the 'positivism' of Milton Friedman, whose theory, as we have seen, is not clearly distinct – at least as regards its basic principles – from Popper's 'critical rationalism'. *A fortiori* one cannot accept Carnap's positivism, with its assumption that scientific theories are defined and distinguished from metaphysical theories by the elimination of unobservables on principle.

Does this mean that we must renounce positivism? No, it does not. That would be to admit that all theories are equivalent, which contradicts common sense. We know that the theory of the 'great Sage' is unacceptable. The central intuition of positivism must therefore be preserved: theories may be more or less valid; an explanation of a phenomenon may be scientific or it may not. These principles must be maintained if we wish to avoid the trap of 'anything goes'. But we cannot be content with the criteria propounded by the 'hard positivists'.[7]

To sum up the discussion so far:

1. One cannot accept Carnap's definition of scientificity based on the potential elimination of the unobservable.

---

7   'Throwing the baby of science out with the positivist bathwater', authors like Hübner (1985) and Atlan (1986) contend that mythic and scientific thought propose incommensurable and therefore equally valid explanations of the world.

2. One cannot admit that congruence with reality is the only basis for evaluation of a scientific theory; nor that a theory's confutability by reality defines its scientificity.
3. In contrast to Friedman and the other 'hard positivists', one cannot accept that the unobservables introduced into a theory can be treated as 'black boxes'. On the contrary, their acceptability and their quality determine the acceptability of the theory.
4. This acceptability is assessed in the light of the fact that these unobservables may be evoked with regard to all the types of phenomena that differ from the phenomenon under examination.

This discussion thus enables definition of what I would call a 'moderate' or 'soft' positivism characterized by the following features.

1. There are theories of a scientific nature and theories of a non-scientific nature.
2. A scientific theory must be amenable to evaluation in terms of its congruence with reality. Ideally, it should be constituted in such a way that it does not include incongruences with reality.
3. Those of its elements and propositions which cannot be subjected to the congruence test must be considered acceptable, in the sense that they may be cited in explanation of other phenomena. The more numerous these phenomena, the more solid the guarantees that they offer to 'unobservables'.

3. The neo-positivist programme in the social sciences

Why is Huygens' theory of the pendulum a 'good' theory? Because it satisfies the above principles. Why is the theory of the 'great Sage' or of 'President Lincoln' a bad theory? Because it violates one or other of these principles.

If the 'neo-positivist' definition that I have just proposed is accepted, then theories just as robust as Huygens' are to be found in the social sciences. In order to prove this contention, I shall describe one theory in detail and outline another. This point is essential, because it confirms that the notion of 'scientificity' need not be defined in any other manner in the case of the human and natural sciences. It settles the first controversy of positivism in the Weberian way (I shall return to this point later).

Like every good scientist, Tocqueville did not concern himself with explanation of anything but enigmatic phenomena. In other words, he considered that phenomena whose explanation was immediate could not by definition be the object of scientific inquiry. Scientific sociology could not engage in the pedantic description of what spontaneous sociology understands perfectly well.

The phenomenon of American religiosity has been regarded as profoundly enigmatic by numerous great sociologists. Why? Because it challenges the 'evolutionary' law propounded by Comte, Tocqueville himself, Durkheim and Weber which stated that modernity would give rise to what Schiller, Balzac and Weber called 'disenchantment of the world'. This 'law' is well grounded, although it is crude and admits to exceptions – the American one for example. It is all the more enigmatic because the United States is the society in which, according to the principles that inspire the law in question, 'disenchantment' should have been most pronounced. Why is the most modern, and also the most materialistic, society the most religious of those of the West?

The enigma is sufficiently disconcerting to have been explored by Adam Smith, Tocqueville, Max Weber and many modern authors. But the latter do not seem to have added anything of importance to the findings of the three classical authors. Rather as if the theory of the pendulum concluded with Huygens, one has the impression that the manifold theory of Smith-Tocqueville-Weber amply embraces the exception of American religious experience.

According to Smith, American religiosity may be explained by the fact that, given the diversified supply of religion in the country, every individual could find a body of dogma matching his/her aspirations in the innumerable sects imported by successive waves of immigration. Conversely, when the religious supply was monopolistic as it was in Smith's Britain, those who for some reason or other could not accept a certain aspect of dogma or worship had no option but to quit the community of the faithful. Smith's explanation probably accounts for part of the American exception. And it may also explain why today the countries with the highest rates of atheism are those in which, like the Scandinavian countries, there is a church which enjoys almost total monopoly and is also the state religion. Smith's theory therefore explains both the American exception and other phenomena: different rates of atheism in particular.

Yet it accounts for the American exception only in part. Tocqueville added numerous insights to complete Smith's account. The fragmentary nature of the American religious institutions (a multitude of sects without one dominant church) has effects other than those envisaged by Smith. It has given less plausibility to the competition between the spiritual and the political manifest, for example, in France during the 1789 Revolution.

Consequently, the American sects have preserved the essential social functions (health, education, 'solidarity') that in the European nations have been transferred to the state. The federal nature of the American state and the limits imposed on federal powers have exerted influence in the same direction. The outcome has been that an American citizen finds the religious institutions in day-to-day life. In what circumstances would it be possible to develop negative sentiments in their regard?

Moreover, the multitude of sects has given rise to great tolerance of 'dogmatic beliefs'. Since these beliefs differ from one sect to another, the idea has arisen that dogmatic truths depend to a large extent on personal opinion. This valorization of personal interpretation is latent in Protestantism, while it is reinforced in situations in which there are numerous sects.

This phenomenon has given rise to a crucial effect: since dogmatic beliefs are highly diverse, the common base of American Protestantism is more 'moral' than 'dogmatic' in nature. Catholics and Protestants in particular identify more with the moral values of Christianity than with the dogmatic assertions that contest the scientific interpretation of the world. Consequently, American religiosity has suffered much less from scientific progress than has French religiosity.

Weber adds a crucial element to this theory (Boudon, 1993). The importance of the egalitarian myth in the United States (which stems from the fact that America is a country of immigration) means that the symbols of language, clothing or other features that denote social class are much less evident than in France or Germany. But since there is obviously a social stratification in the United States, and since everyday social life requires that one must know 'who one is dealing with' – that is, one must be able to locate others in the social scale immediately – it is important to have symbols of stratification. The distinctions evinced by clothing, language, gestures, official signs of distinction (like decorations or more or less high-sounding titles), and so on, do not have the importance in the United States that they do in Germany or France. In that country it is religious affiliations which act as 'functional substitutes' (to use Merton's term). Why can they perform this function? Because, owing to the United States' history of immigration, there is a correlation between religious affiliation and position in the system of social stratification, in that a group is more likely to be represented in the elite if it belongs to a less recent wave of immigration.

If the Smith-Tocqueville-Weber theory of the American religious exception has not often been challenged, and has only been revised in its details, this is because, like Huygens' theory, it furnishes a satisfactory explanation of the phenomena examined. And at the same time it continues to inspire a flow of complementary studies (Chaves and Cann, 1992).

Why is this theory satisfactory? Because its empirical propositions are congruent with reality (it is true that there are sects in the United States, and a dominant religion in France, England and Germany; it is true that the functions of education or solidarity are more frequently undertaken by the religious institutions in the United States than in France or in Germany; and it is true that atheism is more widespread in Britain than in the United States; and so on). In short the Smith-Tocqueville-Weber theory of the American religious exception comprises a set of propositions whose congruence with reality can be verified and which from this (Popperian) point of view are perfectly acceptable.

But on the other hand this theory comprises (like Huygens' theory) numerous propositions that are difficult to verify and are absolutely not verifiable empirically: when a person disagrees with a dogmatic system, s/he tends to look for another one (Smith); a person cannot feel negative sentiments towards institutions whose services s/he values (Tocqueville); when a person belongs to a community, and opinions diverge on topic A and converge on topic B, s/he tends to define the community on the basis of B (Tocqueville); competition increases hostility (Tocqueville); elementary interaction inevitably involves symbols of stratification (Weber); and so on. All these propositions are as unamenable to direct verification as the existence of the forces that move the pendulum. Yet they are acceptable, because they are propositions for which one can find a thousand applications in other cases. These 'psychological' or 'sociological' statements are as easily acceptable as Huygens' 'physical' statements.

In short, the Smith-Tocqueville-Weber theory is a good theory, and it is a theory which is 'good' according to the criteria set out above.

This example suffices to show that the social sciences contain numerous theories that can be verified according to exactly the same principles as used to verify a theory in the natural sciences.

The Smith-Tocqueville-Weber theory is as acceptable as Huygens' theory and for the same reasons: because it fully satisfies the Popperian and non-Popperian criteria that define the neo-positivist programme outlined above.

It would not to be difficult to find numerous examples of this type. I have analysed elsewhere (Boudon, 1990) the scientific debate on explanation of magical beliefs. It is easy to show that, among the competing theories, there is one that predominates over the others according to the criteria of the neo-positivist programme and which for this reason is much more acceptable.[8]

Obviously, when I talk of 'soft positivism', I am using my own terms, not Weber's. And even less Tocqueville's, who in fact never discussed his methodology. However, even though Weber did not consider himself a positivist, he constantly affirmed the capacity of sociology – as he saw it – to be as robust as the natural sciences. On the other hand, he seems to have been very aware – both in his analyses and in his theoretical texts – that sociology as he conceived it does not depart from the procedures used by the other sciences. By insisting that sociology's overriding goal should be discovery of the real causes of collective phenomena, he adhered to the central tenet of positivism. When he asserted the principle that it is necessary to banish 'collective phantasms', have collective phenomena derive from individual acts, beliefs or attitudes, and view the real causes of these acts, beliefs or attitudes as residing in their 'meaning for the actor', he described a framework which permits the sociologist to avoid introducing unacceptable 'unobservables'. He believed that these principles were sufficient to make sociology a science like any other. The sociologist must identify the causes of the phenomena studied, constructing theories congruent with reality and whose non-observable elements are acceptable. The 'existential preoccupation' of which he speaks in his theory of magic – the preoccupation with survival at the basis of the magic spells used by the farmer and the fisherman – is no more directly observable than Huygens' forces. But who would raise the minimum objection against this notion? If they are examined carefully, the theories propounded by Tocqueville or Weber (as well as others, of course) to explain the innumerable enigmatic phenomena that they studied are always based on a set of 'psychological' propositions like the one I have just mentioned, and which on the one hand are not directly verifiable and, on the other, are easily acceptable because, like Huygens' 'forces', they convey notions (like the 'preoccupation with survival') indispensable for explanation of phenomena.

Like Weber, Tocqueville was convinced (judging from his analyses) that collective phenomena derive from the behaviours and convictions that actors adopt and which are meaningful to them, and he wanted this reconstruction to be controlled. All his assertions concerning the reasons for human behaviour strove for acceptability. Thus in *Ancien régime*, he refused to consider the

---

8   However, it should be pointed out that a theory may be accepted or rejected for reasons entirely extraneous to its validity. The theory of the 'primitive mentality' fascinated scholars at the beginning of the twentieth century and then disappointed them because of its Eurocentrism.

enthusiasm for Reason with a capital 'R' that characterized the French at the end of the eighteenth century as resulting from a 'contagion': if this were the case, why were the English immune to such enthusiasm? If there had been a contagious effect, why was the success of the notion of Reason so rapid? In short, Tocqueville used Popperian criteria to decide categorically among the possible alternative theories. But on the other hand, he took great care to show that the attractiveness of the notion of Reason for the peasants most distant from intellectual debate was explained by the fact that they regarded it as comprising ideas that were evident to them. Here as elsewhere, Tocqueville sought to relate more complex collective phenomena to simple psychological propositions; for a good scientific theory requires that propositions that cannot be verified empirically should nevertheless be acceptable.

The foregoing discussion raises another issue. We have just seen that it is not difficult to find robust theories as much in the social sciences as in the natural sciences. Then, why is it so frequently claimed that the social sciences in general and sociology in particular are essentially different from the natural sciences, and in particular that they obey entirely different principles of verification? The first controversy on positivism divided sociologists into two camps: the dualists who asserted the absolute specificity of the social sciences, and the monists (like Weber) for whom the social sciences and sociology could be subjected to the same principles of verification as the natural sciences. The second controversy on positivism, that of the 1960s, resumed the debate, and the dispute has periodically erupted since then.[9]

4. Explanation and interpretation

It was in the course of the first controversy on positivism that the arguments were presented most clearly. Recent developments of the debate have given rise to arguments of increasingly byzantine complexity but which, as soon as one manages to grasp their meaning, largely reproduce those of the first controversy.

The main contention of the dualists in the first controversy was that, while the natural sciences aim at explanation, the social sciences aim at interpretation. Thus the natural sciences seek the *causes* and the social sciences the *meaning* of the phenomena that they study. The above examples demonstrate the summary nature of this distinction: Tocqueville and Weber

---

9   Passeron (1991) defends a point of view close to the dualist view in the first controversy on positivism.

sought the causes of the American religious exception; Lévy-Bruhl and Durkheim sought the causes of magical beliefs. Moreover, as we have just seen, in their search for causes, the social and natural sciences obey identical criteria, rules and principles of verification. It is for this reason that one may talk of 'neo-positivism' with regard to Weber and Huygens. The fact that, unlike atoms, human beings are capable of imagination and intentionality affects neither the nature of the procedures that yield a good explanation nor the criteria that permit one to accept or reject that explanation, to judge it valid or otherwise.

The confusion and the enduring controversy derive from the fact that the social sciences often *also* ask questions for which they do not seek an explanation but an interpretation. Was the French Revolution a good or a bad thing? Was 1793 contained in 1789? Was Stalin inevitable? Is European civilization in decline? Is modern painting the death of art?

A question depends on interpretation when the answer to it necessarily involves value-judgements. To provide a less crude example than those just given, let us take the work of the biographer. As Simmel (1984: 104-8) points out, when writing a biography a historian must seek to unify the innumerable data available to him/her on the basis of a set of guiding principles. Once s/he has chosen these principles, the historian emphasises some facts and under-emphasises others. Another historian who has chosen other unifying principles will give different weight to the same facts. The two biographies will consequently be incompatible, so that both of them can be considered valid without one being deemed superior to the other. This is a typical example of an interpretative situation. On principle, there cannot be a single answer to the question asked. The definitive biography of a historical personage is an impossibility. Nor, moreover, can a historian claim objectivity. A biography may be more or less fair but it cannot be objective. Since it cannot be objective, the very idea of a definitive biography, of a biography that annuls all the others, is unthinkable, whereas it is possible to imagine, for example, a definitive theory of the American religious exception. Furthermore, a biographer must inevitably introduce value-judgements into his/her work by considering one biographical fact to be 'important' and another one to be 'secondary'. Of course, no objective criterion can be associated with these adjectives.

This process of interpretation is naturally not exclusive to the work of the biographer. The historian of the French Revolution finds himself or herself in the same situation. S/he must choose guiding principles and classify arguments in the order of importance determined by those principles. His/her interpretation may be more or less fair but it will not be unique and objective. The 'dualists' of the first controversy on positivism were right when they insisted that when the social sciences investigate the *meaning* of an event, they address a type of question which has no equivalent in the natural sciences. Because a life or an event does not have a unique meaning, the history of the French Revolution is constantly resumed and revised, like the biography of Louis XIV or Peter the Great. Generally, these new works do not arise from the discovery of new facts; instead, they derive from the fact that, by definition, a new point of view is always possible and that the present is understood in the light of the past. It is due to Stalin that Peter the Great is viewed in a new light.

On the other hand, it should be pointed out that a situation of *interpretation* may arise even when causal questions are asked. This is because the causality of certain states of affairs is so complex that it is impossible to reconstruct the set of causes responsible for them in their entirety, even less to gauge the relative importance of individual causes objectively. When Marx saw the conquest of Latin American as an important cause of the decline of feudalism and the advent of the bourgeois world, he stated a true proposition. The conquest led to an influx of precious metals which fuelled chronic inflation. While the feudal lords could hardly adjust their rent to keep pace with inflation without incurring the risk of a peasant revolt, the bourgeoisie could invest, assume debts and enrich themselves because they discharged their debts with devalued money. But, although there is no doubt as to this cause, it is impossible to gauge its importance with respect to other causes, like the religious factors cited by Weber or technical innovations. Objective reconstruction of the set of causes responsible for the ascent of the bourgeoisie is therefore impossible. On the other hand, one can state with absolute certainty that the conquest of Latin America contributed to the affirmation of the bourgeoisie. Here the dimensions of interpretation and explanation merge together.

The origin of the confusion distinctive of the repeated disputes concerning positivism is therefore not difficult to determine. The dualists forget that the social sciences and sociology in particular ask questions relative not only to interpretation but also to explanation. The monists commit the symmetrical error: they forget that the social sciences also ask questions about interpretation. Once we have realized that the dualists and monists commit the classic error of metonymy, we can discard hundreds of pages of useless 'epistemology'.

The confusion also derives from the fact that there are those who confuse positivism with some variants of what I have called 'hard' positivism. Now this positivism is no longer acceptable with regard to the social sciences and the natural sciences. Contrary to Friedman, one cannot treat the axioms that describe the behaviour of social or economic actors as a black box.

On the other hand, many of the questions asked by classical and modern sociology aim at explanation. As the example of the American religious exception shows, the sociologist may in this case pursue the same goals of rigour and objectivity as the biologist or the physicist.

5. The case of Durkheim

There remains a final case to consider: that of Durkheim. I shall not dwell on this matter because I have discussed it thoroughly elsewhere (Boudon, 1994b). In his doctrinal writings and especially in *Les Règles*, Durkheim embraced a 'hard positivism' (eliminate the unobservable, determine the relations among observables). Like Friedman many years later, he viewed the social actor as a black box which it is pointless and even dangerous to open. Comte convinced him that psychology should be entirely excluded from sociology. The sociologist's task, therefore, was only to establish relations of the type 'if A then B' which tie the observable to the unobservable (for example, there are fewer suicides in the countryside than in the city; more among Protestants than among Catholics; and so on).

In practice, however, Durkheim realized that it was not enough to rely on correlations. If one is induced to 'form the hypothesis' that the variable city/countryside is correlated with suicide rates, this is because there are reasons to believe that the situation of people in cities is different from that of people in the countryside. One is therefore induced to introduce unobservable terms, even psychological 'hypotheses' which strive for realism although they cannot be verified. But in this case one shifts from 'hard' to 'soft' positivism.

The same applies to Friedman. The 'hard positivism' that he defends on paper is in reality untenable. If anything can effectively be the 'psychological' hypothesis of the economist, it could not lead to consequences congruent with reality, except by chance. In short, it is necessary for 'psychological' hypotheses to have a certain realism. This entails that there cannot be any whatever hypothesis, and consequently that it cannot be treated as a black box.

6. In short

'Hard positivism' is therefore indefensible apropos the social and natural sciences. But it is essential to realize that there is room in sociology for a 'soft positivism', in the absence of which one would have to admit, against all the evidence, that legends and myths are explanations of the world just as valid as scientific theories. The conception of sociology that I place under the heading of 'soft positivism' is that set out by Tocqueville or Weber (in their analyses, not in their doctrinal works).

The case of Durkheim enables me to insist on another point. The desire to make sociology a scientific discipline presupposes a definition of science. Durkheim created a particular and contestable conception of science, and it is from this that the ambiguities of his thought derive. But Durkheim's error has been repeated numerous times in other forms. Thus, some have defined science as the production and analysis of quantitative data. Others, dazzled by the case of physics and celestial mechanics, contend that there can be no science without mathematization but forget that biology or zoology are full-fledged sciences but rely on mathematics only marginally. Yet others, smitten with the deductive character of mathematics, seek to apply the principles of economics indiscriminately to all sectors. The list could be extended even further. But all these conceptions of science are metonymic in character: they take the part for the whole. Physics is not all science, it is but one science among others. Mathematization is proper to only some scientific disciplines. Only some disciplines can put themselves forward as fully deductive; the ability to predict and make forecasts is distinctive of only some of them. All these features, sometimes elevated to the status of criteria for scientificity, characterize specific scientific disciplines. But they have the advantage of furnishing simple criteria with which to create straightforward linkages. Scientificity, in fact, consists in producing explanations of phenomena which strive for robustness and realism: which are the two objectives that 'soft positivism' is able to combine.

Moreover, one must acknowledge the existence of an area of *interpretation* which evades every positivist conception of knowledge. Thus the theories of modernity belong to the interpretative genre, and sociology is the direct heir of the philosophy of history, which is a paradigmatic example of that genre.

It is disastrous to consider assertions which in fact concern interpretation as constituting explanation. The horrors of nazism and communism also had a cognitive origin. They were possible because race and class were asserted as universal causes by certain *interpretations* which managed to pass themselves off as *explanations*.

Bibliography

Atlan, H. (1986), *À tort et à raison: intercritique de la science et du mythe*, Seuil, Paris.

Bell, D. (1995), 'Social Science: an Imperfect Art', *The Tocqueville Review*, vol. XVI, no. 1, pp. 3-24.

Berger, P.L. (1994), 'Does Sociology Still Make Sense?', *Revue suisse de sociologie*, vol. XX, no. 1, pp. 3-12.

Boudon, R. (1990), *L'art de se persuader des idées fragiles, douteuses ou fausses*, Fayard, Paris.

Boudon, R. (1993), 'European Sociology: The Identity Lost?' in B. Nedelmann and P. Sztompka (eds), *Sociology in Europe. In Search of Identity*, Aldine de Gruyter, Berlin, pp. 27-44.

Boudon, R. (1994a), 'Relativiser le Relativisme', *The Tocqueville Review*, vol. XV, no. 2, pp. 109-29.

Boudon, R. (1994b), 'Durkheim et Weber: Convergences de méthode', in M. Hirschhorn and J. Coenen-Huther (eds), *Durkheim, Weber, Vers la fin des malentendus*, L'Harmattan, Paris, pp. 99-122.

Busino, G. (1993), *Critique du savoir sociologique*, Puf, Paris.

Chaves, M. and Cann, D. (1992), 'Regulation, Pluralism and Religious Market Structure: Explaining Religious Vitality', *Rationality and Society*, vol. 4, no. 3, pp. 272-90.

Chazel, F. (1993) 'L'esthétisme sceptique et ses limites en historie de la sociologie', *Revue française de sociologie*, vol. XXXIV, no. 2, pp. 173-95.

Cuin, C.H. (1997), *Durkheim d'un siècle e l'autre*, Puf, Paris, pp. 265-88.

Durkheim, E. ([1895] 1972), *Les règles de la méthode sociologique*, Puf, Paris.

Hempel, C. (1965), *Aspects of Scientific Explanation and Other Essays in the Philosophy of Science*, Free Press, New York.

Hübner, K. (1985), *Die Wahrheit des Mythos*, Beck, München.

Lepenies, W. ([1985] 1990), *Les trois cultures. Entre science et littérature l'avènement de la sociologie*, Éditions de la Maison des sciences de l'homme, Paris.

Passeron, J.C. (1991), *Le raisonnement sociologique: l'espace non-poppérien du raisonnement naturel*, Nathan, Paris.

Simmel, G. ([1892] 1984), *Les problèmes de la philosophie de l'histoire: une étude d'épistémologie*, Puf, Paris.

Turner, S.P. and Turner, J.H. (1990), *The Impossible Science. An Institutional Analysis for American Sociology*, Sage, London.

2 Post-classical sociology or the twilight of sociology?

MICHEL WIEVIORKA

Introduction

Classical sociology is behind us, and its zenith was undoubtedly in the 1950s, the heyday of functionalism triumphant. The grandiose theoretical schema elaborated by Talcott Parsons as early as the end of the 1930s with *The Structure of Social Action* was an ambitious attempt to articulate the thought of classical authors in the field, beginning with Max Weber, Emile Durkheim and Vilfredo Pareto, as well as the economist Alfred Marshall. Parsons' endeavour, in fact, constituted the highest level of integration that sociology has ever known. Parsons' thesis of convergence made him the theoretician of the intellectual unity of the major trends in sociological thought prior to him, the incarnation of a synthesis that his predecessors could not have foreseen. Yet his theory has proved to be something of a giant with feet of clay: since the 1960s it has been challenged from outside sociology by the social movements that emerged in the United States and undermined its validity, and from within sociology by the onset of trends which, while renewing the approaches of the discipline, also entailed the destructuring and therefore the failure of Parsons' synthesis.

To think of the age of Parsons as the culmination of classical sociology, therefore, is in the first instance to suggest that since the middle of the twentieth century the discipline has undergone an ever-deepening crisis which has bred centrifugal tendencies and worked towards its disintegration. But it has also given rise to a profound examination of the future of sociology. Is it condemned to self-destruction until it loses all importance in the intellectual sphere? Or, instead, is it not called upon to transform itself, to change, to enter a post-classical era assuring itself a respectable place in social analysis? Does the perspective of a gradual disengagement, of an *updating*, which is far from over, imply the pure and simple abandonment of the major paradigms of the subject; or on the contrary does it require us also to consider the continuities which would make the continued use of the word 'sociology' legitimate and desirable?

1. The beginning of the disintegration of classical sociology

In the 1960s and 1970s, it was still possible to put forward a relatively integrated image of sociology on the basis of four cardinal points (Touraine, 1986: 134-43; Wieviorka, 1986: 149-55).

A first set of publications continued to draw their inspiration from Parsonian functionalism. At the end of World War Two, numerous researchers who had come from every part of the world to follow the teachings of Parsons and his school subsequently contributed to the diffusion of his ideas. To a greater or lesser extent influenced by the latter, they helped to internationalize them and to form imitators in their own societies. The influence of functionalism long remained substantial, and in countries very distant from the United States, including those of the Communist bloc where academic sociology, the only discipline that could be represented at international meetings like those organized by the International Sociological Association, remained under the sway of functionalist theory. By developing the image of a society which could take the ideal form of an integrated pyramid with values at the top, then norms, and finally roles and role expectations, by examining the phenomena of social stratification and social mobility, and by proving able to deal with both left-wing, and to some extent Marxist, as well as right-wing variations, functionalism did not suddenly disappear from the intellectual scene. In the 1970s and 1980s, important studies like that of Jeffrey Alexander (1982) sought to salvage whole sections of it, and to develop a neo-functionalism capable of responding to some of the most forceful criticisms brought against Parsons' theory. But this endeavour failed to restore the intellectual supremacy enjoyed by the functionalism of the 1950s.

A second body of research was part of a critical approach associated mainly with structuralism. In the aftermath of the social and political movements of the 1960s, which the mere mention of the year 1968 suffices to symbolize, references to Marx, to Nietzsche and to the second Frankfurt school gave rise to work in which a critical approach was developed. To some extent, the latter was able to adapt to functionalism or to create links with it – at the time, moreover, references were made to 'structural functionalism'. In its critical versions, Nicos Poulantzas' Marxism, and in particular that of Louis Althusser, denounced the state and its machinery as in the service of capital, and analysed the reproduction of relations of production, giving rise to research mainly in the sphere of urban sociology, with Manuel Castells in particular, and, in France, at least, in the sphere of education with Christian

Baudelot and Roger Establet. Elsewhere, the neo-Marxism of Pierre Bourdieu, more sensitive to the cultural dimensions of the reproduction of social domination, exerted an influence that has never been gainsaid. Apart from Marxism, other trends in critical thought were manifest in the work of Michel Foucault and his exposure of the microphysics of power and its ubiquitous exercise, and also in Erving Goffman's analysis of total institutions like the psychiatric asylum, while the work of Herbert Marcuse – in particular his description of one-dimensional man – enjoyed considerable success by virtue of its popularity with the student movement.

A third important trend in sociology was an interest in political systems, strategy and human rationality, with applications in two areas: the analysis of international relations, peace and war, conducted in particular by Thomas Schelling and Raymond Aron, and the analysis of large organizations by, for example, Herbert Simon and Michel Crozier.

Finally, a fourth important tendency in sociology placed conflict at the centre of collective behaviour, with the focus on actors and social movements. This may have been inspired by a form of Marxism, in particular that of the early Marx, rather than the theory that followed the 'epistemological break' to which Althusser refers. Though this tendency departed markedly from functionalism in the work of Alain Touraine, it did not completely break away from it – as one might infer on reading, for example, the work of Lewis Coser on conflict, the inspiration for which was Marx but also Georg Simmel (Coser, 1956, 1967).[1]

The structuring of sociology presented here in summary form was not an outright challenge against the domination of functionalism, and in any case it did not lead to total break-up, even if debates assumed a particularly acute ideological content, especially in the countries where Marxists and non- or anti-Marxists squared off against each other, sometimes paradoxically. Just as one could move fairly easily from a 'Marxist' representation of social classes to another based on the strategies of social stratification, so a protagonist of Marxist thought like Gramsci – the great rediscovery of the early 1970s – could be read from a functionalist perspective. But obviously, what might still be taken in the 1960s as a major crisis in American functionalism, well analysed at the time by Gouldner (1971), was in fact the beginning of the decline of the theory that embodied the maximum possible integration of classical sociology.

---

1   These two texts have been combined in the French translation *Les fonctions du conflit social*, Puf, Paris, 1982.

2. Disarticulation

The first phase of disintegration described above gathered considerable momentum in the 1970s. As the paradigms of functionalism declined in popularity, the other mainstream sociological approaches changed: they diversified, and thereby created space for newcomers, even though new appearances merely masked a return to modes of thought long tried and tested.

The critical approach reached its apogee in the 1970s. It was all the more popular because it seemingly provided scientific support or legitimation for political movements of leftist or radical persuasion. It then went into decline, concomitantly with leftism itself, and ideologies of rupture whether revolutionary or otherwise faded away. Neo-liberal thought was gaining ground and the end of the Cold War was on the horizon. Nevertheless, the critical approach did not completely disappear at this juncture; rather, it tended either to rigidify into analyses of alienation and false consciousness which denounced the authorities and focused on inexorable forms of determinism rather than on social life, or it became disassociated from sociology, fuelling hypercritical trends which claimed to represent post-modernism – I shall return to this topic later – or specific real-life forms of challenge, for example in gay and lesbian studies.

The sociology of decision-making, as Alain Touraine writes in his preface to the French translation of Hans Joas' book *La créativité de l'agir*, has 'made considerable advances in the study of strategies which are rational, but elaborated in complex and largely unpredictable environments' (p. iii). At the same time, strategic thinking applied to international relations and war was destabilized by the rise of international terrorism, then Islamism, the tendency towards the privatization of violence, the weakening of numerous states, the increased number of so-called 'low-level' conflicts, the blurring of distinctions between civil and military populations in most situations of armed violence: the world of Clausewitz, still of fascination to Raymond Aron, had passed, the classical rules of war were obsolete, and most threats and challenges were unprecedented and therefore unexpected. The end of the Cold War intensified the consequences of this evolution.

In short, the sociology of decision-making, and more broadly what can be called political sociology, were forced to envisage very limited strategies, because the actors who shaped them had only a very feeble capacity to relate them to highly uncertain systems of action. Sociologists in this field encountered increased difficulties because there seemed to be very little correspondence between the actor and the system.

In parallel with this apparent de-coupling of actors and systems in sociology, and with the emergence of thought of a certain critical importance but tending towards pure denunciation, as well as other strands of strategic significance but concerning very restricted issues, approaches hitherto much more in the minority began to move to the fore. Some of them related to symbolic interactionism and to a phenomenology varyingly expressed by what is sometimes called the Palo Alto school, with strong references to Erving Goffman or by ethnomethodology. They studied the interactions through which social life is constructed, leaving aside everything to do with history and politics and concentrating on the experience of everyday life. A distinct variation on these approaches was the 'conventions' approach (Luc Boltanski and Laurent Thévenot), which sought to explain how collective logic is constituted on the basis of agreements and compromises among actors, not through their games but rather the premises on which their agreements and compromises are grounded. Other trends in the wake of functionalism and of Marxism sought to fill what they deemed to be a sociological vacuum by suggesting the complete opposite of a grand system, and by developing the idea that sociology can only be based on the postulate of methodological individualism. By reducing social behaviour to that of individuals in the market, these trends matched the spirit of the times and accompanied the neo-liberal ideological, political and economic surge of which they were the sociological expression. They argued that analysis must begin with individual behaviours in explanation of social life, which, they maintained, is organized, structured and transformed on the basis of their aggregation. These utilitarian theories also developed the idea of the pernicious effects and unintended outcomes of action consequent on the aggregation of individual calculations and interests – an idea which Albert Hirschman showed in masterly fashion to be profoundly reactionary (Hirschman, 1991).

Finally, sociological thought reached its nadir at the beginning of the 1980s, when rejection of the major systems of which Parsonian functionalism and Marxism had been the two main exponents became a vision of social life which was desocialized, reduced to a clash among individuals and the image of the social vacuum.

3. The post-modern epoch

Is the destructuring of classical sociology more than simply a manifestation of the crisis of modernity as it was superseded by the onset of a post-modern era?

It took some ten years for this hypothesis to be developed and then generate important international debate in the 1980s.

The first phase involved the issues discussed at the end of the 1960s, when mention was first made of a post-industrial society (Daniel Bell, Alain Touraine). In a context of major cultural and social change, the first elements and the first variants of the post-modern critique of modernity, in particular of its post-colonial and post-national aspects, began to take shape.

From Auguste Comte to Max Weber, classical sociology had been intimately associated with modernity, which it endeavoured to analyse, to the point that one may call it modern sociology. From the end of the 1970s onwards, the period of hypotheses and discussions on post-modernity was to constitute a watershed, not so much because it proposed new analytical tools but because of the historical diagnosis that it proposed. The theoreticians of post-modernity did not invent new categories; they were not at the origin of the wide-scale introduction of new paradigms, whether in the social sciences or elsewhere, primarily in architecture. They stressed the urgent need to analyse a historic change characterized mainly by a split with everything articulated by modernity, or with what could still be envisaged as associated with it. The distinctive features of post-modern thought in its innumerable variations were firstly that it uncoupled the founding categories of modernity, thereby asserting the irremediable separation of objectivity and subjectivity, of the market and technique, on the one hand, and cultural specificities on the other. Secondly, against the inheritance of Enlightenment philosophy, it sided largely with the proponents of conviction, identities and cultural specificities. Post-modernism, from this point of view, theorized the shift from the modern project to impose reason over tradition to a challenge raised against rationality itself. The result was images of a shattered modernity or, in the expression widely used today, of 'multiple modernities' – to quote the title of an important colloquium held in Jerusalem in July 1999. In instances where modernity had campaigned against beliefs, post-modernity posed the question of knowledge, writes Serge Moscovici, to the extent that 'our post-modern vision in the main takes up a number of features which used to be associated with anti-modernity' (1995: 64).

In certain cases, the post-modern thesis, encouraged to move in this direction by the misadventures of the 'deconstructionist' school of thought, seems to end up with the negation of any sociological project. For a certain number of authors, the crisis of modernity inevitably resulted in the demise of sociology, in the explosion (which was itself post-modern) of the discipline into a large number of fairly closed sociologies, introspective because they were linked exclusively to a specific identity – 'black sociology', 'gay and lesbian studies', and so on – yielding the image, within the discipline itself, of a tendency to discard the universal values of reason and the specificities of culture on the basis of a radical challenge against universalism. Numerous protest groups claimed, in fact, that universalism comprised a broad set of phenomena of domination, and that it was the ideological shaping of specific interests, the discourse of whites adapting to the poverty and exclusion of blacks, of men continuing to oppress women, of American arrogance, and so on. Thus the recurrent theme of the crisis of sociology became that of the discipline's decline and disintegration, for example in the work of Irving Louis Horowitz (1994).

But if post-modern thought affords the image of a profound challenge against the project itself of modern or classical sociology, this is also because it accounted, in its own way, for phenomena engendering not only the cultural fragmentation of numerous societies but also the crisis of their institutions, and ultimately the exhaustion of their capacity to ensure their integration. Not only has the theme of de-institutionalization achieved considerable resonance in the sociological literature; also and especially it is the notion itself of the demise of the idea of society explored, for instance, in a series of books by Georges Balandier (1985, 1989, 1994). Can we still speak of society if the relationships among individuals and groups are no longer regulated by institutions and political mediation, or by organized negotiations, but solely by the market, by the clash of cultural specificities or violence? Classical sociology was interested in societies for which one could postulate or envisage a degree of correspondence among values, norms and roles, and in which the institutions played a central role. Its tendency towards evolutionism gave rise to the idea that every sub-set in society was defined by its place in modernization as a whole, in the universal process of progress. This correspondence increasingly seems to be artificial, and it is gainsaid by the facts, while the idea that there is 'one best way' towards progress or stages in economic growth appears to be pure ideology.

If we take the critique of modernity to its extreme, post-modern thought has sometimes insisted, for example with Jean-François Lyotard, on the demise of the 'grand narratives', beginning with those developed by social movements, of which the working class movement was the paradigm. It has also developed the idea of a loss of overall meaning, for example with Jean Baudrillard. This, however, has invigorated debate within sociology, rather than challenging its existence as a discipline. Thus, although aware of the problems discussed by the 'post-modern' school, but refusing to accept the images of the world to which it has led, some sociologists have preferred to consider the conditions under which the elements disputed by post-modernity might be re-articulated. This issue is at the core of Jurgen Habermas's work on communicational forms of action, and it is also addressed by Alain Touraine, for whom:

> without Reason, the Subject is enclosed in the obsession of its identity; without the Subject, Reason becomes the instrument of power (...) is it possible for the two figures of modernity which have either fought each other or mutually ignored one another, to finally speak to one another and learn to live together? (Touraine, 1992: 17).

Whatever the case may be, sociological thought properly speaking has never been particularly distant from political philosophy and moral philosophy. This poses an important question in so far as sociology has often seemed to lag behind them, as if the central focus of the debate no longer resided in sociology but in philosophy. I shall return to this point below.

Today, the discussion on post-modernity has gone full circle, or it has been taken over by shallow thinkers and transformed into a new form of casuistry. The theme has proved short-lived, while a second major discourse concerning the way out of modernity, and therefore out of classical sociology, has consolidated around the theme of globalization.

4. Thinking out globalization

Throughout the world, globalization is an economic, political and cultural theme rather than a specifically social one. Returning in some respects to topics central to debate at the beginning of the twentieth century, in particular among Marxists (Rudolf Hilferding, Rosa Luxembourg), analysis examines the power of the multinationals, which were particularly pervasive in the 1960s and 1970s. Criticism of contemporary forms of the internationalization of capitalism and, in the first instance, of financial capital, has provoked lively discussion between economists and critics of the economy concerning its nature, its newness, its intensity and its very reality.

Globalization challenges states and their capacity, or their will, to implement economic policies which are national or set in a regional context (Europe for example), thereby making economic policy a central issue of political debate. In cultural affairs, globalization is conveyed by a dual process of cultural homogenization (under North American hegemony) and fragmentation. This has provoked heated debate, with particular regard to the concerns aroused by the recent rise of Islam and the success of Islamism since the Iranian revolution. Here the obligatory reference is to Samuel Huntington's thesis on the 'clash' of civilizations. Finally, globalization has had major effects on social life in the strict sense, which is inseparable from flexible capitalism, to use Richard Sennett's expression (1998). It bears down on the existence itself of workers, on their personalities, marginalizes large numbers of people throughout the world, and generates sometimes substantial inequalities.

For sociology, the theme of globalization is too often a facile and universal explanation, an explanatory principle which is not in fact particularly social and which takes the place of sociological analysis. It is alleged that there is a world-wide mechanism driven by international capitalism which knows no creed or law, whose functioning inevitably exacerbates social inequalities, the destructuring of nation-states, radicalization and the risk of clash among cultural identities. This assertion might suggest analysis of the actors and the logic of globalization, but this is a task for economists and political scientists. It gives rise to a lazy form of sociology, which conceives social facts in terms of responses or reactions to the evolution of a system, neglects every institutional and political mediation between the system of globalization and those subjected to it, and underestimates the capacity for action of all the actors between the global elites and those who in one way or another undergo the effects or the consequences of their strategies.

Sociology will not advance if it restricts itself to a conception of globalization as a general principle for explanation of contemporary social problems. A principle of this sort entails that everything is due to the system, or to processes and mechanisms that are almost abstract because their protagonists are so far away; it introduces the idea of an a-social form of determinism in which the implacable forces of international capitalism, disembodied, or embodied in elusive actors outside any social relationship, are alleged to shape, uncontrolled and with impunity, a world of social inequalities and a combination of cultural massification and radicalized expressions of introverted identities. Moreover, it constructs the image of a world in which states and nations are either condemned to impotence or are subordinate to an imperial power, to North American hegemony. A world in which, if there is no violent uprising, there is little room and relevance for the political action of the states, nations and parties that structure institutional life. A world which has reached the end of history, not as Francis Fukuyama (1999) posits because of the theoretical triumph of the market and of democracy, but because of forms of cultural hegemony and economic domination which forbid any challenge against them.

On the other hand, no matter how debatable the various formalizations available may be, the advance of globalization provides sociology with the occasion to move upstream from classical sociology while resisting the ravages of post-modernism. Modern sociology has, in the main, been built around the idea of society – a society often conceived as a whole and whose divisions, structural conflicts or tensions inherent in social mobility and social inequality in no way prevent us from thinking about its unity. From the point of view of modern sociology, the social corpus is both one and plural, and its unity can be defined in cultural terms, and then primarily by reference to the idea of nation, or in political and institutional terms with reference to the state. Society, nation and state constitute the three integrated 'registers' that define modernity, according to Daniel Bell (1976), and they constitute the framework of traditional sociological analysis. The classical sociological literature constantly shifted between these registers, to the point that it sometimes considered them to be identical. Now with debate on post-modernity, and even more so on globalization, considerable changes apparent since the 1960s in each of these registers have challenged the idea of a close correspondence between society, nation and state.

On the one hand, each of these notions must be re-examined. Some scholars speak, as we have seen, of the end of the idea of society, others of states being superseded or even disappearing. What is the nature of a state whose decisions are subordinate not to the interplay of relations among states but to the decisions taken by the economic actors who shape the global economy? Yet others argue that we have entered a post-national age and propose, following the historian Eric Hobsbawm in particular, the hypothesis of the historical decline of the nation. If the scale of social, economic or cultural problems coincides with that of a nation or of a state, they seem only amenable to political solution at a level above or beyond action at the local (for example municipal) level or regional level by political systems which extend beyond the nation-state, for example in the context of Europe and its institutions, or by transnational or international organizations.

It is no longer possible to postulate the systematic unity of society, nation and state, either as the sole reality for sociological analysis or as the only dimension that is possible or desirable. The classical social relations specific to the industrial age, with its conflicts and its negotiations, and their forms of institutionalization set within a national framework (welfare state, or social democracy, for example) have weakened, or even dissolved as a result of the economic opening of the market. Mass consumption and the strategies of the producers of cultural goods make light of frontiers. The main contemporary cultural phenomena operate at a global level, whether in the form of a re-enchantment of the world through religion – a phenomenon of which Islam and Islamism are only one example among many – or of an increasingly massive and complex diaspora. Numerous actors learn, like the ecologists of the 1970s and 1980s, to think globally, even if they act locally, and their internationalism is much more deeply rooted in projects and activities which escape the national framework of action than it was at the time of the working-class movement, the internationalism of which was either abolished at its most decisive stages, for example in Europe with the war in 1914, or else corrupted with real communism.

Globalization, if one does not restrict oneself to the lazy view of it as the *deus ex machina* of sociological analysis, is a set of processes which invite us to consider, on the one hand, the new forms assumed by social relationships, states and institutions, and collective cultural identities, and on the other, the disassociation of these sub-entities. In the continuing debate initiated by post-modern thought, the introduction of the theme of globalization enables us to shift analysis from the general, the global, the universal, to the singular, the local, and the individual him/herself - to the 'subject'. It is also important in so far as it enables us to distance ourselves from the more cut-and-dried conclusions of post-modern thought.

Post-modernism, as a positive identification with the radical critique of modernity, developed in a context which was still that of the Cold War. Where East and West, capitalism and communism embodied two opposite and even conflicting versions of reason, post-modern thought introduced another division, another opposition, between the formal universalism of reason and of law embodied in the market and science, as well as in human rights, and the relativism of difference at work in the diversity of cultures or in the power of convictions rooted in concrete contexts. Post-modern thought reflected the cleavages that beset modernity; it also signified political and historical choices, opting for personal authenticity and the cultural difference among communities. Then came the fall of the Berlin Wall, the collapse of communism and the end of the conflict between the two versions of reason represented by East and West. The great debate that pitted these two forms of universalism against each other is no longer relevant; whence derives the idea of the End of History, relaunched in 1989 by Francis Fukuyama. But the debate that opposes the universalism of human rights and the market against the relativism of the post-moderns, although it may help us to understand some extreme forms of tribalism and violence, hardly corresponds to the actual experience of the great majority of the inhabitants of the planet, for whom the authenticity of cultures, religion, memory, the valorization of their difference, operate in a world in which they also succumb to the enticements of the market and claim their human rights. The theme of globalization introduces the idea of the economic and financial unity of the world in which we live, while also recognizing the importance of the plurality and heterogeneity of the cultural and social forms to which it gives rise or reinforces. It invites us to reject the choice between the thesis of uniformity alone, as symbolized by the idea of the End of History, and the thesis of the most extreme consequences of differentialism and cultural fragmentation embodied, for example, in the idea of a 'clash' among civilizations. When analysed carefully, globalization does not signify implacable opposition between McDonald's and the Jihad, but rather participation in a social life where McDonald's and the Jihad are two complementary versions, simultaneous and most of the time closely linked, of our present and future.

5. The subject

When considering these two aspects of the contemporary world, we cannot content ourselves with the observation that they are simultaneously distinct and (apart from extreme cases of oppression or violence) co-present. We must specify the forms and extent of their articulation. The latter cannot be on the side of the system since, as analyses of globalization indicate, and as the first post-modern thinkers pointed out, the general tendency is for the registers to separate, thereby disassociating reason and cultures, destructuring the relatively integrated entities formed by national societies and their states. The articulation or the re-articulation of the subjective and the objective, the universal and the specific, reason and cultures, and so on, cannot be envisaged from above, at the heart of the systems or sub-systems, the logic of which moves in the opposite direction. This is why some researchers seem to have abandoned the project of thinking it through, directing their attention primarily to systems without actors – a case in point being Niklas Luhmann – or reducing the actor to a false consciousness, or to an alienation which wholly subordinates him/her to the authority of those in power and whose categories s/he internalizes. This is also why the most promising approach is to work from the bottom up, from the person in the singular, not as an individual participating in collective life like a consumer acting in the market, but as a subject. It is perhaps exploration of this perspective that will reinvigorate sociology.

Although it did not neglect the systemic point of view, throughout the last twenty years of the twentieth century sociology never in fact interrupted a process – chaotic perhaps – of 'a return to the subject'. Admittedly, the subject had never been completely abandoned or lost from sight. But particularly after the 1960s, when functionalism fell into disrepute, the orientations that predominated either denied or minimized the subject. It was critical sociology, associated with the diverse variants of structuralism, that went furthest in this negation by asserting the 'death of the subject'. In its Marxist (Louis Althusser), neo-Marxist (Pierre Bourdieu) or non-Marxist and Nietzschean (Michel Foucault) versions, structuralist thought attacked authority, domination and alienation. It denounced the illusion of reference to the subject, the error of believing in the autonomy of the subject; and it ignored the mechanisms, instances and other structures that rule and determine the existence of the dominated. Political sociology has since turned its attention to strategic, rational forms of behaviour developed in an increasingly unpredictable world. It has been dominated by utilitarian paradigms which rely on instrumental, albeit bounded, rationality and which leave little room for the creativity of actors and their capacity to constitute themselves as the subjects of their own existence: rationality is not subjectivity, and although calculation or interest are characteristic of the rational individual, they do not necessarily make him/her into a subject.

Similarly, the various tendencies that constitute the galaxy of symbolic interactionism, (which, as we have seen, includes phenomenological sociology), with authors sometimes grouped together under the headings 'Palo Alto school', 'ethnomethodology', and so on, have taken less interest in the subject (or in intersubjectivity) than in interactions, usually discussed with no reference to history and politics and often with regard to a very small number of individuals. For Erving Goffman, the most eminent exponent of symbolic interactionism, the individual subject was little more than the capacity to adapt according to the situation, and in an interactive context in which knowing how to ensure the face-to-face presentation of self is what matters.

However, sociologists are now rediscovering the subject. Indeed, the main thesis propounded by this essay is that by focusing on the subject, sociological analysis will be much better equipped to enter the twenty-first century.

In the first instance, the idea of the 'subject' is opposed to any sort of determinism, and also to the idea that action is the outcome of objective decisions, of laws for example, as positivist thought contended. It is likewise opposed to hypercritical modes of thought which view social behaviour as no more than the expression of structural domination. In this sense, the thought of Pierre Bourdieu, as evident in his book on *La Domination masculine* (1998) is strongly alien, if not hostile, to the idea of subject, unlike that of Michel Foucault which evolved considerably in later years.

Being a subject is being the actor of one's own existence. It is creating one's personal history, giving meaning to one's experience. But we should not confuse the abstract and analytical category of the subject with the concrete and historical reality of the human person. The subject, as the term is used here, following Alain Touraine (Dubet and Wieviorka, 1995), is the capacity to relate the registers which, in the life of an individual person, appear to him/her as separate and which, if not related, are in danger of becoming totally distinct with, on the one hand, his/her participation in consumption, the market, in paid employment, access to instrumental reason, belonging to an 'objective' world, and on the other, his/her cultural identity, access to work as a creative activity, his/her religion, his/her memory, his/her experience, his/her beliefs, his/her subjectivity.

Put otherwise, in each individual, the subject is the capacity to struggle against the domination of instrumental reason, against the universalism of the rule of law and reason, when, instead of bringing emancipation, the latter ultimately negate the individual, turning him or her into a soul-less consumer, an agent manipulated by the cultural industries or by advertising, a worker subjected to Fordism, deprived of autonomy in work and dispossessed of the fruits of his or her activity. The subject is also and simultaneously the capacity to withstand subordination to the community, to liberate oneself from group law when confronted with the injunctions of a memory, norms and roles laid down by a culture, a religion or a sect. The subject is the assertion of personal liberty. But this is only part of the definition; and it must immediately be completed by what constitutes the other side of the subject: its capacity not so much for defence and protest as for constructive involvement: its creativity. The subject is also the ability to choose, to participate, to consume, to be a rational individual, while at the same time opting for the identity, the community and the memory of one's choice. The subject is the capacity simultaneously to link the two separate registers of modernity together, and to rely on one rather than the other. On the one hand, it is the strength and freedom to struggle against markets and consumption and against pure liberalism in the name of a conviction, a culture, a subjectivity, community solidarities and moral values; on the other, it is the use of reason and individualism to avoid falling under the sway of communities. The subject is the link which enables the individual to reconcile universalism and particularism, the objective and the subjective, rather than opposing them. It should be added that a definition of this kind necessarily includes a complementary – and fundamental – characteristic, namely that there can be no personal subject without the recognition of the subject in the Other.

6. The utility of the concept of the 'subject'

If we take the subject as the point of departure for analysis, a number of perspectives open up. The first of them, which are fairly simple, consists in the direct study of the subject's activity, the subject as it operates in individual practice, in institutions and in collective action. Here the concept is an analytical tool which highlights the concrete; a hypothesis which, if relevant, should yield new, or renewed, knowledge about the subject.

6.1 Corporeality

The human being is not only a soul; it is also a body, and in the past twenty years sociology has paid increasingly close attention to the body. The latter is no longer uniquely what nature, then society, make of it. On the one hand, it is and will increasingly be what each individual endeavours to make of it: a body which is built and not only acquired or scarred by life, a body which is shaped, transformed as a result of efforts to work on it and control it. This point of view relates to the classical analyses of Norbert Elias on civilization as the individualist process of control and interiorization of pulsions and affects. But it also, and primarily, gives rise to the idea of the increased capacity of humans to modify their corporeality and to develop a creative activity on the basis of their bodies, or with their bodies, in sport, dance and drama, for example, as in the analyses of certain pioneers of *cultural studies* like Stuart Hall or Paul Gilroy. On the other hand, the body is susceptible to suffering and to alteration: it is on the body that domination is physically exerted; the body is an integral part of a subject which, even before it constructs itself, must preserve itself, exist, defend itself, sometimes desperately.

The reference to the corporeal subject, both as the material envelope of a heightened creativity and as the raw material on which domination is exerted, is inseparable from sensitivity to pain and to suffering. It requires closer consideration of the points of view of victims, the ill, or those who suffer; it reminds us of the increasing refusal to reduce medicine to the technical and scientific treatment of illness. It entails that the health system must take full responsibility for the ill and those close to them. It makes the issue of euthanasia impossible to ignore.

6.2 The institutions

The study of institutions also has much to gain from the introduction of the subject's point of view. Classically, the institutions are conceived of as the locuses of socialization, of order and of public service. They thus give material form to the abstract idea of society by simultaneously ensuring the compliance of individuals with the general values of society, the maintenance of public order and community solidarity. Today this conception of institutions is fading because they find it increasingly difficulty to perform their traditional functions and are becoming de-institutionalized. But should this induce us to conclude that they are finished? Once again, the theme of the subject enables us to think in terms of *updating* and therefore of change. Instead of disappearing or withdrawing into a conception of their roles which is by necessity increasingly authoritarian and repressive, the institutions may emerge as the condition and the locus in which subjects are constituted and shaped. In the past, for example, the family was, in part at least, the institutional means by which, theoretically, values and a cultural, perhaps even material, heritage were transmitted; it was a sphere of socialization. The family now increasingly appears to be one among the many institutions that are likewise part of democracy, and in which affective and caring relationships are developed. It is thus the locus of production and valorization of subjects, and consequently the locus for learning about personal autonomy and respect for otherness. It is still an institution, but it loses some of its sacred nature; it ceases to protect possible subjects and becomes the very condition, desacralized but highly valorized, for their constitution and their functioning.

Let us consider another important institution: the school. According to the classical view, the school socializes children into individuals who comply with the norms and expectations of society. It shapes them according to the needs of the labour market; it develops awareness of their future civic or family duties and, more broadly, those of the national community. But the school is increasingly a setting in which teachers and administrators focus on the pupil and determine that s/he must be not only taught but also heard. As the school is de-institutionalized, it becomes an arena of exchange and communication, while preparing the pupil to assert his/her autonomy, to retrain during his/her life-course, and to confront new situations. It seeks to constitute the child as a subject, and not just as the recipient of teaching syllabuses and education programmes. Obviously, this does not mean that the teacher need do nothing more than to listen to pupils.

We thus discern an area of study for sociology: to wit, institutions, not only as regards their crisis or difficulty in performing their traditional functions, but also from the point of view of the subject, whether the latter consists of the personnel of institutions (which on this view cannot be reduced to impersonal agents) or the persons that they administer, manage or serve (clients, users, and so on).

One might criticise the above discussion (of the body, the family and the school) as sustaining an ideology which pertains if not to the affluent at least to the middle classes. And one might also find empirical evidence to support such criticism. But the problem, for those who wish to project themselves into the future, is precisely that the working classes, and *a fortiori* the most deprived members of society, have greater difficulty than others in gaining access to corporeal expression, the democratic family, a good school, or more generally to institutions which respect the subject. In this case, sociology must consider which conditions are conducive to the democratic production of ever more numerous and active subjects: it is a matter, to use Robert Fraisse's apt expression, of considering what 'policies for the subject' (1995: 551-64) might involve.

6.3 Social movements

Similar arguments apply to collective action, and to the highest level of its sociological expression: social movements. The contemporary movements that best enhance the subject are those in which cultural assertion and the demand for recognition of the actor's specific nature are linked together in a struggle to reduce social domination and hierarchy – those which combine cultural and social demands. In some instances, the actor is defined primarily in terms of identity and culture, which gives rise to a social movement which is not socially determined and is ultimately a middle-class form of expression, or even of dominant groups able to combine economic liberalism (of which they take advantage) with community assertion. In others, cultural dimensions give way to purely social considerations in the struggle against exclusion and poverty. In yet other cases, the excluded – landless peasants, the poor, and the marginalized – imbue their action with religious or ethnic meanings. The introduction by sociology of the 'subject' into each of these struggles must provide an authoritarian viewpoint: the more actors are able to demand cultural recognition and social justice, the greater their demand for respect and equal access to society's resources, the more they stress the individual's moral dignity and physical integrity, the more it becomes likely that they can invent the future and approach the concept of tomorrow's social movement. Those who are radical and violent confine themselves to mere declarations of a cultural existence; or yet again, the more they restrict themselves to solely economic demands, the less their action appeals to the subject, to his/her autonomy and complex capacity for involvement/non-involvement. Or, at least, there is less scope for their action to enable the direct expression of the subject. Which introduces another order of problems.

7. The absence of the subject and its prohibition

As said, the subject is never totally conveyed in concrete action. Not only is its assertion never complete, entire and, so to speak, 'pure', but in practice it is always mingled with other dimensions of action. And very often it is impossible for the subject to be translated into action: its expression is banned; it is deprived of the resources that would enable it to shape and assert itself directly; its formation involves complex processes, including a phase of disengagement and possible breach of the norms. This is why the hypothesis of the 'subject' may provide the key to understanding in terms of something that is missing. There are two situations which warrant attention here.

7.1 Violence

The first case concerns situations in which the action seemingly contradicts the image of a subject in action. These situations arise in particular when barbarism and extreme violence are perpetrated by individuals and groups which constitute the dominant elite, with a capacity for oppression which culminates in non-recognition of the subject in the Other: the dominated or subordinated population. The latter's existence is negated, and its members therefore behave as non-subjects, or even as anti-subjects. Racism, for example, is a naturalization of the Other which constitutes a negation of otherness equivalent to prohibiting the Other from being a subject. Racism is rarely pure, nor is it exclusively instrumental; rather, it is based on doctrines, ideologies and prejudice, and when it materializes, it is accompanied by discourse which seeks to legitimize or justify it. Racism is not self-sufficient because its proponents know, perhaps confusedly, that the negation of subjectivity imposed on the Other puts a price on their own subjectivity.

On the basis of the example of racism, it is possible to envisage more elaborate analyses in which certain dimensions of barbarism or violence – which in other terminology we could describe as 'evil' – are incomprehensible if we do not introduce the viewpoint of the subject. The traditional paradigms are singularly lacking here, as regards the perspectives of either instrumental rationality or culture. Thus, an exclusively utilitarian analysis which treats violence as an instrument or a resource cannot on its own explain the cruelty and the excess which accompany all experiences with a degree of significance. Nor can analysis which focuses on culture, tradition and community on its own give adequate explanation of political processes, calculations by actors and the rational nature of their acts. The destruction of the Jews by the Nazis, for example, has been analysed as an extreme form of modernity, reduced to rationality, bureaucracy, or to use Hannah Arendt's words, to the 'banality of evil'. Other analyses have focused on German culture at the time, and – this is the thesis of Daniel Goldhagen (1996) – on the profound resonance of an anti-Semitism which was only waiting for favourable conditions to emerge. But the perspective of the 'subject' may enable us to articulate these two types of approach by suggesting, for example, that anti-Semitic culture was due to frustrated nationalism, a dissatisfied subjectivity, or that the extreme cruelty of the extermination camps and of their guards enabled the murderers, as Primo Levi has put it, to be less conscious of the weight of their crimes. In order to move from the thesis of extreme rationality to that of a degree of cultural determination, it may be useful to introduce the idea of a frustrated subject, but also of a subject which does away with itself in barbaric acts which only excesses of cruelty paradoxically enable them to perform. The cruelty which accompanies genocide and other forms of ethnic cleansing is, from this point of view, characteristic of the psychological activity of a subject who is not a subject, or no longer one, and now comes closer to the figure at the opposite extreme: the *anti-subject*. This obviously does not mean that there is never any instrumentality in cruelty, inasmuch as the latter may also be used as a resource.

7.2 Privation

A second situation corresponds to cases in which individuals or groups are from the outset defined by privation, oppression, domination and rejection. In these difficult and sometimes impossible circumstances, they are prohibited from constituting themselves as subjects by authorities that they may or may not be able to identify. These individuals and groups may display forms of protest behaviour or discourse, an endeavour to provoke conflict with an adversary, if one can be recognized. But in these situations we also observe silence and, in the last resort, self-destruction. Here again the hypothesis of the prohibited subject sheds light on the matter. The sociology of work, for example, has long understood that when working-class action which is allowed and institutionalized is unable to develop within a firm, shirking or absenteeism are forms of behaviour whereby workers seek indirectly to express their desire to control their work and the fruits of their creative activity. It is also well known that alcoholism and suicide amongst workers owes much to the inability of the most deprived of them to give meaning to their existence, to construct themselves as actors of their production and as protesters against their masters. Similarly, if examined in the light of the hypothesis of a subject which is negated, maltreated, despised and subjected to arbitrary forms of racism or injustice, revolts and urban violence find an explanation which is a useful complement to the classical arguments couched in terms of crisis, dysfunction, or of calculation or the 'mobilization of resources'.

In short, it seems that a promising approach for sociology as it enters a post-classical age is to focus on the subject and possibly on its opposite, the anti-subject.

8. Is the disintegration of sociology inevitable?

The questions just discussed concern some of the hypotheses that sociology might envisage developing - or at the very least testing – in order to confront the changes now transforming social life and intersocietal relations. But sociology is not extraneous to the fields that it studies; by necessity, the sociologist is always directly or indirectly involved in his or her object of study. The foregoing analysis, if it has any relevance, calls for consideration of the discipline itself, its place in the public arena, and of the possible political involvement of the sociologist.

8.1 A universal discipline

In the years of the Cold War, sociologists endeavoured to preserve unity at the planetary level by refusing, in the name of universal values, and more specifically of reason, to sever the links between East and West. When able to do so, Western sociologists helped their colleagues in the East to exist as sociologists, and to resist total subordination to the discipline of regimes which, in so far as they recognized sociology, made it into a purported 'science' compelled to serve as an instrument of those who wielded power. One of the main functions of the International Sociological Association, in particular, was to maintain what were often vital links with sociologists in the East, helping them to survive and to prevent their international presence from being reduced to delegations of apparatchiks in the pay of zealous totalitarian regimes. Under the banner of reason, but also, if the need arose, of resistance, the unity of the discipline transcended the frontiers of political regimes and the interplay of geopolitics. Moreover, as we have seen, the functionalist paradigm, pre-eminent in the West at least until the 1960s, largely dominated sociology in the East as well: beyond the obligatory references to Marxism-Leninism, the latter long found its main inspiration in Parsonian categories. The rejection of a total cleavage between the West and the East took place under the hegemony of North-American sociology, even though some of its protagonists were highly critical of functionalist paradigms. This relationship dominated by a sociological tradition was all the more apparent because, outside the Western countries (including Latin America) and Soviet Europe, itself under American influence, there was almost no tradition and teaching, far less research, that was specifically sociological. The West therefore exercised near monopoly, if not over the production of knowledge, at least over the elaborating or propounding of paradigms. And although there may have been some discussion of the crisis in sociology, for example in Gouldner's classic book, this was due to tensions and transformations internal to sociology in the West. Sociologists were still few in number, and they were largely concentrated in Europe and in North and Latin America.

Today, everything has changed: the Cold War is behind us. However, in addition to what has just been said about East-West relations, brief mention should be made of the countries in which sociology has been alive and active in political situations which have then evolved substantially. I cite Chile as an example, where the experience of *Popular Unity* mobilized numerous sociologists, who were then repressed under Pinochet's military dictatorship, followed by a return to the market and democracy. In that country a vigorous debate was launched by J. J. Brunner, a sociologist who had entered politics and was a minister in the Frei Government at the time (1997) when he announced the twilight of sociology. Thereafter the discipline was said to be less able to give an account of the present than novels, journalism, the cinema or television. Should we see this criticism as the jaded opinions of a sociologist who had become a politician and who was dispassionately observing the discrepancy between sociological analysis and reality? Or, on the contrary, should we view it as the ideology of a thinker who contested dictatorship but then allegedly settled into a neo-liberal system, where he is now endeavouring to draw a veil over the past? Whatever the case may be, in a situation of this kind, sociology seems either to be under threat or forced to take refuge in the ivory tower of academe, and in any event has lost much of its meaning in the face of major political and economic changes (Montero-Casassus, 2000). Sociology is a subject which, throughout the world, has tens of thousands of practitioners engaged in producing and disseminating its knowledge, not to mention the much larger number of people who have been trained in sociology and use it, in one way or another but not as sociologists, in publishing, journalism, management, and so on. And just as it is undergoing considerable development,[2] the discipline is subject to tensions – for several reasons and on several registers.

8.2 Experts or critics?

The model itself of the concrete practice of sociology – as has always been the case, but in increasingly radical manner today – is split between two main camps. On the one hand, a tradition which assumes the appearance of critical sociology more frequently than it claims to adhere to models of gradual, negotiated, reforming change declares that sociology must intervene in the main discussions in the public arena; that it is an integral part of the life of ideas; and that, generally speaking, it is never very far from political or social action. This conception entails greater commitment by the researcher, who is not just defined by his/her role in the production of knowledge but assumes more normative roles – classical themes, to be sure, whether in the case of the Frankfurt school, or of Marxist sociology, so active in the 1960s and 1970s, or of Max Weber's concerns set out in his celebrated lectures on *Wissenschaft als Beruf* and *Politik als Beruf*. Today, however, the theme has been totally overhauled, given the end of yesteryear's struggles, the historical decline of the working-class movement, the twilight of the classical figure of the politically committed intellectual, the collapse of communism, the demise of the struggles for national liberation and, more profoundly, the rejection – although there is nothing to say that it is definitive – of ideologies of rupture

---

2   Which does not exclude situations where enrolments are declining, especially at the major American universities (Horowitz, 1994).

and revolution. For numerous sociologists the corollary of this rejection is the opposite temptation of 'serving the Prince' and becoming an expert or an intellectual for the constituted powers, or an institutionalized actor. Thus, the question of the sociologist's political commitment, for those who wish to continue the project of direct intervention in the life of the public arena, depends on his/her capacity to avoid two extreme temptations. S/he must steer a middle course between outright rejection, protest or denunciation as a mode of analysis, a hypercritical involvement, on the one hand; and on the other, the expertise which cuts him/her off from people's expectations, opposes him/her to protesters who challenge order or reason, and the risk of being an instrument of legitimation at the service of dominant actors or instituted social and political forces.

For many, the commitment of sociology is an ethical and professional obligation which seeks to navigate between these two extremes. I have insisted on the utility of adopting the viewpoint of the subject, a viewpoint that sheds light on this problem as well. The sociologist who refuses either to promote ideologies of rupture or to be adviser to the Prince, or to contest institutional powers, or, quite simply, to comply with the dictates of money and the market, can become the intellectual actor of liberation. His/her task is thus to produce the knowledge that enables social and political actors to constitute themselves into collective subjects while respecting and valorizing individual subjectivity.

The sociologist who places the subject at the core of his/her thought and action demands change in the classic forms of commitment. S/he is at odds with the heroic figures of the past. But s/he also differs from the expert all the more powerful today in his/her guise as a professional. The professional sociologist is an expert, a specialist; s/he possesses knowledge and expertise that identifies him/her with rationality and which s/he will use not in ideological political debates but to furnish technical services to politicians, entrepreneurs, trade unions and other organizations, public authorities and state structures, while also ensuring reproduction of the discipline by teaching sociology or writing textbooks. To over-simplify, European sociology still entertains the classic concept of commitment, with a fairly substantial willingness to endorse nineteenth-century principles. European sociologists view themselves as intellectuals: they intervene in public debate; they contribute to the editorial pages or political columns of the media; they participate in discussion with philosophers and historians. By contrast, sociology in the United States of America tends to be more strictly professional. Nevertheless an increasing number of European sociologists work as consultants or advisers, while American sociologists divide among numerous tendencies or splinter groups, some of which are   aggressively militant and highly committed. These two conceptions of sociology – politically committed or professional – have so far managed to co-exist and even to communicate. But it may be that schism is just around the corner. In several countries, the growth of the discipline has produced large sub-sets of sociologists with so much material at their disposal that they have no need to talk to each other. In this case, the outcome may be a cleavage between sociologists concerned with changing the world and those others insulated by a professionalism which cuts them off from socially crucial debate and locks them into massive and powerful networks where they are defined solely by their corporatist or professional interests. Increasingly, economic pressure and the acceptance of the market principle by academic authorities – particularly in countries where universities enjoy substantial autonomy from the state – mean that sociology must compete, sometimes for its very existence on the curriculum, with other disciplines for funding and demand, and this is a requirement which certainly does not encourage political involvement.

8.3 Fragmentation

In so far as sociology proceeds in a world both globalized and fragmented, there is a risk that the discipline itself will become globalized and fragmented. In actual fact, the globalization of sociology has subjected it to the hegemony of North American sociology, its language and categories. The danger thus arises of a sociological universalism which imposes its ethnocentricism, with a *de facto* impoverishment of the production of knowledge.

The contrary danger is that of disintegration, with the constitution of national and regional strongholds distinct from this universalism and which define themselves in relation to it on the basis of pure opposition, if only linguistic. We thus see the emergence of breakaway groups in Asia or in the Arab-Muslim world; and although the associations of francophone, lusophone or other sociologists are not connoted by radical struggle against imperialism or North American hegemony, they are nonetheless open to such radicalization. This is a major challenge to be addressed by sociology. Those who consider the issue, like Immanuel Wallerstein during his presidency of the International Sociological Association (1994-1998), have sought remedies to ensure that English (and the imposition of its thought patterns) does not dominate other languages with necessarily more slender resources, but is instead used jointly with them. It has been suggested, for example, that the passive use of languages other than one's own should be promoted. Thus, at a meeting, each participant would speak in his/her mother tongue while the others present would be expected, not to express themselves in all the languages used, but to understand them. Sociologists discuss cultural diversity at length and the interest and difficulties of multiculturalism: their discussions would be more persuasive if they themselves could devise ways to communicate while recognizing linguistic diversity. Sociologists consider how to reconcile the universal and the particular, rather that opposing them in an antithesis typical of post-modernity and a globalized world: it is by putting their own house in order, by settling the problem for themselves, by learning to live with their linguistic differences that they will acquire greater credibility. This is a particularly important issue, for it affects the very core of the discipline. If the internationalization of sociology, instead of encouraging the superseding of national or other specificities, is in danger of ultimately reinforcing them, then it would be appropriate to question not only the political, but also the intellectual and epistemological status of regional, national, even local sociological production. We must pursue the debate which, in the 1980s, took the form of an opposition between the universalism of a sociology which extended in a uniform manner throughout the entire world and the project of 'indigenism' which leads to the multiplication of 'indigenous sociologies', in the words of Akinsola Akiwowo (1999: 155–60).

Should we consider, as Jean-Michel Berthelot wonders, that 'the social and cultural determination of knowledge must be applied to sociology as it is to other systems of knowledge' (1998: 23), with the danger which he himself points out of 'subjecting sociological knowledge to the exclusive determination of its context of production (which amounts to) asserting its *relative* value'? Is the problem not rather to learn to reconcile different points of view, by ceasing to set them in diametrical opposition, while also not endeavouring to merge one in the other?

Here another essential point requires making: these questions are global, but they also arise within each national sociology, and in particular in the Anglo-Saxon world, where whole areas of knowledge are becoming autonomous – in communication, town planning, studies on health, criminology, and so on – as pointed out by the authors of an article devoted to these problems in the journal *Sociologie et sociétés* (Bernard, Fournier and Saint-Pierre, 1998: 3), who also note that 'new intellectual and social perspectives, like feminism, cultural studies, post-modernism or gay and lesbian studies are literally taking the place of sociology on the shelves in the bookshops'.

8.4 Between political philosophy and the natural sciences

The above remarks raise a number of questions relative to sociology itself and its internal transformations. To these questions could be added a further set concerning the future relations of sociology and other spheres of knowledge, and which could be extended to the problems of its place in relation to various actors on the social scene, beginning with the media – although I shall leave this particular point aside.

There is no reason whatsoever to postulate the stability of the present division of disciplines in the order of knowledge. In the recent past, the attempt to develop socio-biology has shown that it is possible to challenge Durkheim's well-known dictum that it is appropriate to explain the social by the social, by studying social behaviour *qua* natural behaviour; this attempt has exerted only a limited and highly unequal impact, depending on the country concerned. But everything which deals with the human body, on the one hand, and with ecology on the other, suggests that important transformations will in the future affect the relationship between nature and culture, and compel sociology to think of nature in other terms, and to consider its own relationship with the 'hard' sciences. Above all, now that we can no longer consider the individual to be a creature of nature with his/her needs or aggressiveness, and while we are moving away from the idea that the role of society is to restrain and control these needs or this aggressiveness through socialization, we observe that the natural sciences are making great advances, also in areas which are usually part of the humanities and social science. The cognitive sciences and neuroscience in particular are suggesting approaches which have already, in many respects, absorbed a part of what used to be psychology; they could equally well in the future, basing themselves on the extraordinary progress of computer science, encroach on the terrain of sociology. A decisive test will be the way in which the paradigm of complexity as developped, for istance, by Edgar Morin, and the impossibility of prediction now increasingly accepted by the so-called 'exact' sciences will, or will not, become imperative in sociology as well.

Moreover, disciplines close to sociology are changing. For example, anthropology, which in some cases has turned its attention to Western societies, does so with the aid of tools forged in the study of colonial or exotic societies. Its objects, but also its methods, bring it closer to sociology, as is apparent when a social anthropologist studies urban conflicts, the functioning of political institutions, or family relationships in a European setting: thus the use of the method of participant observation is equally valid for both disciplines. It is true that there is a considerable distance between social anthropology and sociology, and that the former has long been primarily concerned with the existence of systems of order and the reproduction of societal entities, while sociologists have been more interested in crisis and in change. It is also true that anthropology has been more marked by structuralism than has sociology; but it is developing, and it too is opening up to the 'subject'.

Similar considerations apply to history, in particular when it decides to take an interest in the present, with the risk of encroaching on sociology's terrain, or when it enters into tension with memory, which is associated not only with places but also with persons and groups who refer to their subjectivity, which may be somewhat unhappy. Similarly, the more open sociology becomes to the subject, the more absurd it is to distinguish it totally from psychology. At the very core of the social sciences, it is very likely that processes of decomposition and recomposition of spheres and competence will be at work in the future; and some of these processes are already visible.

The problem becomes even more complex when we consider the relations between sociology and moral or political philosophy. One may ask whether sociology does not risk being squeezed between the natural sciences, which are expanding, and moral and political philosophies which have the immense and paradoxical advantage over sociology of being able to indulge in the articulation of theoretical analysis and normative proposals without having to concern themselves with the production of empirical knowledge relative to the problem under consideration. Thus, we observe that the contemporary debate on multiculturalism has indeed seen sociologists participating actively in the discussion. But the latter have been completely dominated by political philosophers. The specific contribution of sociologists in a debate of this kind should be to furnish knowledge about the way in which cultural differences are reproduced and produced, about the tensions which these processes induce within the societies in question, or yet again, to give an account of the work by the actors concerned on themselves. But this they do not do to any great extent, instead venturing into terrain where political and moral philosophers are much more at their ease, and putting forward and discussing concepts of the just and unjust, of good and evil, and suggest policies.

Sociology is in difficulties here in so far as it hesitates to decide between political commitment and what I have called 'professionalism'. If sociology becomes politically involved, it runs the risk of being caught up in discussions where its production of a specific form of knowledge gives way to more philosophical and political concerns. And if it shifts towards the expert or the professional, or again if it is too narrowly restricted to a phenomenology of what exists, it runs the risk of being excluded from public debate, where actors want to know more about good and evil, the just and the unjust, than about the mechanisms and the interplay of actors through which community life is transformed.

Bibliography

Akiwowo, A. (1999), 'Indigenous Sociologies. Extending the Scope of the Argument', *International Sociology*, vol. 14, no. 2, pp. 115-38.

Alexander, J. (1982), *Theoretical Logic in Sociology*, Free Press, Berkeley.

Balandier, G. (1985), *Le Détour: pouvoir et modernité*, Fayard, Paris.

Balandier, G. (1989), *Le Désordre: éloge du mouvement*, Fayard, Paris.

Balandier, G. (1994), *Le Dédale: pour en finir avec le XXème siècle*, Fayard, Paris.

Bell, D. (1976), *The Cultural Contradictions of Capitalism*, Basic Books, New York.

Bernard, P., Fournier, M. and Saint-Pierre, C. (1998), 'Présentation. Au-delà de la crise, un second souffle pour la sociologie', *Sociologie et Sociétés*, vol. XXX, no. 1, p. 3.

Berthelot, J.M. (1998), 'Les nouveaux défis épistémologiques de la sociologie', *Sociologie et Sociétés*, vol. XXX, no. 1, pp. 8-27.

Bourdieu, P. (1998), *La Domination masculin*, Seuil, Paris.

Coser, L.A. (1956), *The Functions of Social Conflict*, The Free Press of Glencoe, Glencoe.

Coser, L.A. (1967), *Continuities in the Study of Social Conflict*, Free Press, New York.

Dubet, F. and Wieviorka, M. (sous la direction de) (1995), *Penser le sujet. Autour d'Alain Touraine*, Fayard, Paris.

Fraisse, R. (1995), 'Pour une politique des sujets singuliers', in F. Dubet and M. Wieviorka (sous la direction de), *Penser le sujet. Autour d'Alain Touraine*, Fayard, Paris, pp. 551-64.

Fukuyama, F. (1999), 'La post-humanité est pour demain', *Le Monde des Débats*, no. 5, pp. 16-20.

Goldhagen, D. (1996), *Hitler's Willing Executioners, Ordinary Germans and the Holocaust*, Alfred A. Knopf, New York.

Gouldner, A.W. (1971), *The Coming Crisis of Western Sociology*, London, Heinemann.

Hirschman, A. (1991), *The Rhetoric of Reaction: Perversity, Futility, Jeopardy*, Harvard University Press, Boston.

Horowitz, I.L. (1994), *The Decomposition of Sociology*, Oxford University Press, Oxford.

Joas, M. (1999), *La creativité de l'agir*, Cerf, Paris.

Montero - Casassus, C. (2000) 'Crépuscule ou renouveau de la sociologie: un débat chilien', *Cahiers Internationaux de Sociologie*, vol. 108, pp. 38-56.

Moscovici, S. (1995), 'Modernité, sociétés vécues et sociétés conçues', in F. Dubet and M. Wieviorka (sous la direction de), *Penser le sujet. Autour d'Alain Touraine*, Fayard, Paris, pp. 57-72.

Sennett, R. (1998), *The Corrosion of Character. The Personal Consequences of Work in the New Capitalism*, Norton, London.

Touraine, A. (1986), 'Sociologies et sociologues', in M. Guillaume (sous la direction de), *L'Etat des sciences sociales en France*, La Découverte, Paris, pp. 134-35.

Touraine, A. (1992), *Critique de la modernité*, Fayard, Paris.

Wieviorka, M. (1986), 'Le déploiement sociologique', in M. Guillaume (sous la direction de), *L'Etat des sciences sociales en France*, La Découverte, Paris, pp. 149-55.

3 The challenge of multiple modernities

SHMUEL N. EISENSTADT

1. Re-examination of some assumptions of classical sociology and of studies of modernization

Modern sociology as it developed in Europe in the nineteenth century – and later also in the United States – was focused on the understanding of modernity as it took shape in Europe.

It assumed that the basic contours of modernity as they emerged in Europe did indeed constitute the model of modern society. It assumed also, without fully examining this assumption, that the modern nation-state as it crystallized in Europe constituted, as it were, the natural format of modern society, that indeed it was the very epitome of the embodiment of the institutional and cultural programme of modernity.

These assumptions were most clearly formulated in the theories of modernization and the convergence of industrial societies, with strong roots in classical sociological analyses, and they assumed, even if only implicitly, that the basic institutional constellations that came together in European modernity, and the cultural programme of modernity as it developed in the West, would 'naturally' be ultimately adopted in all modernizing societies. Studies of modernization and of the convergence of modern societies assumed that this project of modernity, with its hegemonic and homogenizing tendencies, would continue in the West, and that with the expansion of modernity, it would prevail throughout the world. Implicit in all these approaches was the assumption that the modes of institutional integration attendant on the development of such relatively autonomous and differentiated institutional spheres would be largely similar in all modern societies.

The reality that has emerged proves to be radically different. Current developments in all or most societies indicate that the various institutional arenas – economic, political and familial – exhibit relatively autonomous dimensions that come together in different ways in different societies and in different periods of their development. Indeed, developments in the contemporary era do not bear out the assumption of 'convergence'; they have

99

emphasised the great diversity of modern societies, even of ones similar in terms of economic development, like the major industrial capitalist societies – those in Europe, the United States and Japan. Sombart's question 'Why is there no socialism in the United States?' formulated in the first decades of this century was the first, albeit still only implicit, recognition of this fact. Far-reaching variability developed even in the West: within Europe itself, and above all between Europe and the Americas comprising the United States, Latin America, or rather the Latin Americas (Sombart, 1976).

The same applied a fortiori to the relation between the cultural and structural dimensions of modernity. A very strong – even if implicit – assumption of the studies of modernization, namely that the cultural dimensions or aspects of modernization (the basic cultural premises of Western modernity) were inherently and necessarily interwoven with the structural ones, became highly questionable. While the different dimensions of the original Western project constituted the crucial starting point and constant frame of reference for the processes that developed in different societies throughout the world, developments in these societies have now gone far beyond the homogenizing and hegemonic dimensions of the original cultural programme of modernity.

Modernity did indeed spread to most of the world, but it did not give rise to a single civilization, or to one institutional pattern, but rather to the development of several modern civilizations, or at least civilizational patterns (that is, civilizations sharing common characteristics) which still tend to develop different albeit cognate ideological and institutional dynamics. In other words, it gave rise to multiple modernities. Moreover, far-reaching changes which go beyond their original premises of modernity have been taking place in Western societies.

2. Modernity as a distinct civilization: the cultural and political programme of modernity

Thus close re-examination or reappraisal of the assumptions of studies on modernization may yield understanding of some of the problems facing sociology today. The central focus of such re-examination is recognition that the modern and contemporary world is a world of multiple and continually changing modernities, and changing institutional formations thereof especially in the nation-state.

Such reappraisal should be based on several considerations. It should be based first of all on acceptance that the expansion of modernity must be viewed as the crystallization of a new type of civilization – not unlike the expansion of great religions, or the great imperial expansions of the past. However, because the expansion of this civilization almost invariably combined economic, political and ideological aspects and forces, its impact on the societies to which it spread was much more intense than in the majority of historical cases.

This expansion spawned a tendency – rather new and almost unique in the history of mankind – towards the development of universal, world-wide institutional and symbolic frameworks and systems. The new civilization that emerged first in Europe later expanded throughout the world, creating a series of international frameworks or systems, each of them based on certain of this civilization's basic premises; and each rooted in one of its basic institutional dimensions. Several economic, political, ideological, almost world-wide systems – all of them multi-centred and heterogeneous – emerged, and each generated its own dynamics, its continual change in constant relation to the others. The interrelations among them were never static, and the dynamics of these international frameworks or settings gave rise to continuous changes in the societies concerned.

Just as did the expansion of all historical civilizations, so that of the civilization of modernity undermined the symbolic and institutional premises of the societies involved, opening up new options and possibilities. As a result, a great variety of modern or modernizing societies developed, sharing numerous characteristics but also evincing marked differences.

The modern project, the cultural programme of modernity as it developed first in Western and Central Europe, brought about an obvious shift in the conception of human agency, of its autonomy, and of its place in the flow of time. It exacerbated the tensions between the constructive and destructive potentialities of the construction of social orders, highlighting the challenge of human autonomy and self-regulation and of consciousness thereof.

All these were indeed modern societies and regimes, sharing basic premises of modernity, especially a refusal to take the legitimacy of the social, ontological and political orders for granted, constant reflexivity and contestation against them, and the insistence that active participation in the construction of these orders was possible. The core of this cultural programme has been perhaps most successfully formulated by Weber. To quote James D. Faubian's exposition of Weber's conception of modernity:

> Weber finds the existential threshold of modernity in a certain deconstruction: of what he speaks of as the "ethical postulate that the world is a God-ordained, and

hence somehow meaningfully and ethically oriented cosmos..."

...What he asserts – what in any event might be extrapolated from his assertions – is that the threshold of modernity has its epiphany precisely at the legitimacy of the postulate of a divinely preordained and fated cosmos has its decline; that modernity emerges, that one or another modernity can emerge, only as the legitimacy of the postulated cosmos ceases to be taken for granted and beyond reproach. Counter-moderns reject that reproach, believe in spite of it....

One can extract two theses. First: whatever else they may be, modernities in all their variety are responses to the same existential problematic. Second: whatever else they may be, modernities in all their variety are precisely those responses that leave the problematic in question intact, that formulate visions of life and practice neither beyond nor in denial of it but rather within it, even in deference to it.

Other responses are possible: "traditionalizing" and "countermodern" responses among them... Other responses may even be more satisfying. So at least they seem to be, if not for most, still for man among us... The world is certainly not yet all modern. It is not likely ever to be (Faubian, 1993: 113 –15).

It is because all such responses leave the problematic intact that the reflexivity which developed in the programme of modernity went beyond that which crystallized in the 'axial civilizations' (Eisenstadt, 1982: 294-314, 1986). The reflexivity that developed in the modern cultural programme focused not only on the possibility of different interpretations of the transcendental visions and basic ontological conceptions prevalent in a society or civilization, but came to question the very givenness of such visions and of the institutional patterns related to them. It gave rise to awareness of the multiplicity of such visions and patterns and of the possibility that they can be contested.

Concomitantly, closely related to such awareness and central to this cultural programme were the emphasis on the autonomy of man, on his or her – but in the programme's initial formulation certainly 'his' – emancipation from the fetters of traditional political and cultural authority, and on the continuous expansion of the realm of personal and institutional freedom, of human activity, creativity and autonomy. In parallel, the programme entailed heavy emphasis on autonomous participation by members of society in the construction of the social and political order and its constitution; on the autonomous access of all members of society to these orders and their centres. The programme required a conception of the future in which various possibilities realizable by autonomous human agency, or by the march of history, were opened up.

From the conjunctions of these different conceptions there developed a belief that society can be formed by conscious human activity.

This common core of the modern programme also gave rise to a distinct political programme. It entailed radical transformation of the parameters and premises of the political order, of its legitimation, and of conceptions of the accountability of rulers, basic attitudes to tradition and authority, as well as the basic characteristics of centres and of centre-periphery relations. The central purpose of this political programme was breaking down the traditional legitimation of the social and political order, and opening up different possibilities for legitimation and contestation vis-à-vis the ways in which the political order was be constructed by human actors.

The basic characteristics of the modern programme – the combination of an open future with the belief that society can be formed by conscious human activity – also shaped the premises of the modern political order and of collective identities and boundaries. The core of the political programme of modernity was the breakdown of the traditional legitimation of the political order; with the concomitant opening up of different possibilities for construction of that order and contestation of the ways in which it was constructed. It combined rebellion, protest, and intellectual antinomianism, together with strong orientations to centre-formation and institution-building, giving rise to social and protest movements as a constant component of the political process (Eisenstadt, 1999a). It entailed the combination of the charismatization of the centre or centres with the incorporation into the latter of themes and symbols of protest which became components of modern transcendental visions as basic and legitimate components of the premises of those centres. Themes and symbols of protest – equality and freedom, justice and autonomy, solidarity and identity – became central to the modern project of humankind's emancipation. It was the incorporation of such themes of protest into the centre that heralded the radical transformation of various sectarian utopian visions into central components of the political and cultural programme (Eisenstadt, 1999b; Seligman, 1989).

In parallel, construction of the boundaries of modern collectivities and collective identities was continually problematized in reflexive ways (Shils, 1975: 111–26; Eisenstadt and Giesen, 1995: 72–102; Eisenstadt, 1998: 229–54). Collective identities and boundaries were not taken as given or preordained by some transcendental vision and authority, or by perennial customs. They constituted foci not only of reflexivity but also of contestation and struggle, often couched in highly ideological terms and promulgated above all by different – above all national or nationalist – movements. Such contestation focused first on the relative importance of the basic components of collective identities – the civil, primordial and universalistic and transcendental 'sacred' ones – and on the modes of their institutionalization. Second, the contestation focused on the extent of the connection between the construction of political boundaries increasingly defined in territorial terms and those of cultural collectivities; and third, on the relations between the territorial and/or particularistic components of these collectivities and broader, potentially universalistic ones.

Concomitantly, a crucial component in the construction of collective identities was society's self-perception as 'modern', as carrying forward a distinct cultural and political programme – and its relations from the point of view, to other societies – both societies which claim to be (or are seen to be) bearers of this programme and various 'others'.

The programme and civilization of modernity as it first developed in the West was from its very beginning – this being the case of all great civilizational visions, for instance those of the axial civilizations – beset by internal antinomies and contradictions and tensions, giving rise to continual critical discourse which focused on the relations, tensions and contradictions between its premises and between these premises and institutional developments in modern societies.

The importance of these tensions was fully understood in the classical sociological literature – Tocqueville, Marx, Weber or Durkheim – and it was later taken up in the 1930s, above all by the Frankfurt school and so-called 'critical' sociology, although this focused mainly on the problems of fascism, to be then neglected by post-Second World War studies on modernization. It has recently returned to the fore to constitute a continual component of the analysis of modernity (Joas, 1996: 13-27, 1999: 457-72; 501-4; Tiryakian, 1999: 473-90; Roxborough, 1999: 491-500; Giddens, 1985).

The tensions and antinomies that developed within the basic premises of this programme were, first, those between totalizing and more diversified or pluralistic conceptions of its major components (the very conception of reason and its place in human life and society, and of the construction of nature, of human society and its history); second, between reflexivity and the active construction of nature and society; third, those among different evaluations of major dimensions of human experience; and fourth between control and autonomy.

The tension most critical from the point of view of the development of the various cultural and institutional patterns of modernity, and of the possible destructive potentialities thereof, was that between absolutizing totalization and more pluralistic multi-faceted visions and practices – between the view that accepted the existence of different values, commitments and rationalities and the view which conflated such different values and rationalities totalistically, with strong tendencies towards their absolutization. In the cultural-ideological dimension of the modern programme, the most important such conflations of different rationalities was the one often identified as the principal message of the Enlightenment – the sovereignty of reason – which subsumed value-rationality (*Wertrationalität*) or substantive rationality under instrumental rationality (*Zweckrationalität*) in its technocratic mode or under a totalizing moralistic and utopian vision.

In modern political discourse and practice these tensions solidified around the problem of relations between, on the one hand, the legitimate plurality of discrete individual and group interests and of different conceptions of the common good and social order, and on the other, totalizing ideologies which denied the legitimacy of such pluralities.

One major form of totalistic ideology that developed in modernity emphasised the primacy of collectivities perceived as distinct ontological entities based on common primordial and/or spiritual attributes – above all national collectivities. The other such totalistic ideology was Jacobinism, the historical roots of which went back to medieval eschatological sources, and the essence of which was a belief in the primacy of politics and in the ability of politics to reconstitute society, and the conviction that society could be transformed by totalistic mobilized participatory political action (Eisenstadt, 1999). Whatever the differences between these collectivistic and absolutizing ideologies, they were all deeply suspicious of the open political process and of institutions, especially the representative institutions and free public discussion, and also of strong autocratic tendencies and the endeavour to exclude others and demonize those excluded.

These various tensions in the political programme of modernity were closely related to those among the different modes of legitimation of modern regimes, especially but not only of constitutional and democratic polities – namely between, on the one hand, procedural legitimation in terms of civil adherence to rules of the game, and on the other, in different 'substantive' terms, a marked tendency to promulgate other modes or bases of legitimation, above all, to use Edward Shils' terminology, primordial, 'sacred' – religious or secular – ideological components (Shils, 1975: 111-26).

In the construction of collective identities and collectivities, these tensions were manifest in the contradictions between tendencies to the absolutization of primordial and/or Jacobin universalistic components of collective identities as against a more open or multi-faceted approach to such construction; between the closely related tendencies to homogenize social and cultural spaces and the construction of more multiple spaces allowing for heterogeneous identities. Given the strong territorial orientations of these components of collective identity, the struggles centred on their construction were closely related to struggles among states, and to an extent unprecedented in comparison with 'pre-modern' civilizations.

All these tensions, but especially that between the totalizing and more pluralistic conceptions of constitution of human society, history and nature and of the place of human agency in these constructions, between some type of an overarching 'logocentric', usually some 'grand narrative', and a more pluralistic conception of the meaning of life and the construction of society, between emphases on different dimensions of human existence, between control and autonomy, existed from the very beginning of the promulgation of the cultural programme of modernity; and they constituted a constant component in the development and continual reconstruction of this programme.

3. The crystallization of multiple modernities

All these antinomies and tensions developed from the very beginning of the institutionalization of modern regimes in Europe. The continual prevalence of these antinomies and contradictions also had – as the classics of sociology were fully aware but as studies of modernization have largely forgotten or neglected – far-reaching institutional implications, and it closely interwove with the different institutional patterns and dynamics that developed in different modern societies.

It was around these various tensions and contradictions that there developed the different modern institutional-cultural patterns: multiple modernities. They first arose in Europe, where they focused on the cleavages between utopian and civil orientations. Principles of hierarchy and equality competed in the construction of the political order and political centres. The state and civil society were seen as separate entities by some. Collective identity, very often couched in utopian terms, was differently defined. The variety of the resulting societal outcomes can be illustrated by the different conceptions of state that developed on the continent and in England. There was the strong homogenizing 'laicization' of France, or, in a different vein, of the Lutheran Scandinavian countries, as against the much more consociational and pluralistic arrangements of Holland and Switzerland, and to a much smaller extent of Great Britain. The strongly aristocratic semi-feudal conception of authority in Britain contrasted with more democratic, even populist, views in other European countries (Kuhnle, 1975; Rothstein, 1996; Thompson, 1960; Geyl, 1958; Beloff, 1954; Daalder, 1971: 355-70; Bergier, 1974; Lehmbruch, 1972; Lorwin, 1971: 141-75; Steiner, 1974).

These tensions between the constitutional and destructive potentialities of modernity became even more visible with the expansion of modernity beyond Europe to the Americas. The first radical transformation of the premises of the cultural and political order took place with the spread of modernity to the Americas. There, distinctive modernities reflecting novel patterns of institutional life emerged, with new self-conceptions and new forms of collective consciousness. It is important to note that these modernities, Western but significantly different from those of Europe, developed first, not in Asia (Japan, China, or India) or in Muslim societies, where they might have been attributed to the existence of distinct non-European traditions, but within the broad framework of Western civilizations. They reflected a radical transformation of European premises.

As said, these tensions and contradictions became even more evident with the spread of modern civilizations beyond the West and Europe to the Americas. With the dynamics of continually developing international frameworks or settings, several new crucial elements became central to the constitution of modern societies. Of especial importance was the relative place of the non-Western societies in various – economic, political, ideological – international systems which differed greatly from that of the West. It was not only Western societies that were the 'originators' of this new civilization. Beyond this, and above all, there was the fact that the expansion of these systems, especially in so far as it took place through colonialization and imperialist expansion, gave the Western institutions hegemony over these systems. But it was in the nature of these international systems that they generated dynamics which gave rise to political and ideological challenges against existing hegemonies, as well as to constant shifts in the loci of hegemony within Europe, from Europe to the United States, then also to Japan and East Asia.

But the economic, military-political and ideological expansion of the civilization of modernity from the West throughout the world was not the only factor responsible for this process. No less important (possibly even more so) was the fact that this expansion gave rise to continual confrontation between the cultural and institutional premises of Western modernity and those of other civilizations – those of other axial civilizations, as well as non-axial ones – the most important of which was, of course, Japan. To be sure, many of the basic premises and symbols of Western modernity as well as its institutions – representative, legal and administrative – were seemingly accepted by these civilizations, but at the same time far-reaching transformations in them took place and new challenges and problems arose.

The attraction of these themes – and of many of the basic political institutions – lay in the fact that their appropriation permitted many groups in non-European nations (especially elites and intellectuals) to participate actively in the new modern (that is, initially Western) universal tradition, while also selectively rejecting many of its aspects as well as Western 'control' and hegemony. The appropriation of these themes made it possible for these elites and broader strata of many non-European societies to incorporate some of the universalistic elements of modernity in the construction of their new collective identities, without necessarily giving up either specific components of their traditional identities (which were often couched in universalistic, especially religious terms which differed from those that predominated in the West) or their negative attitudes towards the West.

The attraction of these themes of political discourse to many sectors in the non-Western European countries was intensified by the fact that their appropriation in these countries entailed the transposition to the international scene of the struggle between hierarchy and equality. Although initially set out in European terms, it found resonances in the political traditions of many of these societies. The transposition of these themes from Western Europe to Central and Eastern Europe and then to non-European settings was reinforced by the combination, in many of the programmes promulgated by these groups, of protest with institution-building and centre-formation.

This transposition was engendered not only by the higher hierarchical standing and hegemony of the Western countries in these new international settings, but also by the fact that the non-Western civilizations were put in an inferior position in the evaluation of societies promulgated by the seemingly universalistic premises of the new modern civilizations.

Thus various groups and elites in Central and Eastern Europe and in Asia and Africa were able to refer to both the tradition of protest and the tradition of centre-formation in these societies, and to cope with problems of reconstructing their own centres and traditions in terms of the new setting. The most important aspect of the expansion of these themes beyond Western Europe, and of their appropriation by different groups in non-Western

European societies, lay in the fact that it made it possible to rebel against the institutional realities of the new modern civilization in terms of its own symbols and premises (Eisenstadt and Azmon, 1975).

But the appropriation of different themes and institutional patterns of the original Western modern civilization in non-Western European societies did not entail their acceptance in their original form. Rather, it entailed the continuous selection, reinterpretation and reformulation of such themes, giving rise to a continual crystallization of new cultural and political programmes of modernity, and the development and reconstruction of new institutional patterns. The cultural programmes that continued to develop in these societies entailed different interpretations and far-reaching reformulations of the initial cultural programme of modernity, its basic conceptions and premises. They entailed different emphases on different components of this programme, on its different tensions and antinomies, and the concomitant growth of distinct institutional patterns. They entailed the constant construction of symbols of collective identities, their conceptions of themselves and of their role, and their negative or positive attitudes to modernity in general and to the West in particular.

These differences between the various cultural programmes of modernity were not purely 'cultural' or academic. They were closely related to basic problems inherent in the political and institutional programmes of modernity. Thus, in the political realm, they were closely bound up with the tension between the utopian and the civil components in the construction of modern politics; between 'revolutionary' and 'normal' politics, or between the general will and the will of all; between civil society and the state; between individual and collectivity. These different cultural programmes of modernity also entailed different conceptions of authority and of its accountability, different modes of protest and of political activity, of questioning the basic premises of the modern order and different modes of institutional formation.

The foregoing considerations concerning the multiple programmes of modernity do not of course gainsay the obvious fact that in many central aspects of their institutional structure – whether in occupational and industrial structure, in the structure of education or of cities, or in political structures – very strong convergences developed in different modern societies. These convergences generated common problems, but the modes of coping with these problems (that is, the institutional dynamics attendant on the development of these problems) differed greatly between these civilizations.

But it is not only in the societies of Asia or Latin America that developments have occurred which go beyond the initial model of Western society. At the same time, in Western societies themselves new discourses have developed which have greatly transformed the initial model of modernity, undermining the original vision of modern and industrial society with its hegemonic and homogenizing vision. There has emerged a growing tendency to distinguish between *Zweckrationalität* and *Wertrationalität*, and to recognize a great multiplicity of different *Wertrationalitäten*. Cognitive rationality – especially as epitomized in the extreme forms of scientism – has been dethroned from its hegemonic position, and so too has the idea of the 'conquest' or mastery of the environment – whether of society or of nature.

The growth of European modernity and its later expansion was by no means peaceful. Contrary to the optimistic views of modernity as inevitable progress, the crystallizations of modernities were constantly riven with internal conflict and confrontation rooted in the contradictions and tensions attendant on the development of the capitalist systems and, in the political arena, on growing demands for democratization. The development of modernity bore within it destructive possibilities that were often voiced, somewhat ironically, by some of its most radical critics, who considered modernity to be a morally destructive force, emphasising the negative effects of certain of its core characteristics. All these factors were compounded by international conflicts exacerbated by the modern state and imperialist systems. War and genocide were scarcely new phenomena in history. But they became radically transformed, intensified, generating specifically modern modes of barbarism. The ideologization of violence, terror and war – first and most vividly apparent in the French Revolution – became the most important component in the construction of modern states. The tendency towards such ideologies of violence became closely related with the fact that the nation-state became the focus of symbols of collective identity (Joas, 1996, 1999).

The Holocaust, which took place in the very centre of modernity, became a symbol of its negative, destructive potential, of the barbarism lurking at its very core.

4. The processes of globalization and transformation of the classical model of the nation-state

The multiple and divergent instantiations of the 'classical' age of modernity crystallized during the nineteenth century, and above all in the first six or seven decades of the twentieth, into very different territorial nation- and revolutionary states and social movements in Europe, the Americas, and, after

World War Two, in Asia. The institutional, symbolic, and ideological contours of modern national and revolutionary states, once thought to be the epitome of modernity, have changed dramatically with the recent intensification of the forces of globalization. These trends, especially manifest in the growing autonomy of world financial and commercial flows, have intensified international migrations and the concomitant development on an international scale of such social problems as disease, prostitution, organized crime and youth violence. All this has reduced the control of the nation-state over its own economic and political affairs, despite continuing efforts to strengthen technocratic, rational secular policies in various arenas. Nation-states have also lost a part of their monopoly over internal and international violence (always only a partial monopoly, in fact) to local and international groups of separatists or terrorists. The processes of globalization are also evident in the cultural arena, with the hegemonic expansion, through the mass media in many countries, of what seem to be uniformly Western, above all American, cultural programmes or visions (Friedman, 1994; Hannerz, 1992; Marcus, 1993; Smolicz, 1998: 1-18).

The ideological and symbolic centrality of the nation-state, and its position as the charismatic locus of the major components of the cultural programme of modernity and collective identity, have been weakened; new political, social, and civilizational visions, new visions of collective identity, are being developed. These novel visions and identities have been promulgated by a variety of new social movements, all of which, however different, have challenged the premises of the classic modern nation and its programme of modernity that hitherto occupied the unchallenged centre of political and cultural thinking.

The first such movements to develop in most Western countries – the women's movement and the ecological movement – were both closely related to or rooted in the student and anti-Vietnam War movements of the late 1960s and early 1970s. They were indicative of a more general shift in many countries, whether 'capitalist' or communist, away from centre-oriented movements to ones with a more local scope and agenda. Instead of focusing on the reconstitution of nation-states, or on resolving macro-economic conflicts, these new forces – often presenting themselves as 'postmodern' and 'multicultural' – promulgated a cultural politics or a politics of identity often conceived as multiculturalism, and they were oriented to the construction of new autonomous social, political, and cultural space (Eisenstadt, 1999). Somewhat later, fundamentalist movements emerged within Muslim, Jewish, and Protestant communities, and they managed to occupy centre stage in many national societies and, from time to time, the international stage as well. Communal religious movements have similarly developed within Hindu and Buddhist cultures, generally sharing strong anti-modern and/or anti-Western themes (Marty and Scott Appleby, 1991, 1993, 1994, 1995; Eisenstadt, 1999). A third major type of new movement to have gathered momentum, especially in the last two decades of the twentieth century, consists of particularistic 'ethnic' movements and identities. First apparent in the former republics of the Soviet Union, these have also emerged in horrific manner in Africa and in part of the Balkans, especially in former Yugoslavia.

All these movements have developed in tandem with, and indeed have accelerated, far-reaching social transformations, and they have helped to consolidate new social settings and frameworks. To mention just two of the most important of these settings, the world now sees new diasporas, especially of Muslims, Chinese, and Indians. New types of ethnic minority have come to the fore since the collapse of the Soviet Empire, with Russian minorities emerging as vocal forces in many of the successor states of the Soviet Union and in the former communist countries of Eastern Europe.

All these processes have reduced the control of the nation-state over its own economic social and political affairs, despite the continual strengthening of 'technocratic', rational and secular policies in various arenas, such as education or family planning. Concomitantly, the model of the nation-state has lost its symbolic centrality. At the same time, the nation-state has ceded some of its monopoly over internal and international violence to local and international groups of separatists or terrorists, with no nation-state, or even the concerted action of several of them, being always able to control the constantly recurring occurrence of such violence.

Indeed one of the common denominators of many of these new movements and settings is that they do not see themselves as bound by the homogenizing cultural premises of the classical model of the nation-state – especially by the places allotted to them in the public spheres of such states. It is not that they resist being 'domiciled' in their respective countries; indeed, part of their struggle is to become so domiciled, but on rather new – as compared to classical models of assimilation – terms.

In these and many other settings, new types of collective identity have emerged which go beyond the models of the nation- and revolutionary-state, and are no longer focused on them. Many of these hitherto 'subdued' identities – ethnic, local, regional and transnational – have moved, though in a highly reconstructed way, to the centre of their respective societies, and often into the international arena as well.

They have contested the hegemony of the older homogenizing programmes, claiming their own autonomous place in central institutional arenas – educational programmes, public communications, media outlets. Increasingly successful in advancing far-reaching claims for redefinition of citizenship, and the rights and entitlements connected with it, they are forces to be reckoned with. In these settings, local concerns and interests are often brought together in new ways, going beyond the model of the classical nation-state, choosing alliances with transnational ones like the European Union, or broad religious identities rooted in the great religions of Islam, Hinduism, Buddhism, or the Protestant branches of Christianity. Simultaneously, we witness the continuing decomposition of the relatively compact image offered by traditional belief systems of lifestyles defining the 'civilized man' – all connected with the emergence and spread of the original programme of modernity (Eickelman, 1983: 13-30, 1993; Piscatori, 1996; Hefner, 1998: 83–104). It is indubitable that significant and enduring shifts are taking place in the relative position and influence of different centres of modernity, and that they move back and forth between West and East. This has inevitably produced increased strife between these centres over their degree of influence in a globalizing world (Tiryakian, 1991: 165-80, 1996: 99-118).

Concomitantly, there have developed processes of the constant decomposition of the more or less compact image of the 'civilized man', of the life-worlds and the lifestyles associated with the promulgation of the original nation-state and programme of modernity. There is much greater pluralization and heterogenization in such images and representations. In tandem there have developed new interpretations of modern collective identities – far-reaching reinterpretations of national identity and of modern social spaces or, for instance, of cities or urban settings – all of them redefining modernity in their own distinct terms.

In all these settings and movements, tensions between pluralist and universalist programmes, between multi-faceted as opposed to closed identities, and the constant ambivalence of new centres of modernity towards the traditional centres of cultural hegemony, have constantly articulated, attesting to the fact that, while these new movements have gone beyond the model of the nation-state, they have not gone beyond the basic problematics of modernity. They all are deeply reflexive, aware that no answer to the tensions inherent in modernity can be final – even if each in its own way seeks to provide final, incontestable answers to modernity's irreducible dilemmas. They have reconstituted the problem of modernity in new historical contexts, and in new ways. They strive after the world-wide reach and diffusion, especially through the media, of the movements themselves. They are politicized, formulating their contestation in highly political ideologies and terms. The problems that they face, continually reconstructing their collective identities with reference to the new global context, is a challenge of unprecedented proportions. The very pluralization of life spaces in the global framework endows them with highly ideological absolutizing ideas, and at the same time brings them into the central political arena. The debate in which they engage may indeed be described in 'civilizational' terms; but these same terms – indeed the term 'civilization' itself as constructed in such discourse – are already couched in modernity's new language, utilizing a totalistic, essentialistic and absolutizing lexicon. When such clashes intersect with political, military or economic struggles, they may rapidly become violent.

Reconstruction of the various political and cultural visions across the spectrum of collective identities on the contemporary scene entails a shift in the confrontation between Western and non-Western civilizations, between religions and societies, but also a shift in the relationship of these confrontations with the Western cultural programme of modernity. As against the apparent, if highly ambivalent, acceptance of modernity's premises and their constant reinterpretation characteristic of the earlier reformist religious and national movements, most contemporary religious movements – including fundamentalist ones and most communal religious movements – seemingly engage in a much more intensively selective denial of at least some of these premises. They take up a markedly confrontational attitude towards the West, indeed to anything conceived as Western, seeking to appropriate modernity and the global system on their own, often anti-Western, terms. Their confrontation with the West does not take the form of seeking to become incorporated into a new hegemonic civilization. It is instead an endeavour to appropriate the new international global scene and the modernity for themselves, celebrating their traditions and 'civilizations'. These movements have attempted to dissociate Westernization from modernity, denying the Western monopoly on modernity, rejecting the Western cultural programme as the epitome of modernity. Significantly, many of these same themes have also been espoused, though in different idioms, by numerous 'post-modern' movements (Eisenstadt, 1999).

5. Re-examination of basic concepts of sociological analysis: civil society and the public sphere

All these developments attest to the weakening, transformation, or decay of the 'traditional' or classic nation-state – above all to the uncoupling of its basic components – citizenship, collective identities, and the construction of public spaces and modes of political participation. They also entail far-reaching changes in the construction of public spheres and in the relations between civil society and the political sphere – both in different states and on the international stage, where many new local, translocal and international public spaces have taken shape. In these spaces the new modes of constitution of the civil society in relation to the state, of public spheres and new conceptions, far-reaching claims to the redefinition of citizenship and the rights and entitlements connected with it have been advanced.

Thus, all these developments, which evince a new phase in the crystallization of multiple modernities, call for reappraisal of many of the concepts – notably civil society, nationalism – and assumptions that have guided sociological analysis, and they raise some of the most important challenges faced by sociology in the twenty-first century. I shall illustrate these challenges by examining two such concepts – civil society and public sphere – and then 'nationalisms'.

Various notions of civil society were proposed and elaborated in different European contexts in the seventeenth and eighteenth centuries, especially within the intellectual tradition of what came to be called the Scottish Enlightenment but also earlier by such scholars as Pufendorf. However, the revival of interest in this concept in contemporary social science has been largely and somewhat curiously restricted to the particular conceptualization of civil society formulated mainly by Hegel in a continental European setting in the period of transition from absolutist monarchies to nations and states. This conceptualization certainly did not apply to other European societies such as those of the Scandinavian countries, Holland, or even England in which the influence of 'society' over the 'state' was much greater than in German states, or even in France (Eisenstadt and Schluchter, 1998, and the references therein).

Whatever its strengths and weaknesses, the discourse on civil society long remained dormant in the social science literature – to be revived after the break-up of the Soviet Empire and the promulgation of the concept of civil society as a norm for Middle- and East-European societal reconstruction. This revived discourse was attended by closer attention to the concept of 'public spheres' in the period after the Second World War – a concept set out in Jürgen Habermas' Structural Transformation of the Public Sphere, a book which has gained further recognition in contemporary debate (Habermas, 1989). In that discourse, the concepts of public sphere and civil society were often coupled, overlapped, almost conflated, often with no clear distinction between them. Moreover, in the contemporary debate the strong assumption has developed that the development of a public sphere and civil society is the crucial condition for the formation and development of constitutional and democratic regimes (Cohen, 1999: 208-48).

A look at the available historical and contemporary evidence shows that these assumptions are very problematic. First the relations between civil society, public sphere and the political arena are much more variable than these assumptions envisage. The concept of a public sphere implies that there are at least two other spheres from which the public sphere is more or less institutionally and culturally differentiated: the official sphere and the private one. It is, therefore, a sphere located between the official and the private spheres. It is one in which collective improvements, the common good, are at stake. This also applies to the official sphere. But in the latter this activity is carried out by groups that do not belong to the ruler's domain. Rather, the public sphere draws its membership from the private sphere. It expands and shrinks according to the shifting involvements of such membership, as Albert O. Hirschman has demonstrated with regard to modern development (1970, 1982). Public spheres tend to develop dynamics of their own which, although closely related to that of the political arena, are not coterminous with it and are not governed by the dynamics of the latter. Instead, they develop in different ways in different societies, and in different relations not only to the rulers but also to what has been often called 'civil society'.

Hence these two concepts – public sphere and civil society – should not be conflated. The public sphere must be regarded as lying between the official and the private. And it must also be regarded as a sphere that expands and shrinks according to the constitution and strength of those sectors of society that are not part of the rulership. Civil society entails a public sphere, but not every public sphere entails a civil society of the economic or political variety defined in contemporary discourse, especially as it developed in early modern Europe through direct participation, whether by corporate bodies or through a more or less restricted suffrage of the political process in which private interests played a crucial role. We expect that every civilization with some complexity and literacy will see a public sphere emerge, but one not necessarily of the European civil society type (Eisenstadt, 1987).

But whatever the differences with respect to the relations among public sphere, civil society and the political arena, in all societies these relations have entailed constant conflict on power, authority, its legitimation and accountability.

However, the autonomy of the ulema, the hegemony of the Sharia and the constant yet variable vitality of the public spheres in Muslim society did not imply autonomous participation in the central political arena, as one might deduce from more recent discussion of civil society. They did not entail direct autonomous access to the political domain, or to be more precise, to the domain of rulership; nor to the decision-making process of rulers as it developed in Europe, in parliaments and corporate urban institutions, although needless to say some – often very forceful – attempts to exert such influence did develop in many Muslim societies. In matters of concrete, especially foreign or military, policy, as well as in internal affairs like taxation and the keeping of public order and in supervision of their own officials, the rulers were quite independent from the various actors in the public sphere.

A central ideological component of the upholding of the moral order, of the cohesion of the community, even if concretely, pragmatically, it constituted a necessary condition for the implementation of sharia. There thus developed in Muslim, especially Sunni, societies a highly interesting decoupling between construction of the public sphere and access to decision-making by the rulers and the relation between an autonomous and vibrant public sphere and the political arena. Or to be more precise, the rulers developed in Muslim societies in directions which differed greatly from those in Europe (especially Western and Central). For that matter, they also differed from those of the other Asian civilizations that developed: India, for instance, where the political order did not constitute a major arena for implementation of the predominant transcendental and moral vision, where sovereignty was highly fragmented, and where rulership was to a very large extent embedded in a very flexible caste order (Goodwin Raheja, 1988: 497-522; S. Rudolph and L. Rudolph, 1967, 1987; Wink, 1994) which gave rise to vibrant public sphere with a relatively strong access to the rulers; or China, where it was the political order that constituted the major arena for implementation of the transcendental visions, and where it was the rulers, together with the Confucian literati that constituted the custodians of this order, with very limited scope for an autonomous public sphere (Wakeman Jr., 1998: 167-90; Woodside, 1998: 191-220; Eisenstadt, 1992).

Such variability in the construction of civil society and the public sphere, and in their relations with political arenas, can also be identified in nation-states of the classical period of modernity, and even more so in the contemporary scene.

6. Re-examination of basic concepts of sociological analysis: heterodoxies and the construction of collective identity

Similar considerations apply to the analysis of nationalism. No matter how interesting and pressing the problems of nationalism may be in Eastern Europe, in communal conflict and strife in India, or in civil wars in several African states, the issues of nationhood and nationalism appear rather limited in scholarly terms if not set against the backdrop of national identity as just one construction of collective identity, and in historical terms a rather late and by no means all-pervasive one (Eisenstadt and Schluchter, 1998).

Many of the recent theories of nationalism veer between viewing it as either a constant manifestation of primordiality or as an 'imagined' community that developed in modern times only in response to the expansion of capitalism, industrialism and imperialism. A closer look at the historical and contemporary evidence indicates that collective identities in general are not naturally given but culturally constructed, and that such construction has always constituted a basic dimension of the constitution of society. This approach also runs counter to the implicit assumptions of most classical sociological and anthropological positions that such construction is ephemeral or secondary to power or economic relations.

Collective identities are constituted through the cultural construction of boundaries, which allows a distinction to be drawn between those who belong and those who do not. Maintaining boundaries, however, requires ongoing interpretive efforts through which solidarity and trust are created among the members of the collectivity. A central aspect of such construction is the promulgation and definition of the attribute of 'similarity' among its members. The distinction also poses the problem of how to manage the crossing of established boundaries. The stranger can become a member, and a member a stranger. Religious conversion and excommunication are obvious illustrations of these possibilities.

The construction of collective identities is influenced or shaped by codes through which the ontological or cosmological premises and conceptions of the social order prevalent in a society influence the definition of the main arenas. The major codes of the construction of collective identity are primordiality, civility, and sacredness.

The construction of collective identities has characterized all human societies throughout their histories, and it has been effected in all societies by the interaction among special social actors. It has constantly occurred in different historical settings, including the axial civilizations as well as non-axial ones like Japan (Eisenstadt, 1995). However, the development of universal 'religious' collective identities, as distinct from political and 'primordial' ones, was the achievement of the axial civilizations. Throughout the history of these civilizations, continual changes in the composition of the elite gave rise to important changes in the constitution of collective identities. In many of them one of the most important of these developments was the transformation of more ecumenical conceptions into vernacular ones. Outside Europe, this happened not only during the period from the sixteenth to the eighteenth centuries but sometimes much earlier and sometimes much later.

While it is obvious that the construction of the collective identities that arose in the modern era – designated as nations or nation-states – evinces very distinct characteristics, in order to understand its specificity one must analyse the features shared by this construction with other modes of such construction, and also compare it with other modes in different historical settings and periods.

As said, the construction of collective identities has been effected in all these societies by interaction among special social actors – the proponents of the solidarity of collectivities, other elites and broader sectors of society. In the history of mankind, this construction has occurred in different historical settings, including that of the main axial civilizations, two of which – the Chinese and the Indian – are the focus of our research, as well as a society or civilization like Japan which was constantly impacted by these axial civilizations. It was in the latter, in close connection with their tendency to expansion that there developed new 'civilizational' or 'religious' collectivities, distinct from political and from 'primordial' ones, and yet continually impinging on them and interacting with them and giving rise to a continual reconstruction of their respective collective identities. These processes of reconstruction were carried forward by continual struggle, contention and interaction between the new autonomous cultural elites which were the proponents of the axial vision and the protagonists of the solidarity and political elites of the different continually reconstructed 'local' and political communities.

Throughout the history of these civilizations, constant changes in the composition of these various elites gave rise to far-reaching changes in the constitution of collective identities of the societies that developed within these civilizations. One of the most important of these developments, which took place in many of these civilizations in the sixteenth to eighteenth centuries, was the already-mentioned shift from an ecumenical conception of the civilizational collectivity to more territorially centred ones. The history of the construction in Europe of this type of collective identity or consciousness from the sixteenth century onwards, leading to the formation of the territorial states – ultimately the nation-state – has been studied in great detail. As pointed out above, a parallel emphasis on territoriality developed in the realm of Islam in the Ottoman Safavid and Mogul Empires; in China under the Ming and Ching, and in Vietnam; in Japan under the Tokugawa, and even in South-East Asia. But this parallel development did not necessarily mean – contrary to what many contemporary studies assume – that the pattern of relations between this emphasis on territorial boundaries and other components of collective identity, especially the primordial ones, and their relations with the centres of society developed in the same direction as they did in Europe. Rather distinct patterns of collective identities, the basic components of collective identity – civil, primordial and cultural-universalistic in their relations to territory – developed at the time in India, in China or South-East Asia. Great differences also arose in these societies with respect to the extent to which the centre promulgated strong symbolic and affective commitments and distinct cultural programmes. In all these societies, such developments entailed different relations with the dynamics of the public spheres that developed in these societies.

The construction of collective identities as brought about by different combinations and concrete specifications of the basic codes and subcodes mentioned above has traversed human history in all human societies. The construction of collective identity interwoven with economic political and processes has taken place in different institutional arenas, whether territorial, communal or religious, and in different economic and different political-ecological settings – be these small city states or great kingdoms.

Of crucial importance to the construction of collective identities are inter-societal, intercivilizational contacts. No 'society' exists as a single enclosed system. The populations which live within the confines of what has been designated a 'society' or a macro-societal order are never organized into one 'system', but rather into several systems, including political systems, economic formations, different ascriptive collectivities, and civilizational frameworks. Each of these 'systems' or frameworks with their flexible boundaries is sustained by different coalitions. These different structures and patterns evince different patterns of organization, continuity and change. They may change within the 'same' society to different degrees and in different ways in various areas of social life. Moreover, only very rarely are the members of such a population confined to any single 'society' – even if one such 'society' seems to be the salient macro-order for them; usually they live in multiple settings or contexts.

The importance of such 'international' forces or inter-societal interactions in the construction of collective identities is especially visible in the disintegration of relatively narrow tribal or territorial units resulting from the formation of the Great Archaic empires – Ancient Egypt, Assyria, or the Meso-American ones – and later the Axial-Age civilizations. These processes of disintegration and reconstruction of collective identities were in all cases connected with advances in agricultural and transport technology, with the growing mutual impingement of heterogeneous economic (nomadic, sedentary, etc.) and ethnic populations, with some degree of international political-ecological volatility in general, and with processes of immigration and/or conquest in particular. All these cases of growing internal structural differentiation involved the concomitant growth of new, broader collectivities, and of new patterns of collective identity.

The construction within such different settings of the collective identity of any single society or group usually entails selection and redefinition of some of their broader themes and codes and their different combinations. This selection takes place through a process of contestation and struggle among different social actors acting in a particular social situation and within a framework of symbolic acts. Different coalitions of such actors tend to select and reconstruct these themes or codes.

Such processes of the construction of collective identities within the broader international context also entail the crystallization of a multiplicity or plurality of collectivities and collective identities, both among different collectivities and within any relatively closely defined macro-collectivity. The nature of this plurality or heterogeneity differs greatly according to the constellations of codes and themes by which the different collectivities, above all the respective macro-collectivities, are constituted, according to the nature of the broader international settings within which they develop and the interaction between these settings and the various internal groups and elites, especially the interaction between the respective bearers of such orientations in each setting, and between them and other – political and economic – actors.

7. Some considerations on the applicability of basic concepts of sociological analysis in the contemporary scene

The plurality and indeed multiplicity of collectivities and collective identities have developed in different ways in different civilizations and historical settings – in the ancient kingdoms and city states, in axial civilizations, in modern territorial and nation-states and in contemporary settings – and they call for constant re-examination of both the assumptions that have guided sociological analysis and the concepts used by it (Eisenstadt and Schluchter, 1998). Such re-examination must provide clues to the applicability of Western social concepts. We cannot avoid their use, but we can make them flexible, so to speak, through differentiation and contextualization. Such an endeavour entails the development of diverse perspectives in order to analyse these civilizations and encourage intercultural dialogue among them.

Thus, the use of concepts like 'primordial', 'civil' and 'sacred' as components of collective identities is helpful as long as we do not presume that the way in which these components were elaborated and combined in Europe constitutes the evaluative yardstick for other modernizing civilizations and societies. The construction of collective identities may develop in many different directions, depending, among other factors, on the main symbols available, and especially on the relative importance of religious, ideological, primordial, and historical components among those symbols; the conception of the political order and the relation between the political order to other societal orders; the conception of political authority and its accountability; the nature of the public sphere; the conception of the subject; and the modes of centre-periphery relations.

If we use such concepts as 'political order', collective identity and 'public sphere' to compare historical and modern civilizations, we must take care to avoid the pitfalls of both Western- and Eastern-centredness. Such a fallacious position can be found, for instance, in the Nihonjinron literature, with its claims concerning the incomparable uniqueness of Japan. We cannot identify uniqueness without making comparisons. For instance, there is the attitude of 'inverted orientalism' sometimes to be found among the more critical of Western and Japanese scholars. This 'inverted orientalism' developed in reaction to the Nihonjinron literature, giving rise to the denial of the validity of certain Japanese categories of thought as applied to the analysis of Japanese historical and contemporary experience. The approach proves to be rather paradoxical, since it goes against the exploration of those categories emphasised by the critics of the 'orientalist' approach.

The existence of debate around these problems attests to the intricacies of comparative research, and it is also indicative of some of the major challenges facing sociological analysis in the twenty-first century. The root of these problems is not only the fact that, at least until recently, most of the scholars who addressed these problems came from the West but also the fact that this type of research has developed almost entirely – Ibn Khaldun notwithstanding – separately from the Western modern discourse. The adoption of various critical stances toward the earlier 'orientalist' literature – in the West, in India, in Japan, and elsewhere – has remained part of this discourse, and the continuous reconstruction by its intellectuals in on-Western countries has greatly transformed it. But for the most part these interventions have not gone beyond the confines of this discourse. Whether it will be possible to do so in the future is one of the major challenges for sociology in the twenty-first century.

Bibliography

Balazs, E. (1968), *Chinese Civilization and Bureaucracy. Variations on a Theme*, New Haven Press, New Haven.

Beloff, M. (1954), *The Age of Absolutism: 1660-1815*, Hutchinson & Co., London.

Bergier, J. (1974), *Naissance et croissance de la Suisse industrielle*, Francke Verlag, Bern.

Cohen, J. (1999), 'Trust, Voluntary Association and Workable Democracy: The Contemporary American Discourse of Civil Society', in M. Warren (ed), *Democracy and Trust*, Cambridge University Press, Cambridge.

Daalder, H. (1971), 'On Building Consociational Nations: The Case of the Netherlands and Switzerland', *International Social Science Journal*, vol. 23, pp. 355-70.

Eickelman, D. (1983), 'Changing Interpretations of Islamic Movements' in W.R. Roff (ed), *Islam and the Political Economy of Meaning*, Croom Helm, London, pp. 13-30.

Eickelman, D. (ed) (1993), *Russia's Muslim Frontiers: New Directions in Cross-Cultural Analysis*, Indiana University Press, Bloomington.

Eisenstadt, S.N. (1982), 'The Axial Age: The Emergence of Transcendental Visions and the Rise of Clerics', *European Journal of Sociology*, vol. 23, no. 2, pp. 294-314.

Eisenstadt, S.N. (1986), *The Origins and Diversity of Axial-Age Civilizations*, Suny Press, New York.

Eisenstadt, S.N. (1987), *European Civilization in a Comparative Perspective*, Norwegian University Press, Oslo.

Eisenstadt, S.N. (ed) (1992), *Kulturen der Achsenzeit II. Ihre Institutionelle und Kulturelle Dynamik, Teil I. China, Japan*, Surhkamp, Frankfurt am Main.

Eisenstadt, S.N. (1995), *Japanese Civilization. A Comparative View*, University of Chicago Press, Chicago.

Eisenstadt, S.N. (1998), 'The Construction of Collective Identities. Some Analytical and Comparative Indications', *European Journal of Social Theory*, vol. 1, no. 2, pp. 229-54.

Eisenstadt, S.N. (1999a), *Paradoxes of Democracy: Fragility, Continuity and Change*, The Woodrow Wilson Center Press and the Johns Hopkins University Press, Baltimore.

Eisenstadt, S.N. (1999), *Fundamentalism, Sectarianism and Revolutions: The Jacobin Dimension of Modernity*, Cambridge University Press, Cambridge.

Eisenstadt, S.N. and Azmon, Y. (1975), *Socialism and Tradition, Atlantic Highlands*, Humanities Press, New York.

Eisenstadt, S.N. and Giesen, B. (1995), 'The Construction of Collective Identity. Some Analytical and Comparative Indications', *European Journal of Sociology*, vol. 1, no. 2, pp. 72-102.

Eisenstadt, S.N. and Schluchter, W. (1998), 'Introduction: Paths to Early Modernities – A Comparative View', *Daedalus*, vol. 127, no. 3, pp. 1-18.

Faubian, J.D. (1993), *Modern Greek Lessons: A Primer in Historical Constructivism*, Princeton University Press, Princeton.

Friedman, J. (1994), *Cultural Identity and Global Process*, Sage, London.

Geyl, P. (1958), *The Revolt of the Netherlands*, Barnes and Noble, New York.

Giddens, A. (1985), *The Nation-State and Violence*, University of California Press, Los Angeles.

Goodwin Raheja, G. (1988), 'India: Caste, Kingship, and Dominance Reconsidered', *Annual Review of Anthropology*, vol. 17, pp. 497-522.

Habermas, J. (1989), *Structural Transformation of the Public Sphere*, MIT Press, Cambridge.

Hannerz, U. (1992), *Cultural Complexity*, Columbia University Press, New York.

Hefner, R. (1998), 'Multiple Modernities: Christianity, Islam, and Hinduism in a Globalizing Age', *Annual Review of Anthropology*, vol. 27, pp. 83-104.

Hirschman, A.O. (1970), *Exit, Voice and Loyalty: Responses to Decline in Firms, Organizations, and State*, Harvard University Press, Cambridge.

Hirschman, A.O. (1982), *Shifting Involvement: Private Interest and Public Action*, Princeton University Press, Princeton.

Joas, H. (1996), *Die Modernitat des Krieges*, Leviathan, vol. 24.

Joas, H. (1999), 'The Modernity of War: Modernization Theory and the Problem of Violence', Symposium on War and Modernization Theory, *International Sociology*, vol. 14, no. 4, pp. 457-72.

Joas, H. (1999), 'For Fear of New Horrors: A Reply to Edward Tiryakian and Ian Roxborough', Symposium on War and Modernization Theory, *International Sociology*, vol. 14, no. 4, pp. 501-3.

Kuhnle, S. (1975), *Patterns of Social and Political Mobilizations. A Historical Analysis of the Nordic Countries*, Sage, London.

Lehmbruch, G. (1972), *Proporzdemokratie: Politisches System und politische Kultur in der Schweiz und in Österreich*, J.C.B. Mohr, Tübingen.

Lorwin, V. (1971), 'Segmented Pluralism, Ideological Cleavage and Political Behavior', *The Smaller European Democracies*, Comparative Politics, vol. 3, pp. 141-75.

Marcus, G. (ed) (1993), *Perilous States. Conversations on Culture, Politics, and Nation*, University of Chicago Press, Chicago.

Marty, M.E. and Scott Appleby, R. (eds) (1991), *Fundamentalisms Observed*, University of Chicago Press, Chicago.

Marty, M.E. and Scott Appleby, R. (eds) (1993), *Fundamentalisms and the State. Remaking Polities, Economies, and Militance*, University of Chicago Press, Chicago.

Marty, M.E. and Scott Appleby, R. (eds) (1993), *Fundamentalisms and Society. Reclaiming the Sciences, the Family and Education*, University of Chicago Press, Chicago.

Marty, M.E. and Scott Appleby, R. (eds) (1994), *Accounting for Fundamentalisms. The Dynamic Character of Movements*, University of Chicago Press, Chicago.

Marty, M.E. and Scott Appleby, R. (eds) (1995), *Fundamentalisms Comprehended*, University of Chicago Press, Chicago.

Piscatori, J. (1996), *Muslim Politics*, Princeton University Press, Princeton.

Rothstein, B. (1996), *The Social Democratic State. The Swedish Model and the Bureaucratic Problem of Social Reforms*, University of Pittsburgh Press, Pittsburgh.

Roxborough, I. (1999), 'The Persistence of War as a Sociological Problem', Symposium on War and Modernization Theory, *International Sociology*, vol. 14, no. 4, pp. 491-500.

Rudolph, S. and Rudolph, L. (1967), *The Modernity of Tradition. Political Development in India*, University of Chicago Press, Chicago.

Rudolph, S. and Rudolph, L. (1987), *In Pursuit of Lakshmi: The Political Economy of the Indian State*, University of Chicago Press, Chicago.

Seligman, A. (ed) (1989), *Order and Transcendence*, E.J. Brill, Leiden.

Shils, E. (1975), 'Primordial, Personal, Sacred and Civil Ties', in E. Shils (ed), *Center and Periphery, Essays in Macrosociology*, University of Chicago Press, Chicago.

Smolicz, J. (1998), 'Nation-States and Globalization from a Multicultural Perspective. Signopsis from Australia', *Nationalism and Ethnic Politics*, vol. 4, no. 4, pp. 1-18.

Sombart, W. ([1906] 1976), *Why Is There No Socialism in the United States?*, ME Sharpe, New York.

Steiner, J. (1974), *Amicable Agreement Versus Majority Rule: Conflict Resolution in Switzerland*, University of North Carolina Press, Chapel Hill.

Thomson, D. (1960), *England in the Nineteenth Century*, Pelican Books, London.

Tiryakian, E. (1991), 'Modernizaton: Exhumetur in Pace' (Rethinking Macrosociology in the 1990s'), *International Sociology*, vol. 6, no. 2, pp. 165-80.

Tiryakian, E. (1996), 'Three Cultures of Modernity: Christian, Gnostic, Chtonic', *Theory Culture and Society*, vol. 13, no. 1, pp. 99-118.

Tiryakian, E. (1999), 'War: The Covered Side of Modernity', Symposium on War and Modernization Theory, *International Sociology*, vol. 14, no. 4, pp. 473-89.

Wakeman, F. Jr. (1998), 'Boundaries of the Public Sphere in Ming and Qing China', *Daedalus*, vol. 127, no. 3, pp. 167-90.

Wink, A. (1994), *Al-Hind: The Making of the Indo-Islamic World*, Paper Presented at the International Symposium on Indian Studies, November 28–December 2, Kovalam.

Woodside, A. (1998), 'Territorial Order and Collective Identity Tensions in Confucian Asia: China, Vietnam, Korea', *Daedalus*, vol. 127, no. 3, pp. 191-220.

4 Modern societies as knowledge societies

NICO STEHR AND VOLKER MEJA[1]

Introduction

John Stuart Mill, in *The Spirit of the Age* (1831), gave voice to his growing conviction that the intellectual accomplishments of his age made social progress somehow inevitable (Cowen and Shenton, 1996: 35-41). But progress in the improvement of social conditions is not, Mill argued, the outcome of an 'increase in wisdom' or of the collective accomplishments of science.

It is linked to a general diffusion of knowledge:

> (m)en may not reason better concerning the great questions in which human nature is interested, but they reason more. Large subjects are discussed more, and longer, and by more minds. Discussion has penetrated deeper into society; and if greater numbers than before have attained the higher degree of intelligence, fewer grovel in the state of stupidity, which can only co-exist with utter apathy and sluggishness (Mill, [1831] 1942: 13).

Mill's observations in the mid-nineteenth century, a period he regarded as an age of moral and political transition, and in particular his expectation that increased individual choice (and hence emancipation from 'custom') would result from a broad diffusion of knowledge and education, chimes with the notion of present-day society – the social structure that is emerging as industrial society gives way – as a 'knowledge society'.

Economic capital – or, more precisely, the source of economic growth and value-adding activities – increasingly relies on knowledge.

The transformation of the structures of the modern economy by knowledge as a productive force constitutes the 'material' basis and a major justification for designating advanced modern society as a 'knowledge society'.

This type of society is characterized by the penetration of all of its sphe-

---

1   In addition to a range of other problems of modern societies as knowledge societies, the specific issues taken up in this essay are discussed at greater length in the following two volumes: Stehr, 2000a and 2000b.

127

res by scientific and technical knowledge.[2] The greatly enhanced social, political and economic significance of science and technology calls for an analysis of the increasingly central role of knowledge. A century from now historians, Lester Thurow has observed, will look back on the current era of 'man-made brainpower industries' as the third industrial revolution, symbolized by the fact that the world's richest man, Bill Gates, controls no natural resources, but instead ' a knowledge process' (Ledwith, 1999).

Knowledge has of course always had a major function in social life. That human action is knowledge-based might even be regarded as an anthropological constant. Social *groups*, social *situations*, social *interaction* and social *roles* all depend on, and are mediated by, knowledge. Relations among *individuals* are based on their knowledge of each other.[3] Indeed, if (as in the interactionist tradition in sociology) such a general notion of knowledge is regarded as the foundation of social interaction and social order, we find that the very possibility of social interaction requires situation-transcendent knowledge of individuals engaging in social action. Power too has frequently been based on knowledge advantages, not merely on physical strength. Societal reproduction, furthermore, is not just physical reproduction but has always also been cultural: that is, it involves reproduction of knowledge. In retrospect, even some ancient societies (Rome, China, the Aztec Empire) that gained and maintained power in part as a result of their superior knowledge and information technology may be described as knowledge societies of sorts. Ancient Israel was founded upon its law-like Torah-knowledge, and in ancient Egypt religious, astronomical and agrarian knowledge served as the organizing principle and basis of authority. In this sense, knowledge has had an important function throughout history, and humans have always lived in 'knowledge societies'.

But in present-day society knowledge has clearly become much more fundamental and even strategic for all spheres of life, greatly modifying and in some cases replacing factors that until recently had been constitutive of social action.

---

2   An extended discussion of the term 'knowledge' is contained in Stehr (1994: 5-17, 2000a). Robert Lane (1966:650) first employed the term 'knowlegeable society', but it was Peter Drucker (1969) who first specifically referred to 'knowledge society', a term used later also by Daniel Bell (1973) and, more recently, by Gernot Böhme (1997). There have been various other attempts to find a term suited to describing the new type of social structure, including 'science society' (Kreibich, 1986), 'information society' (Nora and Minc, 1980), 'postindustrial society' (Bell, 1973), 'postmodernization' (e.g. Inglehart, 1995), 'technological civilization' (Schelsky, 1961), and 'network society' (Castells, 1996).

3   See Georg Simmel's ([1908] 1992: 383-455) analysis of the secret and the secret society in his *Soziologie*.

1. Knowledge as capacity for action

We define knowledge as *capacity for action*. The term 'knowledge' is derived from Francis Bacon's famous observation that knowledge is power. Bacon suggests that knowledge derives its utility from its capacity to set something in motion. Bacon's term *potentia*, that is, *capacity*, is employed to describe the power of knowing. More specifically, Bacon asserts at the outset of his *Novum Organum* that 'human knowledge and human power meet in one; for where the cause is not known the effect cannot be produced. Nature to be commanded must be obeyed; and that which in contemplation is the cause is in operation the rule'.

The definition of knowledge as capacity for action has multi-faceted implications and consequences. *Capacity* for action signals that knowledge may in fact be left unused, or that it may be employed for 'irrational' ends. The thesis that knowledge is invariably pushed to its limit, that it is often translated into action without regard for its possible consequences – as argued, for instance, by C.P. Snow (Sibley, 1973) – is a typical view among observers of technological development. However, the claim that science and technology invariably push for the practical implementation of scientific and technical knowledge does not give proper recognition to the context of implementation of such knowledge. Such a conception of the immediate practical efficacy of scientific and technological knowledge, furthermore, vastly overestimates the inherent practicality of the knowledge claims fabricated in science.

Drucker (1969: 269) has proposed a competing definition of 'knowledge' that identifies knowledge with action and views knowledge as emerging from action. He observes that knowledge as 'normally conceived by the "intellectual" is something very different from "knowledge" in the context of "knowledge economy" or "knowledge work"... Knowledge, like electricity or money, is a form of energy that exists only when doing work. The emergence of the knowledge economy is not, in other words, part of "intellectual history" as it is normally conceived. It is part of the "history of technology", which recounts how man puts tools to work'.

The definition of knowledge as capacity for action indicates that the material realization and implementation of knowledge is open, that it is dependent on (or embedded within) the context of specific social, economic and intellectual conditions. Inasmuch as the realization of knowledge is dependent on the active elaboration of knowledge within specific networks and social conditions, a definite link between knowledge and social power becomes evident because the control of conditions and circumstances requires social power. The larger the scale of a project, the greater the need for social power to control the actual realization of knowledge as capacity for action. While it may be possible to build a nuclear generating station in North Korea, this is difficult to imagine in present-day Austria or Germany.

Knowledge constitutes a basis for power. As Galbraith (1967: 67) stresses, power 'goes to the factor which is hardest to obtain or hardest to replace ... it adheres to the one that has greatest inelasticity of supply at the margin'. But knowledge as such is not a scarce commodity, though two features of certain knowledge-claims may well transform knowledge from a plentiful into a scarce resource:

1. What is scarce and difficult to obtain is not access to knowledge per se but to *incremental knowledge*, to a 'marginal unit' of knowledge. The greater the *tempo* with which incremental knowledge ages or decays, the greater the potential influence of those who manufacture or augment knowledge, and, correspondingly, of those who transmit such increments;

2. If sold, knowledge enters the domain of others, yet remains within the domain of the producer, and can be spun off once again. This signals that the transfer of knowledge does not necessarily include the transfer of the cognitive ability to generate such knowledge, for example the theoretical apparatus or the technological regime that yields such knowledge-claims in the first place and on the basis of which it is calibrated and validated. Cognitive *skills* of this kind, therefore, are scarce.

The elimination of time and space as significant elements in the production of knowledge has paradoxically injected time and location into the interpretation and use of knowledge. Since the validation process of knowledge cannot usually refer back to the original author of the claim, the interpretative tasks carried out by 'experts' becomes increasingly crucial. Knowledge must be made available, interpreted, and linked to local circumstances. The extent of the linkages delineates the limits of the power of scientific and technical knowledge. Such limits are an inevitable part of the fabrication of scientific knowledge, and knowledge-based occupations attain increasingly greater centrality. Knowledge is defined by individual actors as well as by the legal, economic, political or religious constructs that have managed to gain authority. Increasingly, it is experts, counsellors and advisers who define knowledge and who mediate between the distribution of knowledge and its seekers.

2. Knowledge and the transformation of the economy

The emergence of knowledge societies signals first and foremost a radical transformation in the *structure of the economy*. Productive processes in *industrial society* are governed by factors that – relative to the increasing importance of the exchange of symbolic goods – have greatly changed and for the most part declined in significance as preconditions for economic growth: the dynamics of the supply of and demand for primary products or raw materials; the dependence of employment on production; the importance of the manufacturing sector that processes primary products; the role of manual labour and the social organization of work; the role of international trade in manufactured goods and services; the function of time and place in production and of the nature of the limits to economic growth. The most common denominator of the changing economic structure is a shift away from an economy driven and governed by 'material' inputs into the productive process and its organization, towards an economy in which the transformations of productive and distributive processes are increasingly determined by 'symbolic' or knowledge-based inputs. The development and impact of modern information technology exemplifies these transformations (and not just in the sphere of economic activities). They include the dematerialization of production that represents diminished constraints on supply, lower and still declining cost, and a redefinition of the social functions of time, place and the increasing acceleration of change (Perez, 1985; Miles, Rush, Turner and Bessant, 1988).

The economy of industrial society, in short, is primarily a *material economy* on the way towards a monetary economy. Keynes' economic theory, particularly his *General Theory* (1936), reflects this transformation of the economy of industrial society into an economy substantially affected by monetary matters. But, as more recent evidence indicates, the economy described by Keynes is best understood as a *symbolic economy*. The structural changes of the economy and its dynamics increasingly reflect the fact that *knowledge* is emerging as the leading dimension in the productive process, the primary condition for its expansion and for change in the limits to economic growth in the developed world. In the knowledge society, most of the wealth of a company, for example, is embodied in its creativity and information. It is therefore not surprising that a 'chief knowledge officer' is increasingly part of the management teams of companies. In short, for the production of goods and services, with the exception of the most standardized commodities and services, factors other than 'the amount of labour time or the amount of physical capital become increasingly central' (Block, 1985: 95) to the economy of advanced societies.[4]

The focus of social science analysis must increasingly be the peculiar nature and function of knowledge in social relations, on the carriers of such knowledge as well as on the resulting changes in power relations and sources of social conflict. In sociology, however, virtually all classical theorists have been proponents and even architects of scientism. This even applies to the ways in which knowledge is conceptualized in theories of society designed to capture the unique features of present-day society. For example, Bell (1968: 156-7) acknowledges that 'every modern society now lives by innovation and growth, and by seeking to anticipate the future and plan ahead'. Innovations are driven by theoretical discoveries, while the commitment to growth is linked to the need to plan and forecast. Bell is optimistic that science (including social science) will fulfil these expectations. 'The rise of macroeconomics, and the new codifications of economic theory, now allow governments to intervene in economic matters in order to shape economic growth, redirect the allocation of resources and ... engineer a controlled recession in order to re-deploy resources'. Indeed, toward the end of the 1960s, Keynesian economics and interventionist economic policies appeared to have solved for the foreseeable future the problem of planning and controlling national macroeconomic developments. Yet only a few years later, the economic profession and entire governments bemoaned the absence of any economic policy to deal with the problem of simultaneous unemployment and inflation. The Keynesian consensus gave rise to what may be regarded as the persisting crisis in economics and economic policy. Bell's claim that the social sciences will be able to deliver and implement ('codify') useful practical knowledge has proved overly optimistic.

In a recent analysis of cross-sectional data on the values and beliefs of the publics in forty-three societies representing 70 percent of the world population, Ronald Inglehart (1995) proposes that the dramatic shift in the direction of social change in the past quarter of the century is clear evidence that we have entered an era of post-modernization. Its origins can be found in the unprecedented achievement of economic security coupled with the welfare state safety net of Western Europe and North America, but also incipiently Southeast Asia. The cultural and political feedback that may be observed in these societies manifests itself in a decline of the authority of religion and of the state, a persistence of individualism, an emphasis on non-economic values, and a shift from scarcity values to security values, as well as

---

4   See especially Drucker (1986) and Lipsey (1992).

a rejection of authority. In the political realm, post-modernization is linked to democratization. Finally, a diminished confidence in the social role of science and technology is noted as a characteristic attribute of the emerging post-modern worldview. Inglehart's post-modernization analysis gives primary weight to certain economic accomplishments, especially the achievement of economic security for large segments of the public. The level of economic security attained corresponds to equally unprecedented levels of subjective well-being. Precisely because publics in advanced societies take their material existence for granted, 'they are not aware of how profoundly this supposition shapes their worldview' (Inglehart, 1995: 385). Although Inglehart refers to a wide spectrum of cultural changes as indicative of post-modernization, he stresses, in contrast to most other post-modernity theorists,[5] that it is economic transformations which make post-modernization possible.

3. Knowing and the known

Even in quite recent discussions on the impact of science on society (Holzner, Dunn and Shahidullah, 1987), this impact still tends to be conceptualized restrictively. In most conventional accounts, science is said to generate, first and foremost, if not exclusively, new types of possibilities, resources or constraints for practical action. The concept of knowledge employed in our context is broader: science and technology permit new forms of action but also eliminate older forms of action; they affect the experience of action while also assuring the 'survival' (in the sense of continued relevance) of existing forms of action; and on occasion they even affirm traditional action.

The crucial point about knowledge societies is that science and technology possess strong attributes that permit effective resistance to uni-dimensional and homogeneous transformations and all efforts to monopolize science and technology as a capacity for action. Science and technology have important enabling features that can be harnessed not only by those who are already powerful. They increase the number of available strategies, heighten flexibility, or restrict the ability of those in positions of power to exercise control. By the same token, these features can also constrain by limiting choices, reducing options, and imposing penalties and risks. It is by no means a self-contradiction to argue that knowledge societies can simultaneously

---

5   On the material foundation of post-modernity and its neglect in theories of post-modernity see Stehr, 1997.

become more standardized and more fragile. It is important not to overstate the extent to which science and technology are forces that operate as means of control and regulation, constraining human agency and delimiting social action. They do all of these things, of course, but there are other consequences as well. Perhaps the most significant outcome is an increase in the essential fragility of society. Science and technology not only enter the fields of social action of groups interested in maintaining the *status quo*, but they also enter the domain of opposing social forces and are employed for entirely different purposes. The emergence of knowledge societies does not mean that societies are becoming uniform social and intellectual entities. Knowledge as a capacity for action encourages the co-existence and interdependence of historically distinct forms of social organization and thought.

Demonstrating the significance of knowledge for social action, particularly in advanced societies, requires a sociological concept of knowledge. What in fact is it that we know? Knowing represents a relation to things and facts, but also to laws and rules. Knowing involves participation: knowing things, facts, rules means 'appropriating' them, including them in our field of orientation and competence. Knowledge can of course be objectified: that is, the intellectual appropriation of things, facts and rules can be established symbolically. In order to know it is not necessary to come into intimate contact with the things themselves, only with their symbolic representations. This is precisely the social significance of language, of writing, printing, and data storage. Most of what is called knowledge and learning today is not direct knowledge of facts, rules and things, but objectified knowledge. Objectified knowledge is the highly differentiated stock of intellectually appropriated nature and society that constitutes society's cultural resource. However, such participation is subject to stratification: the life chances, the life styles and the social influence of individuals all depend on access to the stock of knowledge at hand. Modern societies have made dramatic advances in the intellectual appropriation of nature and society. There exists an immense stock of objectified knowledge that mediates our relation with nature and with ourselves. In a general sense, this advancement used to be seen, in earlier contexts, as a form of modernization and rationalization that would eventually lead to a 'unity of civilization'. This second nature now overshadows the primary nature of humans. The real and the fictional merge and become increasingly less distinguishable.

It is only after the societal significance of such opposites and oppositions has been understood that the full sociological significance of knowledge can become clear. Such a perspective leads to the realization that knowledge is increasingly the foundation of authority, that access to knowledge becomes a major societal resource as well as the occasion for political and social struggles.

Although knowledge has always had a social function, it is only recently that scholars have begun to examine the structure of society and its development from the point of view of the production, distribution and reproduction of knowledge. Applied to present-day society, the question arises if knowledge can provide a foundation for social hierarchies and stratification, for the formation of class structure, for the distribution of chances of social and political influence and also for personal life; and, finally, whether knowledge may prove to be a normative principle of social cohesion and integration, even though the variations and alterations in the reproduction of knowledge appear to be enormous. Paradoxically, efforts to entrench necessity in history or to eliminate the role of chance from history has produced, at least at the collective level, the very opposite tendency. The role of chance, ambiguity and 'fragility' at the collective level is an increasingly important aspect of the way society is organized.

Knowledge is a peculiar entity with properties unlike those of commodities or secrets, for example. Knowledge exists in objectified and embodied forms. If sold, it enters other domains – and yet it remains within the domain of its producer. Knowledge does not have zero-sum qualities. Knowledge is a public as well as private good. When revealed, knowledge does not lose its influence. While it has long been understood that the 'creation' of knowledge is fraught with uncertainties, the conviction that its application is without risks and that its acquisition reduces uncertainty has only recently been challenged. Unlike money, property rights, and symbolic attributes such as titles, knowledge cannot be transmitted instantaneously. Its acquisition takes time and is often based on intermediary cognitive capacities and skills. But acquisition can be unintended and occur almost unconsciously. Neither the acquisition nor the transmission of knowledge are always easily visualized. The development, mobility and reproduction of knowledge resists regulation. It is difficult to censor and control knowledge. While it may be reasonable to speak of limits to growth in many spheres and resources of life, the same does not appear to hold for knowledge. Knowledge has virtually no limits to its growth, but it does take time to accumulate.

Knowledge is often seen as the collective commodity *par excellence*; for example, the ethos of science demands that it is made universally available, at least in principle. But is the 'same' knowledge available to all? Is scientific knowledge, once transformed into technology, still subject to the same normative conventions? The answer provided by one economist is that technology must be considered a 'private capital good'. In the case of technology, disclosure is uncommon, and rents for its use can be privately appropriated (Dasgupta, 1987: 10). But the potentially unrestricted universal availability of knowledge makes it, in peculiar and unusual ways, resistant to private ownership (Simmel, [1907] 1978: 438). Modern communication technologies ensure that access becomes easier, and may even subvert remaining proprietary restrictions; however, concentration rather than dissemination is also possible and certainly feared by many, including the late Marshall McLuhan.

4. Knowledge concepts: classical and modern

The nature of knowledge – long before this became a central concern in the classical sociology of knowledge that is associated especially with the names of Max Scheler and Karl Mannheim – has been a major preoccupation of philosophy at least since Graeco-Roman times. Plato, for example, in *Theætetus* adopts a scientific approach to knowledge and cognition. The recognition, however, that knowledge in the broadest sense is context-dependent and constrained by social factors is of more recent origin, as is sociology itself. Sociology could only arise after the dogma of a congruence between natural and social inequality had fallen into disrepute. The philosophers of the French and Scottish Enlightenments recognized that all social differences have social origins and are thus the result of factors subject to human control. They were fully aware that a wide range of social, economic and political factors share the genesis, structure, and content of human thought, thereby anticipating one of the major propositions of the sociology of knowledge.

In contrast to philosophy, which has generally attempted to demonstrate that the constitutive components of cognition are *a priori*, and that scientific knowledge in particular is warranted by direct experience unaffected by social conditions, thus placing knowledge on a firm, uncontested foundation, the classical sociology of knowledge investigated the interconnections between thought, knowledge-claims and social reality, and it was concerned with intellectual and spiritual structures as inevitably different in different social and historical settings. Yet even Karl Mannheim regarded the scientific knowledge produced in the – for the most part quantifiable – natural and physical sciences as largely detachable from the historical-social perspective (Mannheim, 1936: 290), and he therefore regarded it as highly problematic to subject scientific and technical knowledge to sociological analysis. Mannheim nevertheless thought that the sociology of knowledge was destined to play a major role in intellectual and political life by examining the conditions that give rise to competing ideas, political philosophies, ideologies and diverse cultural products. He persistently pursued the idea that sociology of knowledge is central to any strategy for creating a rapprochement between politics and reason, and this pursuit connects his various essays in the sociology of knowledge.

In more recent decades, accompanied by the development of the sociology of science, a sociology of scientific and formal knowledge still regarded as highly improbable by the classical sociologists of knowledge is now considered a real possibility, and there is new interest in finding a satisfactory solution to the question of how the relation between the structure of human groups and consciousness arises, is maintained and evolves, and thereby changes the course of social evolution. There is also a new interest in the issue of the growing power of knowledge in industrial or post-industrial society (Bell, 1973; Elias, 1989), and a shared emphasis on the increasing importance of specialized forms of knowledge, as well as on the power of the carriers of knowledge.

Knowledge, as we have argued, has always played a significant role in human history. Human action has to a greater or lesser extent always been steered by knowledge, and power has almost always also resulted from knowledge advantages. But now knowledge is assuming a greater significance than ever before. Advanced industrial societies in particular may increasingly be regarded as 'knowledge societies'. A thoroughgoing scientization of all spheres of human life and action, the transformation of the traditional structures of domination and of the economy, as well as the growing impact and influence of experts, are all indications of the rapidly increasing role of knowledge in the organization of modern societies.

Adam Smith and Karl Marx still understood modern society (and the economy) primarily in terms of property and labour. Their conceptualizations have been quite representative of social, economic and political theory in general. Work is seen as property and as a source of emerging property. In the Marxist tradition, capital is understood as objectified and encapsulated labour. In relation to these attributes, individuals and groups define their membership in society. As a result of their declining importance in the production process, especially in the sense of their conventional economic attributes and manifestations (for example, as 'corporeal' property like land and manual work), the social constructs of labour and property are themselves undergoing change. While the traditional features of labour and property have certainly not disappeared, 'knowledge' has emerged as a new principle that to some extent challenges as well as transforms property and labour as the constitutive mechanisms of society. Theories and classifications of societies have tended to mirror these quintessential social mechanisms in their respective constitutive principles, with which they have hoped to capture the 'reality' of a particular historical era. Thus capitalist society was initially analysed as a society of owners of the means of production. Later the focus shifted to some extent to labour itself. Now 'knowledge' is increasingly emerging as a constitutive principle.

Among the social thinkers, to mention only a few representative figures, who have sought to analyse and explain the apparent transformation of modern society are Radovan Richta (1969) and his colleagues, who date these transformations to the scientific and technological revolution of the 1950s. Daniel Bell (1973), by contrast, traces the 'symbolic' onset of post-industrial society to the end of World War II, when a new consciousness about time and social space first emerged. Bell, in fact, elevates theoretical knowledge to the axial principle of society, since codified theoretical knowledge becomes 'the director of social change' (Bell, 1979: 164). Block and Hirschorn (1979: 368) regard the 1920s as the period of emergence of forces typical of post-industrial society (information, knowledge, science, technology), especially in regard to their manifestation in production. Aron's theory of industrial society (Aron, 1966), which encompasses both socialist and capitalist forms of economic organization, stresses the extent to which science and technology shape the social organization of productive activities. The major transformations in both modern society and the modern economy that concern all these social thinkers, are – curiously enough – only marginally reflected in present-day economic theory. For the classical economists, from Smith to Ricardo and Mill to, above all, Marx, economic change induced by technical developments was one of the salient and taken-for-granted sources of the dynamics of the economic system.

Our knowledge about knowledge is not particularly sophisticated or comprehensive even today, despite (but also because of) a restrictively defined sociology of knowledge. The range, volume and the forms of knowledge made available especially by the sciences impact forcefully on the very fabric of modern society and, in fact, have become virtually the only source of *additional knowledge*. The change in the volume of added knowledge dramatically enlarges the available options of social action, as well as the dependence of the future on the volumes of decisions that need to be made. Investment in and the distribution and reproduction of scientific knowledge, together with the production of knowledge, are clearly bound to become ever more significant.

One reason for the deficit in our knowledge about knowledge may be located in the fact that scientific discourse has developed a kind of naturalistic attitude toward its own knowledge. Scientific discourse has generated a self-understanding of its knowledge that generally tends to overestimate not only the objectivity of its own claims but also the immediate as well as unmediated social relevance of scientific knowledge. Scientific discourse also tends to resist self-critical analysis, especially as regards positions that challenge the dominant taken-for-granted assumptions and conceptions of science. In short, our knowledge about knowledge has until recently been derivative of and referential to the dominant philosophies of science. Paradoxically, these perspectives have overestimated the power of knowledge and/or failed to examine the reasons for the possible authority of knowledge in modern society. Theories of post-industrial society, of the technical-scientific revolution and of scientific-technical civilization, but also critical social theory and the theory of modern society as a network society, have generally deferred to the traditional self-conceptions of the sciences.

In any case, and quite apart from the alleged bias towards action rather than reflection in everyday life that was of great concern to Simmel, the number of well-explicated categories of and theoretical approaches to knowledge in sociological discourse has been limited. As a result, there is little to be gained from an overly extensive exegesis of theoretical traditions. We have moved surprisingly little beyond Max Scheler's ([1925] 1960: 13-49) sociology of knowledge conceptualization of the different forms of knowledge. Later explanations often read like a variation on Scheler's categorization, although their Schelerian ancestry is not often acknowledged or even recognized. Scheler distinguishes between:
1. knowledge of salvation (*Erlösungswissen*),
2. cultural knowledge or knowledge of pure essences (*Bildungswissen*),
3. knowledge that produces effects (*Herrschaftswissen*).

Following logic widely employed in social science discourse, the most frequently employed conceptions of different forms of knowledge are dichotomies. Dominant here is the differentiation between scientific and non-scientific knowledge. The distinction has been unchallenged for so long that it has not been modified or elaborated for decades. In addition, a dichotomy that resonates strongly with the separation between scientific and non-scientific knowledge is often invoked. It distinguishes between specialized (expert) and everyday (lay) knowledge. Specialized knowledge is often almost completely identified with scientific and technical knowledge.

5. Scientific knowledge and its limits

The assumption that the increased social importance of knowledge in the end undermines its exclusiveness seems eminently reasonable. Yet the opposite appears to be the case, and therefore raises anew the question of the persisting basis for the power of knowledge. Despite its reputation, knowledge is virtually never uncontested. In science, its contestability is seen as one of its foremost virtues. In practical circumstances, the contested character of knowledge is often repressed and/or conflicts with the exigencies of social action. A critical analysis of the limits of scientific knowledge requires an understanding of the special nature as well as the similarities of scientific and non-scientific knowledge and action. Classifying scientific knowledge as a unique form of human knowledge is of little value. Such a classification is too closely linked to now obsolete epistemological conceptions of science, and to such notions and ideals as universality, experience, rationality, necessity and practicality. Conceptions of scientific knowledge that adhere to such notions tend to deny that scientific knowledge is socially based, and that it is a collective as well as historical enterprise. But the notion that scientific knowledge, unlike other forms of knowledge, is not bound or limited institutionally has to be questioned in light of the conditions necessary for the reproduction of scientific knowledge-claims outside the circumstances of their initial discovery. It is by no means certain, in other words, that it is only the influence of conventional forms of knowledge that contracts as the functional differentiation of society progresses and once powerful institutions such as religion as well as institutionally based knowledge in general diminish in importance.

Knowledge-claims, furthermore, not only take on features derived from the material conditions of their production, but they also reflect institutionally-bound cognitive attributes. These attributes include, importantly, a suspension of the pressure to act as constitutive of scientific discourse. Knowledge produced within the scientific community is released from the tasks it must perform outside science. One of the most salient attributes of everyday life-situations is, by contrast, the persistent pressure to reach a decision, to observe a specific rule, to follow a particular course of action by discarding alternative possibilities, or to provide an account of completed action *ex post facto*. This suspension of the constraint to act within scientific discourse may be described, on the one hand, as a virtue of intellectual activity taking place under privileged conditions which moderate the effect of the pressing interests, rapidly passing opportunities and ambiguous dependencies of everyday contexts on the production of scientific knowledge-claims. On the other hand, the result of this suspension of the pressure to act is that scientific knowledge takes on qualities of incompleteness, provisionality, fragmentariness or expansiveness that reduce its effectiveness as knowledge in circumstances in which action is the foremost requirement. As Durkheim, ([1912] 1965: 479) observed so well: 'Life cannot wait' (Gehlen, [1940] 1988: 296-7). In most social contexts the need to act takes precedence over the need to know. Perhaps there exists, as Simmel (1890: 1) surmises, an anthropological constant in the form of a general and widespread preference among humans to 'do' something rather than merely to 'know' about something. Knowing, in turn, may require prior doing. In his lectures on 'Pragmatism and Sociology', Durkheim, ([1955] 1983), discussing the scientific status of the discipline of sociology, refers to similar issues when he provides reasons for the relative scientific backwardness of sociological knowledge. Durkheim emphasises that the fragmentary and uncertain knowledge of sociology must inevitably produce scepticism or doubt about the contingencies of practical action in the social world:

> (s)ociety cannot wait for its problems to be solved scientifically. It has to make decisions about what action to take, and in order to make these decisions it has to have an idea of what it is (Durkheim, [1955] 1983: 90).

Scientific knowledge, by contrast, is generally produced under conditions that consider 'waiting', distancing, careful reflection, the elimination of time-bound constraints in reaching a decision or even the deliberate abstention from judgement until 'evidence' is available, to be distinct attributes of the validity and the virtue of such knowledge-claims. By reducing and even eliminating urgency as a part of the production process of scientific knowledge, gains from the point of view of epistemological ideals contrast with deficiencies from the perspective of everyday life where the urgency to act is a constitutive characteristic.

Laboratory studies of the production of scientific knowledge (Latour and Woolgar, 1979; Knorr-Cetina, 1983) also show that the knowledge-claims produced by science, which are neither based on nor expressive of a unique form of rationality or logic, result primarily in claims to non-local knowledge. Indeed, the site of production of scientific knowledge does not differ greatly from the sites of production of conventional or everyday knowledge. Scientific rationality, once it appears outside the boundaries of the scientific community – for instance, in the form of expert knowledge in the determination of curricula, the allocation of public funds for research, or as expert witness or counsel – is therefore often followed by severe public disappointment because the scientific knowledge fails to deliver the expected reliability and lead to collective consensus (Barnes, 1972).

In addition to these considerations, a logic that is less stringent than the logic of logic (Bourdieu, ([1980] 1987) can be assigned to practical contexts. In such situations, the social-scientific analysis of everyday contexts reduces the urgency to act. The result might be called a 'depragmatization' of everyday contexts or the elevation of practical circumstances to the level of theoretical contingencies. At the same time, the depragmatization of everyday contexts through social-scientific discourse makes visible those features of everyday life that resist theoretical transformation. Among them are aspects of a practical logic, such as the ease of operation and control, subjective adequacy, economy and its practical persuasiveness represented in the union of a totality of judgements and their ambivalence. This opposition between practical and theoretical logic leads Bourdieu to the radical conclusion that any theoretical reconstruction of practical situations amounts necessarily to a distortion of the 'truth' of praxis.

The peculiar character of practical circumstances is that they resist theoretical reconstruction because the truth of praxis resides in fact in a blindness to its own truth. Scientific discourse and praxis have different purposes and they serve different functions.

Whether scientific/technical knowledge is particularly effective in practice, as most of its proponents argue, is not at issue here. The collective capacity to act, the extent to which our existential circumstances are socially constructed, has certainly increased immeasurably. But this does not mean that the capacity to act of particular units of the collectivity, for example the individual, small groups or even such large entities as nation-states, has thereby been greatly enlarged.

On the contrary, the potential to act at the collective level and in a cumulative manner coexists with an increasing inability even of large and in the past often powerful social formations to control, let alone determine, their own fate.

In a different context, Karl Mannheim observed in *Ideology and Utopia* that there is hardly any sphere of life about which we do not have scientific knowledge, as well as skills and methods for communicating this knowledge:

> '(i)s it conceivable then', Mannheim asks, 'that the sphere of human activity on the mastery of which our fate rests is so unyielding that scientific research cannot force it to give up its secrets? The disquieting and puzzling features of this problem cannot be disregarded. The question must have already occurred to many whether this is merely a temporary condition... or whether we have reached, in this sphere, the outermost limit of knowledge which can never be transcended' (Mannheim, [1929] 1936: 110).

We conclude on a perhaps even more ambiguous note. Their conviction about the relentless success of science and technology has for long led social scientists to ignore the problem of the inherent limits of scientific knowledge. In his famous novel, *The Man Without Qualities*, written at about the same time as *Ideology and Utopia*, Robert Musil brilliantly captures the intrinsic dilemma that remains with us even today: 'The truth is that science has developed a conception of hard, sober intellectual strength that makes mankind's old metaphysical and moral notions simply unendurable, although all it can put in their place is the hope that a day, still distant, will come when a race of intellectual conquerors will descend into the valleys of spiritual fruitfulness' (Musil, [1930] 1979: 48).

Bibliography

Aron, R. ([1966] 1968), *The Industrial Society. Three Essays on Ideology and Development*, Praeger, New York.

Barnes, B. (1972), 'On the Reception of Scientific Beliefs', in B. Barnes (ed), *Sociology of Science*, Penguin, Harmondsworth, pp. 269-91.

Bell, D. (1968), 'The Measurement of Knowledge and Technology', in E. Sheldon and W. Moore (eds), *Indicators of Social Change. Concepts and Measurements*, Russell Sage Foundation, Hartford.

Bell, D. (1973), *The Coming of Post-Industrial Society. A Venture in Social Forecasting*, Basic Books, New York.

Bell, D. (1979), 'The Social Framework of the Information Society', in M.L. Dertouzos and J. Moses (eds), *The Computer Age: A Twenty-Year View*, MIT Press, Cambridge, pp. 163-211.

Block, F. (1985), 'Postindustrial Development and the Obsolescence of Economic Categories', *Politics and Society*, vol. 14, no. 1, pp. 71-104.

Block, F. and Hirschorn, L. (1979), 'New Productive Forces and the Contradictions of Contemporary Capitalism', *Theory and Society*, vol. 7, no. 3, pp. 363-95.

Böhme, G. (1997), 'The Structure and Prospects of Knowledge Society', *Social Science Information*, vol. 36, no. 3, pp. 447-68.

Bourdieu, P. ([1980] 1987), *Sozialer Sinn. Kritik der theoretischen Vernunft*, Suhrkamp, Frankfurt am Main.

Castells, M. (1996), *The Rise of the Network Society*, Blackwell, Oxford.

Cowen, M.P. and Shenton, R.W. (1996), *Doctrines of Development*, Routledge, London.

Dasgupta, P. (1987), 'The Economic Theory of Technology Policy', in P. Dasgupta and P. Stoneman (eds), *Economic Policy and Technological Performance*, Cambridge University Press, Cambridge, pp. 7-23 .

Drucker, P.F. (1969), *The Age of Discontinuity. Guidelines to our Changing Society*, Harper & Row, New York.

Drucker, P.F. (1986), 'The Changed World Economy', *Foreign Affairs,* vol. 64, pp. 768-91.

Durkheim, E. ([1912] 1965), *The Elementary Forms of Religious Life*, Free Press, New York.

Durkheim, E. ([1955] 1983), *Pragmatism and Sociology*, Cambridge University Press, Cambridge.

Elias, N. (1989), *Studien über die Deutschen. Machtkämpfe und Habitusentwicklung im 19. und 20. Jahrhundert*, Suhrkamp, Frankfurt am Main.

Galbraith, J.K. (1967), *The New Industrial State*, Houghton Mifflin, New York.

Gehlen, A. ([1940] 1988), *Man. His Nature and Place in the World*, Columbia University Press, New York.

Holzner, B., Dunn, W.N. and Shahidullah, M. (1987), 'An Accounting Scheme for Designing Science Impact Indicators', *Knowledge*, vol. 9, pp. 173-204.

Inglehart, R. (1995), 'Changing Values, Economic Development and Political Change', *International Social Science Journal*, vol. 145, pp. 379-403.

Keynes, M. (1936), *The General Theory of Employment, Interest and Money*, Macmillan, London.

Knorr-Cetina, K. and Mulkay, M. (eds) (1983), *Science Observed. Perspectives on the Social Study of Science*, Sage, London.

Kreibich, R. (1986), *Die Wissenschaftsgesellschaft. Von Galilei zur High-Tech Revolution*, Suhrkamp, Frankfurt am Main.

Lane, R.E. (1966), 'The Decline of Politics and Ideology in a Knowledgeable Society', *American Sociological Review*, vol. 31, no. 5, pp. 649-62.

Latour, B. and Woolgar, S. (1979), *Laboratory Life. The Social Construction of Scientific Facts*, Sage, London.

Ledwith, S. (1999), *Thurow sees U.S. Recession after Tech-Driven Boom*, Reuters News Agency (September 24th).

Lipsey, R.G. (1992), 'Global Change and Economic Policy', in N. Stehr and R. Ericson (eds), *The Culture and Power of Knowledge: Inquiries into Contemporary Societies*, Aldine de Gruyter, Berlin, pp. 279-99.

Mannheim, K. ([1929] 1936), *Ideology and Utopia. An Introduction to the Sociology of Knowledge*, Brace and Company, New York.

Miles, I., Rush, H., Turner, K. and Bessant, J. (1988), *Information Horizons. The Long-Term Social Implications of New Information Technology*, Edward Elgar, London.

Mill, J.S. ([1831] 1942), *The Spirit of the Age*, University of Chicago Press, Chicago.

Musil, R. ([1930] 1979), *Man Without Qualities*, Picador, McGraw-Hill, London.

Nora, S. and Minc, A. (1980), *The Computerization of Society*, Mass., MIT Press, Cambridge.

Perez, C. (1985), 'Microelectronics, Long Waves and World Development', *World Development*, vol. 13, pp. 441-63.

Richta, R. et al. (1969), *Civilization at the Crossroads: Social and Human Implication of the Scientific and Technological Revolution*, International Arts and Sciences Press, New York.

Scheler, M. ([1925] 1960), 'The Forms of Knowledge and Culture', *Philosophical Perspectives*, Beacon Press, Boston, pp. 13-49.

Scheler, M. ([1926] 1980), *Problems of a Sociology of Knowledge*, Routledge, London.

Schelsky, H. (1961), *Der Mensch in der wissenschaftlichen Zivilisation*, Westdeutscher Verlag, Köln.

Sibley, M.Q. (1973), 'Utopian Thought and Technology', *American Journal of Political Science*, vol. 17, pp. 255-81.

Simmel, G. (1890), *Über sociale Differenzierung. Soziologische und psychologische Untersuchungen*, Duncker & Humblot, Leipzig.

Simmel, G. ([1907] 1978), *The Philosophy of Money*, Routledge, London.

Simmel, G. ([1908] 1992), *Soziologie. Untersuchungen über die Formen der Vergesellschaftung*, Gesamtausgabe Band 11, Suhrkamp, Frankfurt am Main.

Stehr, N. (1994), *Knowledge Societies*, Sage, London.

Stehr, N. (1997), 'Les limites du possibles: La postmodernité et les sociétés du savoir', *Sociétiés,* no. 58, pp. 101-24.

Stehr, N. (2000a), *Knowledge and Economic Conduct: The Social Foundations of the Modern Economy,* University of Toronto Press, Toronto.

Stehr, N. (2000b), *The Fragility of Modern Societies,* Sage, London.

5 Freedom versus control in post-modern society: a relational approach

PIERPAOLO DONATI

Introduction

Modern sociological theory was born from specific reflection on the antithesis between freedom and social order (the latter in the sense of control), as polarities irreducible to one another and within which social life unfolds. Freedom is generally thought of as the possibility of action unbound by conditioning. By contrast, order (control) is understood as a constraint that conditions action from the outside. Conditioning and constraints are first conceived as naturalistic, then as normative, and finally as mechanical.

The point to which I wish to draw attention is that, to moderns, freedom is outside control (that is, extrinsic to its forms). Social control *as such* cannot make one free, cannot be a component of freedom; it can only increase or diminish chances of freedom, which is built on other foundations. Freedom lies in the subject (individual, collective or historical), while social control lies in external constrictions (in the form of rules either structural, normative or functional).

The previous statement may be mitigated by saying that both liberty and control are conceived within a shared framework characterized by rationality, contractuality and conventionalism. One assumes that both sides of the distinction may and must be made increasingly rational, contractual, conventional. What this means is explained by the competing concepts of rationality, contract and conventionalism.

Some have observed that Western social thought, compared to other cultures, takes freedom ('liberation' of the subject, beginning with the individual) as a priority and as a limitation of control. But this may not be true. Of course, only in the West do we find radically libertarian theories unknown to other societies. But it would be stretching the point to maintain that modern sociological thought interprets society only as a process of liberation, or conversely only as a process of control, although these unilateral temptations are widespread.

We can instead state that modern sociological theories still differ today as to the side of the distinction (freedom/control) from which they choose to observe society: some see society from the side of freedom and as a function of freedom (I will call these *lib* theories), while others see it from the side of control and as a function of social control (I will call these *lab* theories). In both cases, however, social aspects are defined and analysed according to conceptual categories that are substantially identical (refer to the same meanings), and they fall within the same binary distinction.[1]

As modernity develops, the '*lib/lab* complex' increases, and the two poles – *lib* and *lab* – enter increasing synergy. Sociology legitimates a configuration of society in which *lib* and *lab* fuel each other, however antithetical they may appear. It is this framework that should be highlighted.

Observing social reality from a *lib/lab* standpoint has certain consequences: (i) it gives to theoretical paradoxes, and (ii) it contradicts many aspects of empirical reality. Modern and contemporary social theories raise these two sets of problems. In an attempt to respond to them, sociology transforms its very nature: from an explanatory and/or interpretative narration of social reality, seen as a phenomenon that emerges independently, it becomes a means for the paradoxical construction of social reality itself.

Those who have sought a non-paradoxical composite of freedom and control within the paradigms of modernity, specifically Talcott Parsons, have failed. No matter how hard they try, sociological theories which refer to the classics (up to and including Parsons) fail to see how freedom and control can be reconciled, in the sense of mutual support or at least significant reciprocal relations. Freedom and control are assumed to be two tracks – infinitely parallel – along which sociological theory runs, but nothing is said about how they are intrinsically connected. Sociology therefore finds itself constantly called upon to resume discussion on the categories of freedom and control. In doing so, it generates theories that are by necessity anti-modern, neo-modern or post-modern.

This highlights the fact that modernity has made a bet. It has configured the relationship between freedom and control as a *synergic antithesis* between the two terms of the distinction. But today this bet seems about to be lost. In

---

1   The fundamental binary distinction is that between freedom and equality. Some might object that these are not antithetical terms, since 'equality of the conditions of freedom' also exists. But one might reply that the conceptual category 'equality of the conditions of freedom' is paradoxical, and therefore does not eliminate the binary nature of the lib/ lab distinction. Indeed, sociological analysis reveals that the processes which encourage liberty are contrary to social equality, and conversely that social controls are introduced to reduce the inequality deriving from the existence of certain freedoms.

Western society today, the contingencies for both freedom and control are increasing; both sides tend to go their own way; meaningful bonds no longer hold – at least those that were considered meaningful until recently.

The relationship between liberty and control spirals endlessly and finishes in a void, or it is limited by forms of self-understanding (*lib/lab*) which prevent society from developing new stable and meaningful relations. If the *lib/lab* logic is extended to all forms of social life, in fact, it generates catastrophes. If instead it is restricted to the inhibition of further possibilities for synergy, it may give rise to degenerative processes: a regression to pre-modern forms of social life or a leap into post-modern destructuring. Managing the freedom/control coupling grows increasingly problematic.

At the end of the twentieth century, numerous scholars are reintroducing a neo-modern reading of society understood as a system which can increase freedom and social control simultaneously, making it both rational, contractual and conventional. But this is a delusion. The synergy no longer acts as a criterion for society as a whole (because its logic consumes what is human in the social much more than it can produce it). At most, the *lib/lab* logic may be reproduced in strictly limited sectors. The binary distinction of freedom/control is no longer able to explain the dialectic between civil society and the state that lay at the foundation of the modern era. The freedom/ control distinction is reduced to a mere conceptual pair-term, analytical in nature, which no longer has the meaning or the functions that it comprised in modernity. One may therefore surmise that modern sociological theories which reason in terms of *lib/lab* contain ideological biases based on a type of society which, with the twenty-first century on the horizon, is obsolete.

In truth, the crisis of the dialectic between freedom and control suggests that we are entering a post-modern era which will induce substantial changes in the most general assumptions of sociological theory. The society of globalization changes the categories of modernity. Freedom, it is argued, manifests itself as 'new subjects', and control as 'new social rules'. New theories and new social rules come into being. But even these representations are inadequate for interpretation of what is happening – the passage to the post-modern – because they fail to grasp the novel features of the social realm. Theories that remain within the *lib/lab framework* see subjects and rules but *not the generation* of society. Generating society becomes – for the first time in human history – the construction of a network of communicative relations.

The thesis developed here is that the passage from modern to post-modern society is distinguished by the need to adopt a *relational approach* to the freedom/control distinction which is *post-lib* and *post-lab*, post-individualistic, and post-holistic. An approach of this kind may shed clearer light on the historically unprecedented aspects of social formation now taking place.

1. *Lib* and *lab* meet and shake hands

In modern sociology, despite the debates between *lib* and *lab* thinkers (or, if one prefers, between methodological individualism and holism), society is viewed as a historical process consisting in individual and/or collective liberation from the ascriptive ties of the community (*Gemeinschaft*) and a move towards progress in which reason, whether individual or collective, micro or macro, of action or social systems, leaves its contractualist mark on society.

In this scenario, freedom is understood as freedom *from* (thus as an opening of contingencies of existence, not merely dependencies) rather than as freedom *for* something or someone. Social control is understood as external, coercive regulation rather than as intentional and purposeful choice based on a moral conscience inherent in subjects and their relationships.

It might be objected that this is simply the positivist, functionalist side of sociology, so to speak. This may be so, but the point is that in modernity no great Western sociological theory appears immune to creeping positivism, which pervades even those theories intended to be non-functionalist or even anti-functionalist (Marxian ones, for example).

Why is positivist functionalism considered to be limiting and simplistic, but then permeates every theory and ends up the winner?

I believe the reason is that *lib* and *lab* theories are not true opposites. Instead, they are largely *complementary*: they 'dance together', so to speak. It is this 'dance' that fuels positivist functionalism. Freedom and regulation, whether individual or collective, work together in a certain manner (defined below) to build the symbolic and institutional complex (*lib/lab*) that constitutes the collective conscience of our times and 'good system governance'. The categorical imperative states: we must expand all freedoms on the sole condition that they do not constrain anyone; and good governance is an expansion of all possible freedoms as long as they are 'compatible' with one another and with the concurrent principles (equality and solidarity) that act as external constraints.

1. From a methodological standpoint, this means that individualism and holism 'shake hands', that they support and complement one another.

2. From an applied standpoint, this means that society is a trade-off between freedom and control arranged along the individual-government axis, and involving continuous negotiation between the market and the state.

Empirical research too uses the same lens. To give an example, anyone wishing to prove that school choices are individual rather than controlled by the system are able to do so, but they are then forced to admit, on empirical findings, that the growth of individual freedom does not alter stratification structures (Boudon, 1979). Individualism and holism meet and shake hands.

This is the *lib/lab* paradigm inherent in modernity. It proposes a synergy between freedom and social control that constitutes the 'engine' of the entire historical-social formation. This engine works as follows: social control is used to free individuals, and freedom is used to make control more rational and functional to progress, under the assumption that one can be freed from the constraining nature of social relationships without jeopardizing the social order.

Still today, Western sociological theory conceives society in these terms: as a *struggle* between *forces of freedom* representing a propulsive (innovative) thrust generally free of any need for a priori ethical justification, and the forces of social control which brake that thrust (self-preservation) and generally require justification, which must become increasingly technical-functional. The burden of proof is on control. The brake concerns the public sphere, and it must only be used when the private freedom of others is violated, not before and not for any other reason. The fuel for the machine of history is the liberty/control distinction used as a synergic antithesis between the private and public.[2]

The engine of the modern machine, thus configured, is fuelled by potentially infinite energy – or at least this is how it is represented. 'Progressively' removing constrictions on freedom, making it potentially unlimited, entails the creation of an inexhaustible source of resources. If one is then able, in complementary fashion, to invent a form of social control that does not block the liberation process, but instead uses control to expand freedoms, then social control itself is no longer an insurmountable obstacle but rather the mere identification of temporary limits and functionally necessary mechanisms to ensure that the freedom machine runs smoothly. Those forms of society that interrupt this process are viewed as deviations,

---

2   By this expression I mean the use of the public to privatize the private, and vice-versa, the use of the private to publicize the public. It is important to emphasise that this comes about through the development of one based on the development of the other, according to a mutual system/environment relationship.

pure accidents, temporary halts or stopovers.

This is how we interpret, on the one hand, the political dictatorships (whether communist, fascist, Nazi, or of other type) that eliminate freedoms, and on the other, those forms of 'rampant' or haphazard capitalism ('casino capitalism') which do not guarantee equal freedoms for all. In the light of the lib/lab paradigm, dictatorships and unregulated capitalism are 'unintentional effects' which must be once again subjected to the (same) freedom/control distinction. Modernity is convinced that the lib/lab machine can be expanded by progressive upgrades. It rejects the idea that this logic has extra or meta-social constraints or limitations, and that each new cycle may generate situations more problematic than before.

This is how the West represents itself – as the best of all possible worlds – and it is reassured by dominant sociological theories that this is indeed the case.

The West believes it has harnessed the freedom/control antithesis as the engine of history. The engine of society has certain analogies with one driven by nuclear energy: it is considered to have practically unlimited resources, and it achieves extremely high performance, although with some inherent risks. This is how the globalized society of communication is conceived. It is assumed that the risks are generally controllable. Note: controllable, which re-introduces the same distinction in what has just been distinguished. The problem of discovering what might be achieved by changing the distinctions of this arrangement is systematically avoided.

This configuration has characterized modern sociological theory from the nineteenth century to the present. Indeed, my thesis is that a theory is considered the more 'modern' the more it assumes this very configuration. To avoid it means risking the development of a pre-modern or anti-modern sociology.

The dance in which lib and lab 'shake hands' is still the prevailing arrangement of Western society. In the meantime, however, its limits have become apparent. We are gradually realizing that it prevents the observer from seeing beyond the – quite limited – horizon where it appears that all possibilities have their place, while instead the opposite occurs.

Indeed, many possibilities have by no means been thematized or discussed, and many of those that have been prove to be more virtual than real. In short, one realizes that the lib/lab approach does not see morphogenesis within society as an emerging associative or surplus form that combines freedom and control according to means that evade modern logic.

2. The modern concept of the freedom versus control dialectic leads to paradoxes and contrasts with empirical reality

The lib/lab configuration begins to be seriously questioned when it displays systematic malfunctioning, and thus when one realizes that it can no longer operate structurally.

There are many crisis paradigms. Most of them note that a development machine encounters structural limitations in its external and internal environments (Hirsch, 1995). One cannot exploit nature indefinitely (physical resources). One cannot make the ecosystem indefinitely artificial. One cannot polarize social relationships indefinitely between total isolation or total constriction, on pain of pathological repercussions.

Yet not everyone sees that critical results are the product of specific relationships between freedom and social control that generate vicious or perverse circles. What I wish to emphasise here is that the lib/lab complex by itself gives rise to unsolvable paradoxes which contrast strongly with the needs and experiences of daily life. Let us examine these two aspects.

Firstly, describing society specifically as a synergic antithesis between freedom and control generates unsolvable paradoxes which take two forms: 1. freedom contradicts itself; 2. social control loses its legitimacy. Let us examine these separately.

1. The exaltation of freedom as the absence of restrictions – in particular normative restrictions – internal to agency and its subject thwarts freedom and eventually causes its self-destruction.

Early modernity still used a concept of freedom that meant interdependency, and hence the choice of the environment on which to depend. But the symbolic code that modernity generates states that this is a purely temporary limitation, because freedom as such consists of the possibility to abandon interdependency or the choice of dependencies. Is it perhaps not true that money, with the freedom to choose a specific transaction, must also bring increased freedom as the ability to evade other constraints for further transactions? The guiding rule of society is no longer a pattern of value, but the convertibility of anything into anything else (Donati, 1991: chap. 4).

As long as this process remains confined to limited groups of people (the modern elite), only the highest social classes experience a lifestyle in which freedom is an end in itself. Only they, for the moment, display the paradoxes. When the process becomes a mass phenomenon, the whole of society takes on the characteristics of a 'deviant majority'. We are witnessing the 'drift of liberalism' (Schooyans, 1991) within a social arrangement in which freedoms cancel each other out. One must then conclude that the civil society born of the Protestant Reformation no longer exists (Seligman, 1992), that it has faded away or defeated itself. The very idea of civil is questioned. To generate a civil life one must create new social institutions which – far from encouraging a 'lightening of ethics', as Gehlen (1986) believes – manage to intertwine freedoms and controls through morally significant relationships between them. When the old relationships fail, one must seek new rules for the creation of social institutions that reflect an ethic of freedom not entirely detached from control. But the resources and possibilities remains limited. Since it is imperative to be modern, and since we are modern to the extent to which we do not seek rules able to constitute freedom from within, but only mechanisms able to reduce the undesired effects of freedom, then social norms are unintentionally configured as vicious circles within the system of freedom. In short, many private behaviours are permitted, but their public effects are punished or condemned (as happens when a country permits the use of drugs in the private sphere but punishes those who sell them and condemns those who become drug-addicted).

2. Something similar takes place as regards control. A concept of social control as external and coercive towards action and its subject removes all substantial legitimacy from the social order and renders the mechanisms (institutions and rules) that should ensure it functionally ineffective.

The more social rules are separated from the subjects' motivations and interior aims, the more they are perceived as purely artificial and constrictive, and therefore meaningless; they become purely a technical necessity, which may in turn be artificially reduced.

There are abundant indicators of these outcomes. One may cite: the collapse of conditional normative orders (based on norms such as 'if x occurs then do y'); the collapse of the institutional welfare state; the fact that the law has changed from the guarantor of social order to a source of social disorder. In these various instances, social control is first delegitimized in terms of aims and values, then reduced to a technical matter and thus subject to procedural rules that chase their own tail. For example, the welfare state was created to achieve greater social justice, but it was then reduced to a functional matter of redistributing resources, and therefore subjected to rules of efficiency which not only made entitlements depend on the existence of a surplus of economic resources which were necessarily always scarce, but could be pursued even outside a certain political-institutional arrangement, thus making the ethos of welfare more and more evanescent.

The control machine begins to waver. The phenomenon may be described as the emergence of an order based on chaos or entropy (Forsé, 1989), or as a differentiation that creates more problems than it solves (Luhmann, 1984). Some, using different terminology, speak of the death of public goods, while others declare the death of privacy. But few see that these demises are produced by that very modernity that exalts the lib/lab synergy: that is the pursuit of greater freedom through controls exerted as a function of non-normative freedoms.[3]

Secondly, the lib/lab code contradicts the empirical evidence and the subjective experiences of daily life.

Modern sociology describes the relationship between freedom and control as a synergic antithesis that always achieves a new and better balance. But that is not how matters actually stand.

In common sense experience, the growth of freedom is always problematic, as is the growth of social controls. To conceive of society as a 'society of individuals' (Elias, 1936-39) with increasing 'individualization', i.e. as a society capable of 'individualizing individuals' (Beck, 1992) according to increasingly less constricting rules, appears to be highly misleading, for at least two reasons: (i) firstly, because it underestimates the fact that the individual is prey to new herd instincts, new forms of alienation and orgiastic and herd group dynamics; (ii) secondly, because it does not mention the fact that new forms of institutionalizing individuals appear that are not functional to the subject's freedom (in the end, what else have many authors such as Foucault and Donzelot told us?).

It is beyond doubt that new freedoms appear on the one side, and new controls on the other. Nevertheless, their growth is not parallel. Most of the time it is asymmetrical in space and time, and remains highly problematic in the rules that guide social processes. The idea that social control may be configured in such a way as to ensure greater individual freedoms without significant relations between freedom and control leads to forms of systemic control which cause the schizophrenia typical of daily life in our times.

---

3 By 'non-normative' freedoms I mean those freedoms that are purely negative (i.e. intended as freedoms 'from' something or someone). Negative freedoms see the alter only as a limit and constraint to ego's action. By contrast, positive (i.e. normative) freedoms are those that are oriented towards (they are 'for') something or someone. The latter see the alter not merely as a limit, but as a condition and resource for ego's agency. In this case, ego is free to act insofar as s/he can promote alter's freedom as a condition and resource of his/her own action. Contrary to the unrelated concept of negative freedoms, the positive concept emphasises the relational nexus between ego and alter, which becomes the focus of sociological interest. Of course, positive freedom does not negate negative freedom; on the contrary, it guarantees it.

The experience of contemporary men and women is that they live between two entirely discordant levels of reality. On the one hand, they are theoretically free to do anything they like, on the condition that it remains private. The culture of globalization reinforces this feeling in individuals, which is that they may 'privately' enter the realm of virtual reality, so to speak. On the other hand, when they deal with the facts, men and women find that the opportunities to satisfy their social needs are socially limited and structured. Many specific freedoms and identities are denied. The ideology of egalitarian control ensures that men and women have the same freedoms and opportunities, but in practice the opposite occurs. Social freedoms and opportunities are gendered, or differentiated by gender, and the egalitarian viewpoint prevents us from seeing the new inequalities that are generated. And yet the globalizing machine of modernity provides a representation that denies this fact. It may admit the existence of inequality only as a temporary situation, while waiting for the synergic lib/lab antithesis to continue further, and thus engender forms of control that ensure more freedom.

The conclusion is that, in the globalization processes currently under way, the ideology of freedom masks widespread non-freedoms, and the ideology of equality masks new inequalities.

Social control is not functional to many freedoms nor to many equalities that one would like to pursue from the standpoint of human needs and rights.

3. Attempts to reconcile freedom and control conducted within modernity

In the course of its history, lib/lab thought has tended to represent society as a construction in which everything works out in the end, thanks to the fact that conflicts may be brought back to rationality through the synergic antithesis of freedom/control. It may be said that this attitude constitutes the sociological mainstream still today.

Parsons' theory represents the point of greatest morphostatic equilibrium in modern sociological thought between freedom of action and the need for social order, between private and public, or to use the words of Alexander (1983), between substantial and formal voluntarism. Parsons was the last of the moderns to theorize that contact between reason and revelation which, according to many (Seligman, 1992), is the origin of the modern spirit and its idea of freedom (civil society) regulated through a system (state) conceived as a structural form of conditioning needed in order to achieve common goals. In

Parsons, the societal community can combine freedom and control only because it has something that transcends both. It embodies the spirit of a freedom that is born 'from within' social actors, and it can be reconciled with the social system because it rests on a cultural system with religious roots. But Parsonian theory is no longer able to justify this arrangement, which appears to be grounded in an unduly normative vision of society. Because of the way in which the theory (the AGIL schema) is formulated, it absorbs and rationalizes the transcendent element, the vital source (of values) of the system. Within the logic of Parsons' AGIL, the subject of freedom gives way to the determinations and structural limitations of social action. Indeed, in Parsons it is already evident that society (even as civil society) is an immense contraption that secularizes transcendent (i.e. religious) concepts and values.

With Parsons and immediately thereafter ended the dream of the starry heaven above that is reflected within us. The Kantian spirit of modern sociology dissolved. It was no longer so easy to reconcile freedom and control. The lib/lab synergy could no longer be considered a normally functioning process. Normality became the fact itself that the mutual conciliation of freedom and control no longer worked.

Parsons thought that freedom consisted of individuals internalizing the value patterns and control mechanisms of the Protestant ethic and Freudian schematics through socialization. This ethic no longer exists, and Freudianism has been overturned. Consequently, this train of thought was 'modern' only in part, for it also reflected a number of pre-modern convictions. Specifically, modernity thinks that freedom cannot be founded (constituted) on control. This is the exact point where Parsons fails, and must be abandoned.

It becomes clearer why and how Parsons never found a way out of the dilemma that lies at the heart of all modern sociological theory, and which can be expressed by the question: how is it possible to limit the (modern) social system's demand to control all areas of human life, beginning with the claim that something precedes the system and legitimizes its institutions?

Parsons' theory still assumes that: 1. freedom and control work within a certain symbolical framework of values, and 2. they augment each other by respecting the famous cybernetic hierarchy. But both of these conditions have collapsed today. Thus the question becomes: how can the social system develop. or even survive, if it globalizes contingencies and searches for its regulatory form within this globalization? Parsons' theory is by now unable to answer this question.

Sociology in recent decades is a declaration of the failure of Parsons' theory as the apex of modern theorization on the freedom/control dilemma.

Three alternatives have arisen since Parsons:

1. one may run the risk of being anti-modern, and thus reject the thesis that freedom and control are merely external limitations on each another, thereby making use of connections and interdependencies that bind freedom and control together under the aegis of some or other structure or prerequisite or meta-social requirement.

2. one may define oneself as neo-modern, thereby reintroducing the synergic antithesis between freedom and control in search of new forms of compatibility achieved by adjusting re-selected mixes and contingencies.

3. or one may enter the post-modern, further destructuring the two terms and their relationships.

These are three different ways to criticise the modern view of society and foresee the post-modern.[4] Of course, various configurations of mixes between these three modes are also possible. And indeed the real post-modern is a mixture of these three 'pure' types of response. Let us briefly examine them.

1. The anti-moderns claim alternative systems for distinguishing freedom/control from those employed by modernity. They highlight that society performs selective reductions of complexity which differ from those typically used in modernity. These distinctions and selections generally have a 'community' thrust (indeed, the category includes many of the so-called 'communitarians'). There is no lack of traditions in this sense. Polany founded one, Le Play another. Marx, Durkheim, Mauss could be considered the fathers of yet other traditions, all couched in different terms. But, apart from the observation that only a few schools today adopt approaches that reject a lib/lab interpretation of contingency, most relevant here is the fact that contemporary sociology has developed a new sensibility. Reasoning about our society requires something more than simply recalling a classical perspective. It requires the ability to point out more highly differentiated and complex means to reduce the globalization of contingencies. Anti-modern cannot be pre-modern. And many of the above-mentioned schools seem unable to avoid these pitfalls.

2. The neo-moderns distinguish themselves by reinterpreting society within

---

4   It is not difficult to place the various currents of today's social and philosophical thought within these three responses to the crisis of modernity. They may be easily classified in terms of morphogenetic theory (Archer, 1995): the first category includes the neo-communitarians (who commit errors of downward conflation); the second includes the neo-liberals (who commit errors of upward conflation); and the third are the neo-relationists (who commit errors of central conflation).

the *lib/lab* synergy more loosely and with a few variations. Many of them repeat Parsons without Parsons' faith. They are uncertain as to exactly what parts of Parsons should be preserved, and which of them must be changed. But they essentially propose bringing multi-dimensionality under the primary assumptions of Parsonian thought, which means opening the theory to greater contingency. They also seek to reconcile freedom and control in the form of *lib/lab* democracy. But to what extent is this possible when the basic assumptions of control in the cybernetic hierarchy of the AGIL framework fail? This is not at all clear. And thus the freedom/control dialectic is now even more uncertain, more replete with indeterminacy. Alexander (1994) attributes its existence and development to the ability of cultural traditions to produce and reproduce, but this solution appears highly problematic. Habermas pointed it out long ago, proposing his own solution of an 'unlimited community of discourse', which in turn is utopian.

The neo-moderns expand the contingencies of freedom and controls, but in doing so lose certain essential prerequisites for the preservation of both. They realize that freedoms must have independent subjects, but the latter are by now a ('deviant') minority, since most individuals are prey to systemic mechanisms and pervasive heteronomous pressures. They still search for forms of control that should meet functional needs, but a functionalist explanation of control encounters a chronic deficit of meaning where modernity is carried to extremes. In short, the neo-moderns attempt to re-launch modernity without the myths and illusions that gave modernity its forward thrust. They strive to 'purify its spirit'. But, I believe that the attempt is conceptually backward compared to the phenomena concerned.

The neo-moderns prove themselves unable to grasp the new.

3. Those who instead draw the radically coherent consequences of the loss of normativity in social systems are followers of post-modern thought, whose greatest departure from the humanistic tradition is systemic neo-functionalism. Luhmann (1984) elaborates a theory intended to deal with the crucial problem implicit in neo-modern thought: making the freedom/control relationship depend on the ability of traditional cultures to regenerate. With Luhmann, freedom is placed radically outside the system, in the so-called system environment, where the human subject may fluctuate as desired. For him, communication is enough to create control. There is no longer need for culture as a necessary prerequisite and framework to organize the relationship between freedom and social control.

Neo-functionalism thereby reaches a decisive turning point in the direction of a *radically contingent* relationism between freedom and control. With Luhmann, sociology proves itself ready to be placed in that crucible of post-modern thought that severs all human ties between freedom and control. In this light, Luhmann appears to be simultaneously the grave-digger of modernity and the lark of post-modernity. This lark, however, has no wings; Luhmann's post-modernity cannot take flight. Beyond the metaphor, it is unable to indicate any cultural innovation complete with a sense of humanity. It cannot distinguish the human-social from the inhuman-social. But on the contrary, this is the core problem of the post-modern world.

The difficulties that modernity encounters in managing the freedom/control relationship foster a multitude of theories based on paradoxes and contradictions between the two terms of the relationship.

It would require a great deal of space to deal with this topic thoroughly. Here, I shall concentrate on the fact that the end of modernity is revealed by its inability to fulfil its promises summarized in the triad of freedom/equality/fraternity. From this standpoint, one realizes that the *lib/lab* complex (freedom/equality) has made solidarity residual and continues to corrode the primary and secondary forms of social integration (non-systemic). The *lib/lab* complex systemically empties the fabric of sociality (Donati, 1993). Society discovers that it is a powerful machine that turns life into merchandise. The appearance of the post-modern is marked by the need to reintroduce the third pole (solidarity) within a historical context in which the freedom/control combination has taken on the abstract form of *general intellect* (of Marxian memory) that appears and materializes more each day in the globalization processes implemented by the new communication technologies.

The crisis of the *lib/lab* complex is manifest as soon as one has to appeal to some form of social solidarity – not occasional or marginal – and realizes that the *lib/lab* set-up does not provide for it. Then, and only then, when one realizes that the destruction of solidarity has exceeded the critical points of social cohesion, does it become apparent that *lib/lab* sociology can describe society only as a paradox. The crisis emerges gradually, asymmetrically in various systems and social institutions, and at different rates in different societies. But, at a certain point, one is led to wonder: what it is that holds society together? Within the model of Western modernization, beyond the threshold where solidarity is radically eroded, the existence of sociability, as a reality *sui generis*, may no longer be assigned to freedom or control, nor to a combination thereof, simply because the modern definitions of freedom and control implode. The only remaining alternative is to conceive of sociological theory as the construction (and management) of paradoxes.[5]

The dialectic between freedom and control becomes something else in relation to the dream of primitive modern civil society. The reconciliation between freedom and control appears increasingly despairing, because the two realities separate beneath the figure of an environment (containing freedoms) that fluctuates around the system (containing control) without the two being able to communicate. Sociology must choose whether to continue to reason within this framework or consider an alternative.

In this regard, my thesis is that many of today's attempts to examine the relationship between freedom and control end up by merely taking note of implosions, irrationalities and distortions, rather than seeing positive aspects. They do not go beyond the crucial boundary of modernity, which is not to see the origination and originality of the social sphere as a reality *sui generis*. I shall demonstrate this with reference to a peculiar analysis of society, concluding with a reflection on the theoretical implications of my discourse which suggests a change in the paradigm of how the freedom/control relationship is understood in post-modern society.

4. The limitations and obsolescence of the *lib/lab* paradigm: must we think in terms of subjectivity and communication rules?

In late modernity, the freedom/control dialectic meets structural and cultural limitations beyond which it may not go.

What are these limits? We may summarize them briefly by stating that the late-capitalistic arrangement:

1. identifies control with mere technical needs, or functional mechanisms, which should be managed by impersonal systems (regulated through negotiations between the state and the market);
2. identifies freedoms using the yardstick of market freedom, thus generalizing freedoms by analogy with mercantilism;
3. makes all associative spheres of social solidarity (i.e. non-profit oriented actors, otherwise called 'social private' spheres) residual, allowed only to survive in the most marginal sectors of society;

---

5   Neo-functionalists offer several paradigmatic versions of this. Alexander (1997) sees civil society as prey to a paradoxical nemesis between freedom and control, the particular and the universal, rather than as an expression of a functional synergy between them. Luhmann (1990) sees society as a paradox in itself and elaborates what he calls 'eurialistics', understood as a strategy to prevent being blinded by it.

4. weakens the civil culture of the life-world – that is, debilitates the civic
   commitment of families and informal networks, through privatized and
   standardized forms of consumption and behaviour.

The *lib/lab* arrangement now rests on a process of ethical non-differentiation;
or, put otherwise, on ethical-cultural relativism (unlike other societal
systems, ethics does not have an internal symbolic code of differentiation).

This is the background against which advanced society, as it enters the
twenty-first century, no longer represents itself as the best of all possible
worlds, but only as one of the many possible variations of one world which is
infinitely 'otherwise possible'.

Indeed, many old problems remain unsolved, and others arise that the *lib/
lab* arrangement cannot deal with. These problems concern:

1. the crisis of the welfare state induced by the growth of freedoms
   guaranteed regardless of the negative consequences of private behaviours
   (Mead, 1986),
2. the overflowing of markets beyond national boundaries and other control
   apparatuses (Scott and Urry, 1987; Offe, 1988),
3. the unregulated dynamism of the mass-media networks which create what
   is called the new global society (de Kerckhove, 1997),
4. the increasing risk of amoral behaviour by subjects, against the
   increasingly 'mechanical' nature of control systems which have long
   ceased to rely on the purposive, intentional motivations of subjects in
   areas of behaviour like drug taking and selling, environmental pollution,
   the diffusion of hazardous lifestyles, the perverse effects of the mass
   media – especially television – on people and their communicative
   relationships (end of the Mandeville paradigm in relationships between
   the private and public spheres) (Beck, 1992).

All this shows that the lib/lab paradigm no longer explains what is happening
in many areas of social life. It no longer interprets the deepest meaning of
problems, no longer offers viable solutions for their management with an
acceptable degree of satisfaction.

The inadequacy of the paradigm is revealed in the fundamental
subsystems of society.

1. Politics no longer has control over the supporting structures of society
   (state and market), and tends to close itself into a self-referential political-
   administrative subsystem, while on the other hand it would be necessary to
   examine the political nature of the various spheres of life.
2. New civil and human claims for freedom emerge which cannot be derived
   from market freedoms or generalizations thereof but instead lead to other

spheres and require other generalized symbolic means (different from money).

3. New intermediate social formations arise, with a subjectivity of their own which cannot be located on the individual-state axis, the pivot of modern citizenship.

4. An ethical question concerning nature has emerged ('ecology') which cannot be related to political ethics (which remain governmental) or business (market) ethics: that is, the two ethics whose symbiosis has formed the hinge of government in the modern system.

The *lib/lab* distinction becomes obsolete as the guiding distinction of society precisely when it is no longer able to see:

1. the developments within each subsystem of society,
2. the relations that change the relationships among these subsystems,
3. the emerging effects of their interaction.

An analysis of all these matters would require more space than is available here. However, the end result is that the *lib/lab* arrangement must be confined to its own terrain. The *lib/lab* code must be functionally specialized and limited to a few concrete mechanisms of social protection which safeguard the basic acquisitions of modernity in the form of a minimal safety net. These functions can no longer act as the guiding functions of the societal system. To go further, society needs a fundamental change in the guiding distinctions upon which social institutions are built.

At the present time, the passage to new paradigms of relationship between freedom and control is marked by a language and symbolic codes that refer to the interplay between the subjectivity of the actors and social rules mediated by the 'world of communications'.

The post-modern society tends to be described and interpreted within the framework comprising the subjectivity of actors and communications system (with its symbolic codes, means and rules of communication).

This is the system against which I shall compare the emerging phenomena of today: in the increasingly apolitical climate that pervades society in the form of *autós* (need to render autonomous the links between freedom and control within each sphere of life); in the development of new, alternative markets (known as 'social' markets since they are non-profit); in the appearance of new social networks and aggregations; in the emergence of new cultures of difference. All these phenomena are barely present or entirely unforeseen by the *lib/lab* arrangement.

The framework that I call 'communications paradigm' takes cognizance of these new phenomena. But how does it interpret the changes under way? It offers many answers but, generally speaking, communicationists believe:

1. that the apolitical character of society may be resolved by allowing the rules to emerge from the 'community of discourse' of subjects and from so-called communicative hyper-cycles; however, it remains to be seen whether this will give rise to a re-politicization of the social sphere or produce an additional deficiency in the political character of society;
2. that freedoms may be managed by translating them into new forms of communication, including new, non-monetary forms of 'money'; here again it remains to be seen whether these means will activate a new sociality or, on the contrary, force the social context of communication into latency, thereby distorting social reality;
3. that the new subjects must be understood as communicative actors, no longer protagonists of historical revolutionary battles nor activators of collective resources, but rather bearers of new cultural codes in which identity and interests blend in a vital-existential manner;
4. that the relationships between society and nature may be re-thought as 'clean ecological communication'; but it remains to be seen whether it will be possible to avoid the further artificialization of nature itself, beyond limiting the Faustian exploitation thereof.

The new paradigm of globalization centred around subjectivity and social rules mediated by communication on a planetary scale certainly revises the *lib/lab* logic as a logic of modernization. But in turn, it leaves the relationships between freedom and control hanging. Often, the communications system is once again viewed as the product of administrative and market demands, into which it is difficult to introduce elements of *Lebenswelt*.

At the end of the twentieth century, a representation of society as the world of communication – or rather, as an infinite number of cohabiting worlds of communication – becomes dominant.

One wonders how and to what extent this new paradigm manages to go beyond the limits of the *lib/lab* arrangement.

It acquires a few advantageous features, but also persistent weaknesses. The gains lie in the fact that the subject is now seen as freer to express his/her internal self and relate to others. The weaknesses persist in the fact that this paradigm once again finds it difficult to account for the social pathologies that derive from the progressive scission between freedom and control, understood respectively as interior and exterior, intimate relationships and generalized relationships, private and public. Managing these cleavages solely through mere communications further reduces the ability of actors to relate to each other. The logical consequence is the various theorems of the death of the subject and the implosion of social ties (Taylor, 1989).

My thesis is that the two paradigms – *lib/lab* and communications – certainly contain discontinuities. The paradigm of society as communication lends itself better than the previous one (*lib/lab*) to grasping of new social aspects. But I also believe that the communications paradigm does not offer an adequate view of freedom and control as social relations.

In the new communications paradigm, freedom resides in the subjects and control in the procedures of the communication system. But, one wonders, what relationships exist between the subjects and the communication system? Supporters of the paradigm take up two distinct positions.

On the one hand, there are those who maintain that only thing common to subjects and the social system is communication and no more than communication. They assure us that communication can act on its own as a vehicle for both freedom and control, making both of them more contingent, because freedom and control take on the nature of pure communication. This seems to dissolve the paradoxes and contradictions towards non-virtual reality.

On the other hand, there are those who affirm that the 'society of communication' is by no means such. They note that communication is always embedded in social relations which precede and extend beyond subjects and the communication system. They emphasise that freedom and control are achieved in a context where choices do not depend on pure communication, and even less do they correspond to pure contingencies. This raises the view of a truly 'relational' society, as opposed to the relationistic (non-relational) fading society of the 'pure' communicationists (who reduce relations to simple communication).

On the one hand, the view of pure communicationists prompts the observation that freedoms, far from having content, are increasingly formal and empty, and do not create that minimum of political 'glue' upon which the vitality of the spheres of daily life depend. They even find it difficult to direct exchanges towards a social end. Daily life dissolves into a globalization that is a standardization of the mind. The rules which exert social control appear increasingly impersonal and systemic, and increasingly less pertinent to the life-world and social interaction. The world of the media does not show (does not generate!) those spheres of social integration and symbolic cultures (ethos) needed to fill the void left by the modern.

On the other hand, freedom and control can relate only in certain contexts and under specific conditions in such a way that they express action directed towards values and capable of social integration. Note that this takes place:

1. in personal care services and within a new professional ethic of social work conceived as services to the *alter* while respecting his/her characteristics, potential, and membership;

2. in service organizations, where private freedoms are enacted for the purposes of community utility rather than solely for the instrumental interests of the members of those organizations;

3. in social relationships that assume a new attitude towards 'nature', considered not as a mere physical ecosystem but as a symbolic referent that offers new mediations of meaning for human life.

These environments and types of social relations have something in common which reveals the novelty of the social sphere. This is the reality *sui generis* of society when expressed in an *original* and *originative manner*.

Original because social relations arise in specific and independent ways outside the systemic regulations of the state-market complex.

Originative because social relations come into existence through an otherness of symbolic exchange that is not imposed from outside nor is an aim unto itself, because it has giving as a need-order, as a pattern of value, as a rule and as a medium.

Why create caring relationships, why respect actors for their differences and peculiarities, why work for the good of others, why celebrate the value of nature? Because, in all these cases, the relationship between freedom and control is configured with a relational structure and culture of symbolic exchange whose paradigm lies in giving, and not elsewhere.

One wonders whether someone who makes a gift is free or forced to do so. From a common sense viewpoint, the answer is that the first to do so, on his/her own spontaneous volition, is free, while s/he who reciprocates is in some way obliged to do so by the norm of restitution. But this distinction does not hold. Within the giving circuit it is difficult to track down the 'first' move. Who or what is the *primum movens* of giving? The subject's freedom or the norm of reciprocity as a symbolic exchange? If we admit that an individual may be totally free as a speck, an atom, which moves throughout the emptiness of social space as it pleases, then the *primum movens* is the individual. But an individual of this kind does not exist in the social field (Archer, 1995).

Anyone who gives a gift responds to internal and eternal needs that are born and live in a context of relationships within which only the gift has meaning (Caillé, 1996).

The gift is a relationship in itself where the subject's freedom encounters social constraints. Each impulse takes place in a social environment and achieves social reality, but it is not imposed in an entirely binding fashion on that concrete individual. This human freedom lies within social determinism but at the same time transcends it.

This observation takes us beyond simply noting that human beings move freely within social determinism (Gurvitch, 1963). We find that the system of social relevancy has changed.

The society of communication goes beyond the *lib/lab* concept if and to the extent that it performs two operations: first, it makes 'other' freedoms and 'other' forms of control possible; second, it relates them according to a new symbolic code.

If it does so, this is because it posits the relationship as the underlying assumption of a new metaphysics of the social world, after Western technology has replaced the classical, rational ontology of beings.

There are many different ways to interpret and enact society *as a social relationship* between freedom and control (thus with different AGIL-relationships). Only a few of them are innovative. Among them are those marked by instrumental motives (which remain within the A-G complex), and those marked by symbolic exchange motives (mutual giving) which stem from L–I. As Mauss has shown (Caillé, 1996), only reciprocal giving can generate new forms of sociability, while instrumental motives are more likely to lead to its consumption.

The new civil society is born as a place where human relationships are taken seriously.

In order to provide care, to organize a collective service, to respect and enhance nature, it is necessary to make specific choices. In these domains, one must develop social relationships in which freedom and control *penetrate each other* and thus remain *interdependent, inter-penetrated and interactive* according to new processes.

Civility emerges to the extent that human relations become significant 'otherwise' in the sense of taking on the significance of a good in itself, and to the extent that this *'relational good'* is pursued as such.

In short, this is my thesis. Society is (and is becoming) post-modern if and to the extent that it takes the originative and original nature of social relations seriously, sees them and enacts them, placing communication within the relationship and not making the relationship a by-product or superstructure of communication (as late modernity does).

For this type of society to emerge, freedom and control must distinguish themselves and rejoin relationally (as happens within the logic of reciprocity), rather than acting as a binary division that proceeds by progressively excluding one side from the other through the logic of *re-entry* (Spencer Brown, 1979).

Only if matters are viewed in this light can one realize that post-modern society is divided into many social spheres which differ because they conjugate the meaning of freedom and control – and their relationships – differently. In particular, we can distinguish four types of spheres:

1. market spheres, where freedom means competition for profit and control is assigned to the pricing system;
2. government spheres, where freedom is represented by exercising the right to vote and control is entrusted to obedience of laws;
3. service spheres, where freedom means symbolic exchange and control lies with associative social exchange rules;
4. the spheres of family and informal networks, where freedom is an action of mutual giving and control is entrusted to the rules which make this relationship valuable.

This multitude of intertwining spheres is the foundation of a new societal configuration.

5. A relational approach to freedom versus control dilemmas in post-modern society: possible scenarios

I have described the crisis of late-modern society as resulting from the peculiar, synergic antithesis between freedom and control that has been postulated since the beginning of modernity. I have also maintained that this symbolic code (*lib/lab*) can no longer act as the guiding code for the entire societal system and becomes a mechanism for highly limited choices in specialized social sectors.

I shall now draw the theoretical implications of this interpretation of society beyond modernity.

The overall premise is the assumption that the freedom/control relationship is an antithesis only in particular instances. The antithesis – especially when synergic – is only one of the possible reductions of the relational dilemmas between the two poles. It lends itself to description of the relationship between state and market, but not of relations within and among the other spheres of life. Generally speaking, a complex, multi-faceted relationship arises between freedom and control.

When this reality takes on a new appearance, we enter the after-modern world[6] where alternative relating processes emerge because the relationship between freedom and control may now be seen and enacted with much greater degrees of contingency on both sides. This contingency is selectively reduced in different ways, according to the communication contexts, *since these are relational contexts*. That this type of society raises new problems, and even immense risks, is intrinsic to its relational nature.

From a theoretical standpoint, it thus emerges that freedom and control are not simply two dimensions inherent in every social relation; rather, they are social relations themselves and must be conjugated differently in different social environments.[7] We must define freedom and control as social relations, and do so without making their interaction with other relations and dimensions of social action – such as for example with solidarity – antithetical or even perverse.

Freedom lies not only outside control but also within it; freedom is a form of control and its source of justification. Control not only offers greater or lesser opportunities for freedom but also constitutes it, in the sense that it creates the various forms and degrees of freedom itself.[8]

Freedom and control work together and are not mutually exclusive alternatives. Instead they are contexts and opportunities which develop each other reciprocally. To see this, we must consider the freedom/control distinction as a relationship of social relations. But how is it possible to consider freedom and control as social relations?

1. As far as freedom is concerned, modernity has viewed it as a social relationship that may be enacted in many ways. By introducing new distinctions (differentiations), it has made unique relational universes possible.

First example. By introducing the *distinction between freedom 'from'* (negative) and *freedom 'for'* (positive), it has on the one hand expanded

---

6   The term 'after'-modernity means simply what comes historically after the modern era at the moment when the basic criteria of social action and organization no longer refer primarily and exclusively to the concepts of freedom and equality as envisaged by the modern Enlightenment. The concepts of freedom and control, lib and lab, become only two operators among many. They are not absolute but must be referred to other principles which, in turn, may prove to be more important. I introduce the term 'after'-modern in order to avoid the many ambiguities inherent in 'post'-modern discourse.

7   To claim that freedom and control are social relations themselves means that they can be conceived as AGIL-relationships, which in turn means that freedom must have its own internal controls, while control must have its own internal freedoms. Or, otherwise stated, one cannot disconnect freedom and control entirely, one can only redefine the relations among their components.

8   To use the philosophical language of Erich Przywara (1962), one might say that modernity (from Kant to Parsons) adopts a logic of 'above-within' that negates the reciprocal, thus the logic of the 'within-above'.

negative freedoms into demands for non-interference, and on the other opened new horizons of positive freedoms as needs to achieve significant goals.

Second example. By introducing the *distinction between procedural freedom* and *substantial freedom*, it has on the one hand increased the possibilities for automatic social relations, and on the other made new relationships of significant human intention possible.

The *lib/lab* complex, however, still almost exclusively sees the first side of these relationships. It mainly sees negative and procedural freedoms, while it has great difficulty in seeing positive and substantial ones.

This explains why much of sociology has observed freedom essentially in the form of the contingency inherent in 'money' (as a generalized symbolic means), freeing the adaptive function (the A of AGIL) from the rules of input/ output exchange and from all forms of self-restriction, thereby making all social relationships abstract and instrumental. By doing so, sociology has obscured the reverse processes, those through which new embodied, value-based, closely intertwined and at the same time self-restricting social relationships have produced social forms outside those regulated according to the *lib/lab* logic.

Many sociological theories have failed to realize that the social relationship is a mutual action, and have thus ignored the fact that vital associative worlds produce positive and substantial freedoms outside the state-market complex.

2. The same applies to control. Modernity generated new distinctions of social control; that is, it created control as a social relationship that can be played out in many diverse ways.

First example. By introducing the *distinction between systemic control* and *social integration control*, it has on the one hand built new rules without human intentional meaning, and on the other created room for norms otherwise laden with significant intentional meaning.

Second example. By introducing the *distinction between hetero-control* and *self-control*, it has on the one hand been able to construct impersonal apparatuses of social security and regulation, and on the other to explore the worlds of internal regulation (mainly biopsychological and only marginally conscience-based).

The *lib/lab* complex still almost exclusively considers the first side of these relationships: it sees systemic and coercive control towards subjects, while it has difficulty in seeing the control of informal rules within subjects and social actions.

This explains why sociology has ended up by viewing the social domain as that which negates the authenticity of the self (i.e. society as a powerful machine that denies bio-psychological identity or 'individuality'), rather than that which makes it possible.

Modernity tends to articulate freedom and control as opposite, negatively correlated dimensions, which define a sort of *'relational hyperbola'* between *refero* and *religo*[9] in which they may develop only inversely (fig. 1).

In modernity it is assumed that if freedom is expanded along the *refero* axis, then control is reduced along the *religo* axis, and vice-versa. It is always difficult to find a point of balance on the hyperbola (this difficulty gives rise to the constant reduction of the social world to a series of problems only, to wit, the well-known process of *Problematizierung*). Consequently, society is described as an antithetical oscillation between *statu nascenti* movements and processes of institutionalization.

In the course of developing this dynamic, the forms of social control tend to liberate freedoms insofar as this is possible. As long as the game remains within certain limits, it is possible to find mix solutions while remaining on the hyperbola. But it is no longer possible beyond certain thresholds. The asymptotic development of control must expunge freedom in the system environment (thus outside institutions).

The same applies to the asymptotic development of freedom, which confines controls to its environment (thus only within system operations). In one direction, freedoms are placed outside the social sphere (thus outside social institutions), and in the other social control becomes only systemic (i.e. mechanical) and is deprived of justifying values.

The *lib/lab* complex thus ends up by stretching the social sphere asymptotically towards 'polar layouts' dominated by control (along the *religo* axis of functional limitations) or freedom (along the *refero* axis of merely symbolic references).

I suggest that this formula for reading modernity may be generalized using the AGIL diagram to represent post-modern society as a relational society born of modernity (fig. 2).

In representing society as a hyperbolic organization (interpreted according to the AGIL diagram: fig. 2), the space of relations between freedom (*refero*) and control (*religo*) delineates the scenarios for both micro and macro social forms emerging in post-modern societies.

---

9   On these dimensions, which refer to the Weber (*refero*) and Durkheim (*religo*) traditions, see Donati (1991). The expression 'relational hyperbola' is explained and treated within the modern cultural and philosophical context by Cevolini (1997).

We have eight possible 'hyperbolic escapes'[10] (fig. 2):

a G --> A: decisional (political) freedom is asymptotically reduced to the economic mechanisms of the market;

b A --> G: the mechanisms (constraints) of the market are cancelled out by free political decisions;

c G --> I: decisional (political) freedom is reduced to the rules of social exchange in the so-called third sector;

d I --> G: social exchanges in the third sector give way to political decisions;

e L --> A: informal relationships take on the characteristics, especially the restrictions, of the market;

f A --> L: the market is cancelled out within the network of informal relationships;

g L --> I: informal networks give way to third-sector organizations;

h I --> L: third-sector organizations accentuate their nature as informal networks.

Fig. 1   The relational hyperbola of modernity[11]

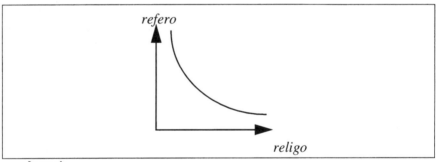

Legend:
refero = symbolic (value and intentional references = freedoms)
religo = functional (adaptive and regulative constraints = controls)

---

10   A 'hyperbolic escape' may be defined as follows: if the AGIL-system is reduced to one dimension (*refero* or *religo* in one of these two poles), the other dimension is placed in its environment (the asymptote corresponds here to the re-entry of the systemic differentiation according to Luhmann). For example, if the love relationship becomes 'pure' (one of pure intimacy as though suspended in a normative vacuum) – or put otherwise, when the love relationship is reduced to the pure L of AGIL- then the institution (the *religo* in the couple) is placed outside the AGIL-system formed by the pure love relationship (in other words, the social institution of the couple becomes only one of the many possibilities represented on the horizon of the pure love relationship).

11   The distinction *refero/religo* is, in its turn, relational. To understand this, take for instance the dilemma of competition (marketization) versus social control (welfare provisions). This dilemma can be articulated by positing these two poles either as *refero/religo* or as *religo/refero* respectively, depending on the point of view of the observer/ actor of the situation (who stresses one as freedom and the other as control). The hyperbola in fig. 1 becomes specified only when it is articulated within fig. 2.

Fig. 2   The relational nature of post-modern society

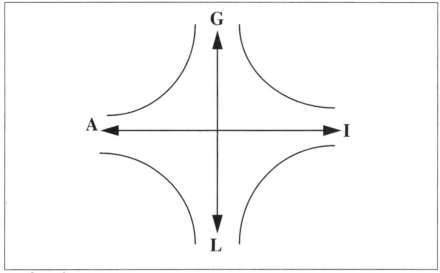

Legend:
refero (L-G axis) = culture (symbolic and significant)
religo (A-I axis) = structure (adaptive and regulative)

To describe society as a relational-hyperbolic pattern of social forms is an alternative to a description based on the functional primacy of one of the four functional prerequisites A, G, I, L. The functional primacy of one of the four poles is no longer possible (as Parsons and Luhmann still believe) for the entire society. Only trends are possible, as asymptotic convergences of the hyperbolas on one of the relational poles (A, G, I, L around fig. 2), which however cannot – as a single dimension – ever absorb the others, which are forced to develop in other social spheres. To develop a code for the freedom-control interaction in one direction (in a certain relational sphere) means pushing for other codes of that interaction to be developed in other directions (in other relational spheres).

If we consider the vertical axis in fig. 2 (*refero*) as culture and the horizontal axis (*religo*) as structure, we can summarize the four possible response scenarios to modernity as follows. Social forms may:
1. *remain on the hyperbola*, i.e. in some intermediate point; this is the neo-modern scenario that still bases itself on the *lib/lab* model;
2. *escape* into the *refero* for G or L through charismatic movements characterized by a purely intentional ethic (even irrational); in these cases,

pre-modern types of political movements may emerge (in that they un-differentiate the system in the G pole) or cultural movements of post-modern action (which give primacy to latency values in L); in these instances, affirmations of freedom prevail over demands for control;

3. *escape* into the *religo* for A or I; in the first instance we have hyperfunctionalism, in the second new social markets;

4. finally, they may *produce a morphogenesis* of the social (and therefore of the societal system) through relations emerging from the interaction of all of these dimensions. This is *after-modern society*. Its main feature consists in going beyond the modern forms of social differentiation through new competitive as well as solidarist games among the different dimensions of social relations, thereby generating social forms unknown to the previous society. These new forms will be vital in so far as they are original and originative, as said earlier. Of course, strains, conflicts, and even struggles will not disappear. Quite the opposite.

The new society will result from this 'game'. Paths 2 and 3 remain 'exceptional', in my view, in the sense that they may occur in spatially and temporally limited spheres of the social realm. As far as the general framework of the societal system is concerned, the global challenge is played out between paths 1 and 4.

All this may be stated in yet another way. We may hypothesise that society changes its structure from a hyperbolic configuration typical of the modern to a relational configuration typical of the post-modern.

In the former, freedom and control are played out as a synergic antithesis, while in the latter they are played out relationally (i.e. as an emergent property of reciprocal action). The underlying theoretical hypothesis, which will obviously require a great number of empirical studies for its verification, states: the more freedom and control differentiate, the less they become separable and must be newly *bound* and *referred* to one another. This may happen by remaining on one of the four hyperbolas; in this case, solutions to social issues will be still 'modern' (although making room to 'other modernities'). But it may also happen that a new relational AGIL-complex is born (when both constraints and references change for the entire AGIL-system). In this case, solutions to social issues will be after-modern, in the sense that they will escape from the synergic antithesis between freedom and control. Freedom and control will be configured as qualitatively new relationships, with new cultural (*refero*) and structural (*religo*) dimensions. Thus society will rediscover its relational nature, and hence the fact that it is made up of relationships where 'relationship' itself implies references and constraints which interconnect in a manner *sui generis*.

In conclusion: the more society becomes post-modern, the more each relationship (each sphere of social relations) must be based on its own guiding distinction that sees freedom and control not as identifiable or collective attributes in an antithetic contraposition, but as characteristics of differentiated, specific networks of relationships that are regulated (and regenerated) on the basis of an autonomous nexus between freedom and control.

I do not believe that the debates on agency and structure, between subjectivity and rules, have highlighted this new reality clearly enough.

They have undoubtedly shed light on many aspects of the morphogenesis now under way (Burns and Dietz, 1992). But they have failed to see the overall relationality of the social sphere. Most of them have reduced the new relational quality of society to a single hyperbola. By way of just one example, consider the 'pure relationship' theorized by Giddens (1992), which represents an escape from a pre-imposed social structure through the hyperbolic paths that tend asymptotically toward the flight to pure latency (L in fig. 2).

Perhaps by adopting a relational paradigm, sociology will see how the norms of freedom and control lie neither simply in individuals (as 'abstract' subjects) nor in systems ('fully structured'), but in social relations, when they are taken seriously for what they are: real (fully social) reciprocal actions among subjects.

Herein lies the novelty of civil society, which beyond modernity no longer coincides with the forefront of political democratization, but rather with social subjects that express a new civilizing process (Donati, 1997).

The political expression of this project is 'societal citizenship', understood as citizenship distinct from the governmental sense of the term. Societal citizenship is constructed as the co-growth of freedom and control within a framework of social solidarity, through distance relationships between civil society and the state, rather than as an ascriptive emanation of the nation-state (implemented, as in modernity, through the principle of progressive inclusion of the populace).

Social relationality is the new 'glue' of society, not the state, an abstract normative system, or an abstract adaptation system. It may perhaps be called 'the political' (*le politique*) of social exchanges, as opposed to 'the politics' of the political party system (*la politique*) (according to the distinction drawn by Caillé, 1993). But only if we see that the political stuff of society consists of its 'relational glue', and if we are able to observe it in adequate manner. 'The political' has become simultaneously more global and more local, meaning that it has spread throughout all relational dimensions of society and at the same time has differentiated within each societal sphere, according to autonomous intersections (nexuses) between freedom and control. In the twenty-first century, society will be able to manage 'the political' only as a form of relationality unknown to the moderns.

Bibliography

Alexander, J.C. (1983), *The Modern Reconstruction of Classical Thought, Talcott Parsons*, Routledge, London.

Alexander, J.C. (1994), 'Modern, Anti, Post, and Neo: How Social Theories Have Tried to Understand the 'New World' of 'Our Time'', *Zeitschrift für Soziologie*, Special Issue, vol. 23, no. 3, pp. 165-97.

Alexander, J.C. (1997), 'La società civile democratica: istituzioni e valori', in P. Donati (a cura di), *L'etica civile alla fine del XX secolo: tre scenari*, Leonardo, Milano, pp. 107-56.

Archer, M. (1995), *Realist Social Theory: The Morphogenetic Approach*, Cambridge University Press, Cambridge.

Beck, U. (1992), *Risk Society. Towards a New Modernity*, Sage, London.

Boudon, R. (1979), *La logique du social*, Hachette, Paris.

Burns, T. and Dietz, T. (1992), 'Cultural Evolution: Social Rule Systems, Selection and Human Agency', *International Sociology*, vol. 7, no. 3, pp. 259-83.

Caillé, A. (1993), *La démission des clercs. La crise des sciences sociales et l'oubli du politique*, La Découverte, Paris.

Caillé, A. (1996), 'Ni holism ni individualisme méthodologiques. Marcel Mauss et le paradigme du don', in L'obligation de donner. La découverte sociologique capitale de Marcel Mauss, *Revue du MAUSS*, no. 8, 2° semestre, pp, 12-58.

Cevolini, A. (1997), *L'iperbole relazionale della modernità*, Doctoral Thesis, Faculty of Political Sciences, University of Bologna, Bologna.

Connolly, W.E. (1991), *Identity/Difference: Democratic Negotiations of Political Paradox*, Cornell University Press, Ithaca.

De Kerckhove, D. (1997), 'I nuovi media e la società civile', in P. Donati (a cura di), *L'etica civile alla fine del XX secolo: tre scenari*, Leonardo, Milano, pp. 83-106.

Donati, P. (1991), *Teoria relazionale della società*, Angeli, Milano.

Donati, P. (1993), *La cittadinanza societaria*, Laterza, Roma-Bari.

Donati, P. (1997), 'Alla ricerca di una società civile. Che cosa dobbiamo fare per aumentare le capacità di civilizzazione del Paese?', in P. Donati (a cura di), *La società civile in Italia*, Mondadori, Milano, pp. 22-80.

Elias, N. (1936-39), *Über den Prozess der Zivilization*, Haus zum Falken, Basel.

Forsé, M. (1989), *L'ordre improbable. Entropie et processus sociaux*, Puf, Paris.

Gehlen, A. (1986), *Urmensch und Spätkultur. Philosophische Ergebnisse und Aussagen*, Verlag GmbH, Wiesbaden.

Giddens, A. (1992), *The Transformation of Intimacy. Sexuality, Love and Eroticism in Modern Societies*, Polity Press, Cambridge.

Gurvitch, G. (1963), *Déterminismes sociaux et liberté humaine. Vers l'étude sociologique des cheminements de la liberté*, Puf, Paris.

Hirsch, F. (1995), *Social Limits to Growth*, Routledge, London.

Luhmann, N. (1984), *Soziale Systeme. Grundriss einer allgemeinen Theorie*, Suhrkamp, Frankfurt am Main.

Luhmann, N. (1990), 'Sthenography', *Stanford Literature Review*, vol. 7, no. 1-2, pp. 133-7.

Mead, L. (1986), *Beyond Entitlement. The Social Obligations of Citizenship*, The Free Press, New York.

Offe, C. (1988), *Disorganized Capitalism*, Polity Press, Cambridge.

Przywara, E. (1962), *Schriften: Analogia entis. Metaphysik. Ur-Struktur und All-Rythmus*, Johannes Verlag, Einsiedeln.

Schooyans, M. (1991), *La dérive totalitaire du libéralisme*, Editions Universitaires, Paris.

Scott, L. and Urry, J. (1987), *The End of Organized Capitalism*, Polity Press, Cambridge.

Seligman, A. (1992), *The Idea of Civil Society*, The Free Press, New York.

Spencer Brown, G. (1979), *Laws of Form*, Dutton, New York.

Taylor, C. (1989), *Sources of the Self: The Making of the Modern Identity*, Harvard University Press, Cambridge.

PART II:
THE NEW REALITIES OF TODAY: COSMOPOLITAN SOCIETY, GLOBALIZATION, ETHNICITY, NATIONALITY, IMMIGRATION

6 The cosmopolitan society and its enemies

ULRICH BECK

Introduction

The title of this chapter 'The cosmopolitan society and its enemies' is, of course, a reminder of the famous book *The Open Society and its Enemies* written by Karl Popper in reaction to the fascist assault on freedom and democracy and published in 1945. For Popper, too, the Open Society is a cosmopolitan society and its enemies are Marxism and Fascism, both of which advocated closed societies.

Once upon a time, it was possible to believe in all the splendid Enlightenment values – progress, universal laws, perpetual peace, the Kantian '*sensus communis*' – unproblematically. I am always moved by how firmly Kant and Popper believed that all the diverse human cultures were bound to transcend their conflicts of interest and achieve some sort of federal world-state – the United Nations as an 'idea of reason', if you like. I think those values are still open to us; they are even becoming more important in what I call the 'second age of modernity'. And I also think that the current fashionable anti-Enlightenment rhetoric, such as we find in some theories of post-modernity, is both ethically and politically disastrous. There is a need for a second Enlightenment to understand the shift in global relations and to highlight key concepts and conjunctures different from those embedded in the classical narrative of modernity. Hence I am reading and confirming Popper against Popper.

There are indeed many enlightening ideas in Popper's *Open Society*. But as an antidote to tribalism Popper envisions a 'democratic cosmopolitan empire' (to me a contradiction in terms), having in mind, for example, the British Empire. Hence his argument provides an ideal backdrop to investigation of the dilemmas of cosmopolitanism (Hacohen, 1999).

There is, for example, the *tribal dilemma* of cosmopolitanism: all attempts to open up the ethnic ghetto seem to produce and enforce it. Even more than this, as Popper himself experienced to his cost, defining yourself as a member of the cosmopolitan community can be counteracted by the violent ethnic self-definition of others who force you to be a Jew. 'I do not consider myself as an assimilated German Jew,' Popper argued, 'this is how the Führer would have considered me'. Ascribed ethnic identities, because they tend to be violent, have the dreadful power of self-fulfilment. They awaken the bloody nightmares of history.

The title of my chapter, again, is 'The cosmopolitan society and its enemies'. Accordingly, I shall discuss three questions:

What is a 'cosmopolitan society'?

Who are its enemies?

But I shall start with a methodological question:

What is a cosmopolitan sociology?

1. What is a cosmopolitan sociology?

Let me begin by attempting to nail a pudding to the wall, so to speak: that is, define what I mean by 'globalization' (Beck, 2000a). Globalization does not exist or happen as such; it is not a linear process, but a reflexive and dialectic one in which the global and the local (or the universal and the particular) do not exist as cultural polarities but are combined and mutually implicating principles. These processes are both historically variable and multi-dimensional. They not only involve interconnections across boundaries and the dissolving of other boundaries but transform the quality of the social and the political *within* nation-state societies. They also significantly change consciousness and identities: issues of global concern are becoming part of the everyday local experience and 'moral life-world' of the people. They provoke conflicts throughout the world. To treat these profound changes simply as myth is to rely on a superficial and unhistorical understanding of 'globalization', on misunderstandings of *globalism*. The study of globalization and 'globality' (that is, the everyday global consciousness of the global) (Albrow, 1995) constitutes a potential revolution in the social sciences.

For the social sciences, globalization raises fundamental questions of redefinition, reinvention and reorganization. First, of course, there are conceptional problems. By these I mean, for example, the declining ability of the sociological classics to make sense of a dramatically changing economy and society. Second, there are methodological problems: most of sociology is based on a *methodological nationalism*. This term can be defined by explicit or implicit assumptions about the nation-state as the container of social processes and the national order as the key to the understanding of major social, economic and political processes (Taylor, 1996). Third, there are organizational problems: what transnational structure of cooperation does sociology need in order to explore and understand the emerging worlds of transnational flows, networks, socioscapes, life-forms, identities, classes and power structures? A sociology that remains happily glued to its own society and times will not have much to contribute.

So what will be the space of sociological imagination, theoretical argument and empirical investigation in the Global Age, if it is not the nation-state society? Göran Therborn (2000) distinguishes very interestingly between the universal and the global. He argues that, for classical sociology, the space was the social space of humankind. But now we are entering a new space of sociological imagination, namely *globality*, which means reflexive globalization, a global everyday experience and consciousness of the global. For Therborn a 'global sociology' treats the globe as a set of divergent cultures and modernities and not only as the territory of humankind in the evolution of modernity.

Therborn writes that 'globality entails a turn away both from provincial self-centredness and from the exotic gaze of the coloniser (and of the colonised). There is no longer any legitimate centre-point, from which to look out and to communicate to the rest of the world. Vistas, experiences, conceptualisations from all parts of the globe will be brought into networks of global inter-communication. Extra-European cultural experiences and language skills will be important assets here, and new links to comparative linguistic will be opened up … A global sociology amounts to a fundamental turn of imagination as well as of investigation, from the nation and a North Atlantic space of reference to a global social cosmos with no naturally given privileged observation post and no absolute time'. And he concludes: 'Globality has potential implications for social studies as revolutionary as Einstein's theory of relativity had for Newtonian physics'.

I totally agree. But a tiny question remains to be answered: how to research the global? Is not the total global, so to speak, a bit too global? And would not a sociology of the global necessarily transform sociology into philosophy and metaphysics *without* any systematic empirical reference for falsification? Hence the following question must be framed and answered: How can an empirical sociology of the global be possible?

Curiously, I believe that there is a simple answer to this question, but it is impeded by common images and misunderstandings of globalization. These are the paradoxes of globalization.

The first one is that globalization is about globalization. This is not true.

Globalization is about localization as well (Robertson, 1992; Tomlinson, 1999). One cannot even think about globalization without referring to specific places. One of the most important consequences of the globalization discourse is the recovery of the concept of 'place'. It is the global-local relationship which Robert Robertson has in mind when he talks about 'glocalization'. The implication for empirical sociology is that glocalization happens not 'out there' but 'in here' (Giddens, 1994). Therefore sociology can investigate the global locally.

How this works is becoming clearer if we pick up on a second misunderstanding of globalization, which sees it as an additive and not substitutive aspect of nation-state society and sociological analysis. In the globalization discourse, one often finds the assumption that globalization only changes the relations between and beyond national states and societies ('interconnectedness'), but not the inner quality of the social and political itself ('cosmopolitization'). But globalization includes globalization *from within*, globalization *internalized*, or, as I prefer to say, 'cosmopolitization of nation-state societies'. Thus a third misunderstanding can be cleared up: under conditions of globalization, the national is no longer the national. The national must be rediscovered as the *internalized global* (Beck, 2000c).

As Saskia Sassen (2000) puts it: 'Of particular interest here is the implied correspondence of national territory with the national, and the associated implication that the national and the non-national are two mutually exclusive conditions. We are now seeing their partial unbundling'. Sassen argues 'that one of the features of the current phase of globalization is the fact that a process happens within a territory of a sovereign state does not necessarily mean that it is a national process. Conversely, the national (such as firms, capital, culture) may increasingly be located *outside* the national territory, for instance, in a foreign country or in digital spaces. This localisation of the global, or of the non-national, *in* national territories, and of the national outside national territories, undermines a key duality running through many of the methods and conceptual frameworks prevalent in the social sciences, that the national and the non-national are mutually exclusive'.

From this one can draw the most important implication. There is no need for the global to be investigated totally globally. We can organize a new purposeful historical sensitive empiricism on the ambivalent consequences of globalization in cross-national and multi-local research networks. But what kinds of concepts and categories can we use for this purpose? Do we have to invent and coin new ones?

It was Kant (1964: 12) who argued: 'Anschauungen ohne Begriffe sind blind; Begriffe ohne Anschauungen sind leer'. Intuitions without concepts are blind; concepts without intuitions are empty. If it is true that the meaning of the national and the local is changing through internalized globalization, then the most important methodological implication for *all* sociology is that normal sociology categories are becoming *zombie* categories, empty terms in the Kantian sense. Zombie categories are the living-dead categories which blind sociology to the rapidly changing realities inside nation-state containers and outside as well (Beck, 2000).

The purpose of my distinction between a first and a second age of modernity is *not* to introduce a new problematic evolutionary form of periodization based on either-or epochal 'stages'; when everything is reversed at the same moment, all the old relations disappear for ever and entirely new ones move in to replace them. The main purpose of the distinction between a first age and a second age of modernity is twofold: first to position the question of new concepts and frame of references by, second, criticising conventional sociology as an empty-term sociology, as zombie sociology. At the Munich research centre on Reflexive Modernization, of which I am the head, we are conducting long-term research on subjects such as the following: How does the meaning of 'class' change under conditions of individualization and globalization? How does the perception of global risk transform the concept of 'rationality' in science and law? How are the concepts of 'employment' and 'labour' being dissolved and redefined in the global information economy? Has the concept of the state already been converted into a super-supra-inter-post-neo-trans-nation state?

Let me provide an example. Sociologists have written textbooks and conducted research on the class structure of Britain, France, the United States, Germany, and so on. But if we look at how a class-based sociology defines class categories, we find that it depends upon what is happening in families, in households. Empirical definitions of class identity are founded on categories of household defined by either a male (head) of the household or at least the leading person in the household. But what is a 'household' nowadays (in the West), economically, socially and geographically, under conditions of living apart together, normal divorce, remarriage and transnational life forms? High mobility means more and more people are living a kind of *place polygamy*. They are married to many places and different cultures. Transnational place polygamy, belonging to different worlds: this is the gateway to globality in a person's life.

We need descriptions and descriptive categories for economic flows and social networks of people and groups who live transnationally. We need a fresh, actor-directed view of globalization – globalization *from below*. We have to explore the connections between old patterns of identity and the new means to give them expression.

Hence, at the research centre in Munich we are conducting research on such questions as the following: What is a household? If there is no clear relationship between household and family, where does one start? If one does not know what a 'family' is, maybe one could start with a 'couple'. But what is a 'couple'? The French sociologist Jean-Claude Kaufmann (1994) provides a very sophisticated answer: a couple is not when two people are living together nor when they are having sex. Something else must be added: a couple begins when two persons have bought one washing machine (not two!). Why? Because then they quarrel about 'Dirty Laundry' (the title of Kaufmann's marvellous book). Who washes for whom? What counts as dirty? What as clean? What happens in each case, if he says yes and she says no?

These questions seem easy to resolve, but we all know what huge and fundamental battles they can provoke. What makes them seem bewitched? There are at least two reasons. First these questions are embarrassing, they cannot be discussed. We cannot negotiate about everything. There has to be suspension of doubt in order to interact on an everyday basis. But the second problem is that the dirty laundry argument is not really about dirty laundry. It is about identity and the mutual recognition of the other. You forgot about my dirty laundry, which actually means: you forgot about me and therefore I want to divorce you.

This is one of many reasons why I find a reflexive self-critical sociology so exciting, a sociology which must start all over again and redefine its basic research units, its categories, and its frame of reference.

But merely criticising conventional sociology as trapped in territorially biased zombie categories is not enough. That would be 'post-ism' or 'de-ism' or 'beyond-ism'. Everything is 'post', 'de' or 'beyond'. These terms only state what is *not* the case, they do not state what *is* the case. If there exists a strong case for rupture scenarios at present, what has sociology to offer? Do we manage to pose great questions? Do we have a challenging hypothesis of the coming new social structures and conflicts? We must distinguish between a nation-state sociology based on a container theory of society and a cosmopolitan sociology which tries to redefine the sociological frame of reference under conditions of globalization, and so on. If we set out to do this for the purpose of empirical research, there are two concepts in the making.

First *interconnectedness*, beautifully explained and with rich empirical documentation in the work of David Held and colleagues, especially in their latest book *Global Transformations*. But this idea of interconnectedness somehow still presumes the territorial units of states and state-societies which become increasingly interconnected and networked.

The other concept is *cosmopolitization*, and this is what I am currently working on (Beck, 2000c). Cosmopolitization must be clearly distinguished from cosmopolitanism. Cosmopolitanism is a broad, ancient, rich and controversial set of political ideas, philosophies and ideologies. It was in part an ideological construct, and as such it had the abstract, even artificial, aura that Heinrich Heine described as a 'kingdom of the air'. Cosmopolitization on the other hand is a frame of reference for empirical exploration of globalization from within – globalization internalized. It is a kind of class analysis which takes globalization on board. Like class analysis as propounded by Marx, it combines a descriptive analysis of social structures with the assumption that this analysis gives us a key to understanding the political dynamics and conflicts of the social world. I shall return to this point shortly.

But cosmopolitan sociology implies more than a new transnational sensitivity on the part of empirical research (Therborn, 2000). Western sociology, the sociological equivalents of NATO, has most of the money and the intercontinental firepower. What does the rest of the world have? It is not without significance that it contains about seven-eighths of the world's population, and that these seven-eighths are no longer subjects of colonialism and have their own centres of higher education and research, however short of financial resources many of them may be. Secondly, transnational immigration and education is creating a quite significant new stratum of educated transnationals.

They have personal knowledge of both East Asia and California, of Latin America and Anglo America, of South Asia and England, of the Arab world, Africa and France, of Turkey and Germany and the United States, to mention only a few of the largest combinations. These people are raising standards of a cosmopolitan redefinition of social science.

The London School of Economcs is the best example of this. And should and could not this institution be or become a place and resource for a cosmopolitan renaissance of sociology?

2. What is a cosmopolitan society?

As is often the case in history, cosmopolitization is being experienced and reflected upon as *crisis* – crisis of cosmos (nature), crisis of *polis* (paradigm of nation-state politics) and globalphonia. To illustrate this I shall concentrate on the latter phenomenon.

We must now recognize and act upon the new global market risk highlighted by the Asian crisis of 1998, which demonstrated the social and political dynamics of the *economic* world risk society (Beck, 2000b: 6). The global market risk is a new form of 'organized irresponsibility' because it is an institutional form so impersonal as to have no responsibilities, not even to itself. Enabled by the information revolution, the global market risk allows the near-instant flow of funds to determine who will prosper and who will suffer.

But, like the global technical risk, the global financial risk cannot be kept to one side; it floods and transforms itself into social and political risks; that is, risks for the middle class, mainly the poor, even the elites.

Today, the components of the global market risk can be illustrated by the Asian crisis, just as in 1986 the basic aspects of global technological risk could be illustrated by Chernobyl. Somehow, in fact, the Asian crisis is an *economic Chernobyl.*

1. Two conflicts, two logics of distribution are interconnected: the distribution of *goods* and the distribution of *bads*;
2. the foundations of 'risk calculation' are undermined: damage to millions of unemployed and poor people cannot, for example, be compensated financially; the insurance principle collapses – it makes no sense to insure oneself against a global recession;
3. the 'social explosiveness' of global financial risks is becoming real: it sets off a political dynamic and change that undermine nation-state bureaucracies, challenges the predominance of globalism, the free-market ideology; and it is being superseded by its opposite – a *politicization* of the global market economy.
4. Risk conflict always involves the question of responsibility; hence the need for 'responsible globalization' becomes a word-wide public and political issue; the need to reconcile turbo-capitalism with social justice and ecological norms at either the national or international level is moving onto the political agenda; new options are emerging: some want to reverse the last decade of liberalization; others want to discourage excess inflows of 'hot' money by increasing the perceived risk to lenders; and some even

argue that if we are to have a globalized economy, a single world currency would be advisable.

Thus cosmopolitization comes into being as people recognize themselves as involved and victimized by the global risk regime.

As said, cosmopolitization denationalizes national societies from within. The resulting 'post-national constellation' (Habermas, 2000) has many dimensions. Favoured national industries are bought by 'foreigners'. We live in a world in which nobody knows who owns what. Neither do we know where the objects that we buy and consume come from. The same holds at the biographical level. The old logic by which one could deduce a person's place of birth, nationality, mother tongue and passport merely by looking at them is no longer valid. People still apply this logic, of course, but it increasingly gives rise to embarrassing mistakes. This is what happens when state, society and territory loosen their connections but we still insist on equating them in our thoughts.

There is now a 'world culture', we are told, but we had better make sure that we understand what this means. Not a homogeneous space of symbols, meanings and expressions but the confrontation with fundamental differences everywhere and the necessity to live (with) these contradictory certainties somehow – often with violent outbursts. It was Friedrich Nietzsche (1910) who spoke in this sense of 'The Age of Comparison', by which he meant not only that the individual was free to pick and choose among competing traditions and heritages, but even more significantly that the various cultures of the world were beginning to interpenetrate. And he predicted that this process would continue until ideas from every culture stood side by side in combination, contradiction and competition, everywhere and always.

Those who so wish can look around and see, even in a country like Germany, how far post-nationalization has progressed (Beck and Beck-Gernsheim, 2000). For example, there has been an enormous increase in dual-national marriages in Germany: in 1997 every sixth marriage included at least one spouse of foreign citizenship. And we find the same when we inspect the results of those marriages: in 1997, one in every five children born in Germany had a mother or father of foreign nationality. In the province of Landshut in lower Bavaria, first-graders were recorded as speaking more than ten different languages.

To look at the same development from another angle, baptism was once the entry ticket to German society (as Heinrich Heine once remarked with bitter irony). But today, even in small Lutheran and Catholic towns, standing next to 'German' churches are 'German' mosques. Today, there are approximately 5000 Moslem members of the German army, so that they naturally need a German Imam.

The list could continue. When will we know that Germany has become post-national? When German policemen have Turkish surnames. When you can hear black people speaking Bavarian. When the nationality of a company can no longer be deduced from the nationality of its workers. When the central bankers have become zombies, bending to the will of the European Central Bank. But all these things, once unimaginable, have already happened. And when German universities, police forces, boards of directors, judges, members of parliament and the government all look like the world-champion French 'national' soccer team, then the country will be entirely post-national. Unthinkable? In the last year of the last century, Germany finally introduced dual citizenship. Two passports, dual loyalty – something that a century ago would have been inconceivable.

Today, people trade internationally, they work internationally, they love internationally, they marry internationally, they research internationally, and their children grow up and are educated internationally – not only are they bilingual, they are perfectly at home in the no-place of the Internet and television. So why should we expect political loyalties and identities to remain bound to a single nation-state? Russian Jews in Tel Aviv are integrated with the daily life of Moscow through cable channels that provide them with Russian films and television shows and daily news programmes. Further down the social scale we see marginalized groups that have maintained their connections across the globe and which display astonishing creativity in evading the barriers of discrimination and state repression. Indeed, especially marginalized groups experience a *transformed* locality into which the wider world increasingly intrudes. They may be the losers of globalization, but this does not mean that they are excluded from its effects. Quite the contrary: it seems that the poor and marginalized – for example, those who live in inner-city areas – often find themselves most closely involved in the most turbulent transformations, while it is the affluent who can afford to retire to rural backwaters that have at least the appearance of a preserved and stable 'locality'. In fact, an entire branch of research has grown up to study what are now called 'transmigrants': people whose social obligations span a distance between their country of origin and their new homeland.

In short, transnationality is not simply the privilege of global players. Across the class spectrum, community is now no longer simply determined by place. This transcendence of distance has been made possible by an information network that connects every place on the globe to any other.

Amongst many other things, this is what makes it possible to live here while also being very much apart. One result of the process is that collective memory is losing its unity and integrity, as Britain is now experiencing: 'Britishness' has been thrown into the air and nobody knows how it will come down, nor how to restore it. Often, the 'national' self-image has become an integration of common enemies, a multi-ethnic friend-foe melange. People that have been transnationalized either through their jobs or their marriages or their political engagements, must now find their bearings in a minefield of mutually exclusive national myths and conflicting bureaucratic regulations. And then there are the tricky questions: for example, what do Turkish Germans have to do with the Holocaust? Or non-Jewish Israelis for that matter?

Consider the changing meaning of key concepts, How, for example, should the concept of *power* be redefined in the conditions of a deterritorialized global economy? The state-labour-capital-relationship becomes a game of cat and mouse. The cat-ness of the economy resides in the fact that its investors, shielded by their institutionalized freedom, are able to supply or shut off the life-blood of state and labour – namely jobs and taxes. All this is determined by the neutral calculus of economic action; but this does not alter the fact that supplying or cutting off the life-blood of society is a kind of super-politics. And the mouse-ness of state power is based on what used to be its strength: its attachment to territory. As it engages in this cruel contest on factors so crucial for survival like jobs and taxes, the state has few cards to play as long as it acts 'nationally' – that is, as a 'sovereign' power, as a single, territorial mouse. This is why the political Europe is *the* experimental answer to the question of globalization.

But the metaphor of the cat-and-mouse game distorts one crucial point: the cat does not want to eat the mouse. And it is exactly this restraint that multiplies the power of the cat. It is time to dispense with metaphor to gain a better grasp on the idea. The crux is that the state does not have to yield to a power marching in, but to the *spectre* of power marching *out*. That is truly deterritorial power. Not imperialism, but lack of imperialism, not invasion but withdrawal by investors, is the basis of global economic power. Not controlling, but refraining from control is what threatens national society and the nation state. States yearn for nothing so much as the invasion of investors, and fear nothing so much as their retreat.

The deterritorialized power of the economy lacks everything that constitutes the territorial power of the state: no military, no means of violence, not even legitimation. Neither the government nor the parliament are needed to gain permission for the entrance or exit of investors. Does this mean that the global economy is acting illegitimately? How could it be? The threat is of *intentional non-interference*. This invisible, non-violent *leaving* neither needs permission nor can have it.

Intentional non-interference: in this formula lies the answer to the question of where the alternative politics of the deterritorialized economy obtains its overwhelming power, and why state politics have so palpably failed in their attempt to raise obstacles against it or to obtain a veto on it. Global investment decisions do not have a control centre, so there is nowhere to put an obstacle. And yet these decisions have binding force. In fact they have the most powerful binding force imaginable: the power of accomplished facts.

We can clarify this schema of how a 'parallel actor' like the global economy exerts its effect by examining the controversies that have recently raged in Germany on the possibilities being opened up by study of the human genome. The point is that even as some of us are engaged in this heated discussion, human genetics is quietly and completely transforming the world through the politics of accomplished facts. The same applies to globalization. If something is prevented from happening here, it will happen over there. And then it will happen here. This proved to be the case when it came to technical innovation: why make life difficult when it is going to happen anyway? The ethical discussion of eugenics is like putting a bicycle bell on the airliner of genetic research, and the same is true of other kinds of technical progress. The bell rings and rings but the plane flies on regardless.

All these different aspects of cosmopolitization must be analysed in detail and by social indicators which must be theoretically developed, of course, and empirically evaluated (for more detailed discussion see Beck 2000c: 79-105). Here, of course, the key question arises. Does the post-national constellation open up chances for a new cosmopolitanism? My answer is 'yes'. But one must clearly distinguish between globalism and new cosmopolitanism. Globalism ignores and evades the otherness of the other, cosmopolitanism acknowledges and empowers the otherness of the other. There are many inimical images of cosmopolitanism. Does not a cosmopolitan culture mean that we all have to become Americans? Is it not a new imperialism? Is it not a memory-less culture? Does it not have a hybrid, eclectic character? Is it not formed from the shreds, and without memory patches, of real existing historical cultures? Is it not a mixture of globalism and post-modernism? These doubts are in fact related to globalism, not to cosmopolitanism.

But matters are not quite so straightforward. One must also recognize the *dilemmas* of cosmopolitanism (as they can be studied in Popper's *Open Society*, for example). Those dilemmas arise from the question: how can we negotiate and combine the universal and the particular? There are three logical answers to this question: imperialistic domination, universalism and a willingness to engage with the other, and all of them give rise to some sort of dilemma.

1. *The imperialistic dilemma*: one particular power tries to dominate the world. This solution found its explosive and self-destructive degeneration in the two world wars in the twentieth century.

2. *The universalistic dilemma*: the first response to the racist argument that those who are different are inferior and cannot be members of the nation is *not* that we ought to respect difference. Rather, it is universalism: that we are all equal humans and entitled to equal rights as citizens. Thus Popper redefined Immanuel Kant's cosmopolitanism into liberal politics and shared some of the problems of his universalism. Kant's and Popper's universalism somehow, in the end, suppresses diversity. Constructing the state as a federation of republics, Kant enforced uniformity, excluding individuals and states not conforming to rational citizenship. According to Kant's vision, there could be only one cosmopolitanism, for there is only one world-wide community of human beings. This raises fundamental questions: How far have varieties of cosmopolitanism been present outside the West? What equivalent forms of cosmopolitan experiences, practices, representations developed, for example, in China, India and the Islamic world?

The third possible answer is a cosmopolitan project which involves different forms and institutional settings: how to acknowledge and empower plurality and diversity by forms and institutions of cross-cultural dialogue, transnational institutions and forms of conflict regulation. This awareness of the world as one of *many* cultural others derives from transnational biographies which include the other, the local, and the global at the same time. But here (3) the *democratic* dilemma arises: how do collectively binding decisions become possible under conditions of transnational plurality and diversity?

And at the same time there arises (4) the *power paradox* of new cosmopolitanism: the prospect of a cosmopolitan project built through powerful international governmental institutions looks rather *poor*; and through the rise of non-governmental organisations *without* institutionalised power it looks rather *optimistic*.

3. Who are the enemies of cosmopolitization?

When the tide of capital and people that cross boarders reaches a certain critical mass, and when global risks are increasingly of the sort that no one nation can control or ignore, then the territorial first principle – the assumption that a state can control the most important things that happen to the people within its borders – ceases to be valid. And the question is, what happens to the ideas and institutions that are premised upon it? What happens to methodological nationalism in the social sciences and in politics? Can politics and democracy exist outside the frame of the nation state? How can we open up the national container in order to conceive of deterritorialized democracy and a self-reflexive cosmopolitan society? How can the basic concepts and institutions of modernity – social justice, the law, democracy and political community, citizenship and civil society – be redefined in an era of cosmopolitanism? Under what conditions and in what form will the successful transformation of politics be possible? And what will the consequences be if we fail?

Post-modernists, system theorists and neo-liberalists disagree about almost everything. But the one point on which they converge is that they all dismiss politics as a subject of serious inquiry. Politicians and activists still take politics seriously, of course, and the subject is still discussed in university departments of political science. But (with some notable exceptions, such as David Held's work on cosmopolitan democracy) (Held et. al., 1999) the answer to whether politics can survive the dismantling of borders has been a peremptory 'no'. Protectionism, in the widest sense of the term, is everywhere. Some want to protect the nation; some want to protect the social welfare state; others to protect democracy; and others still to protect nature. But in each case it is simply assumed that such worthy ends can be achieved only within the nation-state; thus whatever endangers a nation-state endangers those goals as well. And it is precisely this clash between a changing world and an inflexible mode of thought that may be preparing the ground for the enemies of the cosmopolitan society.

I do not believe that the enemies which Karl Popper had in mind will survive in their old forms: communism and fascism. We will not experience a replay of history. But the last century started with a great deal of optimism and finished as the worst in history. And this may happen again. There are new, and possibly no less dangerous, enemies of the open cosmopolitan society already visible at the centre of the West today. The final section of this essay will discuss three of them:

1. Post-modern nationalism,
2. Globalism,
3. Democratic authoritarianism.

Post-modern nationalism. Nations and nationalism derive from the requirements of modern industrial social organization and the pressures of mass-literature and mobility. When this nation-state paradigm of society dissolves from within, this makes for the rebirth and reinvention of the most diverse kinds of cultural, political and religious movement. What we must understand is the *ethnic globalization paradox*: at a time when the world is becoming more unified, interconnected and cosmopolitized, and when the barriers between ethnic groups and nations are lifting, there is a resurgence of ethnicity.

In every corner of the world, ethnic identities are being refurbished and recast. What is so frightening about this ethnic resurgence is that all the different protest movements against globalization, willingly or unwillingly, seemingly enforce an ethnic and tribal reaction to the ambivalences and uncertainties of a post-national second age of modernity. And frightening too is the fact that there is a post-modern turn (and return) of ethnicity. When Ernest Gellner said, 'The profits of nationalism were not near the First Division, when it came to the business of thinking', he had the old nationalism of the first age of modernity in mind.

The claims of various minorities in the United States – gays, lesbians, blacks, women, Hispanics, for instance – are often named 'identity politics'. After Marxism, which reduced the individual to a member of a class, a new collectivism appeared to appoint him/her a member of a minority collective. There is a post-modern paradox in constructing and empowering ethnic identities. They combine what seems to be contradictory: relativism and fundamentalism. There are different tools for each ethnic minority, but as a member of a specific group or minority, one has privileged access to its criteria of truth. Thus, only a member born with the identity can know the history of oppression and the reach for justice which empowers the movement. What we see here are post-modern constructions of fundamentalism through the means of relativism. And this combination is not only used by leftist minority groups, but also by populist movements on the far right across Europe to construct and enforce post-modern ethnicity. These too define themselves 'beyond left and right'. But in this case Adorno is correct to say that s/he who believes that s/he is beyond left and right, is right.

There is a post-modern romance of ethnicity in the making. Take, for example, Tom Nairn and his latest book *After Britain*, which gives all the ingredients. Nairn transforms relativism into fundamentalism, constructing a post-modern narrative on the oppressed victim and the 'purity' of the Scots, calling for complete independence from England and constructing new foreigners and ethnic divides among the four British nations. With post-modern sophistication. Nairn invents a new narrative of ethnic survival and self-determination in the global era, even more empowered by the new significance of the local; and, of course, also because of Europe, which not only weakens the old imperial nation-state but strengthens the regions. According to Nairn, Britain is dissolving from within, which might be the beginning of what historians will call the ethnic Balcanization of Britain.

Where the centre right has grown weak and divided, or has failed to modernize, there has been a resurgence of a xenophobic, racist and embittered populist far right. This has happened, so far, in France, Switzerland and Austria, and it may happen in Germany, if the CDU collapses or is marginalized. Hence, in the post-national constellation the *racist trap* opens up again, revitalized by post-modern ingredients.

Globalism. The vision of a global free market has created a new myth: history is on the side of freedom as never before. The basic idea is that the combination of free markets in giving everybody access to the Internet has created *Weltbürger*, or world citizens.

Or, to put the argument in less fanciful terms: these days, for markets to work well, micro-computers and modems must cover the economic landscape. As a side effect, the state control of information is eroded and citizens are empowered, with the consequence that governments which want prosperity must sooner or later tolerate political freedom.

This evolutionary optimism is contradicted by the facts: the post-modern ethnic revival gainsays it, but also history. In assessing the optimism aroused by the Internet, it helps to remember that much the same thing happened five centuries ago, after Johannes Gutenberg introduced the movable type printing press to Europe. Of course, this is a long story. The printing press did indeed challenge power. What threatened the church was an important technical device that made Luther's reformation possible and placed the old regimes under threat. But there was a significant counter-effect: in many ways European governments grew more absolutist in the century after Gutenberg's invention (Robert Wright).

There are other striking examples. In the nineteenth century Auguste Comte argued that there are two kinds of conquest – either the exploitation of nature by industry or imperialism, or the exploitation of foreign peoples. The former makes money, the latter costs it. For this reason, Comte concluded, the development of industrial capitalism would cause war to wither away. Interestingly enough, Engels also advocated the theory of pacifist cost-cutting: weapons are not only destructive but also unproductive. Modernizing them makes them 'overly expensive and at the same time useless for the purpose of war'. After those theories of 'pacifistic capitalism' the imperial age and the age of world wars began.

There is an important difference between globalism on the one hand and nationalism, socialism, fascism and communism on the other. The old ideologies had and still have an inspirational power which globalism does not possess. The latter is an elite ideology, not one that motivates and activates the masses. The new liberal crusades preach that we must streamline, downsize, flexibilize, and connect with the Internet. But this hardly creates a new feeling of belonging, solidarity and identity. Quite the opposite: the free-world market ideology undermines and supplants democratic politics and political identities.

In the 1970s, Franz Joseph Strauss, the leader of the Bavarian right-wing conservative party CSU, organized his election campaign around the provocative slogan 'socialism or freedom'. Now there is a new political contradiction emerging: 'capitalism or freedom' (Beck 2000d). Global capitalism undermines the culture of democratic liberty by radicalizing social inequalities and endangering basic principles of social justice and security. And it contradicts a cosmopolitan culture in which we assert that we can live together, equal yet different.

Hence globalism, the free market ideology, is a powerful enemy of a cosmopolitan society. And there is the even greater danger that an alliance will arise between post-modern nationalism and global capitalism (a Haider-capitalism in Europe and elsewhere). I do not believe, however, that this will necessarily happen. In the first age of modernity the economy backed the building of nation-state democracies. There may be a project of a cosmopolitan democratic revival of politics in the second age of modernity as well, and it could be forcefully supported by the global economy. Such a vision of a 'cosmopolitan democratic transformation of capitalism' has yet to be invented. And many would believe and argue that the idea is just another 'kingdom of the air'.

A recent United Nations progress report on business and human rights outlines nine core-principles on labour standards, human rights and environmental norms that have already been internationally agreed upon. But these only pay political lip service. There is no political power or structure, no cosmopolitan coalition between states and commerce, which enforces these principles of a global New Deal. The overriding question is whether or not the endeavour to reconcile today's turbo-capitalism with social justice in cosmopolitan democracy can be framed as legislative and institutional proposals, at either the national or international level, with the support of the global financial elites, or only against their radical resistance.

New democratic authoritarianism. In Germany, every clash on fundamental questions in recent years has been provoked by someone who has questioned a national taboo. Why is it taboo to compare the Holocaust with the horrors of Stalinism and ask whether one justifies the other? Why cannot Germans stop acting as if they were criminals of some sort and open themselves up to the 'destiny' that history has prepared for them? Why does the memory of the Holocaust have to be a public affair – why cannot it be a matter between an individual and his or her conscience? Why cannot the misery of humans be fixed by genetic engineering?

These questions give rise to a problematic, and it takes only one more question to show this clearly: would not capitalism work more smoothly *without* democracy? If nation-state institutions are so obviously overwhelmed, then why not remove them – in the name of reform, of course – so that the pressing problems of our time can finally be solved by experts to the benefit of everybody? And while we are at it, why not punish child abusers and violent teenagers by flogging them in public? There would still be room for liberals in a world of this kind. They would limit the punishment to no more than fifteen lashes, and argue that the state should provide a doctor at public expense to examine the offenders after the punishment had been meted out.

It would be a serious mistake not to notice that as the institutions of national democracy have grown weaker and less able to handle the problems faced by the modern state, the capacity for authoritarian solutions has grown stronger. The possibility of achieving consensus by democratic means is vanishing. But the capacity to enforce compliance with state decisions is growing. The means of violence and the means of media manipulation have been both modernized and augmented. It is not hard to imagine how the democratic power deficit could be remedied by high-tech authoritarian means – while preserving democratic facades, of course – because we should remember that this questioning of all our assumptions grows out of the drive towards fundamental democratization. But when democracy questions its own assumptions – when it threatens the taboos that surround democracy – we are threatened with the paradox of *democratic authoritarianism*.

The hunger for boundaries and structure feeds on their dissolution. And the questioning of all assumptions, the drive of modernity towards a *tabula rasa*, is reinforced by the expansion of our technological abilities. Governmental means of monitoring and control are already impinging on basic civil liberties. And the mass media already permit a kind of plebiscite whereby governments can go over the heads of unions, parties and parliament.

When we contrast all these possibilities for the state to increase its power with the continual decline in its present ability to solve the major problems confronting it; when we contrast the anxiety of having our assumptions questioned with the power and firmness that could derive from breaking taboos; then we can understand whence the new authoritarian questions obtain their seductive charm.

Authoritarian questions are themselves a kind of paradox, and it is not easy to nail down what actually defines a question as going too far.

Subverting the Enlightenment. Authoritarian questions exhibit the zeal of the convert. Brought up in the spirit of Enlightenment, their proponents know how to avail themselves of the joy of transgressing boundaries, and they re-direct this weapon at the Enlightenment's own foundations. They turn the tables and act as if it is the heirs of the Enlightenment that are its enemies. Is it not the spirit of the Enlightenment to break down old taboos? Is it not the politically correct establishment that is shying away from hard truths?

Conforming to modernity. While the appeal of authoritarian questions comes from the breaking of taboos, their plausibility derives from their acceptance of the imperatives of globalism. If economic globalization is turning democratic institutions into shadows of their former selves, why continue to complain about what cannot be changed? Why not just accept that our political ideas have to evolve to keep pace with technological change? Realism is invoked to ease our conscience. And once again, it puts the shoe on the other foot. It is not breaking restrictions that needs to be justified; it is rather the restrictions that need to be justified. 'See here,' say the new authoritarians, 'you haven't even a handbrake to stop this thing'. And with that, they triumph over the difficulty of saying 'no'.

The new simplicity. Society is complicated these days, as any seven-year-old who has tried to fit his schedule into those of his divorced parents can tell you. Correspondingly, there is an urge for simplicity, and the new authoritarians satisfy this urge with simple ideas. But what gives these ideas a staying power that they did not use to have is that they can avail themselves of the post-modern critique of humanism and rationality which, by removing reason as a court of appeal in such matters, has allowed the crudest nationalisms and naturalisms to flourish again unchecked. They celebrate, again, a post-modern return to origins.

With authoritarian questions, the crumbling territorial state is trying out its bite-reflexes. The territorial instinct is being acted out intellectually, and it is trying to remove its stigma.

As Ralf Dahrendorf argues, the internationalization of decisions and activities means a loss of democracy. The combination of post-modern ethnic temptations and new democratic authoritarianism adds up to a severe attack on liberty. Therefore it is most important to begin a new political project, one that insists on liberty and redefines the Open Society as a Cosmopolitan Society.

Bibliography

Albrow, M. (1995), *The Global Age*, Polity Press, Cambridge.

Beck, U. (2000a), *What is Globalization*, Polity Press, Cambridge.

Beck, U. (2000b), *World Risk Society*, Polity Press, Cambridge.

Beck, U. (2000c), 'The Cosmopolitan Perspective: Sociology of the Second Age of Modernity', *The British Journal of Sociology*, vol. 51, no. 1, pp. 79-106.

Beck, U. and Beck-Gernsheim, E. (2000), *Juden, Deutsche und ander Erinnerungslandschaften*, Suhrkampf, Frankfurt am Main.

Beck, U. and Willms, J. (2000d), *Freiheit oder Kapitalismus. Gesellschaft neu denken*, Surkampf, Frankfurt am Main.

Dahrendorf, R. (1999), *Whatever Happens to Liberty?*, New Statesman, Sept. 6th, pp. 25-7.

Giddens, A. (1994), *Beyond Left and Right*, Polity Press, Cambridge.

Habermas, J. (2000), *The Postnational Constellation*, Polity Press, Cambridge.

Hacohen, M. H. (1999), 'Karl Popper, Jewish Identity and Central European Culture', *The Journal of Modern History*, vol. 71, pp. 105-49.

Held, D. et. al. (1999), *Global Trasformations*, Polity Press, Cambridge.

Kant, I. (1964), *Critique of Pure Reason*, Macmillan, London.

Kaufmann, J.C. (1994), *Schmutzige Wäsche*, Universitätsverlag, Konstanz.

Nietzsche, F. (1910), *Human, all too Human*, Foulis, London.

Robertson, R. (1992), *Globalization: Social Theory and Global Culture*, Sage, London.

Sassen, S. (2000), 'New Frontiers Facing Urban Sociology at the Millennium', *The British Journal of Sociology*, vol. 51, no. 1, pp. 143-60.

Taylor, P.J. (1996), 'On The Nation-State, The Global and Social Science', *Environment and Urban Planning A.28*, pp. 1917-28.

Therborn, G. (2000), 'At the Birth of Second Century Sociology: Times of Reflexivity, Spaces of Identity, and Nodes of Knowledge', *The British Journal of Sociology*, vol. 51, no. 1, pp. 37-57.

Tomlinson, J. (1999), *Globalisation and Culture*, Polity Press, Cambridge.

Urry, J. (2000), *Sociology Beyond Societies*, Routledge, London.

7 Sociology after the revolution in Eastern Europe: can it survive?

ZDZISŁAW KRASNODĘBSKI

1. Sociology after communism

The beginning of the new millennium was not a particularly spectacular event, in spite of the enormous efforts of the mass media to make it just that. Even the millennium bug was totally overestimated. And the year 2000 does not seem very different from 1999. There has been no Apocalypse, no revolution, no eruption of religious feeling, no eternal peace, no global happiness. On the first day of 2000 business was back to normal. Instead of the war in Kosovo, a war was raging in Chechnya, and the reaction of the West to that war clearly shows that the universal human rights proclaimed in Europe during the NATO intervention in Kosovo was nothing more than wishful thinking or empty rhetoric.

It is therefore obvious that the need to reflect on the future of sociology derives not only from a simple change of the calendar date. There is a widespread feeling that the general context in which sociology operates has changed in recent years, and that sociology must face new challenges. Of course, there are several reasons why we are inclined to believe in such change: the process of globalization, new cultural streams, the development of genetics and computer technology, and so on. But there is also talk of a new epoch because of radical and rapid change in the political situation – the downfall of communism as a global (or at least half-global) system – which is considered a historical watershed. Accordingly, the transition to a new epoch happened, not at the turn of this year but eleven years previously in 1989 and in 1990. It was then that the short twentieth century – which began with a delay in 1914 – came to an early end. However, not only has the object of sociology – the contemporary social world – altered, but change has also had an impact on the discipline's identity by compelling sociologists to revise old and significant patterns of sociological thought. As a consequence, today's sociologists give different interpretations to many processes which were already well visible in the past.

All sociologists and political scientists agree that the events in Eastern Europe have given rise to a historical turn. For instance, David Held, known as one of the proponents of the 'global cosmopolitan democracy', writes as follows:

> (t)he East European revolutions were, without doubt, a historical watershed. The collapse of the Soviet empire, and retreat of communism across Europe, were not only major events of the twentieth century but probably of modern history as well (Held, 1996: 457).

If so, then sociological reflection on modernity is not possible without considering this event and its consequences.

Hence, asking what sociology in the new century will be means asking what it will be after the decline of the Soviet Union, and after communism, after the waning of the socialist hope that has accompanied sociology since its beginnings. One can expect it to be a quite different sociology. As the British sociologist Martin Albrow puts it:

> the reunification of Germany, and perhaps the single market of 1993, mark a watershed as significant as the French Revolution. The creation of supranational entities and the claims of minorities are equally signs of structural change which may signal a coming of decisive point for sociology too. A European sociology for the twenty-first century is likely to be very different from its ninetieth and twentieth century predecessors (Albrow, 1993: 90).

However, one can also hear and read opinions that sociology will not survive in the next century. Immanuel Wallerstein maintains that, due to changes in the world and in the natural sciences and humanities, sociology is no longer a discipline with distinctive boundaries and that it will be replaced by a more general social science (Wallerstein, 1999). Some years ago there was heated debate in Germany on the question: Why today do we need sociology at all? (Fritz-Vannahme, 1996) The impetus for the discussion came from the widespread feeling that although sociology is institutionally well-established, and although there have never been as many sociologists as today, the meaning of sociology has vanished and it has lost its sense of 'mission'.

2. An ambitious undertaking

This crisis seems to be quite natural for sociology, given that complaints about its critical condition have been voiced during its history with astonishing regularity. However, the present discontent and lack of self-confidence seems to be more serious, just because no simple and clear-cut alternative can be offered, as happened for instance when Alvin Gouldner wrote his famous radical critique of academic sociology, hoping that Marxism would rescue it. Today, not only are the empirical and theoretical means by which sociology seeks to achieve its aims viewed with scepticism, but those aims themselves are regarded with suspicion. And this is not only an attitude of the few anti-sociologists that can be found in every period; it is present in the mainstream of sociology.

The almost desperate-sounding question of whether sociology still makes sense is rather unexpected, for it was not long ago that sociologists considered themselves to be the 'creators of sense' (*Sinnproduzenten*). They claimed to have the answer to the major questions of modernity and to offer a solution for its dilemmas. Sociology was a highly ambitious endeavour at the outset. For the first sociologists, almost every problem was a problem that sociology had the tools to deal with; they were convinced that they could offer solutions for problems unsolved by other sciences. Consequently, some philosophers (Karl Jaspers, for instance) warned about the totalitarianism of sociology. Jaspers emphasised that when psychology and sociology do not respect their own limits, they belittle human beings and this leads to anti-human consequences (Jaspers, 1983: 106-17). However, sociology considered itself to be the successor of theology and philosophy and sought to replace these two disciplines with a real science. Social theorists and sociologists discussed the question of whether philosophy was still needed – theology seemed not even worthy of that question. However, it now seems that neither of the disciplines have disappeared, and the willing gravedigger now finds himself in danger.

Sociology was a science with Promethean aspirations (Weiss, 1992), combining two ideas at the same time: being a science of society and paving the way for a new, better society. As a science it aimed to replace the traditional knowledge of social life with scientific inquisitiveness. On the other hand, sociology also had the ambition to change society, to ameliorate it – directly by controlling the people or indirectly by changing their self-consciousness. The need to improve society was based on the conviction that modern society was in deep cultural crisis (Lepenies, 1985; Scaff, 1989; Lichtblau, 1996). Its rationality should at least have given rise to a better (and that often meant) more rational society. Even Max Weber, who – as we know – was much more sceptical about the range and epistemological capacities of sociology than Durkheim, for instance, stressed that cultural sciences, and sociology in particular, enabled modern human beings to be conscious of their situation. However, Weber pointed out that only a thin line separates science from faith, and he knew very well that the cultural sciences, which also include sociology as a *Wirklichkeitswissenschaft*, are based on cultural values, which they presuppose but are unable to reflect or control.

It was sometimes thought that both aims (to study society and to reform it) were in conflict. Improving society apparently contradicted the scientific and rational search for social reality. In order to achieve the status of a science, sociology had to abandon its goal of making the world a better place, and this was reflected in the beginnings of American sociology: 'Scientific techniques should make sociology respectable' and 'purge it of its "social work", "ameliorative", and "journalistic" vestiges' (Turner, 1989: 223). However, it meant above all the replacement of old unprofessional, philanthropic, *ad hoc* amelioration with reform – or revolution – based on scientific knowledge.

In the twentieth century, sociology joined the ranks of the academic disciplines. However, the twentieth century was not only the one in which sociology developed; it was also the bloodiest century in the history of mankind. Modernity and the progress of civilization did not prevent barbarism. The twentieth century was a century of two world wars, of communism, of fascism, and of national socialism – a century in which millions of people were murdered and which experienced the Holocaust. As one prominent British historian has written:

> (t)here are shades of barbarism in twentieth-century Europe which would have once amazed the most barbarous of barbarians. At a time when the instruments of constructive change had outstripped anything previously known, Europeans acquiesced in a string of conflicts which destroyed more human beings than all convulsions put together (Davis, 1996: 897).

Hence, in reference to sociology's initial ambitions of improving the world, one may say that it failed utterly. The world did not become a better place because of sociology. And strikingly, sociology long remained silent on the dark sides of modernity (for instance, the sociology of war was totally neglected). We must admit that the question of the barbarism of the twentieth century is a core issue for sociology. If Zygmunt Bauman is right to argue that modernity itself was the source of both forms of totalitarianism, and if Anthony Giddens is right to maintain that 'modernity is itself deeply and intrinsically sociological' (Giddens, 1990: 43), then sociology must reflect on its responsibility for what happened in the twentieth century. The opening of a new horizon for sociology demands on critical reflection on its own past.

However, rather than deal with this issue, the tendency is now to stress the close connection between sociology and a democratic and pluralistic society. This thesis is often defended *post festum* by sociologists not previously known for their democratic attitudes. One may legitimately doubt whether it is true, although I do not think that it suffices to say that '[t]he idea that social science is inherently democratic is well-intentioned rubbish. A science is neither democratic nor anti-democratic, the users of the science are' (Horowitz, 2000). Of course, the use of a science is decisive, but this does not mean that a certain type of knowledge will be used in one way rather than others.

It is an empirical fact that sociology has not always been on the side of democracy. For several years discussion has been in progress in Germany on the role of sociology during the Nazi era. The previous prevailing belief that almost all German sociologists emigrated when Hitler came to power, and that the rest were compelled to silence, turns out to be too simplistic: there were many sociologists and social scientists who worked for national socialism. However, much more important is the question of the relationship between sociology and real socialism or communism. The question of socialism, of a social organization that could be based on principles other than capitalism, was always central to sociological thinking. After the Second World War, also Marxism became very influential in sociology. If it is true that the third quarter of the twentieth century was the time of 'sociological explosion' (Shils 1980: 134), then one must say that substantial impulse for that growth came from the turbulence of the 1960s, in which Marxist ideas played a significant role. Today it is almost unimaginable, but there were times when a large – sometimes even dominant – group of sociologists considered themselves to be Marxists. 'By the mid-twentieth century, it was somewhat of a truism to say "we are all Marxists now" (Carver, 2000: 71). Marxism promised that sociology would not just be a critique of reality; it was also a general framework in which the divisions among many sub-fields could be overcome. Johannes Weiss has summarized the aspirations of Marxist sociology, showing why it was so attractive to many sociologists in the 1960s and 1970s, even though it was also deleterious to sociology's reputation among the general public:

> (t)he materialistic theory seemed ... to offer a possible way of grasping the 'totality' of social existence in all its complexity and historical dynamism, a way that at the same time generated a fundamental critique as well as both political and, if need be, revolutionary action programs, thus providing a compelling legitimization of the step from analysis to actual deeds (Weiss, 1989: 109).

There was no room in this theory for events like the East European revolution of 1989, for the evolution from real socialism to capitalism and liberal democracy, and not in the opposite direction as the majority of sociological theories predicted: it was a truly liberating revolution of the twentieth century. Paul Berman, in his book *A Tale of Two Utopias. The Political Journey of the Generation of 1968*, which furnishes a moral history of the baby boom generation in the West, maintains that the revolution in Eastern Europe was in some sense a realization of the genuine values of the 1968 movement:

> (s)uddenly it was obvious that the authentic political revolution of our era was now [i.e. 1989], not then [1968]; liberal and democratic, not radical leftist in the '68 style, not imaginary. Here and there the leaders of the revolutions of '89 – a Vaclav Havel in Czechoslovakia, an Adam Michnik in Poland – turned out to be the same heroic persons, now adult liberals, who as young radicals had helped lead the movements of 1968 (Berman, 1997: 18).

The events of 1989 were, however, alien to the mainstream of sociology. They happened in a totally unexpected and unforeseen manner. There was almost no Western empirical research on socialist societies, even at a time when it was already possible, and most theories predicted the downfall of capitalism rather than the crisis of real socialism. One may therefore say that sociology, especially Western sociology, failed. Western sociologists missed one of the important historical events of our era, the decline of communism which put an end to the twentieth century. They missed a chance to 'improve' the world, when the chance really existed. They did not foresee it, they did not do research on it, they did not participate in it intellectually and politically, they did not support it as sociologists. And if anybody rescued the 'honour' of sociology, it was the East European sociologists who joined the opposition movement. This does not mean, however, that sociology was an 'opposition science' in communist countries *per se*. Its role was much more ambiguous. In the first period, sociology was banned as a 'bourgeois science' and replaced by historical materialism, which was considered to be the only real rational and scientific study of the social world and history. Later, sociology was allowed at universities and used in communist attempts to plan social development (Mucha and Keen, 1995). Only in Hungary and especially in Poland was it able to develop relatively free of political instrumentalization and ideologization (Kulcsar, 1989: 121-2). In other countries, it remained a tool of the state and party. As one East German sociologist admitted quite frankly:

> (s)ociology in the GDR is both a product and an intellectual instrument of socialist society and of its leading force, the Marxist-Leninist party, for managing and planning social process (Weidig, 1989: 84).

A Bulgarian sociologist stated:

> (t)he necessity to explain and govern this process, whose context is the socialist transformation of the national society, constitutes the main driving force for belated but rapid institutionalization of sociology as a scientific discipline and a profession in the country (Genov, 1989: 12).

Two leading Soviet sociologists maintained that the aims of Soviet sociology consisted amongst other things of 'overcoming predatory, petit-bourgeois, consumption-only trends which are alien to the Soviet way of life' (Ivanov and Osipov, 1989: 184),

> the blending of nations, nationalities and ethnic groups on the basis of common socio-economic goals and the eradication of nationalist trends (ibid.: 186).

And further:

> sociology is called upon to extend the range of scientific research geared to raising the efficiency of all units of the social mechanism for purposes of accelerating the country's development and above all for deriving the maximum efficiency from the 'human factor' in all spheres of social life (ibid.: 189).

And:

> (s)ociologists are expected to propose optimal ways of combining democratic centralism and maximum initiative from below (ibid.: 188).

A sociology of this kind fortunately failed to achieve its aims. From its perspective, the opposition movement could only be perceived as an obstacle against the modernization of socialism, and as a reactionary danger to social peace. Even in relatively liberal countries like Poland, sociology remained divided: one part of it contributed to the critique of oppression; the other part to legitimization and stabilization of the system. However, although the introduction of some of the ideas of Western sociology was very important in the process of gradual liberalization and emancipation from communism, the most important impulses came from philosophy, theology, history and literature.

After 1989, Eastern Europe had to deal with a new kind of society, one that no sociological theory had ever predicted: post-communist society. A new branch of world sociology had emerged in the form of sociology of transformation. The reality of this still surprises many researchers, if they are undogmatic enough to allow themselves to be surprised. According to one of the specialists in this field:

> (t)he experience of the first decade of post-communism subverts – or at least fails to support – most of the prevailing ideas and paradigms in the analysis of democratization and democracy (Fish, 1999: 795).

In post-communist societies today sociology plays an important role. The opinion that democratic societies need sociology, and that in contemporary democracies there is a permanent need to check public opinions and collective attitudes and feelings, is in a sense true. On the other hand, under such pressure sociology in the new democracies of Eastern Europe is to a large extent reduced to the role of opinion polling.

3. Between Balkanization and banalization

Since 1989, sociology has become a sociology in which Marxism (as one of the mainstreams of twentieth-century sociology) has evaporated. Leading world sociologists like Jürgen Habermas, Anthony Giddens and Zygmunt Bauman no longer call themselves Marxists or neo-Marxists. This has been the first and most important change in the new century.

At the beginning of the twenty-first century only very old-fashioned, stubborn – or maybe non-conformist – sociologists would call themselves Marxists. The question as to whether the former attitudes, convictions and values will find a new form of expression still remains open. What would replace Marxism in the future? At Western universities it was Marxism in different variants that enabled students of sociology to combine academic studies with political commitment and moral conviction. It was a false, misleading synthesis, but can the social sciences be studied and developed without any form of such a synthesis?

In any event, the revolution in Eastern Europe generated a compulsion to change the language with which the late modern world is described. Richard Rorty, who can be considered one of the leading philosophers of the new epoch, wrote in an essay entitled 'The End of Leninism, Havel, and Social Hope' as follows:

> (t)he events of 1989 have convinced those who are still trying to hold on to Marxism that we need a way of holding our time in thought, and a plan for making the future better than the present, which drops reference to capitalism, bourgeois ways of life, bourgeois ideology, and the working class. We must give up on the Marxist blur, as Marx and Dewey gave up on the Hegelian blur (Rorty, 1998: 233).

However, those concepts also belonged to the vocabulary of sociology, and if Rorty is right, then the language of sociology will have to change as well. In fact, we can observe a considerable shift in sociological vocabulary, even though not all theoreticians share Rorty's radical conclusion. This new language should develop in dialogue with Eastern European intellectuals (among them sociologists) because – as Rorty pointed out – such communication forces a rethinking of old dogmas:

> (t)he more Czechs, Poles, and Hungarians we talk to, the more old habits we are going to have give up. For example, we shall have to stop regretting the Cold War, stop excusing the Stalinism of people like Sartre, and start realizing that to a Czech the phrase "the romance of US Communism" sounds as odd as "the romance of the German-American Bund" sounds to a Jew (Rorty, 1998: 237-8).

The sociology of the beginning of the twenty-first century is quite different from that of the beginning of the twentieth. If we compare, for instance, Sorokin's description of sociological theories with a contemporary handbook on sociological theories, we find that the approach of most of the 'schools' that he wrote about, like the 'mechanistic school', 'geographical school', 'biological interpretation', 'anthropo-racial school', 'psychological school', not only disappeared but would today be considered totally unscientific, while their vocabulary would be rejected as reactionary and politically unacceptable (Sorokin, 1928). However, recent handbooks on sociological and social theory also differ from those written in the 1960s or 1970s. New topics have emerged: for instance, globalization, ethnicity, nationalism, gender issues, new media, cultural problems. Generally, one can observe a shift of sociology towards culture. The world since 1989 is often described as pluralistic and multilateral, and this is what sociology, too, has become. In the epoch of the 'politics of identity', when pluralism became the most important idea, sociology adapted to the situation and became diverse itself. One can often hear, indeed, the complaint that the discipline has lost its unity:

> (t)he increasing diversity of sociology on the one hand, its success in the media, civil society and the state, its institutionalization throughout the world, the quantitative increase of the sociological community on the other, make sociology look more solid and it is certainly socially more visible now than in heroic era of the pioneers. It is at same time intellectually Balkanized (Boudon, 1993: 42-3).

The same diagnosis of dissolution has been formulated by Irving Louis Horowitz, who accuses sociology of conformist adaptation to fashionable cultural trends:

> (i)n parody of intellectual pluralism, the field of sociology boasts (in addition to the now mandatory sections on women, the black caucus, and the cluster of other minorities) a variety of organizational shapes and forms, some directly sponsored and others benignly tolerated. These range from associations for the sociological study of Jewry and the Society for Christian Sociology at one pole to gay and lesbian sociological caucus at the other ... In the attempt to promote new forms of the democratic, to deny no one a fair hearing, sociology has become a simulated replica of real-world confusions, rather than an analytical tool for explaining or predicting social behaviour (Horowitz, 1993: 34-5).

According to Horowitz, sociology has given up its scientific ambitions and has become an ideology, or a set of different ideologies, instead of being the study of ideologies that it had been previously (ibid.: 16).

However, this development can also be considered a positive reaction to powerful critique of sociology by post-modern social and philosophical theory, which convincingly criticised scientism, foundationalism, the tendencies toward totalization, essentialism and the insularity of sociological theories (Ritzer, 1997: 17). These arguments became especially powerful and convincing after 1989.

The classics of sociology are losing their influence and seem to be less popular than ever before. Even sociologists like Karl Marx, Emil Durkheim or Max Weber seem to be too Eurocentric or parochial. Perhaps Georg Simmel is the only exception. Clearly divided traditions or schools of sociological thought have to large extent ceased to exist. Randall Collins, who wrote a well-known book on sociological theoretical thought, described its four main traditions, and in a later edition of that book stated:

> (i)n the later decades of the twentieth century, the four streams have been lapping across the edges of each other's channels in various places (Collins, 1994: 294).

Moreover, the boundaries with other social sciences are blurred. The erosion of boundaries among disciplines and the dilution of the identities of disciplines are two reasons why there is an identity crisis in sociology today. Nevertheless, this gives the discipline an opportunity to broaden its horizons:

> (w)hat is ... perplexing nowadays is that there scarcely appears to be an 'inside' (or core) to one's discipline. What we get beneath the title of, say, Sociology is a choice of materials by which a particular version of the discipline is constructed – which means, of course, that it is pretty hard to argue that there is a discipline of sociology upon which all practitioners might agree. Instead of roots of a discipline, there are routes by which academics have arrived at their partial versions of the discipline (Browning, Halcalli and Webster, 2000: 2).

On the one hand, sociology seems to be losing its relatively safe place between social theory and social research. The space 'in between' becomes narrow. Or as Horowitz put it more critically:

> (s)ociology was unable to overcome the twin challenges of abstracted empiricism and grand theorizing (Horowitz, 1993).

On the other hand, sociology has become more interdisciplinary, open to other theoretical insights and vocabularies. Instead of sociological theories, social scientists today talk more generally about the theories of the present or the theories of modernity (Browning, Halcalli and Webster, 2000). One can expect sociology to be enriched, broadened and mixed with other social and human sciences, while its old presuppositions are critically re-examined.

Of course, one can still maintain that the reason for this new development is the fact that sociology has not reached the genuine standards of science, that it still remains at a pre-scientific level of development. Thus, twenty years ago Raymond Boudon complained that

> (i)n many respects, sociology has still to experience its Copernican or Galilean revolution. Some sociologists still have an image of their discipline which is more reminiscent of Aristotelian physics than Galilean physics: their unstated and sometimes unconscious belief is that sociological analysis has more to do with the methods to which Aristotle and the Middle Ages gave the name 'rhetoric' and 'dialectics' than with controlled observation (Boudon, 1980: 35).

Yet, today, quarrels about methods cease to bother sociologists; there is more or less peaceful coexistence among many approaches. One can even say that almost 'anything goes'. The only limit seems to be sociological political correctness. However, although the dominance of methodology in sociology belongs to the remote past, the criticism that sociological imagination and insights are hampered by false pretences of a scientific character (a criticism totally opposite to Boudon's demands) is still partly valid. A question once formulated by Robert Nisbet can be repeated today:

> How many mute inglorious Simmels, how many village Cooley's lie today buried in required sequences of curriculum and in the computer rooms, their talents occupied not by development of ideas and insights but in the adaptation of trivial or well worn ideas to the language of the machine or the endless replication of studies that often shouldn't have been done in the first place. Such servitude is justified on the false and appalling ground that the student can thus be taught the 'method' of science (Nisbet, 1968: 157).

One can only add that 'without the studies that shouldn't have been done in first place' sociology would probably lose many of its institutes and faculties.

In any case, the prediction of future developments made by Raymond Boudon has proved to be false. He maintained that: 'When it [sociology] does exist – about the year 2000, all being well – the type of sociology, still flourishing in France, which depends like Aristotelian science on 'rhetoric' and 'dialectics' and the glossing of new sacred texts will probably belong to the past or – more likely – will carry another name' (Boudon, 1980: 38). Sociology exists, but its Aristotelian character has not changed: there has been no Galilean revolution, and no Newton of sociology has emerged. Waiting for such Messiah would be futile – we know already from Weber and Simmel why there cannot be a Newton of sociology. I think we should take them at their word. And if there has been a revolution in sociology in recent years, it has not been a Galilean or Newtonian revolution but a Nietzschean one (Albrow, 1993).

However, such description of today's sociology partly is misleading. In my view, it is not diversity that is a danger to sociology. Dangerous is uniformity, which still exists despite the discipline's seemingly limitless diversity. The tendency to diversification described by many authors is accompanied by far-reaching uniformization – a side-effect of internationalization and globalization – and to which the dominance of English also contributes (Münch, 1993: 62). Previously, sociology developed mainly within national contexts. Although there was always an exchange of ideas, they emerged first in relatively isolated, particular and idiosyncratic contexts. Now sociology seems to losing its local character and its local and national peculiarities. The same fashionable ideas and authors are read everywhere. Many sociological books are totally separated from any special context. This has given rise to a sociology that is similar in all the countries and parts of the world – a new kind of sociology which is above all addressed to an international community of scholars. There would be nothing wrong with this if there were not the special logic in sociology, in social thought and the humanities by which the more universal their statements, the more they are devoid of content. One can observe this logic in operation at international congresses. The larger the sociological congress, the more banal the papers are. It is like staying at international hotels; the world always looks the same, regardless of whether we are in Europe, America or Asia. On the other hand, there are strict limits on the pluralism of opinions in sociology. Sociologists seemingly represent only one of the political and cultural wings that exist in modern societies, and they systematically neglect phenomena which do not fit with their own convictions. Despite their praised or criticised pluralism and diversity, sociologists seem to repeat the same story in different forms and versions, instead of expressing different attitudes and opinions. The fact that Nietzsche has replaced Marx as their main source of inspiration has not changed the situation.

4. No way out?

If one reads the works of the classical sociologists and their diagnosis of the age, one sees that even if they grasped the main tendencies of modernity, their predictions and visions of the future have proved false. The tendencies which they believed to be already an extreme expression of modern civilization seem to us only a first, modest step towards it. For instance, George Simmel illustrated the discrepancy between subjective and objective culture by using the typewriter as an example. For Max Weber, the fate of modernity depended on the future of coal mines. What they considered to be a time of crisis appears to us to be a relatively traditional, cosy epoch when everything was stable and old-fashioned. Since then, the trends and tendencies observed by the classical authors have become radicalized in an previously unimaginable way. The founding fathers of sociology thought that we could escape modernity, but we know that there is no exit visible in the foreseeable future. We have rather the feeling, as Anthony Giddens puts it, of 'riding the juggernaut' (Giddens, 1990: 151-4) without brakes.

Consider for instance the following prediction made by Pitrim Sorokin:

> (t)he "atomization" of values was replaced by their universalization and "absolutization"; expediency, pleasure, and utility, by duty; licentious freedom, by sanctity of norms and justice; coercion and egoistic contract, if not by all-embracing, all-bestowing, and all-forgiving love, at least by more familial and altruistic relationships. Religion, ethics and law overcame the unbridled sway of force and fraud. God took the place of materialism; spiritual values, that of sensate values ... Purified and ennobled, society proceeded to erect a new house based on the Absolute, God, love, duty, sacrifice, grace, and justice ... Such was the invariable course of the great crises of the past. Such is the way out of our own crisis. There is no other possibility (Sorokin, 1941: 324).

Of course, Sorokin was wrong. There is, however, another possibility. There has been no such turn of events as he postulated (at least until now). On the contrary: we can expect that the negative tendencies criticized by him will develop in the future. Sorokin was convinced that the contractual society could not survive for long. However, today's developed society has become even more contractual and individualized. Most of the influential contemporary philosophers – John Rawls, Ronald Dworkin or Joseph Raz, amongst others – are proponents of this kind of society. Richard Rorty speaks about civilization in which any references to the absolute, eternity, objective truth are and should be eliminated. Anthony Giddens or Ulrich Beck – the most influential global sociologists of the present – talk about a second, reflexive modernity in which individualization and de-traditionalization go much further than they did in the 'first modernity' and human relations become 'democratized'. Which means that they are based on conscious, voluntary contracts.

However, one can argue that all this is only true in reference to the smallest and richest part of world, and even there it refers to only one stratum (the middle class). We can also observe other tendencies or counter-tendencies as well: the continued presence of tradition, re-traditionalization and ritualization, the renaissance of religion, the persistence of local loyalties, of involuntary relationships, of collective identities, and so on. Yet sociology seems to ignore phenomena which do not fit with its new dogmas.

The sociology of the twenty-first century must overcome its contemporary one-sidedness. The problem of today's sociology is not that it is too diverse, but that it is not diverse enough; it has not become too pluralistic, but not pluralistic enough. It should also be more positivistic in the future than it is now. What I observed above still holds true. Many sociologists know sociology better than the societies in which they live. It is very difficult to feel informed about a country if one only reads the sociological literature about it. It may be that contemporary sociologists should repeat the old Husserlian dictum: 'go back to the way that things were before' – back to the real world, the world that we had before research began. Perhaps they should follow Wittgenstein's advice and look, not think; at least they should look more carefully instead of thinking too quickly. Critics of contemporary sociology have noted that it very seldom tells us something unexpected; it does not compel us to change our opinions; nor does it surprise us. The reasons are that sociologists seldom let themselves to be surprised by reality. Too seldom do they leave the university and go out into the 'real world'. They have forgotten the old methods of the sociological masters: participant observation, deep historical analysis, ethnographic description, even experimental design. A more intense use of such methods could lead to a renewal and revitalization of sociology (Hirschauer and Amann, 1997).

This does not mean that sociology should cease its diagnoses of epochs, of great sociological syntheses and interpretations. For this purpose it must renew its former close relationship with philosophy and even theology. It is also expected that the twenty-first century will see sociology having to deal with non-human or para-human intelligent creatures and their social life. The human sociology of humans could then be confronted with fundamental questions about humanity that once seemed to belong to such anachronistic disciplines as theology and metaphysics.

Bibliography

Albrow, M. (1993), 'The Changing British Role in European Sociology' in B. Nedelmann and P. Sztompka (eds), *Sociology in Europe. In Search of Identity*, Walter de Gruyter, Berlin, pp. 79-97.

Berman, P. (1997), *A Tale of Two Utopias. The Political Journey of the Generation of 1968*, Norton, New York.

Boudon, R. (1980), *The Crisis in Sociology. Problems of Sociological Epistemology*, Columbia University Press, New York.

Boudon, R. (1993), 'European Sociology: The Identity Lost?' in B. Nedelmann and P. Sztompka (eds), *Sociology in Europe. In Search of Identity*, Walter de Gruyter, Berlin, pp. 27-44.

Browning, G., Halcali, A. and Webster, F. (2000), 'Theory, Theorists and Themes', in G. Browning, A. Halcali and F. Webster (eds), *Understanding Contemporary Society. Theories of the Present*, Sage, London, pp. 1-21.

Carver, T. (2000), 'Post-Marxism', in N. Browing, G. Halcali and F. Webster (eds), *Understanding Contemporary Society. Theories of the Present*, Sage, London, pp. 71-83.

Collins, R. (1994), *Four Sociological Traditions*, Oxford University Press, Oxford.

Davis, N. (1996), *Europe. A History*, BCA, London.

Fish, M.S. (1999), 'Postcommunist Subversion: Social Science and Democratization in East Europe and Euroasia', *Slavic Review*, vol. 58, no. 4, pp. 794-823

Fritz - Vannahme, J. (ed) (1996), *Wozu Heute noch Soziologie?*, Leske and Budrich, Opladen.

Genov, N. (1989), 'National Sociological Traditions and the Internationalization of Sociology', in N. Genov (ed), *National Traditions in Sociology*, Sage, London, pp. 1-17.

Giddens, A. (1990), *The Consequences of Modernity*, Polity Press, Cambridge.

Held, D. (1996), 'The 1989 Revolutions and the Triumph of Liberalism', in S. Hall, D. Held, D. Hubert and K. Tompson, *Modernity. An Introduction to Modern Societies*, Blackwell, Oxford, pp. 436-65.

Hirschauer, S. and Amann, K. (eds) (1997), *Die Befremdung der eigenen Kultur. Zur ethnographischer Herausforderung soziologischer Empirie*, Suhrkamp, Frankfurt am Main.

Horowitz, I.L. (1993), *The Decomposition of Sociology*, Oxford University Press, Oxford.

Horowitz, I.L. (March 10 2000), *Whose Handmaiden? The Parochial, Chequered Career of the Social Sciences*, Times Literary Supplement.

Ivanov, I. and Osipov, G. (1989), 'Tradition and Specific Features of Sociology in the Soviet Union', in N. Genov (ed), *National Traditions in Sociology*, Sage, London.

Jaspers, K. (1983), *Kleine Schule des philosophischen Denkens*, Pieper, München.

Kulcsar, K. (1989), 'Tradition, Modernization and Sociology: the Case of Hungary', in N. Genov (ed), *National Traditions in Sociology*, Sage, London, pp. 118-34.

Lepenies, W. (1985), *Die drei Kulturen. Soziologie zwischen Literatur und Wissenschaft*, Hanser, München.

Lichtblau, K. (1996), *Kulturkrise und Soziologie um die Jahrhundertwende. Zur Genealogie der Kultursoziologie in Deutschland*, Suhrkamp, Frankfurt am Main.

Mucha, J. and Keen, M. (eds) (1995), *Socjologia Europy Srodkowo–Wschodniej 1956-1990*, IFiS PAN, Warszawa.

Münch, R. (1993), 'The Contribution of German Social Theory to European Sociology', in B. Nedelmann and P. Sztompka (eds), *Sociology in Europe. In Search of Identity*, Walter de Gruyter, Berlin, pp. 45-66.

Nisbet, R. ([1966] 1993), 'Sociology as an Art Form, in Tradition and Revolt', in R. Nisbet, *Historical and Sociological Essays*, Random House, New York, pp. 143-62.

Nisbet, R. (1993), *The Sociological Tradition*, Transaction Publisher, New Brunswick.

Ritzer, G. (1997), *Postmodern Social Theory*, The McGraw-Hill Companies, New York.

Rorty, R. (1998), 'The End of Leninism, Havel and Social Hope', in R. Rorty, *Truth and Progress. Philosophical Papers*, Cambridge University Press, Cambridge, pp. 228-43.

Scaff, L.A. (1989), *Fleeing the Iron Cage. Culture, Politics, and Modernity in the Thought of Max Weber*, Univeristy of California Press, Los Angeles.

Shils, E. (1980), *The Calling of Sociology and Other Essays on the Pursuit of Learning*, University of Chicago Press, Chicago.

Sorokin, P. (1928), *Contemporary Sociological Theories*, Haper & Brothers, New York.

Sorokin, P. (1941), *The Crisis of Our Age. The Social and Cultural Outlook*, Dutton, New York.

Turner, J.H. (1989), 'Sociology in the United States: its Growth and Contemporary Profile', in N. Genov (ed), *National Traditions in Sociology*, Sage, London, pp. 220-42.

Wallerstein, I. (1999), 'The Heritage of Sociology. The Promise of Social Science', Presidential Address, XIVth World Congress of Sociology, Montreal 26 July 1998, *Current Sociology*, vol. 47, no. 1, pp. 1-41.

Weidig, R. (1989), 'Sociology in the German Democratic Republic' in N. Genov (ed), *National Traditions in Sociology*, Sage, London, pp. 81-99.

Weiss, J. (1989), 'Sociology in the Federal Republic of Germany' in N. Genov (ed), *National Traditions in Sociology*, Sage, London, pp. 100-17.

Weiss, J. (1992), 'Die Normalität als Krise. Bemerkung zur 'Entzauberung' der Soziologie', in *Die Europäische Sozialwissenschaften am Ende des XX Jahrhunderts. Demographische, Technologische und Epistemologische Herausforderungen*, Autonome Region Trentino-Südtirol, Trient, pp. 85-98.

8 Globalization and peripheral identity

TALIS TISENKOPFS

Introduction

In the recent vibrant debate on globalization it is possible to distinguish three broad schools of thought which Held, McGrew, Goldblatt and Perraton (1999) refer to as the *hyperglobalizers*, the *sceptics* and the *transformationalists*. For the hyperglobalizers, contemporary globalization creates a new era in which people everywhere are increasingly subject to global forces. By contrast, sceptics argue that globalization is essentially a myth which conceals the reality of the international domination of powerful nations, regional blocs and international organizations. Finally the transformationalists see globalization as the profound change of societies across the globe as they seek to adapt to a more interconnected and highly uncertain world.

If the territorial, economic and political manifestations of globalization are seen from a macrosociological perspective, historical analogues can be found, and this may encourage us to think that globalization is a routine set of changes – ones which bring the world more closely together – something similar to global warming. A microsociological insight into societies, however, shows that the transformations caused by globalization have a fundamental impact on people's everyday lives, identities, and intimacy, and that these effects do not have historical precedents. This means that a more sociologically creative approach would be one in which globalization is seen as a radical shift in post-modern development, during the course of which the basic structures of individual life also change.

Globalization is just another word that can be used to describe how shaky, unfixed and frustrated identity has become as a result of individualization within the continuously opening and interweaving world in which we live.

1. Globalization as combination

Globalization can mean different things to different people. To some it means a growing flow of goods, capital, information and people across borders. Others associate globalization with information technologies and the increasing opportunities that people have to use information. Yet others point out the increasing role of mass media, and the spread of unified cultural products and lifestyles throughout the world. Often, attention is focused on the expansion of free-market capitalism, the growing influence of multinational corporations and international organizations, as well as on the opposite process – the declining role of national states. Admittedly, globalization has some clearly negative aspects: it exacerbates inequality between rich and poor countries and leads to an enormous concentration of wealth and power in a narrow circle of people, corporations and countries. Predominant since the beginning of the 1980s is a powerful line of critical thought based on dependency theory and the theory of world systems, and which, among other things, points to inequality in the global system of capitalism (Wallerstein, 1990).

Facts are the first thing to surprise us when we look at globalization in the world and in each individual country. Globalization is poignantly characterized by facts that indicate the growth rates of markets, technologies and information. According to the *Global Human Development Report* (UNDP, 1999a) the daily volume of transactions in the international currency market grew from US$ 20 billion in 1970 to US$ 1.5 trillion in 1998. Total exports in the world amount to US$ 21 trillion per year and comprise 21% of the world's GDP (in 1970, when the world's GDP was much smaller, the share of exports was only 17%). The share of high-tech production in world trade rose from 12% in 1980 to 24% in 1994. In 1960 computers were 1,000 times more expensive than in 1990. Currently the Internet is used by 150 million people or 2.4% of the world's population. In Canada, which has the highest human development index in the world, the Internet is used by 17% of the population. The volume of direct foreign investments reached US$ 400 billion in 1997, which was seven times higher than in 1970. The number of tourists in the world grew from 260 million in 1980 to 590 million in 1996, which exemplifies Zygmunt Bauman's metaphor of the conversion of a social actor from a pilgrim to a tourist – a person who once used to inhabit the margins of social action but has now moved to its centre (Bauman, 1996). This is a tourist who 'needs more space' and fears fixation.

Still, globalization is more than a spurt of growth. Globalization can be defined as a process that links people, organizations, markets, technologies, finances, information and governance together in one common interactive network stretching beyond the borders of national states. Globalization means that individuals, businesses, governments and non-governmental organizations can all interact with partners in various parts of the world faster, more extensively and more cheaply than ever before. This interaction may lead to the creation of products and ideas that can be distributed across the globe. Hence, globalization is a new way in which people can use common linking networks, skills and knowledge to combine capital, technology, markets and policies in an open world. This gives rise to even closer mutual ties between people and nations.

Combinations are inherent mechanisms of globalization. The combination of human beings, non-human items, technologies and social relations serves to make globalization plural. As Jan Nederveen Pieterse (1995) has put it: 'Globalisation is a process of hybridisation which gives rise to a global melange'. There are as many modes of globalization as there are globalizing agents with their specific identities and goals, which makes it possible to apply an actor network theory in analysis of globalization.

Globalization is a relatively recent phenomenon which structures the world as a whole (Robertson, 1996): formerly, events in the world were not tightly linked and structuration took place within the confines of nation states. In the globalization process an equally important role is played by the acting agents (governments, international organizations, multinational corporations, professionals, students, skilled labour, non-governmental organizations, and others) and capital, information, policies, technology and the market. This body of structure and agency, or this ensemble of resources and action, can be organized into various combinations, so that individuals and organisations involved in global networks are able to construct their own scenarios which correspond to their goals. This is a precondition for the democratization of globalization, a globalization that promotes human development.

Globalization is not only a market of concrete processes in the area of information and technology; it is also a new discourse that explains and actively shapes the contemporary world and influences policy. Participants include mass media, scientists, politicians and other agents of action. The discourse of globalization is based on the contraposition of the cold-war system against the order of an open world (Friedman, 1999). The cold-war world was split between closed and hostile camps, while globalization is characterized by openness. The central idea of the Cold War was that of the border, as symbolized by the Berlin Wall, while the key concept of globalization is integration, which is symbolized by the free market and the Internet. Following the collapse of communism, at the beginning of the 1990s the cold-war world was replaced by an open and internally-linked world order in which the same processes simultaneously affected increasingly more people around the planet.

'The world is 10 years old!' exclaims Thomas L. Friedman. Since the fall of the Berlin Wall, the chopped-up world has been replaced by a new, closely interconnected system called globalization. Free market capitalism, liberalism, international organizations, information and communications technologies, e-mail, the 'e-conomy', life on-line – these have all become passwords for entry into the new and open world. Nothing of the sort could even have been imagined ten years ago, when the fall of communist regimes in Central and Eastern Europe and the restoration of independence in the Baltic States seemed to be the culmination of the goals of these nations for a long time to come. Today, however, Latvia and the other countries of the Baltic region and Central and Eastern Europe are undertaking an even more difficult mission to achieve rapid development and to maintain cultural identities in a world where frontiers are disappearing and competition grows increasingly fraught. Paradoxically, globalization has pushed nationalism into the background of the transformations now occurring in Central and Eastern Europe – the same nationalism which in the early 1990s was the most influential ideology in the entire post-communist space (Gellner, 1992).

2. The driving forces of globalization

The recent publications of the UNDP devoted to analysis of globalization and its human consequences (UNDP 1999a, 1999b) emphasise four driving forces of globalization: new markets, new technologies, new agents and new norms.

2.1 New Markets

In the 1990s globalization mostly took place as a result of the spread of free-market capitalism and free trade throughout the world. The market is encroaching on more and more economic sectors and aspects of life, and it is also expanding geographically. Increasing numbers of national economies are opening to international markets.

Liberal ideologies and policies promote the spread of free-market capitalism. The underlying lesson is that the more a country opens up its economy to competition and market forces, the more efficient it will become, and the more it will flourish. This idea is an invitation to open, deregulate and privatize the economy. The liberal discourse is strengthened by the achievements of market capitalism, since this has proved to be the most effective way to increase wealth. In contrast, other economic systems have been able to distribute wealth more equally, but none has been able to produce it so effectively. This factor sometimes induces liberals to feel an uncritical sense of triumph and to imagine that the free market is the sole recipe for every requirement of social development and the only path that the world should follow.

However, market capitalism has its shortcomings. Although competition and the market can achieve the greatest efficiency, they do not guarantee balanced development and social justice, which are important to the public. The free market creates disproportionate concentrations of wealth and escalates inequality. Jolts in the international financial market during the last years have forced many of its former defenders (for example, the billionaire George Soros and President of the World Bank James D. Wolfersohn) to call for closer international control over financial markets, a battle against the poverty exacerbated by globalization, more attention to social problems, and thinking in broader terms than merely the categories of financial stabilization.

It is important to touch upon one aspect of the free market: namely creative destruction. Increased competition forces companies to merge and fight for a larger share of the market, because otherwise it is impossible to take advantage of innovations and the latest technologies. Those who able constantly to invent something new survive under capitalism, and this leads to the rapid destruction of inefficient companies. Inefficient countries, which are not sheltered by protectionism, are also pushed into backwaters by capitalism. The speed at which innovations become goods and services under the conditions of an open economy is such that businesses must work faster, grow larger, become more efficient and reduce costs. Under these conditions large companies have a greater chance of survival. Under the conditions of globalization, in order to enter and maintain their position in domestic and international markets, businesses must be much more creative, and they are forced to join common supply and sales networks.

2.2 New Technologies

New technologies are the second most important driving force behind globalization. Previous eras of globalization were based on the invention of railroads, steamships and automobiles, which promoted transportation and trade. Modern-day globalization is based on the use of computers, information technologies, microchips, satellite communications, fibre-optic cables, the Internet and falling prices for telecommunications. These technologies make it possible for people to exchange information quickly and to coordinate their actions in various locations around the world simultaneously.

2.3 New Agents

Globalization is facilitated by multinational corporations, governments, certain influential individuals, international non-government organizations, and every regular consumer and Internet user. Multinational corporations are the largest providers of foreign direct investments in the world and among the most influential agents of globalization. Unlike dealers in the international currency market, who engage in speculative transactions in stocks and government securities, multinational corporations invest more in actual companies, especially in the areas of energy and information.

Many countries around the world are competing to attract foreign investors. The long-term factors that promote investment include a developed infrastructure, a skilled labour force, low levels of corruption and bureaucratic obstacles, transparency of bureaucratic procedures and a stable banking system (United Nations Conference on Trade and Development, 1999). These factors are even more important for investors than tax breaks. Latvia, like other Central and Easter Europe countries, is striving to create a favourable environment for investments. In thinking about the investment environment, governments are trying to create conditions that would stimulate the flow of new technologies into the region, so that investment can facilitate an increase in exports and also prevent the creation of manufacturing plants which pollute the environment. It must be borne in mind that the goals of multinational corporations and governments differ. The former seek to increase profits and their competitiveness in the international arena, while a government's task is to promote economic growth.

Governments in many countries around the world are facilitating globalization by implementing liberal economic policies, reducing government control over the market, opening the economy to foreign investment, restricting social welfare schemes, and turning over many public services to the private sector. These policies have some features in common: the privatization of state enterprises, macroeconomic stabilization and reduced inflation, cutting back bureaucracy, reducing budget deficits, lowering import tariffs, lifting limitations on foreign investment, limiting monopolies, facilitating exports, deregulating capital markets, battling corruption, promoting competition in the banking and telecommunications sectors, reforming pensions systems and introducing pension funds (Friedman, 1999). The influence of liberalization and privatization significantly alters perceptions of the role of the state, which is increasingly seen not as an institution that safeguards public interests, but instead as an instrument that serves private interests (The World Bank, 1997).

Not only 'small' but also 'large' agents are important for globalization. Small agents do not have the same large resources at their disposal as governments and multinational corporations, but they can actively participate in global processes. These small agents include scientists, athletes, 'Eurocrats', managers of businesses, students, professionals, non-governmental organization activists, journalists, importers, exporters, skilled workers and other representatives of society. Latvia has a growing number of people whose professional and personal contacts extend beyond its borders, and an increasing number of Latvians are studying, working and living abroad, and for longer periods of time. By becoming involved in international contacts and communities, these people acquire new knowledge and experience, and usually they also improve their material situation and raise their status in Latvian society. However, internationalization can also give rise to a 'brain drain' – that is, skilled human resources leaving the country, which is one of the most severe globalization-related threats to development in Latvia, and in small and peripheral states in general.

2.4 New Norms

The leading and legitimizing idea behind globalization is free market capitalism – an idea which claims that the more market forces are allowed to operate, the more effective and fast-growing the economy will become. It is increasingly recognized throughout the world that the free market is the most efficient institution for organizing societies, and market principles restructure not only the economy but also many other spheres of life. This idea advocates the spread of free-market capitalism throughout the world. If Robinson Crusoe today found himself on a desert island, then globalization would have prepared Internet connections and access to stock markets for him, because someone would have opened, deregulated and privatized the island. Free-market capitalism is being presented as the absolute and liberal truth of the globalized world.

The spread of the free market is accompanied by the spread of liberal democracy. Globalization promotes broader acceptance of democratic norms in the world, and democratic principles are transferred to international relations. In a globalized world, foreign relations are regulated by the multilateral agreements, treaties and conventions which are replacing norms based on the Cold War, the Arms Race and opposition. Particularly, the countries of Central and Eastern Europe are eager to sign multilateral treaties and join international organizations. The fact that ten countries in the region have been invited to begin negotiations on entry to the European Union is perceived in these societies as confirming their strategic choice to join the international community of nations. The countries in the region have all adopted human rights conventions, thereby affirming their readiness to respect individuality and human freedoms.

Governments and international non-governmental organizations unite in joint efforts that cannot be undertaken individually. Examples include international conventions on environmental protection, the preservation of biological diversity, limitations on harmful emissions, prevention of climate changes and protection of the ozone layer. Countries have also signed multilateral treaties on the protection of intellectual property and the free development of communications and services; and a multilateral treaty on investments is currently in preparation. However, many global processes remain without influential monitoring which would ensure adequate control over these processes. This is especially true of the international financial market.

3. Globalization and periphery

Globalization not only offers new opportunities based on intellect and technology to a wider circle of people but it also maximizes both gains and losses. Financial capital, intellectual property and information technologies are being concentrated within a limited group of individuals, organizations and states, and there is a risk that the world may see the establishment of new forms of domination and supremacy. More than 90 % of Internet users live in the world's wealthiest countries and only 0.2 % of them in the world's poorest ones. Sixty of the world's countries have grown poorer since 1980. Twenty % of the world's inhabitants who live in the wealthiest countries produce 86 % of the world's gross economic product, while 20 % who live in the poorest countries produce only 1 % of it. The value of the assets held by the world's three richest individuals exceeds the total value of property and assets possessed by all the world's poorest countries and their 600 million inhabitants (UNDP, 1999a). AIDS, narcotics, international crime and poverty are affecting increasingly larger numbers of people. This circumstance of broadened opportunities combined with distribution is becoming more unequal intra-nationally and internationally, and it embodies globalization's contradictory nature as it creates new problems in human development. Globalization may exacerbate backwardness and inequality for those individuals, nations and territories that do not have access to the new markets and technologies.

Thus globalization may promote the emergence of new territorial and social peripheries with no influence over the driving forces of globalization, and which are excluded from its benefits. Under conditions of globalization, relations between the centre and the periphery are no longer shaped as a configuration of social agents around the central values of society and the dominant power and authority within the confines of a nation state. The centre, which under conditions of modernization served to consolidate society, in the era of globalization is now shifting, changing its location and moving beyond the nation state: it is losing its solidifying power. The centre seems to dissolve because there are so many new and 'external' forces seeking to gain control in society or some segment thereof. Society comes to resemble a supermarket where there is a fierce fight for a market share in every group of products, but where different kinds of commodities do not compete with one another. Put otherwise: society becomes polycentric while the periphery becomes plural. Which means that the global forces may achieve manifold domination over the peripheral zones and groups of society, and that these groups may find themselves aggregately excluded, exploited, and with restricted choices. This is vividly illustrated by the evolution of poverty in the modern world, in which a lack of income still affects the majority of people. These economic manifestations of poverty have now been joined by the lack of access to information and technologies, as well as by growing dependence on knowledge created elsewhere.

The peripheral status of states, territories and regions in a globalized world is determined by several factors: weak national economies, low competitiveness, distance from economic and political centres, weak integration into international organizations, a deficiency of democratic governance, and so on. However, a key social factor is the weakness of integrative links in society. This is clearly apparent in the new democracies of Central and Eastern Europe, where the lack of an integrative centre is still strongly felt, and where there is an absence of what Arend Lijphart has called 'consensual democracy'. Social action is marked by anomie and a lack of norms, and society seemingly does not hold together. Many people act contrary to common sense, the principle of the public good, and the interests of others; and social action draws further away from the centre, rather than moving towards it and consolidating society around common values. Caring for one's own wealth and self-interest without caring for others is elevated into the main principle of action. This disposition of social behaviour hampers the growth of integrative relations in society and obstructs the consolidation of democracy. It also stunts civil society, which is universally weak in post-communist societies. Roland Inglehart's study on the shift in values in the course of modernization and post-modernization (Inglehart, 1997) has shown that modern societies are much more likely to emphasise greater individualism and values which focus on individual freedom, happiness, welfare and self-fulfilment. In the post-scarcity societies of Central and Eastern Europe, such materialistic and individualistic orientations are highly respected, which adds further conflict to situations in which economic inequalities are expanding and poverty is rife.

One of the most important factors creating peripheries and pushing social agents into a secondary role under the conditions of globalization, however, is a lack of opportunities, resources and skills in globalization. People, organizations and even entire countries have no access to new technologies, markets and information. Or access to these critically important resources of globalization is hindered; or else people simply do not know how to use these resources. This distances local agents from forces which have a fundamental influence on their lives. If globalization represents the construction of individual scenarios from elements of knowledge, technology, markets, capital and information, then an inability to join this game of combinations means a relapse into the state of a peripheral and dependent agent.

4. The iron fist of globalization and its critique

The new global regime that has emerged under the influence of free-market capitalism and liberal ideology fosters the conviction that there is no other option available. Communism has collapsed, socialism has been dismantled, and the welfare state has proven ineffective. Paradoxically, people may complain about the negative aspects of the free market and about the iron fist of liberal policies, they may call for a socially responsible policy or a 'third way', but the fact remains that they cannot deny the efficiency of capitalism, and they cannot suggest alternative models of economic development which are just as efficient. Indeed, the strong side of liberal discourse is the convincing evidence that free-market capitalism is the most effective way to create wealth and to raise standards of living. This capitalist argument is mediated, transmitted and adored internationally. Under conditions of globalization, increasing numbers of countries throughout the world are trying to bring the liberal argument into practical policies: reducing government control over markets, repealing subsidies in national economies, opening economies up to foreign investment, and reducing social welfare schemes. This is seen as the route that the entire world must follow. Other theoretical and political alternatives, such as Keynesianism, social democracy and the welfare state, are all regarded as ineffective.

It may be that the implementation of consistently liberal markets brings with it better economic results than do inconsistent market reforms and flirtations with socialism. But the triumph of neo-liberal ideologies in the world nonetheless reminds us of a Darwinist approach to economics – a cynical and dehumanising approach to society.

The absolutization of neo-liberalism may be the point from which critical thinking can start and a search be made for models of development that help to adjust global forces to human goals. Liberal discourse and policies have one obvious weak point: although free-market capitalism induces more rapid economic growth, it generates an enormous concentration of resources and economic inequalities. It does not create the conditions for sustainable development and social cohesion. Competition and the liberal market are the best ways to achieve efficiency, but they do not give rise to equity, democratic participation, civil solidarity, and the equal access to opportunities so important for human development.

Conducting a critique of neo-liberalism – which has now, in fact, established itself as the new global regime – is a fundamental challenge for contemporary social thought as part of the continuing effort to understand capitalism as a theory and as a social system (Albrow, 1997). Since the early 1990s, the United Nations Development Programme has sought to extend the range of development goals beyond merely economic objectives.

By publishing annual *Human Development Reports* on more than ninety countries, the United Nations Development Programme endeavours to promote sustainable human development policies targeted on both economic growth and aspects of life quality: education, health, environmental protection, reduced poverty, gender equality, participation, and others (UNDP, 1999a). Apart from the human development concept, there are other powerful ideas which counter-balance the neo-liberal approach to development; the ideas of universal human rights, the empowerment of people, development through participation, global governance.

Liberal ideologists and politicians largely lack ideas on how people can be mobilized in pursuit of shared development goals. In the meantime, under the aegis of critical thought new alliances of individuals and organizations emerge which stand for the public good and for sustainable development. Examples are the non-governmental organizations that lobby on behalf of the interests and rights of citizens, international human rights organizations, anti-corruption organizations, and yet others. Also to be noted is the growing demand by civil societies for political honesty, transparency and governance closer to the population. The human rights movement throughout the world has undoubtedly made an invaluable contribution to the popularization of such values as individual freedom, equality, minority rights, child protection, women's equality and other values of little concern to free-market capitalism.

The powerful critiques of 'capitalism with its gloves off' that have appeared recently in social thought (Bourdieu, 1998; Chomsky, 1999; Giddens and Christopher, 1998) make it clear that we are about to experience new currents of critical thought which, ironically enough, may be based on a neo-Marxist approach. Critical theory argues that it is possible to envisage a future better than the one based on inequalities of the past and the present. Another sign of present-day critical thinking is an opposition to the structures of domination embedded in and manifested through major social institutions: the lordship of wealthy classes and nations over poor people and the Third World or the domination of politics and economics over people's everyday lives.

Critical theory is seeking dialectically to overcome the gap between structure and agency. Although social structures shape everyday life, knowledge of structures can help people change social conditions (Agger, 1998). In a globalized world not only states, multinational corporations and 'super-organizations' but also ordinary people have the right to create the conditions for their lives. In other words, critical theory takes an in-depth look at globalization and social change 'which starts at home' (ibid.), the purpose being to empower 'small agents'. It may also serve to recognize that life in an open world ruled by a diversity of interests is one in which individuals should develop greater tolerance and skills in order to harmonize self-interest and the public good democratically.

5. Privatization of public space

The institutional foundation of globalization is a free market and its underpinning liberal ideology, which also has an effect on policy. Everywhere in the world where a free market has been established and liberalism has gained the upper hand, revenues increase and economic development accelerates. However, inequality and individualism also increase, social relations become more unstable and life becomes less secure. Liberalism creates new threats to the prevalence of society, as the free market, privatization and denationalization reduce the public sector and society's space of common interests. The impact of liberalization lessens feelings of mutual concern and responsibility among people. As the state withdraws from its former role as society's caretaker, and with civic society under pressure, there is no longer any influential agent to care for the common good. Everywhere in the world, welfare-related state functions and social care are diminishing. In the name of new opportunities, people are more willing to dispense with public interests than individual gains.

Public space is being privatized, with severe consequences for the public good and the common benefit. The realities of Central and Eastern Europe provide a body of remarkable examples which evidence that privatization has narrowed the common and integrative space of society. The state's refusal to provide many kinds of social services to the poor, and its inability to deal with the social problems that have occurred as the result of economic stratification constitute the most commonly cited evidence. The poor are usually left to fend for themselves, in their isolated spaces with limited opportunities. It is not only the negative consequences of transition, but also the economic growth and increase in material well-being, that are accompanied by diminishing collective space. By means of laws and various methods of social and territorial exclusion, private property relations are applied to common space which now becomes detached from the public and is restricted to access by others. A vivid example of this is the way in which parks and gardens in Latvia's capital city of Riga have been used in the last several years. Private attractions and closed parking lots have been erected in some parks, and despite complaints in society, public access to recreational zones has been restricted.

The state withdraws from many sectors of public life and from its responsibility for ensuring public housing, education, healthcare and pensions. The scattering of the state has become common throughout Central Europe, a process which has discredited the public interest and created a gap between population and politics. The public sector crisis reflects the inability of the state to defend the public interest at a time when many people have ended up the losers in transformation and need help. Human development balance sheets in Central and Eastern Europe and the CIS in the 1990s show an increase in registered and long-term unemployment, widening income gaps (the Gini Index has grown constantly in all the countries of the region), and an increase in the proportion of poor in overall populations. At the same time public spending on health and education remains low (UNDP, 1999c). It should be noted that many of the achievements of the welfare state are also being dismantled in Western Europe. The influence of neo-liberalism and globalization brings about a fundamental shift in the idea of the role of the state. The state is no longer seen as a shelter and caretaker for the public interest and the common good, but as an instrument which promotes the private interest. The consequence of this is egoism among politicians, and anti-parliamentarian attitudes and distrust in the state among the population. Governments argue for the privatization of public services, which is all too often set as a goal unto itself, without consideration of whether the results are effective.

In a recent critical book *Acts of Resistance: Against the Tyranny of the Market*, Pierre Bourdieu argues that betrayal of the public interest, egoism in politics and the silence of intellectuals are all parts of a market tyranny. In a period of crisis of confidence in the state and in the public good, two tendencies emerge: corruption among the rulers, which is linked to a decline in respect for the public interest; and a distrust in politics, alienation and apathy among those who are governed (Bourdieu, 1998).

Corruption is a critical indicator of neglect of the public good. According to the global anti-corruption non-government organization, Transparency International, the index of corruption is much higher in the post-socialist transition countries than in the countries of European Union, the OECD or the First World as such (Transparency International, 1999). The transfer of public property to private purposes in the countries of Central and Eastern Europe has been implemented at all costs, and privatization has been worshiped as a state religion. The efforts of governments to serve private interests have frequently led to clientelism and corruption. Political leaders in the region often have a wide circle of friends through which the public interest is placed under private control. These leaders are selfishly concerned with attracting attention to their personalities, and they are eager to appear on television and in the newspapers. Their public image is personal, and it often lacks connection with their public functions. In post-socialist countries it is not at all uncommon to see a contradiction between publicly declared democratic and legal norms on the one hand and the actual behaviour of political and bureaucratic leaders on the other. Fancy cars and elegant government offices paid for with taxpayer money are signs of political egoism, which taken together make it increasingly difficult to determine whether politicians care for the common good.

A critique of the egoism of politics and the retreat of the state serves as a reminder that in a globalizing and liberalizing world there is a need for the greater defence and representation of public interests at all political levels. In other words, under conditions of freedom, individualism flourishes on its own, and more care should therefore be invested in strengthening common values. This can be accomplished by urging people to incorporate respect for others and concern for society's common interests into their own motivations for action and also by promoting civic co-operation.

6. Globalization and everyday life

Globalization is not something removed from everyday existence which exists in some remote, faraway place. Globalization affects the lives of each individual. Today, the work of many is inescapably associated with computers connected to the global web. The global financial market functions simultaneously throughout the world and affects stock prices, currency exchange rates and interest rates in many countries, causing the inhabitants of these countries to worry about their private deposits and pension funds. As free trade becomes more widespread, people are able to fill their everyday consumer baskets with goods produced in various continents. High-tech and science-intensive technologies are quickly commercialized and turned into goods sold in global markets. These goods improve the material aspect of life and also serve to unify people's lives. The global entertainment industry unites people even more than does the global market for goods. Millions of people all over the globe simultaneously watch the Olympic Games on television, or watch the Academy Awards or charity concerts, thereby becoming participants in a world-scale symbolic exchange.

One of the spheres in which globalization has exhibited itself most surprisingly is that of intimacy. Forms of intimacy are undergoing change – the sense of identity, family, love and friendship, interpersonal relations and the relationship between people and time. As communications diversify, new opportunities arise to join new communities, and this raises a serious challenge to existing sentiments of belonging. The pace of life is accelerating and people must juggle an increasing number of tasks simultaneously. A lack of time prevents people from paying sufficient attention to their families and their microcosm, which is the framework for human development.

Globalization not only affects corporate behaviour, it also alters the character of work and careers and, by extension, the rhythm of individual lives, which become more dynamic and less safe (Sennett, 1998). In today's increasingly competitive environment organisations are becoming unstable, and this has an impact on how people work: they work more and more, often managing more than one job, changing jobs, and moving from regular employment into short-term project-type work. In these circumstances employment is no longer long-term and secure, but instead often becomes fragmented. Today's form of work not only provides ways in which to prove oneself but also creates insecurity and stress.

Risk has become part of working. This means that people must constantly keep themselves in top form in order to retain their competitive edge in the labour market. This often happens at the expense of their health, family and free time, in reality narrowing and even damaging other important opportunities in life.

The international demonstration effect is yet another influence on everyday lives. The populations of peripheral countries experience stress as their taste and consumer desires are dictated by global and usually Western standards. The inability to maintain this level of consumption creates stress and leads to corruption. Incidentally, this may partly explain the actions of those officials in the developing countries who squander taxpayers' money. The pressure of international demonstration, in advertising, for example, has been so strong that the rationality and traditions of many societies have been shaken to the core. In just one decade, Western standards of consumption have been applied to the post-socialist and post-scarcity countries of Central and Eastern Europe. Consumer choices have proliferated, and consumer frustrations have deepened correspondingly. For most of those who have difficulty in making ends meet, it is impossible to balance consumer desires with the monetary resources of households.

These everyday experiences suggest that the basic human condition is transforming under the pressures of globalization. Life is being displaced somewhere between locality and globality, social relations are becoming fragmented and short-term, as if they were 'made of biodegradable plastic and designed for recycling' (Bauman, 1996). Identities are individual rather than collective projections, and flexible communities are preferred to stable institutions.

7. Pursuit of opportunity

The human desire to create and take advantage of new opportunities is a feature of contemporary culture and individualization, and no rules exist to prevent it. Globalization has opened up a new level of opportunity for those individuals who have access to the resources of globalization. As Ulrich Beck has argued when discussing the effects of globalization in personal lives, nothing is as useful as the illustration of a woman who splits her life between Munich and Kenya. She changes locations, but also changes the borders of separate worlds, nations, religions, cultures, skin colours and time zones. Beck calls this the multiple location of individual biographies, writing that mobility in the old sense as movement between two points in the social hierarchy or across the landscape is losing its significance. What is coming forth is the *inner* mobility of an individual's life, for which coming and going, being both here and there across frontiers and at the same time has become normal (Beck, 2000).

Zygmunt Bauman has developed a similar argument about mobility as the most powerful and coveted stratifying factor in our late-modern and post-modern times. The freedom to move is not shared by all. Some of us have become truly and fully global, while others are fixed in their locality. Contrary to the optimistic vision of endogenous development, this often means deprivation, segregation and exclusion. Bauman writes: 'Being local in a globalized world is a sign of social deprivation and degradation' and there is 'progressive breakdown in communication between the increasingly global and extraterritorial elites and the ever more 'localised' rest'. Bauman points to an intimate connection among the mobility of individual lives, the speed of travel and social cohesion: new speed and new mobility tend to polarise a society. More to the point, whoever is free to run away from a locality is also free to run away from consequences, 'leaving to the locally bound the task of wound-licking, damage-repair and waste-disposal' (Bauman, 1998a).

The desire to take risks in order to try out new opportunities, and the fear of losses which may be incurred if one stops at what has already been achieved – these are two of the traits of the mobile, post-modern human being. This is a person who never says *no* to new opportunities and, indeed, the word *no* is heard less and less frequently in our fevered age. The article must be finished by next Wednesday; the new project must be started on Friday; the flight is on Saturday; jobs are not yet completed but new ones are on the horizon.

The chase after opportunity and the *yes-culture* have not taught people to limit themselves, and this is particularly true in post-scarcity societies. People agree to take on *one more* job, *one more* project, *one more* market transaction and contract. This formula of life pushes life forward at an ever accelerating pace. By saying *yes*, a herd of mobile individuals mediate through and across social settings in search of multiple benefits that can be acquired on the basis of mosaic and *ad hoc* relations. Attempts to broaden opportunities can give rise to an effect in complete contrast to human development. Jobs are becoming more unstable and more intensive. By working more, people are overburdening themselves, thereby eliciting chronic fatigue and psychological stress. Furthermore, the increased workload is indirectly and unintentionally increasing pressure on others, who feel that they too must raise their level of productivity. Hence, globalization exhibits itself as new opportunities and also as the new stress that people feel in their everyday lives. If at the macro-level, globalization is associated with the disappearance of social controls over the global flows of capital and information, at the micro-level it involves lessening control over one's own mobility.

The achievement of opportunities and the utilization of life chances depend on the competitiveness of the individual. Competitiveness means the individual's readiness to operate within the capitalist system of incentives. This system is ruled by private interest, the profit motive, and the laws of the market. It is in constant motion, always calling for better products and services, for self-improvement, for more work, and for the ability to manage stress. Individual competitiveness is determined primarily by education, qualifications and initiative.

Precisely because not everyone has enjoyed the same opportunities (for example, with regard to privatization) and the same resources, society has become divided into 'losers' and 'winners'. The boundary between these groups cannot be drawn precisely, but it is certainly felt in society. The political elite, the educated and entrepreneurial, the young and the active, businessmen and women, the new professionals brought forth by the market economy, and the growing middle class are among the successful. They have been able to use social transformation to their own advantage, and they are simultaneously the product and the producer of these changes. A second group is made up of those people for whom the changes have brought more losses than gains, and their present circumstances are formed by an accretion of the negative consequences of the transformation.

Social stratification studies show that during the period of post-communist transition, for instance in Latvia, personal prosperity and satisfaction with life has increased for those individuals who have become involved in the private sector either as entrepreneurs or as skilled employees, as well as for those who have a 'multi-active' lifestyle, working at several jobs and creating several sources of income for themselves (UNDP, 1998). This shows that participation in change has been dependent on certain crucial human resources not shared equally by all: education, connections, initiative, and, not infrequently, access to the powers-that-be.

Unfortunately, differences between losers and winners have a tendency to become structurally embedded as the signs of inequality become more closely tied to specific social groups, such as rural residents, pensioners, single mothers, families with numerous children, the disabled, those of pre-pensionable age looking for work and those who lack the will, the skills, or the resources to find alternative employment in a competitive environment. All these groups find themselves in an unfavourable situation caused by a combination of factors: they have lower incomes, greater difficulty in finding work, more limited opportunities for communication, and all the other problems. While the successful, the 'upwardly-globally mobile' keep increasing their material and social welfare, the unsuccessful suffer the negative effects of both transition and globalization, fighting for survival with no particular support from society or the state.

The return of individualism and the retreat of the state make it possible to blame the victims, claiming that they are responsible for their misfortune. The victimization of the poor is a widespread practice in post-socialist countries, where the state has adopted the liberal position that everyone is responsible for themselves. It has shifted the burden of responsibility for their welfare onto the shoulders of individuals before many of them have been ready to support under its weight. It has neglected the fact that the Soviet or socialist regimes made many people dependent on the state's external support. Now these people – finding themselves in crisis, having lost their jobs, or facing the uncertainties of globalization and European integration – do not know how to answer the crucial question: 'What should *I* do now?'.

Until now individual competitiveness has been left to the individual. Some have been able to compete while others have not. The role of the state in the development of individual competitiveness and human resources must become proactive and significantly greater. The process of developing human resources may lead to successful cooperation between major agencies: the state, non-governmental organizations and the private sector, and may lead to the emancipation of public concern about the competitiveness and globalization skills of every individual.

8. Transformation of identity

At the beginning of the twentieth century the classics of social theory maintained that individuality and collectivity, communality and difference were the factors that shaped the basic structure of social identity. Durkheim studied collective consciousness and solidarity while Simmel focused on the subjectivity of the individual. Social identities have always been shaped in the reciprocal or even contradictory interaction between individual and collective.

As the twentieth century passes into the twenty-first, however, social identity is undergoing an unprecedented crisis, one manifest as the growing conflict between the freedom of individual identity, on the one hand, and efforts to preserve common national, territorial, ethnic and cultural identities on the other. The process of globalization, which breaks down the boundaries within which all previous and traditional forms of identity were constructed exacerbates this identity crisis. Indeed, globalization poses an unprecedented challenge to identity. Life in an open society where boundaries are being erased challenges customary social structures and stable forms of collectivity shaped within the framework of a divided world that formed people's understanding of social order, security and the establishment of their personal lives. Globalization poses a challenge to the sovereignty of the national state, to its currency, borders, citizenship, administrative independence and cultural autonomy. In many functions, these institutions are being replaced by transnational structures which establish the conditions for a globalized environment. Many people are not prepared to accept these new structures as determining their actions.

It is only the minority in various societies that operates actively with such global resources as information, finances, higher education, high technology, professional qualifications, innovations, free-market relations and foreign languages. Most people cannot take advantage of these resources and incorporate them into the structure of their action; many simply do not know how to do so. These people see globalization as an external force in which they cannot participate and over which they have no control.

Their attitude toward globalization is based on a sense of insecurity about their future and fear of threats against their common (national, ethnic and cultural) identities.

One issue that exercises numerous small and peripheral countries, including Latvia, is whether participation in globalization and the benefits of an open world will allow for the preservation of the Latvian identity and traditional values with which Latvia differs from other states and nations.

This question is of interest both to those actively involved in globalization and to those who watch from the sidelines.

Zygmunt Bauman has described identity as a dream from which the bourgeoisie has not yet awoken, but which the masses have already forgotten. Bauman is not the only sociologist who has considered the ambivalence of identity. Other theorists define identity as a sense of belonging to a group, a nation, a place or a religion. Yet others stress the difference between identity of *me* and identity of *us*. Researchers in the field of individual identities devote much attention to gender, the body, autobiography and life crises, while sociologists tend to focus more on interaction between identity and environment. The anthropologist Frederik Barth has written that in the process of identification people draw boundaries and identify the *we* group on this side and the *others, them* and *aliens* on the other (Barth, 1969). Nationalism theories add to this analysis, shedding light on group relations, stereotypes and fears of strangers. Some theories view identity as an ethnic and linguistic issue, while others include politics and even technologies in the mix. In the mid-twentieth century, theories of structural functionalism claimed that identities arise from history, but contemporary action theories are more likely to propose that identities actively shape society.

Over the last decade identity has been subject to intense sociological debate, and the upper hand has been gained by those who see identity as something which people establish themselves. People choose the content of their identity in order to justify their actions and to establish societies which meet their objectives. This is possible if we accept that the road towards the future leads through identity and action.

8.1 Identity as a postulate

'Though all too often hypostasised as an attribute of a material entity, identity has the ontological status of a project and postulate. To say "postulate identity" is to say one word too many', writes Zygmunt Bauman. In post-modern times, the catchwords of identity are activity, project and creation. This fairly radical approach to identity allows Bauman to analyse identity as a tool, an instrument and a core project. According to this approach, individual action is built around an identity-opportunity axis. What Talcott Parsons called the action frame of reference – predominantly fixed institutions, norms and relations which determined social action – now has become the dynamism of an agent based on his or her identity and perception of opportunity.

The postulated identity is an acting one. It acts and moves at the same time, it never stops or settles, and it is forever changing location. Bauman elaborates this 'mobility argument' by adding the observation that flexibility makes identities unreliable, and their stories cannot be trusted (Bauman, 1998b). This is a highly paradoxical outcome: the mobile identity may well be detached from the autobiography, which has always been considered a safe domain for individual identity. The best place to consider one's identity is in a transcontinental aeroplane, when time and direction have become confused and one is flying to a city which, in one's memory, is confused with other cities. Thus one comes to understand that identity is travelling. It hangs in the air, and there are many places for it to land.

In the early twentieth century Simmel divided social actors into friends, enemies, strangers, competitors, flirters, wasters, the noble, the adventurous and the poor. He did not, however, list the greatest hero of our time – the traveller. The traveller is no longer the isolated decadent who populated the Berlin salons of Simmel's time.

Today he or she is a purposeful adventurer, a violator of borders who travels from city to city and from country to country. Today's traveller can be an entrepreneur, a risk taker, a manager of an international company who moves the economy and enables the global markets. A traveller can also be the crosser of ethnic, cultural and lifestyle boundaries within a society, the agent of an open society who tears down prejudices and feels free to engage in various groups. However, identity can also be considered in a completely different situation – when you are relaxing in a warm bath or standing in a field and watching an aeroplane fly past you on a quiet evening. This situation reminds us that in addition to travel, an identity also needs a stop, a home, and it longs for some sort of final destination.

As a postulate, identity nurtures activity. Thomas Luckmann and Peter L. Berger have written:

> The world of everyday life is not only taken for granted as reality by the ordinary members of society in the subjectively meaningful conduct of their lives. It is a world that originates in their thoughts and actions, and is maintained as real by these (Berger and Luckmann, 1966: 19-20).

In the post-modern and globalizing society, reality is constructed even more actively via different identity acts and projects, and there are fewer and fewer social areas which are taken for granted.

8.2 Transition towards individuality

Research into agency in post-socialist societies suggests that identity actively drives social change and influences the emergence of new social structures and relationships which reflect the desires and efforts of people towards what they want to become (Tisenkopfs, 1995). People today usually want to be different, and identification is manifested mostly as individualisation. The yearnings of individualism increase, values are aimed at individual self-satisfaction and the self-fulfilment represented by new lifestyles. The significance of traditional social relations and the influence of major groups such as class and nation are forced to recede. It might be said that identity is regrouping in the direction of individuality. Culture, ethnicity, nationality, and state are no longer collective dogmas which people must follow. Rather, they are optional forms of sociation which individuals establish themselves. The ties of collectivity and solidarity are no longer inherited directly under these circumstances but are shaped in free association among individuals on the basis of their professional, political, leisure and other interests.

Latvia's history since the restoration of independence in 1991 has displayed a shift from ethnic nationalism, which inspired the independence movement, to a multiplicity of forms of identity, as well as to new forms of civic collectivity. The desire to pursue individual difference – to obtain and demonstrate specific individual identities and lifestyles which emphasise the unique nature of the person – is a far more powerful desire than the wish to nurture ties of solidarity. These efforts toward individualization are most commonly seen among the young, among the *nouveaux riches*, and among the emerging middle class in Latvia.

The restructuring of identity towards individualism in Central and Eastern European societies has been the inevitable result of the triumph of market capitalism and liberal ideology, as well as being a precondition for them. Individualization has also been fostered by the withdrawal of the state from the public scene. The return of individualism in post-socialist societies has been a means for these societies to return to the Western world (Lauristin and Vihalem, 1997), which is itself experiencing an upsurge in liberal democracy and individualism. Bourdieu (1998) argues that the return of individualism is a kind of self-fulfilling prophecy which tends to destroy the philosophical foundations of the welfare state and, in particular, the notions of collective responsibility and solidarity which were once the fundamental achievement of social thought. The shift toward individualism in the countries of Central and Eastern Europe until very recently when civil societies have started to emerge, has had no alternative, and it has been promoted by the processes of globalization, among other factors.

However, individualism has its limits, and these are set by the existence of a law-based state, as well as by the need for solidarity and social cohesion. The emergence of individualism involves the grevious problem of excessive egoism and intolerance at the expense of social cohesion and integrative relations in society. In Latvia, there are several such identity-related problems. One part of the population – usually those who are better off, more educated, belong to the elite groups and those who take advantage of the opportunities of globalization – care for themselves, and their identities are egoistic. In a society where inequality is on the rise, the egoism of 'haves' and their mobile identities tend to cement inequality with cultural and symbolic means. Another part of the population – usually the poor, 'have-nots' and those excluded from the processes of globalization – are not prepared to recognize a multiplicity of identities. These people long for broad and embracing collective identities which provide them with imagined sense of security. In Latvia these large-scale identities are most often expressed in ethnic form. Many people are unaccustomed to perceiving their identities in the plural, and some adhere to stereotypes of ethnicity, gender and other identities.

Never before in society has there been such a variety of identities; nor has there been such active effort to reach agreement on the basic principles of communal life at the national and global levels. People can freely choose large and small, ethnic and class-based, national and European, closed and open, inclusive and exclusive, friendly and unfriendly identities. The problem today is not a lack of identities; rather, it is a lack of tolerance. Every identity has value to the concrete individual. However, from the perspective of society what is important is social cohesion, which presupposes the inclusion of all members of society and access to opportunities for all. A harmonized society is one in which relationships among individuals are based on a balance between competition and co-operation, not on hate and permanent conflict. This introduces the important issue of the reciprocity of identities and solidarity in a social space.

8.3 Identity, time and space

Identity cannot exist in a vacuum. It needs a shared space in which to establish sympathy and friendship with other identities. Therefore identity is sensitive to the way in which the common space is arranged. The classics of sociology believed that social order is established if people include the central values of society in their actions.

This thesis is true if there are central values in the society. With regard to present-day Latvia there are few truly common values; individuals instead act feverishly and, usually, on their own. In this case, the social space can be analysed from an ethnomethodological perspective which focuses on the regular and reiterated common-sense procedures by which individuals interpret their behaviour. In this case order is shaped not by abstract norms such as 'democratic values', 'free market relations', and so on, but by the repeating of actions, attitudes and judgements. What occurs regularly and most frequently shapes the common space, and human understanding learns to accept it as a new social norm. Partisans of the rule of law can claim, for example, that corruption is a bad thing, but if a considerable number of people have learned that it makes sense to pay a bribe, then corruption becomes the public norm. Doctors and demographers can fret over the fact that the public health is affected by alcohol abuse, but if every fourth man goes to the store to buy vodka, alcohol becomes part of the structure of society. This logic of repetitiveness requires that good things happen in the common space.

The public space in Latvia (and it is no exception in the post-communist landscape), however, is conflicting, and repeated situations in it include scandals among the elite, violations of the norms of law, and alienation between society and administration. Many Latvians feel distanced from it, as if they were not to blame for these failures of an immature democracy. There is a shortage of positive repetition in the common space which would allow people to follow examples of successful development and the building of cohesive relations. There is a lack of critical thinking and participation that would help to structure public space more harmoniously. Is it any wonder that many identities feel lonely and have trouble in finding friendship?

Identities also need a favourable time. It is surprising how many people nowadays suffer from a lack of time, replenishing their space with scattered and, in the end, alienated activities. Identity requires time which people can spend for *themselves* and for *us*. There has to be time to take a walk, to read a book, to enjoy the autumn landscape. Time for love and slow friendship. Identities need time for *them* and *others* as well – to talk to the neighbour, to become involved in public organizations, to participate in community life and take part in all those tiny forms of common activity which strengthen solidarity. There is a lack of such time, skills and money which leads people into social isolation and weakens civil society. Relatives gather less frequently, choirs fall apart. Concerning Latvia, this is the metaphor of two million Latvians scattered across small towns, farms and forests who do not talk to one another. Perhaps this is their bitter Nordic identity and their strength.

Discussing the issues of late-modern society, Anthony Giddens has emphasised the importance of self-reflection in identity (Giddens, 1991). Reflection is the inner clock of identity, and it must keep time. If people only act, if they do not stop, if they run but do not reflect, their identities become fragile. They lose the ability to predict the consequences of their actions and to evaluate risk. A lack of self-reflection impedes people from perceiving the dangers hidden in every segment of risk society – it is one of the reasons for the growing number of traffic accidents. Accidents and traumas are examples of how the aggressiveness of common space and a lack of reflection on the part of the individual lead to dramatic consequences.

8.4 Money and identity

Individualism means that identity today is closely linked to money. Many go so far as to believe that money is the best form of identity. There are those who do not trust in any other identity projects than those that lead to money. Such individuals reject the verbal construction of self, in the belief that verbal identity, unlike money, has no value, and unlike style it has no appearance. For them identity is confusing or even senseless if it does not generate income.

Simmel wrote that money is an important form of human interaction, which must be fulfilled. If this form is empty (that is, if there is no money) there is reason to doubt whether fully vested social interactions among people exist (Simmel, [1907] 1978). The importance of money is proven by those who possess it. The world is changing, and every time it transforms, we have to buy a new entrance pass. That is why money is important – people need it to enter the world, to engage in reciprocal interactions, to become involved in events and relationships, to obtain and maintain their social status. Changes in society determine that money is needed without interruption, and in increasing amounts.

Simmel said that money is a pure quantity, so that its ideal resides in its amount. People want it all and at once. In a financial survey a banker, however, remarked concerning this ideal: 'That's wrong. People need money sufficiently, but without interruption.' The banker was right – it makes no sense to have all of the money, because one cannot participate in everything. The amount of money has to be commensurate with the aggregate of interactions in which an individual is involved. Then it ensures socialization and the widening of interactions.

Globalization is opening up new ways to earn money. To quote Thomas Friedman: 'The global marketplace today is an electronic herd of often anonymous stock, bond, currency and multinational investors, connected by screens and networks', and they can make a million dollars with a snap of their fingers in the stock exchange. Under conditions of globalization, however, not everyone can ensure an adequate increase in their cash flows, and subsequently sustain their social reproduction and the necessary amount of interactions. Many people lack the unique skill of obtaining and increasing wealth and are pushed into the backstage of society. These people are doomed to limited interactions and have little opportunity to nurture and demonstrate the latest lifestyles. Their social appearance is seen at the bread store, shopping quietly. They are the ones who inhabit the corners of society, where the trending developmental rarely manifests itself and where the difficult present is reproduced again and again.

Money is more powerful today than ever before, but it has changed its appearance, becoming invisible. It exists in electronic form as connections and communications. Money has become estranged from the traditional work and values. The way in which it is made nowadays has changed, and so have the human relations around monetary transactions. The traditional ways to obtain money – proper work based on Protestant ethics – are no longer the key ones. Those who wanted to increase their material welfare and build their futures on the basis of traditional work and values in post-communist society were quickly disenchanted and ended up poor. This has been exemplified in the harsh fates of the industrial proletariat in cities and the farmers in the countryside.

Contacts, communication, social and technical networks and *ad hoc* projects are the buzzwords when it comes to making money today. The interactions which money causes are changing. In order to make more money, people engage in more frequent and more varied contacts. Their interactions are shorter, more fragmented and aimed at rational efficiency. When money is earned in this way, people put together the most unimaginable forms and areas of action, and it is difficult to identify social action as a homogeneous and integrated act. A sociologist, for example, can simultaneously be involved in three different projects – one concerning biological farming, one on national identity and yet another on technological assistance to small businesses. The appetite for more money has caused an avalanche of new interactions – fragmentary and fevered – a new model of social action which is virtually a cocktail of purposeful behavioural acts but nonetheless never descends into chaos. The new type of social action is characterized by extreme purposefulness and a lack of time. Many people work at more than one job, they work on Saturdays and Sundays and at night. Some complain: 'I have to run around from one place to another'. Others occasionally send the e-mail message: 'I have bitten off more than I can chew'.

The hunger for more and more money has taken over modern man, and has nearly eliminated the ability to say *no* to new opportunities and chances. On the contrary, people try to take advantage of every chance that they come across, and it would be odd if they did not do so, because these are the chances of their lives which in society may not necessarily be fulfilled.

8.5 Identity and lifestyle

In addition to money and identity, style is the third basic form of life. Unlike the first two, it has a colour, a form, a smell, and it is visible. Style is the balance between money and identity which is difficult to accomplish. Style is the most difficult form of interaction, it requires both money and identity, but not every mix of both results in style.

The basic function of style is to give form to money and to materialize identity in meaningful signs that can be perceived. Style involves eating habits, the manner of speech, the colour of the necktie, fashion, powder and all of the other decorations with which people embellish reality.

Style requires two resources: money to buy and an identity to want. But there is a third resource: the time in which to spend the money, to buy and shape one's life according to one's intention.

Life is more than just money, and a pure time is not yet life unless a person is a philosopher. Those who have achieved a balance between money and time have achieved a good deal. They have sculpted their lives as pieces of art – as a harmony of money and time – and they recognize the value of their lives. In order to achieve this balance, they must have both greed and sentiment. Time comes and goes, leaving behind a specific sense of time – a bittersweet yearning. Those who have greed and melancholy, a passion for money and a longing for the time that is being lost, have a good chance of finding their own style.

All resources of style are limited, but what nowadays is in shortest supply is often not money but time and melancholic feelings; therefore contemporary style, which just like contemporary social action, is becoming eclectic and fragmented. In the early twentieth century the bouquet of style involved Art

Nouveau, Fauvism, Symbolism, Cubism, Expressionism and other forms of *avant garde*, and style was inspired by high culture. Today style is a form of individual self-expression which emerges, manifests itself and vanishes in everyday life. Style comes from life and is a form of life itself. It is born and it fades in the street, in stores, and in the occasional moments when people can be alone with themselves.

8.6 A new structure of identity?

The postulation of identity under conditions of globalization is one of the most difficult challenges facing individuals and entire nations today, because people are forced to strike a balance among fulfilment of their individual lives, their collective belonging, and their common survival in the open world. Globalization focuses attention on the future goals of identity, calling on people to restructure their identities in a way that includes in their structure not only 'traditional attributes', such as origin, language, ethnic background, and national belonging but also the new forces of globalization: technology, information, finances and the market. If ethnic identity is based on ethnic tradition, why cannot a 'globalized identity' be based on the skills to use information and communication technologies?

If identity is a unity of action which integrates knowledge, tradition, innovation, technology and the market, its achievements are rooted in the way in which individuals define their freedom and act correspondingly. If someone feels the spark of entrepreneurship, he or she can include means of production in the structure of his or her identity, mix them up with investment, cover it with the sauce of market relations, scatter a handful of risk over it and release it into the marketplace. The commodification of identity proves that there is someone to buy it. In global capitalism, the market specifies the value of identities, just like the value of commodities, and the value of identity is not determined by sweat or by history. If an identity is not in demand, it may have an inappropriate structure. Perhaps it has not been marketed well or maybe it lacks innovation, or it is based on out-of-date technologies. Or it may be too unique to reach the wider marketplace.

The issue here is whether the contemporary identity crisis – the one being experienced by the populations of peripheral nations – can be overcome by reconfiguring the structure of identity. Can the traditional ethnic, national and cultural confines of identity be expanded to include knowledge, innovation, risk, modern technologies and markets, without losing the solidarity, language and culture characteristic of every social and national community?

The story of identity has been a short one during the last decade. From contemplation of the past, identity is now a category of will, the future and action. The post-modern human condition recognizes action and achievement, and passiveness of identity becomes a burden. In order not to lose out people are seeking to liberate themselves and to reject limitations. The transformation of identity into life-achievement is a new identity practice which individuals, nations and other social agents are learning in the open world. Identity is a project called "life" and it is driven by creative action. Nothing in life is really mandatory. Everything is mere possibility, and identity links one opportunity to the next. Were people or nations born with predestined life courses, there would be no place for identity. Happily, the tracks of life are different, and identity keeps us on the right one.

Conclusion

In the perspective of the twenty-first century, identity is a new unity of tradition, language, knowledge, innovation, technology and market. Many peripheral countries are trying to postulate their national identity by adding to its construction exactly these decisive forces of globalization. The objective of these efforts is to utilize identity in order to achieve greater recognition for small countries in the world, to shape their image, to improve the competitiveness of national economies, and to achieve more rapid development. In Latvia, for example, in elaborating the country's development strategy the government has encouraged public discussion on national identity and its long-term objectives.

The opportunities created by globalization and sought by individuals and countries alike intensify the climate of competition in the world and change notions of what is valuable and desirable. Capital, resources and the entire economy are being transposed to intellectual ground. This increases the role of science and education. More and more people and nations associate their futures with education and technological development, which may compensate for a lack of traditional types of capital and serve as a basis for accelerated development.

Postulating identity in a globalized world means undertaking concrete innovation, overcoming barriers to action and establishing efficient mechanisms which enable achievement of development objectives. One of Latvia's strategic goals under discussion is to achieve a knowledge-based economy and society (UNDP, 1999b). A socio-economic model of this sort, as opposed to one of a country based on agriculture, light industry or transit, would ensure competitiveness for the national economy and the sustainability of human development.

Globalization typically entails the liberalization of trade, internationalization of market and production factors, an increase in direct foreign investments and heightened competition. These factors determine the transition to an economy based on research and technological output. Innovations and state policy that supports them become the essential driving forces of the economy.

In a small country with an open economy like Latvia, vigorous scientific and technological research and creative work are vitally important means to achieve competitiveness and protection. Sometimes they are called the 'new weapons' of the economy as tariffs, quotas and other means of market obstruction lose their former meaning under the conditions of globalization. Globalization offers rapid development opportunities to those countries opening up to the world market and which base their economies on scientific and technological research and innovations.

Latvia, like many other small and peripheral countries, is seeking a development strategy that is innovative and directed toward the future, and which would promote economic growth and sustainable human development. For peripheral states it is important to decide in which sectors to develop scientific and technological research and high-tech manufacturing, as a lack of resources often make it difficult to ensure support for all sectors. It is important to decide which sectors' development will be based on the procurement of technologies and linked with the consolidation of skilled labour, and in which sectors investments should be attracted, thereby promoting the co-operation of multinational corporations with local small, medium-sized and large companies.

Based on the analysis of globalization and human condition, it is possible to draw some conclusions about human development in peripheral states.

The government, the private sector and individuals are jointly responsible for the creation of a competitive economic structure in the country and for the successful advancement of human development. Co-operation between the government, non-governmental organizations and private companies is necessary to achieve greater influence on globalization processes and to obtain control over them. It should be remembered that the economic upswing of small countries has been based on a state policy that actively supports scientific and technological research and tertiary education. The opportunities of individuals to participate in globalization and their control over its processes are broadened by participation in social networks. People have greater possibilities of influencing technology, policies and the market if they are involved in non-governmental organizations and interest groups. Therefore, under the conditions of globalization, an active civil society is one of the most important preconditions for sustainable development.

The globalization opportunities of individuals must be fostered: their access to technology, information, knowledge and finances. Information and communications technologies must be made much more accessible. It is necessary to democratize information and technology. Human development would be advanced if each family had access to computers, the Internet and credit cards. These three resources not only make electronic commerce possible but also broaden the possibilities of obtaining information and education.

The ability of individuals to globalize must be developed, and they need to be trained how to use globalization resources (computers, modern technologies, finances, the Internet and new forms of acquiring knowledge and qualifications), so that they can use these resources to raise their standard of living, improve their education and qualifications, obtain work, tend to health-care needs and achieve consolidation of a civic society.

Primary globalization opportunities, which are associated with finances, capital, technology and labour, and secondary globalization opportunities, which are linked to information, knowledge and social contacts, must be used. As primary globalization opportunities are more limited and financial resources and capital are more difficult to come by, participation in globalization could be achieved by actively involving people in secondary globalization – training them how to use the latest information technologies, promoting education, fostering personal contacts and co-operation.

The democratization of finances is necessary alongside the increased welfare of society. The next step in the development of democracy is wider access to capital and credit to acquire an education, purchase property, make home improvements, and fulfil other needs. Small loans must be made more widely available, and individuals themselves should give more thought to personal savings and establishing pension capital.

In a globalized world, development will be more closely dependent on knowledge and education. Ensuring the education of the population, consolidation of the educational system and introduction of modern forms of study, also in the areas of adult education and retraining, are of primary importance. Policies on science and technological development must be established so that highly specialized technologies with high added value can be developed. More support should be given to science and research that fosters technological innovations and promotes growth in science-intensive production and service sectors.

The conditions of globalization also require the democratization of administration and increased public participation in it. In a free market, many organizations actively lobby the public authorities to take decisions in their favour. However, at times these decisions are geared to the satisfaction of corporate and egoistic interests, and no account is taken of public opinion in the decision-taking process.

Thus, it is possible to subjugate public interests to corporate interests, and this is dangerous for human development. In order to exclude this possibility, the transparency of decision-taking and public participation in the discussion of draft decisions and draft laws must be ensured. Broadened political networks, in which various organised interests are represented and which serve as a setting for dialogue, are one of the forms of policy-making and policy implementation under the conditions of globalization.

Bibliography

Albrow, M. (1997), *The Global Age*, Stanford University Press, Stanford.
Agger, B. (1998), *Critical Social Theories*, Westview Press, Boulder.
Barth, F. (1969), *Ethnic Groups and Boundaries: The Social Organisation of Culture Difference*, Little Brown, Boston.
Bauman, Z. (1996), 'From Pilgrim to Tourist', in S. Stuart and du P. Gay (eds), *Questions of Cultural Identity*, Sage, London, pp. 37-52.
Bauman, Z. (1998a), *Globalisation. The Human Consequences*, Polity Press, Cambridge.
Bauman, Z. (1998b), 'Identity – then, now, what for?', *Polish Sociological Review*, vol. 3, no. 123, pp. 205-16.
Beck, U. (2000), *What is globalisation*, Polity Press, Cambridge.
Berger, P.L. and Luckmann, T. (1966), *The Social Construction of Reality. A Treatise in the Sociology of Knowledge*, Doubleday, New York.
Bourdieu, P. (1998), *Acts of Resistance: Against the Tyranny of the Market*, The New York Press, New York.
Chomsky, N. (1999), *Profit over People. Neoliberalism and Global Order*, Seven Stories Press, New York.

Featherstone, M., Lash, S. and Robertson, R. (eds) (1995), *Global Modernities*, Sage, London.

Friedman, T.L. (1999), *The Lexus and the Olive Tree: Understanding Globalisation*, Farrar, Straus and Giroux, New York.

Gellner, E. (1992), 'Nationalism in the Vacuum' in J. Alexander (ed) *Thinking Theoretically about Soviet Nationalities*, Columbia University Press, New York, pp. 243-54.

Ghai, D. and Hewitt de Alcantara, C. (1995), *Globalisation and Social Integration: Patterns and Processes*. A policy paper commissioned by UNDP for the World Summit for Social Development, United Nations Research Institute for Social Development, Copenhagen.

Giddens, A. (1991), *Modernity and Self-Identity: Self and Society in the Late Modern Age*, Stanford University Press, Stanford.

Giddens, A. and Christopher, P. (1998), *Conversations with Anthony Giddens: Making Sense of Modernity*, Stanford University Press, Stanford.

Held, D., McGrew, A., Goldblatt, D. and Perraton, J. (1999), *Global Transformations*, Polity Press, Cambridge.

Inglehart, R. (1997), *Modernisation and Postmodernisation. Cultural, Economic and Political Change in 43 Countries*, Princeton University Press, Princeton.

Lauristin, M. and Vihalem, P. with Rosengren, K.E. and Waibull, L. (eds) (1997), *Return to the Western World. Cultural and Political Perspectives on the Estonian Post-Communist Transition*, Tartu University Press, Tartu.

Lijphart, A. (1984), *Democracy. Patterns of Majoritarian and Consensus Government in Twenty-One Countries*, Yale University Press, New Haven and London.

Pieterse, J.N. (1995), 'Globalisation as Hybridisation', in M. Featherstone, S. Lash and R. Robertson (eds), *Global Modernities*, Sage, London, pp. 45-68.

Robertson, R. (1996), 'Mapping the Global Condition: Globalisation as a Central Concept', in M. Featherstone (ed), *Global Culture: Nationalism, Globalisation and Modernity*, Sage, London, pp.15-30.

Sennett, R. (1998), *The Corrosion of Character. The Personal Consequences of Work in the New Capitalism*, Norton, London.

Simmel, G. ([1907] 1978), *The Philosophy of Money*, Routledge, London.

The World Bank (1997), *World Development Report 1997. The State in a Changing World*, Oxford University Press, New York.

Tisenkopfs, T. (1995), 'Search for the Centre in a Peripheral Society: A Case Study of Youth Identities in Latvia', *Nordic Journal of Youth Research*, vol. 3, no. 3, pp. 2-19.

Transparency International (1999), *Newsletter*, Transparency International, Berlin.

UNDP (United Nations Development Programme) (1998), *Latvia human Development Report 1998*, UNDP, Riga.

UNDP (United Nations Development Programme) (1999a), *Human Development Report 1999*, Oxford University Press, New York.

UNDP (United Nations Development Programme) (1999b), *Latvia human Development Report*, UNDP, Riga.

UNDP (United Nations Development Programme) (1999c), *Human Development Report for Central and Eastern Europe and the CIS 1999*, The Regional Bureau for Europe and the CIS, Bratislava.

Wallerstein, I. (1990), 'Societal Development, or Development of the World-System?', M. Albrow and E. King (eds), *Globalisation, Knowledge and Society*, Sage, London, pp. 157-72.

9 'Mind' and collective consciousness

STEVEN GROSBY

Introduction

The objects of sociological research are human associations, ranging from those of minimum social distance and relative temporal simultaneity, for example, the intra-generational primary group of friendship constituted by 'face to face' relations,[1] to those of maximum social distance and temporal duration that include past and future generations, for example, a territorially extensive society or even a civilization.[2] Various methods have been employed to investigate these associations, ranging from statistical correlations of data gathered from surveys created by investigators to comparative historical analyses that necessarily employ ideal-typical categories for the selection and organization of factual material.[3] This extensive variety of objects and methods has meant that the criteria demarcating sociology from anthropology, history, sometimes even biology, occasionally social philosophy and philosophical anthropology, and increasingly economics are blurred.

Rather than regretting a disciplinary state of affairs that might, for some, call into question the scientific nature of the discipline of sociology, it should be welcomed; for this blurring of subject matter and methodology may not indicate disciplinary immaturity, but rather indicate the complications involved in the study of human cognition and action, specifically the various attachments formed that are constitutive of respectively various associations. When it is asserted that sociology has only one object or only one method of investigation (as, for example, at times occurs with the theory of rational choice, which, with its assumption that all action is to be understood to be a result of the individual calculation of the most efficient means to the pursuit of the most pleasurable end among other ends that must be assumed to be comparable, collapses sociology into a branch of economics), then sociology

---

1   For the primary group, see Shils (1951).
2   See, for example, Eisenstadt (1963, 1986, 1996).
3   For a brief discussion of the methodological problems involved in comparative historical sociology, see Grosby (1995a).

257

risks wrongly simplifying the contrary tendencies of the human mind and, thus, the complexities of life.

One task facing sociology in the twenty-first century is to revive critically those earlier traditions of sociological analysis that refused to abjure the complexity of life as it is actually lived out of a misguided fidelity to the artificial simplism of a theoretical schema.

It is a task that requires a more realistic understanding of the human mind, its creations, and the bearing of both on collective consciousness and collective behaviour.

1. The tyranny of tradition

One recent expression of this tendency to simplify the complexity of life is the analysis of what is called 'globalization'. It has been argued that the undeniable international expansion of the market place and the technological advances that have made that expansion possible have resulted in a cultural uniformity among all those who have been able to purchase the goods and services offered in the international market. It has thus been concluded that the boundaries between national states and even civilizations and the previously culturally specific patterns of conduct implied by those very boundaries have become increasingly irrelevant as a new international culture has emerged.

Arising to take the place of 'vertical' boundaries between national states, so the argument goes, are so-called 'horizontal' boundaries that putatively demarcate a new cultural uniformity among previously distinct, but now economically similar, strata of national populations that are able to participate directly in the international market place.

This putative breaking up of national cultures is what appears to be meant when increasing numbers of social scientists use the term 'globalization'.

Whatever the undeniable merits of this argument, the impartial observer cannot fail to recognize significant and ubiquitous counter-developments. Ethnic and national attachments, for example, have not yet been undermined by cross-national 'interests' arising from participation in the international market, including, significantly, those areas of the world where an international market for goods and services is most developed, that is, in the industrially and technologically advanced Occident; for example, the devolution of Scotland from the United Kingdom, and such movements of secession as that of Quebec from Canada and Euzkadi from Spain.

To be sure, the situation is contradictory, perhaps as never before, with the European Union as the example of a developing transnational formation, albeit a hesitant one, containing, as it does, conflicting national loyalties.[4] Such a contradictory situation – where relatively rational and rationalizing tendencies co-exist with tendencies that are parochial – is not, in fact, new; rather, it seems historically to be the norm. One recalls, for example, the *Pax Romana,* or Christian Europe of the twelfth century with its canon law when all of Western Europe was, at least in principle, subject to the jurisdiction of the Roman curia as the tribunal of last resort, or the French-speaking royal houses throughout the Europe of the seventeenth and eighteenth centuries – all three of these trans-national examples co-existing with the emergence and consolidation of distinct national cultures in Europe. While the expansiveness of the market is as never before, it nevertheless appears that the rush among many sociologists to embrace 'globalization' as an analytic rubric descriptive of the Occident at the beginning of the twenty-first century may be overly hasty and simplistic.

This simplism that views the Occident and increasingly the world to be culturally homogeneous as globalization putatively sweeps aside various traditions seems, perhaps paradoxically, to be a result of the tyranny of tradition. It is not the tyranny of the tradition of a particular national culture that confines the mind; but rather the tyranny of a particular sociological theory, namely, the theory of the historical movement from, using Tönnies' terms, *Gemeinschaft* to *Gesellschaft,* or, as Henry Sumner Maine (1970: 165) formulated this theoretical perspective, 'a movement from Status to Contract'. Thus, for this influential tradition of sociological analysis, this 'contrast may be most forcibly expressed by saying that the unit of ancient society was the family, of a modern society the individual' (Maine, 1970: 121).[5] As analytical categories designating different patterns of conduct, *Gemeinschaft* and *Gesellschaft* are clearly heuristically useful. Indeed, the analytical clarification and further differentiation of Tönnies' distinction – the so-called pattern variables – was and remains an important contribution of

4   Existing alongside such legal developments as a policy of open borders among members of the European Union are, for example, the French immigration and citizenship laws of 1993 that further restricted both immigration and the right to citizenship, and the recent amendments to Article 16 of the German Basic Law that curtailed the right to asylum in Germany. Attention should also be paid to such recent ominous, nationalistic developments within the European Union as the electoral victories of Jean-Marie Le Pen's National Front in Southern France and the growth of Joerg Haider's Freedom Party in Austria.
5   For an example of a forceful, recent expression of this theoretical tradition, see Coleman (1990).

Talcott Parsons' and Edward Shils' *Toward a General Theory of Action* to sociological theory. However, as an empirically valid description of an unequivocal and ubiquitous development of human collectivities, the distinction between the historically earlier and religiously infused *Gemeinschaft* and the later and putatively secularized *Gesellschaft* should be rejected as antiquated, as a relic of a previous theoretical perspective that has been rendered invalid by subsequent historical developments.

The most manifest of these developments, evident at the beginning of the twenty-first century, are two. The first is the persistence of religious attachments – a persistence described increasingly by some as 'fundamentalism'. One has the sense that some have employed the term fundamentalism in an effort to imply a condition of abnormality that has arisen as a compensatory response to the allegedly unique, massive dislocations of modern life. Such an overly facile interpretation represents an obstacle to a better understanding of the significance of the persistence of religion at the beginning of the twenty-first century. The second development is the persistence of ethnicity and nationality not only in Asia and Africa, but also in the Occident – a persistence that indicates the resilience, however susceptible to transformation, of the attachment to the primordial objects that bear the significance of vitality: territory and varying structures of kinship. The fact that in the last several years there has been a proliferation of journals, books, and series of books devoted to ethnicity, nationality, and religion bears witness to the scholarly recognition of their persistence. Nevertheless, despite this recognition, which could scarcely be avoided any longer, theoretical perspectives still dominate the human sciences which, in fact, deny or seek to deny the realities of this persistence.

Rather than viewing *Gemeinschaft* and *Gesellschaft* as designating pluralistic patterns of conduct that overlap in various ways, as providing the analytical tools to interpret the complicated relation between primordial attachments and those that are relatively rational and universal, the prevailing theoretical apparatus remains a simplistic one that too often views human action today as being entirely within the category of *Gesellschaft*, and, as such, homogeneous. Here, there would seem to be a convergence between a historical analysis that views human action today as being uniform – characterized variously as organic solidarity (Durkheim), *Kürwille* (Tönnies), or market-oriented – and a methodological requirement that must view all action and orientation as being uniform, specifically as being utilitarian. To be sure, many researchers may now be critical of the earlier evolutionary perspective of a Maine, Durkheim, or a Tönnies; nonetheless, many of the assumptions of that theoretical perspective are held firmly today by those researchers. Such is, after all, the theoretical perspective, often unacknowledged, of such widely-embraced analytical rubrics as 'secularization' and 'modernity'. Moreover, this theoretical perspective has also exerted considerable influence on social and political philosophy. For example, the so-called 'argument between the ancients and the moderns' is a distinction that implies that life today is made up entirely of individuals pursuing the maximization of their own individual pleasure. It is a most overwrought distinction.[6] For the theoretical understanding of human action and society to develop further, sociology must view critically such categories as 'modernity'.

2. Mind and the ambiguity of interest

These preliminary comments, which reject an understanding of human action and association as uniform in favour of a recognition of a plurality of incommensurable orientations and associations, are not to be taken as a denial of the likelihood of an elemental behavioural mechanism of the individual avoidance of pain. The subject matter of sociology, however is not preoccupied exclusively with what we have in common with rats, for example; rather, it is preoccupied with the consequences of the existence of the human mind, irrespective of whether or not those consequences are 'emergent properties', and whose imaginary capacities enable it to lay claim to elements of the past as relevant to the present, to lay claim to a vision of the future as a concern of the present, and to lay claim to the image of a past, present, and future of one individual as in some way capable of being shared by another.[7]

---

6 More than sixty years ago, Frank Knight (1982: 84-6), the central figure, if not the founder, of the 'Chicago School of Economics' pointed out the fundamental error of this theoretical tradition that has been most ably represented by Knight's own students, 'the most important single defect, amounting to a fallacy, in liberal individualism as a social philosophy ... is that [it] takes the individual as given ... This is a fundamental error ... From the standpoint of sociology, liberalism is more "familism" than literal individualism. Some sort of family life, and far beyond that, some kind of wider primary group and culture-group life must be taken as they are, as data ... The revolutionary liberals were excessively rationalistic'.

7 As far as this 'sharing' of meaning is concerned so that there exists consensus or collective self-consciousness, I accept such distinctions as that of Frege (1966: 59) between an 'idea' that an individual has of an object and in which the individual has an 'interest', hence often saturated with his or her own feelings, on the one hand, and an object's 'meaning' which is held in common in the mind of each of many individuals, hence 'objective', on the other.

If one collapses the tasks of sociology into those exclusively concerned with the elemental behavioural mechanism of the avoidance of pain and the maximization of pleasure, then one wrongly rejects, or will not be able to understand properly, such pain-seeking orientations as asceticism – especially those pain-seeking ascetic actions on behalf of others – unless one indulges the tautological argument that by seeking pain, one maximizes one's pleasure. The response of the behaviourist to this criticism is that one may choose to sacrifice – an act of ascetic disavowal – an immediate pleasure in the expectation that, by so doing, a greater, future pleasure will be achieved. But, then, how is one to explain, on the basis of such a calculation, decisions and actions as those described in 1 Maccabees 2: 29-38 where Jews chose to die rather than profane the Sabbath by fighting (Burkert, 1998: 7). To be sure, such actions are not those of everyday behaviour; although such actions, which are motivated by ideas about what constitutes a right order, are characteristic of those persistent phenomena, nationality and religion, of the twentieth century that require explanation. Such actions highlight the limitation of a behavioural explanation of human behaviour that excludes motivations for action other than the maximization of one's own pleasure.[8]

Moreover, if one reformulates the behaviour of pain-avoidance and pleasure-seeking as that of the preservation of life (or an 'interest' in the preservation of life), then, as Max Scheler observed, complications immediately arise because of the various ways in which the imaginative capacity of the mind understands that preservation, for example, as the perpetuation of one's own life through one's descendants, or as the preservation of a (often understood as the best) part of life either as a contribution on behalf of humanity or the salvation of the soul. Thus, if we pursue one step further the consequences of the individual's 'interest' in the preservation of his or her life, we see that the individual has an 'interest' in kinship (the family and, although there are theoretical problems here the details of which must be worked out, ethnicity and nationality) and an 'interest' in religion, for example, an interest in everlasting life. These latter considerations pose point-blank a number of theoretical problems at the beginning of the twenty-first century, precisely because of the persistence of those symbolic complexes that are constitutive of ethnicity, nationality, and religion. These theoretical problems are by no means new.

Such problems are similar to those posed by Talcott Parsons (1938) when

---

8   Note however that Mattathias' subsequent decision to fight, if necessary, on the Sabbath (1 Maccabees 2: 39-41) can be adequately accounted for on the basis of the theory of rational choice or some variant of it.

he raised the question, 'How are we to account theoretically for the role of nonempirical existential ideas (which are, for example, constitutive of nationality and religion) in human action?'. Parsons' question, and his answer to it that affirmed the relatively independent reality of such ideas as causes of action, imply that the achievements of the mind, once they are elevated out of the behavioural stream of life, that is, objectivated, take on an existence of their own – an existence to which human cognition and action may be subsequently directed.[9] Furthermore, once one puts aside consideration of the development of the objectivated achievements of the mind out of the tensions or anxieties of life, one is confronted with the fact that to be human is to orient one's actions to or out of consideration of these objectivated achievements. One takes an 'interest' in them. In the recent theoretical traditions of phenomenology and philosophical anthropology, this character of human consciousness has been described in various ways: by Husserl (1977) and Schutz (1973) as an essential property of the ego to have systems of intentionality; by Freyer (1999) as man is a detour-making animal; by Scheler (1961) as man is open to the world, a being capable of taking an ascetic attitude toward the reality of life;[10] by Cassirer (1996) as man, *qua* human, has a will to formation. Karl Popper (1972: 106-90) referred to this relatively autonomous realm of the objectivated achievements of the mind to which the individual orients himself and in which he participates as 'World Three', where 'World One' is the physical world, and 'World Two' is the psychic or psychological world. All of these descriptions of human consciousness agree that there is a cognitive and evaluative component to behavioural orientation; or, in the vocabulary of Parsons' and Shils' *Toward a General Theory of Action*, the 'cathectic mode of action' is empirically inseparable from the cognitive. This means that our actions in the physical 'World One' are, in varying degrees, influenced by our psychological 'World Two' grasp of, our 'interest' in, the geistige 'World Three'. In other words, through the cognitive acts of generalization and discrimination involved in the intentionality toward an object, 'World Three' (or, more accurately, various realms of World Three each with its own horizon of meaning) 'encompasses' 'World One'.

9   To recognize objectivated symbolic complexes and their influence on human action does not invalidate the proper principle of methodological individualism, although it does complicate our understanding of the distinctiveness of individually centered deliberation and action. See Grosby (1995b), Freyer (1999).

10   See also Gehlen (1988).

3. Mind and rationalization

The bearing of these anthropological and philosophical observations on sociology is crucial to a proper understanding of the complexities of human action and cognition. The most fundamental postulate of sociology is that human actions are limited or determined by the 'environment': human beings become what they are at any given moment under the pressures of circumstances which delimit their range of choice and which also fix their objectives and the standards by which they make choices. These choices are determined also by their passions and their interests, and they are also assimilated from the patterns presented by the culture in which they have lived. When one frees oneself to the extent that one can, and acts rationally, all one can do is to pursue one's own interest. This interest lies in the maximization of one's own advantages, the advantages being conceived as wealth, power, or some pleasure (Shils, 1985). This complex idea is at the heart of sociological thought; and it indicates the range of merit of such theoretical perspectives as 'rational choice' and 'sociobiology'.

However, to be human is to be able to disengage or to become independent to some degree from the environment, thereby creating a new environment, or, more accurately, multiple, new environments as described, for example, by Max Weber in *Religious Rejections of the World and Their Directions*. That is precisely what the worlds of, for example, history, religion, art, and science signify: various environments of objective mind, of what Popper called 'World Three'. To be human is further to be able to reflect critically upon these different environments, subjecting them to various standards created or perhaps discovered by the imaginative capacity of the mind. Thus, these various environments, which although products of the imagination are neither phantasms nor imaginary, are, as such, susceptible in varying degrees to being rationalized. This susceptibility to rationalization indicates that there is an ordering principle as an *a priori* property of the mind.[11]

However, these various environments are rationalized not according to one standard as postulated by the theory of rational choice or the preferential calculus of the theory of economic behaviour; rather, they are rationalized

---

11   This paper takes no position on the epistemological status of this rationalizing tendency. Left unanswered is whether this tendency indicates a kind of platonic conception of mind where the mind uncovers or discovers criteria (concepts), as argued by Kurt Gödel (1995: 320-33) ('concepts form an objective reality of their own, which we cannot create or change, but only perceive and describe'); or where the mind creates criteria as seems to be argued by Michael Friedman (1991). The answer to this problem has no necessary bearing on the objective existence of concepts and the latter's influence on human action.

according to the categorial principle that is central to each environment. For example, it is inappropriate to pose the question of the truth value of a judgement as one does in science when examining the appreciation of a work of art. To formulate the same point differently: language refers not only to segments of reality that are accessible to empirical verification but also to those symbolic configurations which, as objects of contemplation, influence human action and are inaccessible to verification, for example, the Garden of Eden or Heaven (Burkert, 1998: 25). This last point deserves to be repeated: the end of this rationalizing or ordering capacity, where the mind seeks – to employ the term of Edward Shils – a 'centre', is not uniform across various fields of content, but rather varies according to the respectively various meaningful centres of each field of content. It is a drive for coherence of the environment or world of meaning at any particular time, given the constitutive categorial principle or principles of the specific environment at that time. As is well known, the recognition of categorially specific rationalizations is found in the work of Simmel, Weber, Husserl, Freyer, Schutz, and many others. Its significance for understanding the complexities of human action has occasionally been obscured by the incorrect theoretical assumption that this underlying principle of mind has resulted in a uniformity of all fields of human conduct.

Not only are the orientations of the mind that result in various environments or 'worlds' of meaning heterogeneous, but the rationalization or drive to coherence of each of many particular environments is limited. It is limited not only by the existence of these other environments – what Max Weber in *Science as a Vocation* referred to as the eternal struggle between the old gods; the degree or extent of rationalization may also be limited by considerations internal to each environment. Thus, for example, in the environment of law, the drive to rationalize the law according to one principle may be limited as a result of the existence of another principle: for example, the tension arising between conceptions of formal and substantive justice. In the environment of religion, the drive for logical consistency may, given the categorial principles of an omniscient and omnipotent deity, result in an overly transcendent, predestinarian monotheism. However, this particular drive for coherence in the world of religion may be limited by the inexpungeable and relatively rational expectation that to one degree or another human beings are capable of influencing their own salvation. This limitation of the degree of rationalization of a particular environment or world of meaning has been obscured by an unwarranted emphasis placed on, and an uncritical acceptance of Weber's writings on bureaucratization, often perceived to be uniform and ubiquitous, in contrast to Weber's more subtle and accurate treatments of the tensions or the antinomies contained within the categorially distinct rationalization of a particular environment or world, for example, that of law or religion.

4. Mind and nationality

It is also likely that such an antinomy or tension exists in nationality as it is constituted around a complex of two meaningful orientations: one being a primordial orientation of kinship; the second being a rationalization through law that is conveyed structurally through the existence of the state. It appears that these two orientations co-exist with one another, not without tension, perhaps as differing levels of collective self-consciousness, constitutive of the nation. An indication of the tensions present among these differing constitutive levels and the limits they place on one another are laws of immigration and citizenship – laws that vacillate between the limiting criteria of kinship and the expansive criteria of legal rights as the latter are subjected to the rationalizing criterion of consistency.

The symbolic complex containing these two meaningful orientations of the mind that are constitutive of nationality vary from one nation to another as greater weight is, in one instance, accorded to one of the orientations at the expense of the other. For example, Japan is an example of greater weight being accorded to the primordial orientation of kinship;[12] while the United States would be an example of greater weight being accorded to the order established through law.

In trying to understand better the relation between these two orientations, one must be careful not to fall victim to a variation of the historical schema of *Gemeinschaft* (kinship) as an initial condition that is followed by *Gesellschaft*; for it is historically quite likely that a relation of kinship may be attributed to a territorially relatively extensive collectivity whose expansiveness is a consequence of the application of a relatively rational legal code.[13] Finally, sociologists should view with scepticism the widely held

---

12   See, for example, van Wolferen (1990: 163-9, 202-4).
13   It is strikingly curious that in his analysis of ethnicity and nationality, Weber (1978: 342, 366) abandoned the rich complexity of his classification when he relegated the shared awareness constitutive of ethnicity and nationality to simply being a response to economic competition. It appears that Weber (1978: 389) did not ponder the significance of his own incisive observation that 'almost any association, even the most rational one, creates an overarching communal consciousness; this takes the form of a brotherhood on the basis of the belief in common ethnicity'.

view that nationality is exclusively a modern phenomenon (Hastings, 1997; Grosby, 1991; Smith, 1998). In ancient, medieval, and modern societies there are examples of relatively extensive yet bounded territories; the rule of law; and the attribution of kinship to those who dwell in that land and who are subject to that law (Grosby, 1995c, 1997).

Thus, Weber's forms of social action and legitimate domination should be not viewed within a framework of a uniform historical development from *Gemeinschaft* to *Gesellschaft*; nor should an analysis of, for example, the rationalization of law or religion overlook the limits of the rationalization of either. That is, as Weber saw, one should not overlook the apparent antinomies or tensions involved as these environments or worlds of meaning are rationalized, or made more consistent along the lines of their central, constitutive, categorial proposition or set of propositions.

These and other observations rightly complicate our understanding of the historical expressions of the heterogeneous orientations of the mind. The mistake of ignoring or denying the existence of the multiple, heterogeneous orientations of the mind, their respectively heterogeneous worlds of meaning, and, as Parsons argued, the bearing of the latter on action became all too apparent at the end of the twentieth century when sociologists stumbled over themselves as they attempted to account for the persistence of what they had once confidently predicted would no longer exist.

Nevertheless, it would, once again, be a mistake if the recognition of these multiple, heterogeneous environments or worlds of meaning led one to reject the postulate fundamental to sociology that human actions are limited or determined by the environment. It would, once again, also be a mistake if the recognition of these multiple environments led one to reject the behavioural assumptions fundamental to economic theory and the theory of rational choice.[14] However, both this postulate and these powerful theories require qualification if they are to take into account such sociologically significant facts at the beginning of the twenty-first century as the persistence of ethnicity, nationality, and religion. Understanding these complications requires: a better and more realistic understanding of mind, both the mind of the individual and the objectivated achievements of the mind; the recognition

---

14 As many have observed, one may agree with Parsons that ideas which have bearing on human action are culturally given, but still recognize that the action influenced by these ideas conforms to a calculus of maximizing preference. Nevertheless, these various, more nuanced attempts to reconcile the criterion of predictability with the explanatory tradition of *Verstehen* have generally overlooked or still deny the conflicts between different worlds of meaning and the limit of the degree of rationalization within each particular world. For an overview of some of the problems involved, see Salmon (1989: 394-9), Boudon (1993a), and especially Boudon (1993b).

and affirmation of those achievements by both the individual and a number of individuals such that they become shared; and a better understanding of the different environments or worlds of meaning and the orientations of the mind responsible for them as to why they not only exist but also persist. Such complications have in the past been understood as the distinctive task of sociology: namely, to understand how it is that a 'we' and a number of different groups exist, or, as Simmel formulated one aspect of this task, 'How is society possible?'.

5. Mind and human associations

The existence of objective mind, variously understood, has long been recognized by sociological theorists.[15] When Durkheim (1974) spoke about 'society' and 'collective representations' as *'sui generis' f*acts that existed external to the mind of any particular individual, he was speaking about objective mind – a recognition which, incidentally, Durkheim held while rightly maintaining the principle of methodological individualism that this reality external to the mind of any particular individual could only be expressed through individual minds. When Simmel in many of his writings referred to 'forms' and 'separate provinces or worlds of meaning', he was referring to objective mind. When in the *Introduction to the Polish Peasant in Europe and America*, W. I. Thomas (1927: 149) wrote about the existence of 'social opinion self-conscious', he was referring to objective mind. When Charles Horton Cooley in *Social Process* (1966: 4-7) argued that there existed 'impersonal forms of life that are organized along lines other than those of personal consciousness', he was speaking about objective mind. When Max Weber recognized that ideas can be the cause of action, he recognized objective mind. And when Weber (1978:19) distinguished the meaning of mathematical reasoning or a rational deliberation about the results of a proposed course of action in promoting certain specific ends from the 'psychic' or 'mental', he also demarcated a realm of objective mind. Perhaps the most differentiated analysis of objective mind, freed from those assumptions of Hegel that limited its analytical rigour, was that of Hans Freyer (1999).

Particularly useful for the study of human associations was Freyer's analysis of the form of objective mind that he designated as a 'social relation',

---

15   For a philosophical treatment of the problem, see Popper (1972: 153-90), Collingwood (1924), and, of course, Hegel (1971).

examples of which are nations, religious denominations, or, indeed, customs. Consider the example of the custom of greeting another individual with a handshake. Two individuals, each with their own interests, happen upon one another. So far, these two individuals are 'interacting'. However, as one extends his or her hand to the other, these two individuals are no longer interacting; they are now 'participating' in a custom of greeting, the meaning of which exists independently of the action of execution; and, in the sense that they 'find' that custom and its meaning already existing, the custom is objective. Even though there is this objectivity, the material of the social relation of the custom of greeting is made up of living human beings who make actual the custom by performing it; its existence, in contrast to, for example, a book, is dependent upon this performance. Thus, the form of objective mind described as the social relation has a dual character: it is at the same time both an inter-individual phenomenon (the two individuals making actual the custom) and a trans-individual phenomenon (the meaning of the custom in which the two individuals participate). The social relation is simultaneously an inter-individual and trans-individual phenomenon.

All human associations, the subject matter of sociology, such as a nation have this dual character of the social relation. They are, on the one hand, forms of life, structures of living human beings, who must fit into the order of the association and who must always make anew this order – hence the marked susceptibility to change exhibited by human associations in contrast to other forms of objective mind like a book or a tool or a work of art – so that the association becomes actual. The objective elements of the nation are its meaningful traditions constitutive of kinship that individuals must make anew through reaffirmation (and, through the process of reaffirmation, modified) so that the nation 'becomes actual', that is, continues to exist. If those traditions are not reaffirmed, then the nation risks breaking up; it may cease to exist.

It may be that the individual decision to affirm, that is, to participate in a tradition (in the above example, the custom of extending one's hand when greeting a person), can be understood as conforming to the principles of rational choice. Likewise, it may be the case that the individual decision to reaffirm or not reaffirm (the decision to emigrate) the traditions constitutive of a nation may be so understood. In both instances, the ends of the action are already given. The givenness of such ends is a common enough recognition of the limitation of the explanatory power of the theory of rational choice. However, other and more complicated problems have been posed: the existence of heterogeneous orientations which, as heterogeneous, limit the explanatory power of a putative relative ordering of outcomes; the extent to which those orientations and their ends may be understood as conforming to the postulates of rational choice; and the limitation of the degree of rationalization within each orientation.

6. Mind, pluralism, and rational choice

These observations raise several problems that require a solution, however tentative. Can the recognition of heterogeneous orientations of the mind that are objectivated into the symbolic configurations constitutive of respectively heterogeneous environments or worlds of meaning be brought into line with a modified understanding of the theory of rational choice and a certain understanding of rationality, albeit a broader one similar to the one argued by Boudon? (1993a, 1993b). And can the postulate fundamental to sociology as to human beings, being both products and victims of the society in which they live, be reconciled with the imaginative capacity of the mind to create environments which may then be further transformed by the mind? Furthermore, if one rejects the currently prevalent naive historicism as represented by such fashionable analytic rubrics as 'globalization', 'secularization' and 'modernity', then how is one to understand the persistence, albeit with considerable variation, of those orientations of the mind that are expressed in, for example, nationality and religion?

An initial approach to these problems may perhaps be found by adapting Simmel's (1918) *Lebensphilosophie* to a recognition of the pluralistic orientations of the mind.[16] Throughout his work but increasingly so towards the end of his life, Simmel asserted the existence of 'inner needs' or 'impulses of life' or 'fundamental dispositions'. However, for Simmel, these various needs, impulses, or dispositions were not reducible to a single one, for example, centred on the individual through the individual's pursuit of self-interest or maximization of his or her own pleasure. They were, in contrast, expressions of qualitatively different states of being. The latter were seen as a consequence of a differentiated human nature: specifically, the human capacity to divide oneself into subject and object,[17] that is, the human capacity to disengage oneself from the immediate environment, including the

---

16   For other recognitions of these pluralistic orientations, see Weber (1946), Shils (1957), and Oakeshott (1991).

17   The recognition of the human capacity to separate oneself into subject and object, for self-consciousness, is, of course, by no means new. It is, for example, the implication of Genesis 3. There is no need, however, to hold to an assumption of a state of original unity that has been subsequently torn asunder.

environment of the individual's own instinctual apparatus.[18] Because this latter capacity of the mind conveys the potential for the formation of meaning (that is, order), we can agree with Simmel that there exists a metaphysical tendency within the individual as an integral part of the human psyche.

The recognition of such orientations that are fundamental to life may represent an essentialism. It is, however, a modified essentialism because the approach seeks to take into account those contradictory developments so manifest at the end of the twentieth century: on the one hand, the international expansion of the market for goods and services, and the apparently attendant movements toward trans-national legal codes; yet, on the other, the persistence of ethnicity, nationality, and religion.

There are three orientations of life. The first is the propagation, transmission, and preservation of life that, following Edward Shils (1957), is to be designated as primordial. The second is the spontaneous character of life that is designated as freedom. The third is the orientation of life towards order. These three orientations of life are manifested in various *geistige* environments or structures of meaning that permeate one another. Regarding the first orientation, the propagation and transmission of life is most clearly expressed in the structure of the family.

The second orientation, the spontaneous, voluntary character of life has been understood as being expressed through play (Huizinga, 1949: 3-13). However, the 'pretend' element of play indicates that this second orientation may be better understood as the capacity to disengage oneself from one's immediate environment, or as Huizinga formulated this capacity, 'when an influx of mind breaks down the absolute determinism' of the environment. This influx of mind would include the capacity for an ascetic stance towards life; that is, in the ability of the individual to say 'no' to any given state of affairs. Ultimately, this second orientation of life is represented by the concept of freedom.

The third orientation of life is the compulsion of the mind to seek a centre, to seek order. It is expressed by the quest for a meaning of life that finds various manifestations, for example, through law or, above all, religion.

This tripartite division can be reconciled with a modified version of the postulates of the 'avoidance of pain' or the 'pursuit of self-interest'. As indicated earlier, one may, for example, reformulate the postulate of 'the

---

18 Schleiermacher (1988) had argued for the existence of two orientations fundamental to the mind: one self-directed; the second externally directed and subject to variation, for example, to nature, to the various collectivities in which one was a member, or to a sense of the infinite.

avoidance of pain' as the individual's 'interest' in the preservation of his or her life, the latter understood as being manifested in the recognition of the primordial significance of vitality and its transmission, hence the individual's 'interest' in kinship. One may decide to sacrifice one's life on behalf of one's family or nation because of the belief in one's continued existence after death through the continued existence of one's family or nation. One's 'interest' in the continued existence of these primordial structures contains, as Frege noted, an element of subjective desire; but that 'interest' necessarily also contains an ideational element that channels the expression of that desire.

The cognitive orientation to order may be understood as a behavioural expression of the avoidance of pain, as one seeks to minimize the anxiety arising from a bewildering multitude of possibilities for action through the formation of order that excludes many possibilities for action. However, here, too, that behavioural expression is channelled along culturally given patterns – a channelling abetted by the institutions that bear that meaning of order. These modest suggestions as to how a recognition of a behavioural heterogeneity might be brought into line with a modified understanding of rational choice are obviously preliminary; and they owe much to the earlier arguments of Simmel, Weber, Parsons and Shils. The broader problem, as I see it, is whether or not the tradition that can be traced back to Plato of an understanding of a uniform orientation of life, but which is now represented – to be sure, with a different set of assumptions – by the view of *homo economicus*, should be maintained or abandoned.

A particular human association may contain a variable combination of the meaningful expressions of these orientations. The structure of the family is constituted by a meaning whose primary referent is the primordial one of vitality and its transmission. However, the national state, as previously observed, contains within its conceptual centre referents not only to vitality – nativity: *natio* – but also to order, for example, law. The consequence of this latter ordering element indicates that the national state has a capacity for a greater degree of rationalization than does the family. This difference in capacity has structural consequences. The structure of the family has remained relatively unchanged throughout the ages. However, for a national state – given, for example, the ordering postulate of 'the equality of human beings' – the structural expression of this postulate has in the Occident undergone a rationalization such that, as Edward Shils (1975a, 1975b) and S.N. Eisenstadt (1987:1-11) have correctly observed, the periphery of the national society has achieved a previously unheard of access to the centre. The conceptual vehicles for this diminution in the distinction between periphery and centre have been the extension of citizenship, democratic elections, and the rule of law. However, as pointed out previously, there is a limit to this rationalization and its structural expression, as may be observed in the continued existence of boundaries, and the inability of the centre to be entirely secularized. This is because the national state is not only a vehicle for the order of life, but it is also a vehicle for the sustenance and preservation of life.

This tripartite schema of the orientation of life and its bearing on the capacity for rationalization may also be observed in the world of religion. The so-called pagan religions of antiquity, insofar as they were nature religions that emphasised the primordial propagation and transmission of life, were relatively resistant to rationalization. The ethical, monotheistic world religions, with their greater but not exclusive emphasis on an order or meaning of life that transcends that of vitality are, in contrast, susceptible to greater rationalization. However, these orientations of life whose primary focus is a relatively rationalized meaning attributed to the existence of life – for example, theodicies that attempt to account for the suffering of the innocent – cannot, as an orientation of life, ignore the concern of vitality. That is one reason why one finds innumerable antinomies within the world religions, for example as expressed in the relation between the world religions and nationality. All human relations, the subject matter of sociology, are characterized in varying degrees by the existence of antinomies arising out of a varying combination of these different orientations.

Those symbolic complexes or worlds of meaning such as mathematics that are most removed from life, its anxieties (for example, the awareness of one's extinction), and its temporal structure are capable of the greatest rationalization. However, in contrast to the world of mathematics, all human associations are, once again, dependent upon life; they have this dual aspect of a 'living objectivity'. Thus, the vast majority of human associations are limited in the extent to which they can be rationalized, as they contain some combination of the expressions of these heterogeneous orientations.

The unsatisfactory imprecision of this attempt to formulate the tripartite schema of the orientations of life is clear. Nevertheless, its merit is that it seeks to take account of the pluralistic orientation of the mind and the attendant objectivations into non-comparable worlds of meaning. It allows for degrees of rationalization, including its limits, of the various worlds of meaning. Finally, it takes as its point of departure the complexities of human associations so manifest at the beginning of the twenty-first century.

Bibliography

Boudon, R. (1993a), 'Toward a Synthetic Theory of Rationality', *International Studies in the Philosophy of Science*, vol. 7, no. 1, pp. 5-19.

Boudon, R. (1993b), 'More on Good Reasons': Reply to Critics', *International Studies in the Philosophy of Science*, vol. 7, no. 1, pp. 87-102.

Burkert, W. (1998), *Creation of the Sacred: Tracks of Biology in Early Religions*, Harvard University Press, Cambridge.

Cassirer, E. (1996), *The Philosophy of Symbolic Forms-Volume Four: The Metaphysics of Symbolic Forms*, Yale University Press, New Haven.

Coleman, J.S. (1990), *Foundations of Social Theory*, Harvard University Press, Cambridge.

Collingwood, R.G. (1924), *Speculum Mentis*, Oxford University Press, Oxford.

Cooley, C.H. ([1918] 1966), *Social Process*, Southern Illinois University Press, Carbondale.

Durkheim, E. ([1898] 1974), 'Individual and Collective Representations', *Sociology and Philosophy*, The Free Press, New York, pp. 1-34.

Eisenstadt, S.N. (1963), *The Political Systems of Empires*, The Free Press, Glencoe.

Eisenstadt, S.N. (1986), *The Origin and Diversity of Axial Age Civilizations*, State University of New York Press, Albany.

Eisenstadt, S.N. (1987), 'Historical Traditions, Modernization and Development', in S.N. Eisenstadt, *Patterns of Modernity*, New York University Press, New York, pp. 1-11.

Eisenstadt, S. N. (1996), *Japanese Civilization*, University of Chicago Press, Chicago.

Frege, G. ([1892] 1966), 'On Sense and Reference' in P. Geach and M. Black (eds), *Translations from the Philosophical Writings of Gottlob Frege*, Basil Blackwell, Oxford, pp. 56-78.

Freyer, H. ([1928] 1999), *Theory of Objective Mind: An Introduction to the Philosophy of Culture*, edited and translated by S. Grosby, with introduction by S. Grosby, Ohio University Press, Athens.

Friedman, M. (1991), 'The Re-evaluation of Logical Positivism', *The Journal of Philosophy*, vol. 88, no. 10, pp. 505-19.

Gehlen, A. ([1950] 1988), *Man*, Columbia University Press, New York.

Gödel, K. ([1951] 1995), 'Some Basic Theorems on the Functions of Mathematics and their Implications', in W. Feferman, D. Jr. Goldfarb, T. Parsons and N. Solovay (eds), *Collected Works III*, Oxford University Press, Oxford, pp. 304-23.

Grosby, S. (1991), 'Religion and Nationality in Antiquity', *Archives Européennes de Sociologie*, vol. XXXII, pp. 229-65.

Grosby, S. (1995a), 'Introduction', *Qualitative Sociology,* vol. 18, no. 2, pp. 139-45.

Grosby, S. (1995b), 'Antinomies of Individuality and Nationality', *Qualitative Sociology*, vol. 18, no. 2, pp. 211-26.

Grosby, S. (1995c), 'Territoriality', *Nations and Nationalism*, vol. 1, no. 2, pp. 143-62.

Grosby, S. (1997), 'Borders, Territory and Nationality in the Ancient Near East and Armenia', *Journal of the Economic and Social History of the Orient,* vol. 40, no. 1, pp. 1-29.

Grosby, S. (1999), 'The Chosen People of Ancient Israel and the Occident', *Nations and Nationalism*, vol. 5, no. 3, pp. 357-80.

Hastings, A. (1997), *The Construction of Nationhood*, Cambridge University Press, Cambridge.

Hegel, G. F. W. ([1830] 1971), *Philosophy of Mind*, Oxford University Press, Oxford.

Huizinga, J. (1949), *Homo Ludens*, Routledge, London.

Husserl, E. ([1929] 1977), *Cartesian Meditations*, The Hague, Martinus Nijhoff.

Knight, F. ([1939] 1982), 'Ethics and Economic Reform', in F. Knight, *Freedom and Reform: Essay in Economics and Social Philosophy*, Liberty Press, Indianapolis, pp. 55-153.

Maine, H.S. ([1861] 1970), *Ancient Law*, Peter Smith, Gloucester.

Oakeshott, M. ([1959] 1991), 'The Voice of Poetry in the Conversation of Mankind', in M. Oakeshott, *Rationalism in Politics and other Essays*, Liberty Fund, Indianapolis, pp. 488-541.

Parsons, T. (1938), 'The Role of Ideas in Action', *American Sociological Review*, vol. 3, pp. 13-20.

Parsons, T. and Shils, E. (1951), *Towards a General Theory of Action*, Harvard University Press, Cambridge.

Popper, K. (1972), *Objective Knowledge*, Oxford University Press, Oxford.

Salmon, M.H. (1989), 'Explanation in the Social Sciences', in P. Kitcher and W.C. Salmon (eds), *Scientific Explanation. Minnesota Studies in the Philosophy of Science*, vol. XIII, University of Minnesota Press, Minneapolis, pp. 384-409.

Scheler, M. ([1928] 1961), *Man's Place in Nature*, Beacon Press, Boston.

Schleiermacher, F. ([1799] 1988), *On Religion: Speeches to its Cultured Despisers*, Introduction, transl. and notes by R. Crouter, Cambridge University Press, Cambridge.

Schutz, A. (1973), *Collected Papers I*, The Hague, Martinus Nijhoff.

Shils, E. (1951), 'The Study of the Primary Group', in D. Lerner and H.D. Lasswell (eds), *The Policy Sciences: Recent Developments in Scope and Method*, Stanford University Press, Stanford, pp. 44-69.

Shils, E. (1957), 'Primordial, Personal, Sacred and Civil Ties', *The British Journal of Sociology*, vol. VIII, no. 2, pp. 130-45.

Shils, E. ([1961] 1975a), 'Center and Periphery', in E. Shils (ed), *Center and Periphery: Essays in Macrosociology*, University of Chicago Press, Chicago, pp. 3-16.

Shils, E. ([1965] 1975b), 'Charisma, Order, and Status', in E. Shils (ed), *Center and Periphery, Essays in Macrosociology*, University of Chicago Press, Chicago, pp. 256-75.

Shils, E. (1985), 'Sociology', in A. Kuper and J. Kuper (eds), *The Social Science Encyclopedia*, Routledge, London, pp. 799-811.

Simmel, G. (1918), *Lebensanschauung, Vier Metaphysische Kapitel*, Dunker & Humblot, München.

Smith, A.D. (1998), *Nationalism and Modernism*, Routledge, London.

Thomas, W.I. ([1919] 1927), *The Polish Peasant in Europe and America*, Alfred A. Knopf, New York.

Van Wolferen, K. (1990), *The Enigma of Japanese Power*, Random House, New York.

Weber, M. ([1915] 1946), 'Religious Rejections of the World and Their Directions', in H.H. Gerth and C.W. Mills (eds), *From Max Weber*, Oxford University Press, New York, pp. 323-59.

Weber, M. ([1922] 1978), *Economy and Society*, University of California Press, Berkeley.

10 Beyond national and post-national models: transnational spaces and immigrant integration

THOMAS FAIST

Introduction

The canonical models of immigrant integration have treated processes of adaptation mainly within the container of national and multinational states. Influential assimilation theories predict that immigrants will melt into the majority core of a society over three generations (Gordon, 1964) provided there is an absence of or decline in large-scale discrimination directed at the newcomers and their children.

The transnational ties of immigrants are even thought to retard successful integration in the immigration country. While the model of ethnic pluralism assumes that immigrants and their offspring retain 'homeland' cultural practices such as language in their new countries of settlement to a certain degree (Kallen, 1996), the theories that can be grouped under this heading do not include immigrant ties spanning the space in between the emigration and immigration countries. Transnational ties are also largely absent in considerations of refugee integration (Stein, 1981).

More recently, the post-modernist surge has proclaimed the borders of sovereign states to be increasingly less relevant or even obsolete for the lives of transmigrants. Radical views consider even relatively immobile persons as metaphorical migrants because the opportunities for mobility have vastly increased – not only of persons but also of information and symbols. In essence, the models of assimilation and ethnic pluralism, on the one hand, and post-modern and post-structuralist approaches on the other, represent the extremes of a continuum regarding the importance of transnational ties for immigrant integration within sovereign national and multinational states.

But although migration researchers have repeatedly established that first generation migrants tend to establish ties criss-crossing the borders of sovereign states (Gmelch, 1980; Thomas and Znaniecki, 1927), this insight has not yet systematically entered the conceptualization of immigrant

277

integration. The bulk of immigrant ties are neither exclusively 'national' nor 'post-national', but 'in-between'. Therefore, this analysis presents the various patterns of transnational ties entertained by immigrants in transnational spaces, and reviews their implications for concepts of integration in immigration countries. To the canonical models of assimilation, ethnic pluralism and post-modernism, it adds a new and thus apocryphal concept of border-crossing expansion of social space.

Examples of immigrants' transnational ties are plentiful: Muslims from Morocco and Algeria who reside in France exchange religious instructors with their countries of origin. These imams have contributed to a pluralization of the French religious landscape; moreover, their second generation sometimes traverses borders to transfer its syncretist practices. The children of Turkish immigrants in Germany travel to their parents' country to start musical careers. In the economic field, nurses from Jamaica work in New York hospitals while their mothers rear their children in the Caribbean; the children, in turn, spend some of their childhood in New York (Brown, 1997). Tellingly, some migrant groups engage in recurrent international migration: for instance, South Korean academics work in the United States while their families stay 'at home'. The children of Pakistani immigrants in the United Kingdom invest in the homeland of their parents, thus using insider advantages such as language and cultural customs in order to reap benefits from relatively lower production costs. In the political realm, Kurdish organizations in Germany, the Netherlands and Sweden have tried to influence Turkish politics and the governments of their respective countries of settlement. Politicians from Mexico, the Dominican Republic and Haiti campaign in Los Angeles and New York during elections (Smith, Guarnizo and Eduardo, 1998), their prospective voters being permanent residents or citizens of the United States. Also, more than a half of all states in the world do not raise objections to their own citizens, or, sometimes also naturalized citizens, holding multiple citizenship (Goldstein and Piazza, 1996: 73). The reality of these transnational exchanges and the growing legal tolerance of multiple membership indicates that migration and return migration are not definite, irrevocable and irreversible decisions. Transnational lives in themselves may become a strategy of survival and betterment.

Ties which concatenate into transnational spaces present an unexpected puzzle for social cohesion, political coordination and cultural practices in the process of immigrant integration. In the past, territoriality as geographical propinquity was thought – among other factors, such as a shared common interest and a common language – to be conducive to the formation of groups and communities. Consider the English trade unions, which first organized along patterns such as cities. Later, trades such as carpenters replaced location as an organizing principle (Simmel, 1955: 128-30). General findings in social network research indicate that geographic distance and infrequent contact increase the difficulty of maintaining strong social ties (Wellman and Wortley, 1990). Social theorists have relentlessly emphasised that to constitute social and political life morally, social transactions must be the conduit through which norms, values, and standards come to be common or shared in nature. Transactions must be regular, frequent and meaningful, and the respective social and symbolic ties must be in sufficiently intimate contact to act and react (Durkheim, 1964: 262). The development of transnational spaces thus offers a unique opportunity to look into the formation of networks, collectives and organizations that span at least two states, and their implications for the integration of newcomers.

These considerations lead to two propositions guiding the conceptual analysis of immigrant life in transnational spaces:
1. Transnational spaces are pluri-local, border-crossing sets of ties among persons, networks, communities and organizations. Transnational spaces and the other names given to these phenomena – such as transnational social fields (Basch et al., 1994) and transnational communities (Portes et al., 1999) – are characterized by a high density and continuity of interstitial ties on informal or formal levels. Some forms, such as diasporas, show a particular longevity which even outlasts a human generation.
2. Over time, transnational links may concatenate into various forms of transnational spaces: contact fields of persons, goods and information; small kinship groups, issue groups and networks; and, finally, transnational communities such as diasporas and borderlands, and transnational organizations. Among the prerequisites for durable transnational spaces, such as transnational communities, are not only border-crossing travel but, even more importantly, sustained long-distance communication, contentious minority politics in the countries of emigration, perceived discrimination on the part of the migrants, and generous multi-cultural policies in the countries of immigration. Looking at the consequences of transnational spaces for immigrant integration, two further propositions emerge:
3. The trajectories of immigrant integration envisaged by the canonical concepts of assimilation, ethnic pluralism and post-modernism hold in certain cases. Other phenomena, such as continuing transnational linkages, need to be categorized in a new and separate conceptual niche.

Even those immigrants who have settled for a considerable time in the immigration country may have strong transnational links and may thus participate in transnational spaces. Assimilation, ethnic pluralism and post-modernism are insufficient because they either espouse a container concept of space or neglect the state borders that separate. However, since growing transnationalization contributes to the plurality of avenues open to immigrant in various states, but is nevertheless always tied to specific places, the concept of border-crossing expansion of space enriches our understanding of immigrant adaptation.

4. There is an elective affinity between the four broad concepts with which to explain and describe immigrant integration (assimilation, ethnic pluralism, post-nationalism and the border-crossing expansion of social space), on the one hand, and the concepts used to describe and explain economic activities, politics (citizenship), and culture, on the other. In the economic sphere the concepts are socio-economic parity with the majority groups, enclaves and niches, global entrepreneurship and interstitial entrepreneurship; in the political realm: national, multicultural, post-national and transnational membership; and in the culture sphere: acculturation, cultural retention, hybridity and border-crossing syncretism. Treated as ideal-typical concepts, each of these captures an important part of immigrant integration.

The concepts of transnational spaces and border-crossing expansion of social space complement the systemic thrust of earlier studies of border-crossing transactions with a focus on the life-world of actors. The first generation of transnational research dealt with the challenge of multi- or transnational companies to the capacity of states to regulate border-crossing economic exchange. This paradigm of transnationalism criticised the exaggerated state-centredness of some theories of international relations. For example, the neo-realist branch of international relations theory claims that states are the only important actors on the international scene, and that they act as politically coherent units (Waltz, 1979). Critics of such perspectives have complained that most exchanges beyond state borders take place independently of governmental control and that non-state actors in the national arena may even compete with nation-states. However, this certainly does not mean that transnational organizations removed states as important actors in world politics. Nevertheless, the transnational focus is able to comprehend multiple relations between economic, social and political actors in different countries in which states do not completely monopolize these relations (Keohane and Nye, 1977: 24-25). The 1990s once again saw a revival of the transnational perspective, this time going beyond economic transactions and delving into transnational solidarity, for example in studies on human rights (Sikkink, 1993), border-crossing social movements (Tarrow, 1996), non-governmental organizations and the consequences of international migration for the life-worlds of mobile persons (Portes, 1995). It is within the context of these latter studies that this analysis sketches the implications of immigrant integration in the immigration countries.

The analysis first defines the concept of transnational spaces, and the main resources of actors in the various types of transnational space. Second, integration in and through transnational spaces goes beyond national container-models of assimilation and ethnic pluralism, on the one hand, and post-national concepts on the other. The analysis presents the main assumptions and predictions of these three canonical models, and the implications of a fourth integration model: border-crossing transactions of social space. These considerations apply to three realms of immigrant integration: membership and participation in culture, economic life and polities.

1. Transnational spaces: definition, concepts and dynamics

Transnational spaces differ from clearly demarcated state territories. 'Space' here denotes the cultural, economic and political practices of individual and collective actors within territories or places. Thus, the term 'space' does not only pertain to physical characteristics, as in a more traditional geographical orientation, but also comprises the ties among actors in pluri-local places, whereas 'place' refers to one specific location. This social-relational understanding of space helps one to comprehend the manifold ties of actors across various states. This analysis focuses on the transnational ties and structures that developed from and in connection with interstate South–North migration.

The smallest analytical units in social spaces are ties, social and symbolic. Social ties represent a continuing series of personal transactions – communication among at least three actors – to which the people involved ascribe common interests, obligations, expectations and norms. Social ties can also be indirect, reaching to persons beyond the immediate realm of direct relations. Symbolic ties are continuing transactions with which the people involved link common meanings, memories, expectations for the future, and representations. Both social and symbolic ties may reach beyond the face-to-face relations between persons by aiming at people speaking the same language, members of the same faith, class, profession, ideology, ethnicity, and nationality.

There are three types of resources flowing through social and symbolic ties that enable individuals to cooperate in networks, groups and organizations. These assets also serve to connect individuals to networks and organizations through affiliations, and – viewing it from the opposite perspective – they enable collectives to integrate members. Thus, these resources can be both personal and group assets, depending on the analytical perspective. We can differentiate the following forms of resources within ties:

1. Reciprocity as exchange: mutual obligations and expectations of the actors, associated with specific social or symbolic ties and based on exchanges and services rendered in the past (Coleman, 1990: 306-9). These obligations and expectations may be an outcome of instrumental activity, for example, the tit-for-tat principle well-known from the Old Testament.

2. Reciprocity as a social norm: what one party receives from the other requires some return (Gouldner, 1960: 160). However, reciprocity as a social norm and other resources should not be limited to dyadic relations. Rather, the smallest set here are triple relations: for example, X extends help to Y not simply because he or she expects Y to return a favour in the future but because X thinks that Y could also extend a favour to a third person, Z (Ekeh, 1974: 206-7). Reciprocity as exchange and as a social norm are two important forms of social capital.

3. Solidarity with others in a group who share similar positions (Portes, 1995: 16). This is an expressive form of social transaction. Solidarity builds upon shared ideas, beliefs, evaluations and symbols. If symbolic ties concatenate into clearly definable communities, they refer to 'collective representations' (Durkheim, 1965: 471). Collective representations can be expressed in some sort of we-feeling or we-consciousness, and refer to a social unit of action. In their ideal-typical form they are cultural communities, such as families, ethnic groups, religious parishes, communities, or nations. Symbolic ties may serve as cultural capital.

Persons can derive three main benefits from assets and capital inherent in social and symbolic transactions: In general, they help members of networks or groups to gain access to more economic, human, social and cultural capital. This crucially depends on the number of persons in a network or a collective who are prepared or obliged to help a person when called upon to do so, and on the number of social and symbolic ties available. Moreover, information is a benefit of social and cultural capital. In general, the information benefits of a large, diverse network tend to be higher than the information benefits of a small and socially homogeneous network. Further, the greater the stock of social and cultural capital, the more control can be exerted to monitor and sanction other actors and subordinates. The basic idea is that the extent to which any particular person is an important link in indirect social and symbolic ties to others matters in controlling the flow of information, authority and power.

Transactions based on reciprocity as exchange, the norm of reciprocity and solidarity have desirable and undesirable effects upon the autonomy of persons. Resources may restrict the degrees of freedom of the persons involved in significant ways. Whilst the norm of reciprocity tends to enhance cooperation, it may also give rise to revenge and retaliation: take the case of clan groups which carry conflicts abroad. And solidarity may not only help to pool energies among kinship members when building a business, but it may also encourage envy and stifle entrepreneurship when the profits are constantly split within the kinship group instead of being also used as funds for reinvestment.

Resources such as reciprocity and solidarity may exist in non-institutionalized and institutionalized varieties. In its institutionalized variants, citizenship in a state constitutes an expression of full and formal membership. It forms a continuing series of transactions, primarily among citizens, regulated by state institutions. Citizenship is the public representation of ties among members, and the loyalties of members in a polity to the corresponding state. Loyalties are a form of solidarity. As an institutionalized form of reciprocity and solidarity, citizenship is usually in short supply among virtually all newcomers to a polity.

This approach to assets in social and symbolic ties goes far beyond conventional network analysis. Network theory is a particular methodology which seeks to explain the behaviour of actors primarily in terms of their position within social structures (White et al., 1976). The emphasis is on the 'syntax' of social and symbolic ties; theoretical statements creep into network methodology only implicitly (Granovetter, 1979: 501). By contrast, the capital approach allows us not only to distinguish density and type of ties but also to give clearer definition to the content of ties, the resources inherent in social and symbolic ties. This is a first step towards complementing the 'syntax' of ties with elements of a 'grammar'. The focus on resources within ties helps to differentiate the type of exchange taking place – be it reciprocity as exchange, as a norm, or as solidarity (Faist, 2000a: chap. 4).

2. Types of transnational spaces

Transnational spaces can be differentiated along two dimensions: their degree of formalization and their durability. The degree of formalization concerns both the internal characteristics of group organization and the extent of common or even shared values and symbols. On the one hand, there are networks that display a low level of formalization, and on the other there are highly formalized institutions. Organizations are characterized by a high extent of formalized relations, for example regarding hierarchy and control. Treated as an overstylized type, communities also display a high degree of formalization; however, not primarily in view of their internal organizational structure but with respect to common values and symbols. They include highly formalized ties expressed in national, religious, communal and family peculiarities. The second dimension represents the potential durability of different kinds of transnational space. The actors' time perspective is of importance – whether it is more short-term or more long-term. There are four types of transnational space: contact fields; small groups, particularly kinship systems; issue networks; and communities and organizations (*Figure 1*). Issue networks, transnational communities and organizations tend to have a greater longevity than contact fields and transnational kinship groups.

Figure 1: Types of Transnational Spaces

Degree of formalization Potential of durability	Low: Networks	High: Institutions
short-lived	*contact fields of goods, persons, information and practices* (1)	*small kinship groups* (2)
long-lived	*networks in established cycles: issue networks* (3)	*communities and organizations* (4)

2.1 Contact fields of goods, persons, information and practices

This category does not only comprise phenomena which finally form the basis for mass action, such as chain migration in migrant networks. In addition to people, ideas and information it also contains social and cultural practices spreading across borders, such as the repertoires of action in social movements (Tilly, 1978: chap. 5). Among immigrants we observe processes that partly point to diffusion from the country of origin to the country of settlement. For example, Kurds in Turkey adopted the tradition of celebrating New Year (*Newroz*) and took it to Germany, where it became an important symbol of Kurdish we-feeling. In order to take the wind out of the Kurdish separatists' sails, so to speak, the Turkish government declared *Newroz* a national holiday in 1996.

2.2 Small groups: kinship systems

Highly formalized and border-crossing relations within small groups like households and families or even wider kinship systems are representative of many migrants of the first generation. Such small groups have a strong awareness of a common home. A classic example of these relations is provided by transnational families who conceive themselves as an economic and solidarity unit and which maintain, besides the main home, a kind of shadow household in another country. Transnational small groups fall back upon resources inherent in social ties like reciprocity, and upon resources existing in symbolic ties like solidarity. Economic assets are mostly transferred from the immigration countries to those who continue to run the household in the emigration state. This type of transnational space tends to be relatively short-lived, although it is internally much more formalized or institutionalized than the contact fields of goods, information, practices and people. As a rule, the remittances of migrants in small relational or household-groups, which are based on reciprocity, occur only as long as the group has not yet re-united in a country or the migrants are still alive.

2.3 Issue networks

Transnational issue networks are sets of ties between persons and organizations in which information and services flow for the purpose of achieving common goals. Often, there is a shared discourse around a specific issue such as human rights or a profession. The access of interested actors to these networks is not rigidly restricted. In this way, issue networks are similar to epistemic communities – a designation frequently used for reciprocal exchange relations between scientists and experts (Haas, 1992). While issue networks look back upon a long tradition in the realm of human rights, and are on the march in ecology, they are also emerging among migrants who have moved from the so-called third countries to the European Union. One instance of the intensification of relations based on issue networks is the 'migrants' parliament' in Brussels which lobbies the European Union on behalf of various immigrant groups.

2.4 Transnational communities and organizations

Communities and organizations constitute highly formalized types of transnational space with an inherent potential for a relatively long life-span. These two sub-types partly overlap. For analytic reasons they should, however, be distinguished: close solidarist and symbolic ties are characteristic of transnational communities, and a more formal internal hierarchy and systematically structured controls of social ties exist within transnational organizations. Transnational communities comprises dense and continuous sets of social and symbolic ties characterized by a high degree of intimacy, emotional depth, moral obligation and sometimes even social cohesion. The development of transnational communities requires forms of capital such as reciprocity and solidarity which extend beyond face-to-face ties. Community on the one hand, and geographical proximity on the other, are partially decoupled. They may describe a wider social-relational space spanning the borders of states. Transnational communities may evolve at different levels of aggregation. The most basic types are village communities in the emigration and immigration states, whose relations are marked by an extended solidarity over long periods of time. Those members of such communities who are abroad or have returned home invest in private or public projects (Engelbrektsson, 1978).

The quintessential form of transnational community is constituted by border-crossing religious groups and churches. World religions, such as Judaism, Catholicism, Islam, Hinduism and Buddhism existed long before modern states came into existence. Also diasporas belong to the category of transnational communities. Diasporas are groups formerly subjected to a traumatic experience which has resulted in the territorial dispersion of their members – examples being Jews, Palestinians and Armenians. Generally, their members have a common memory of their lost homeland or a vision of an imagined one to be created, while at the same time the immigration country often refuses to grant the respective minority full acknowledgment of its cultural distinctiveness (Safran, 1991). Borderlands offer a particularly rich context for emerging transnational communities: for example, along the Mexico-USA and Poland-Germany borders.

Transnational organizations differ from small groups like transnational families in their even greater degree of formal control and coordination of social and symbolic ties. Both state and non-state political organizations are marked by a specific form of bureaucratic rule with efficient instruments of administration and inherent tendencies towards the expansion of their respective spheres of competence and control (Weber, 1988: 498). A first type of transnational organization has developed from issue networks: for example, the Red Cross, Amnesty International and Greenpeace. Another type is transnational enterprises. These companies are differentiated border-crossing organizations with an extremely detailed internal division of labour.

3. The emergence of transnational spaces

Technological progress in transport and communication plays a part in the formation and the endogenous dynamics of transnational spaces. Capitalism has produced unanticipated possibilities in technological development. Technological breakthroughs in the fields of telecommunications and travel occurred as early as the nineteenth century and fostered the growth of the world market (Marx and Engels, 1972: 465). New and improved methods of travel and communication like transoceanic steamship lines or telegraphy offered the necessary, albeit not sufficient, prerequisite for the rise of the North Atlantic space in the nineteenth century within the former European-North American migration system. In short, continuing technological progress in the fields of communication and transport considerably diminished the costs of covering long distances. This tendency even intensified after the end of World War Two. Although relative geographical immobility reigned supreme in a world with only about 2% of international migrants, the migration rate grew by about 1.8% per year between 1960 and 1990, and, though with a slight upward tendency, at an annual average of 2.6% between 1985 and 1990 (Zlotnik, 1999: 22-3). Thus, diverse potentially global structural and technological developments removed the restrictions on territorially confined networks, communities and organizations. However, these processes did not simply give rise to respective global effects; rather, many pluri-local spaces of a transnational type came into existence.

Moving from the transnational to the state level, some of the ceteris paribus conditions which caused the formation of transnational spaces within both the emigration and immigration states can be specified. There were factors generating migration or flight in the countries of origin, and factors or processes which impede or promote transnationalization in the immigration countries. The spread of the nation-state idea through the de-colonizing parts of world after World War Two often entailed flight-generating minority policies and conflicts in the countries of origin. This can be observed, for example, in late-coming nation-states in the 'South', which have usually adapted the alleged European state model of cultural and national homogenization. With regard to ethnic, religious and national categories, highly heterogeneous states emerged, for example in Africa. Among the most important flight-generating factors in the emigration countries have been conflicts concerning national minorities. This claim can be substantiated by numerous examples, ranging from Indian Sikhs in Great Britain, Canada and the United States to Kurds in Germany, to Armenians throughout the world. Similar instances of forced migration occurred during and after the dissolution of former empires, such as the Soviet Union, Afghanistan and Ethiopia, and of multinational states such as Yugoslavia.

Moving from emigration to the immigration states, the denial of acculturation or cultural recognition, and serious obstacles against socio-economic integration are factors conducive to the extension of immigrants' transnational activities. Economic and cultural problems of integration into the immigration country may either coincide or proceed separately. Some immigrant groups, for example, face serious obstacles against their cultural integration, although they are well-adapted from an economic point of view – be it within niches or in the 'core' of society. For example, this was true until the 1940s of the Chinese living in the white settler colonies – the United States, Canada, Australia and New Zealand. There are, however, other cases in which socio-economic exclusion and a lack of cultural recognition have gone hand in hand. Recent examples of immigrants from northern Africa and southern Europe in western Europe attest to this.

Surprising, but only at first sight, multicultural policies have also contributed to the political and cultural transnationalization of immigrants. If immigration states are liberal democracies and do not aim to assimilate immigrants by force, the immigrant minority has a greater chance of maintaining its cultural difference and ties to the country of origin. Multicultural policies in immigration states – such as the institutionalized teaching of the native language as well as the incorporation of religious confessions – possibly supports not only integration but also the maintenance of various transnational communities and organizations. The more liberal or tolerant the respective political regime towards the immigrant minority regarding the maintenance of distinctive practices and institutions, the more likely, ceteris paribus, will be the formation of transnational collectives. Multicultural policies enable immigrants to mobilize resources: as an example, Kurdish immigrants in Germany, Sweden and the Netherlands come to mind. This means that not only do repressive policies and discrimination support transnational ties of immigrants but, in quite contrary fashion, so too do liberal multicultural rights and activities. Overall, a mix of repressive and flight-inducing politics and policies in the emigration countries and a framework of liberal democratic conditions in the immigration states seems to be particularly conducive to transnational mobilization in the political and religious realms of life.

4. Implications of transnational spaces for models of immigrant integration

Conceptually, the model of the border-crossing expansion of social space – derived from the reality of transnational spaces – complements the traditional and fruitful theories of assimilation and pluralism on the one hand, and globalization and post-nationalism on the other. The proposition is that neither nationally-bounded container models such as assimilation and ethnic pluralism, nor limitless ideas of post-nationalism and post-modernism, capture all the facets of immigrant integration in today's world. In essence, assimilation presages a melting into the 'core' of the immigration society, and ethnic pluralism suggests a retention by immigrants of major cultural characteristics beyond the first generation. On the opposite side of the conceptual universe, post-nationalism sees an increasingly strong impact on integration by supra-national regulations and ties spanning the globe, and post-modernism discovers hybrid identities everywhere, turning ever more 'locals' into 'globals'. The border-crossing expansion of social space lies between the 'national' and the 'post-national', emphasising that integration processes occur in the context of interstitial ties created by immigrants (*Figure 2*).

The canonical models of assimilation, ethnic pluralism and post-nationalism or post-modernism, undeniably capture important aspects of the contemporary scene. These approaches, however, cannot account for other phenomena, especially the persistence of transnational ties in border-crossing spaces. In past decades, processes of admission to membership, participation of immigrants, and the willingness of newcomers and natives to integrate have not entirely changed. Yet the processes involved have become more plural and multilayered.

Inspection of the evidence from the wealth of research on immigrant group experiences in the West European, Australian, Japanese and North American contexts in recent years shows an unmistakable trend towards assimilation in the political and economic sphere, although signs of the marginalization of certain groups and of substantial minorities within selected immigrant groups clearly exist as well. Account should be taken of the following three seminal changes in international migration: ongoing international migration flows, albeit guided by restrictive policies on the side of immigration countries; an ongoing communications and transport revolution; and diversifying economic opportunities for immigrants depending on the degree of post-industrial development and the resources of immigrants (for example, working-class migrants as opposed to formally highly-qualified human capital migrants) (Faist, 2000a: 244-52).

Figure 2: Four Models for the Analysis of Immigrant Integration

integration model	assimilation	ethnic pluralism	post-nationalism	border-crossing expansion of social space
prediction *spheres of Integration*	melting into the core of majority society	group diversity	globalization	transnational Spaces
culture	*acculturation:* adaptation to norms and symbols of the majority society	*transplantation:* transplantation of practices and identities from emigration to immigration countries	*hybridization:* *mélange* as a basic social and cultural pattern	*transnational syncretism:* diffusion of culture and emergence of new types and plural loyalites
economy	*socio-economic parity:* socio-economic equity with autochthonous population	*niches and enclave economies:* middlemen occupy distinct economic fields	*global entrepreneurship:* even small companies have chances to operate globally	*interstitial entrepreneurship:* transnational networks and collectives, based on relatives and friends
polity	*national citizenship:* coherent national political culture	*multicultural citizenship:* recognition of cultural differences: polyethnic rights	*post-national membership:* human and citizens rights converge	*dual (multiple) citizenship:* ties of citizens to several states can be complementary

Since growing transnationalization contributes to the plurality of avenues open to migrants and refugees in various states, but is nevertheless always tied to specific places, the concept of the border-crossing expansion of space enriches our understanding of adaptation.

5. Assimilation: melting into the core of majority society

The traditional assimilation model in its various incarnations still offers the most refined description of immigrant integration. Assimilation essentially means the melting of immigrants and their offspring into the majority core of the immigration country in all spheres of public and private life. Often, assimilation theories use stage models to describe and predict the transition from the poverty and discrimination endured by the first generation, through gradual socio-economic upward mobility by the second generation, to the total immersion of the third generation into majority norms and behaviour (Gordon, 1964). This transition of stages is not necessarily smooth; it may take the form of a 'bumpy line' (Gans, 1992).

5.1 Cultural life: acculturation

The idea of melting concerns in particular the socialization of the second generation, and it is the end result of complex processes. The first conceptualization of the assimilation model defined it as

> a process of interpenetration and fusion in which persons and groups acquire the memories, sentiments, and attitudes of other persons and groups and, by sharing their experience and history, are incorporated with them in a common cultural life (Park and Burgess, 1969: 735, 510).

On this view, it would be totally unrealistic to expect assimilation to occur in the first generation. One important contextual variable facilitating melting into the majority core is the decline or absence of strong discrimination against immigrants. This does not necessarily mean that all the ethnic, religious or national characteristics of the immigrants totally disappear. Folklore, of course, does not offer a challenge to assimilation theories. Also, it is even possible that the majority culture will change as a result of immigrant integration. These theories aptly capture the distinctive path followed by the main European immigrants in the United States during the first decades of the twentieth century. Strict immigration restrictions in the 1920s and 1930s, the Great Depression and World War Two helped to create a glasshouse atmosphere in which transnational ties did not matter much for assimilation.

5.2 Economic participation: socio-economic parity with majority groups

Assimilation theories predict that, eventually, the children of immigrants will achieve socio-economic parity with the majority groups. This outcome sometimes but not necessarily implies that employers hire immigrants for certain tasks, or that natives or earlier immigrants move up the occupational prestige ladder and vacate jobs for newcomers. Historically, this pattern applied to US-American immigration history around the turn of the nineteenth and twentieth centuries, and in post-war Europe until the early 1970s. Rapid economic growth demanded ever-increasing amounts of manual labour for the new or expanding smoke-stack industries. When domestic supplies – such as youth, women and peasants – diminished to a trickle, employers generally recruited workers from abroad. For example, industries based on coal, steel and iron radically changed the economic landscape in the Ruhr area of Germany, where Polish workers dug out the black gold, followed decades later by Turks. Originally, many of the descendants of the first-generation immigrants became part of a blue-collar working class. In essence, this is a game of musical chairs or a job queue, when newcomers or minorities find favourable entry positions in the course of upward job mobility among natives or majorities. A well-known example is provided by public service jobs: many Irish were replaced by African-Americans after the 1960s in New York; Americans of Irish descent moved out of the public sector and, moreover, the administration offered additional jobs for entry cohorts (Waldinger, 1986/87). Several decades later, researchers still ask whether new immigrants such as Turks in Western Europe or Mexican Americans in North America will experience a trajectory similar to that of the earlier immigrant generations which entered in periods of rapid capitalist expansion. These are truly very odd questions: while the latter groups came in periods of economic boom after World War Two, the situation has changed dramatically since the 1970s, with a marked shrinking of the pool of blue-collar jobs available to newcomers. This trend has been more visible in countries like Germany, where the service sector did not grow as fast as it did in the United States.

5.3 Political membership: exclusive national citizenship

The most widespread form of full membership is exclusive state citizenship: for immigrants, this is citizenship of the immigration country. Rights, obligations and a sense of belonging more or less exclusively refer to the people of a territorial state which has become the new home for immigrants and into which they become assimilated. This means, of course, that the newly-developed ties of immigrants to the receiving country are the exclusive criterion for naturalization: sufficient knowledge of the country's language(s), a declaration of belief in the constitution, as well as successful integration in the housing and labour markets.

Contemporary immigration states usually regulate the access of the immigrants' children to citizenship in accordance with three different principles, *ius sanguinis*, *ius soli* and *ius domicili*. The ideal-type of ius soli is, of course, always combined with ius sanguinis. Countries like the United States and the United Kingdom come closest to a pure principle of ius soli. By contrast, the Israeli 'Law of Return' represents the clearest manifestation of the principle of ius sanguinis. Germany until 1999, Italy until the 1980s, and Greece may also be cited as countries in which ius sanguinis played an outstanding role. It was these countries that used regulations as ius sanguinis in order to maintain the transnational ties of hundreds of thousands of citizens who had emigrated overseas around the turn of the nineteenth and twentieth centuries. One of the main reasons why the German Reich explicitly insisted on ius sanguinis in the 'Reichs- und Staatsangehörigkeitsgesetz' of 1913 (Law of Membership in the Empire and the State) was to tie the numerous German emigrants in the United States to their country of origin.

The third principle regulating the access of second-generation immigrants' children to full membership is citizenship as an option – what could be called ius domicili: most European countries do not provide genuine ius soli or ius sanguinis rules for the second generation. Ius domicili means that the children have the right to opt for the citizenship of the immigration country in which they grew up, usually around majority age, or that they are allowed to naturalize: this is the case in countries such as Belgium, the Netherlands, and Italy. Ius domicili is very far-reaching in the Scandinavian countries, where it is not tied to birth in the country of settlement. Continuous residence in the country for at least five years suffices. France has a mix between ius soli and ius sanguinis: the second generation automatically receives French citizenship on reaching majority age.

To conclude, the assimilation model carries the historical baggage of questionable ideological assumptions. For example, the normative content of assimilation cannot be understood as a general empirical tendency covering all immigrant groups. Even in the United States there are undeniably groups to which the assimilationist model does not apply; for example, African-

Americans in the urban ghettoes and Mexican Americans in the Southwest. Empirical studies have shown again and again that in this latter region third-generation Mexican Americans lag behind the first generation on a number of indicators like income and social status (Featherman, Hauser and Robert, 1978: 478). Also, assimilation theories find it difficult to handle categories of immigrants who were imported as slaves and experienced discrimination after emancipation (Lieberson, 1981). More to the point, assimilation theories often assume that transnational ties do not contribute to the integration of newcomers and their children, or even delay it (Gordon, 1964) see, however, the sophisticated analysis by Esser, 1980. Numerous groups, such as Greek immigrants, defy this simplistic connection. For example, Greek 'national schools' in Germany have not delayed integration of Greek immigrant children into the educational systems (Hopf, 1987).

6. Ethnic pluralism: group diversity

In contrast to the assimilation model, ethnic pluralism does not display a set of relatively coherent theoretical elements. The ethnic pluralist perspective privileges all those characteristics of immigrants which relate to collective elements such as language, religion and ethnicity, differentiating newcomers and their descendants from natives or majority groups. Historically, this model too was formulated in the early decades of the twentieth century, and was originally based on the experience of European immigrants in the United States (Glazer and Moynihan, 1963). Similarly, this perspective has also disregarded categories of immigrants who came as slaves or experienced internal colonization. One more commonality is that the early formulations of ethnic pluralism assumed a stage process, in this case four periods; but in contrast to the assimilation model it ends in dissimilation (Kallen, 1996: 82, 87): Initially, immigrants try hard to adapt and to move up the socio-economic status ladder. However, since they often experience discrimination they turn to their own traditions, their history and their collective life in a second period. This process then gives rise to the opposite process to assimilation, namely dissimilation – the formation of a separate cultural, political and economic life. The fourth phase is then full-blown pluralism. The earlier an immigrant group arrives, the better its chances of preserving its distinctive character: '... the most early American of the immigrant groups are also the most autonomous and self-conscious in spirit and culture' (Kallen, 1996: 88). Over the past decades ethnic pluralists have discarded notions of quasi-national autonomy for immigrants within immigration states. Nevertheless, newer versions such as multiculturalism have claimed that ethnically or religiously distinctive customs and institutions can help immigrants to adapt to new environments. Placed in a wider perspective, the self-organizing capacities of immigrant communities are a major resource for eventual integration (Breton, 1964).

6.1 Cultural life: transplanted cultures

From an ethnic pluralist perspective, there is no contradiction between integration and cultural plurality. A high degree of cultural autonomy even guarantees a form of adaptation to the country of settlement. The degree of pluralism is variable. While the early pluralists spoke of 'nationality', newer versions have emphasised the 'ethnic' character of immigrant groups, especially regarding cultural retention. Even if members of the second and third generation acculturate – take over the norms and behaviour of majority groups – a large number of them maintain in-group social and symbolic ties, especially in families and neighbourhoods in which the language of the parents is still alive.

6.2 Economic participation: middlemen in niches and enclaves

While ethnic pluralism places strong emphasis on the cultural sphere, several approaches can be subsumed under this heading in the economic and political realm. A specific variant of the pattern are 'middlemen minorities' (Bonacich, 1979). These consist of groups specializing in trade and concentrating in the petty bourgeoisie. Usually, they experience a high degree of hostility in times of economic depression and war: for example, Chinese migrants in mid to late nineteenth-century America. Some successful middlemen minorities connect different economic classes and ethnic groups together (Weber, 1980: 536-7). For example, Indians in Uganda linked the colonial powers and the native population. They established non-redundant social ties, thus acting as a bridge in that the native population and the colonial powers did not communicate directly with each other. Both sides used the Indian intermediaries employed in the colonial administration. This formed one of the key mechanisms with which 'plural societies' (Furnivall, 1948) were integrated.

6.3 Political membership: multicultural citizenship

The proponents of multicultural citizenship argue that in order to participate meaningfully in public life, persons must be assured of a secure cultural background. The supportive framework of cultural groups constitutes such a 'context of choice' (Kymlicka, 1995: 85). Drawing normative and policy implications, the multiculturalists go on to postulate that this context can only be maintained or created by granting special rights to ethnic and religious groups. These special rights necessarily range from rights to political autonomy for indigenous groups – national minorities existing at the time of nation-state formation – to comparatively uncontroversial guarantees for religious practices for immigrants. Proposed are multicultural rights to accommodate the cultural identities and practices of immigrant groups. In particular, polyethnic rights are meant to keep intra-group social and symbolic ties alive and to strengthen them: 1. voting rights for permanent immigrant residents; 2. affirmative action programmes which increase the representation of visible minorities in major educational and economic institutions; 3. revised work schedules so as to accommodate the religious holidays of immigrant groups; 4. bilingual education programmes for the children of immigrants, so that their earliest years of education are conducted partly in their mother-tongue as a transitional phase to secondary and post-secondary education in the dominant receiving country language; and 5. minority group schools such as Muslim schools. On this view, reciprocity and solidarity in cultural groups provide the basis for a collective culture that fosters common and publicly declared narratives and collective representations.

Like the assimilation model, the multicultural approach restricts citizens' solidarities within the confines of a particular state. Unlike the assimilation model, the multicultural approach adds another layer and expands citizens' loyalties to a particular cultural group within the state. It is not a full-fledged model, and it is meant mainly to complement the national model with multicultural elements. Importantly, both assimilation and multiculturalism emphasise common membership in states as containers, albeit with a different emphasis. T.H. Marshall cogently summarized the main underlying assumption, albeit not with reference to these particular models. Analysing the development of welfare states after World War Two, Marshall stated that the recognition of rights must be based on a sense of common membership in a group, thereby embedding reciprocal rights and duties in the solidarities of a collective identity: 'The status of citizenship presupposes ... a direct feeling of membership in a community on the basis of the loyalty towards a culture that is shared by all people' (Marshall, 1964: 92). This notion is indubitably plausible in so far as a collective idea about citizens' rights and mutual duties is closely tied to the solidarity and reciprocity inherent in members' social and symbolic ties. Nevertheless, the question arises as to whether full membership in a political community must be exclusively tied to indivisible loyalty to one and only one state. Since citizenship is not exclusively founded on ties between citizens and the state, but more fundamentally on ties among citizens, the toleration of transnational ties cannot be dismissed out of hand.

While the necessity of a context of choice is a plausible one, it is not self-evident that a particular cultural collective has to guarantee this frame. The concept lacks a clear argument as to why the particular category into which a person happens to be born and raised constitutes the primary group of reference. This criticism is only partly recognized by multiculturalists who argue for cultural and political rights such as extensive self-government in the case of national minorities and only polyethnic rights in the case of immigrants. Moreover, polyethnic rights are essentially good old-fashioned civil rights – they can easily be derived from such well-known principles as the freedom of religion and freedom of speech.

In sum, theories grouped under the ethnic pluralist model offer a sophisticated array of propositions explaining why and how in-group resources and cohesion may be compatible with eventual immigrant integration. They go a long way towards explaining the 'ethnic paradox': concomitant self-organization among immigrants and their eventual integration into the country of settlement (Faist, 1996). Nevertheless, the close focus of the ethnic pluralist model on resources transplanted from the emigration to the immigration countries neglects the emergence of new and syncretist forms of culture and politics in migration and integration processes. In immigration situations, it is very likely that immigrants will draw on the cultures of both the emigration and immigration countries.

7. Globalization: limitless borders

The post-modern and post-national perspectives of globalized lives neither constitute a relatively unified model like assimilation theories, nor do they imply an over-arching idea like integration through group diversity as do ethnic pluralist theories. Instead, post-modern and post-structural perspectives encompass diverse claims, such as the reinterpretation of cultures in a world of decolonization (Appadurai, 1996), increasing chances for small and medium-sized companies in world markets (Fujita, 1998), and post-national membership in political communities.

7.1   Cultural life: hybrid identities

In the realm of cultural integration, post-modernist interpretations of hybrid culture do not form a model of integration, but rather a perspective which analyses societies from the 'fringes'; for example, from the vantage point of post-colonial writers. This is largely an epistemological enterprise. International mobility plays a key role because European colonial history thus migrates back to the centres of economic, political and cultural power. Since post-modern approaches argue against using comprehensive notions such as 'nation' – and thus attack assimilationist ideas such as 'melting into the core' – they advocate strategies of pluralization. However, it is not pluralistic cultures as such – as in ethnic pluralism – but the incommensurability of cultural practices that enjoys conceptual priority (Bhabha, 1995).

Recently, researchers in anthropology and cultural studies have extended the term 'diaspora' beyond its traditional meaning. In the past, 'diaspora' used to denote a forced dispersion of people from their native countries and the longing of the refugees to return to a real or imagined homeland. In post-modern thinking, the term now applies to all those who are characterized by, for example, migration, constant travelling, tourism, and multiple loyalties in different states. Mobile people do not exclusively belong to one community but exhibit patchwork identities with ties to manifold collectives. These *sujets mixtes* allegedly constitute hybrids, showing a cultural *mélange* of languages and symbolic practices (Bhabha, 1994). Great political hopes are vested in these persons with hybrid identities. Supposedly, because of their special position, these diasporists are able to conduct critical examination of the dominating discourses of nation and liberalism (Clifford, 1994). These hybrid transmigrants inhabit the 'in-between' of nations and organizations. According to post-modernists, they mentally and actually live in 'third spaces'; they are neither here nor there.

7.2   Economic participation: small global players

Over the past decades, the extent and variety of economically-based border-crossing transactions by immigrants have increased, for example in the USA-Caribbean migration system. Contemporary studies often deal with transnational economic giants which exert a great deal of political and economic influence: 'global players'. However, one should not jump to the conclusion that transnational enterprises only include huge combines like IBM or Daimler-Chrysler. International South-North migration offers chances to build up middle-class firms (Portes, 1996), for example in the textiles industry. Thus immigrants make use of their insider advantages within reciprocity-as-exchange relations in business. For this to come about, two seminal economic parameters have changed. First, a tightly interwoven world economy gives strong incentives even for family businesses to look for markets abroad. Favourable conditions for border-crossing transactions include a lowering of customs barriers for some products in various countries and, above all, decreasing costs for long-distance transport and communication. This is not only an example of changing economies of scale – the relation between size and efficiency – but also, to create a novel expression, of improved 'economies of scope'. Economies of scope do not primarily concern production quantities but space-time compression. This is a form of flexible 'just in time' production (Harvey, 1989: 147-59). In some of these cases, flows of information and trust as reciprocity become important in kinship groups and tightly interwoven networks of friends – such as guanxi networks among Chinese migrants (Seagrave, 1995: 17).

The second parameter is the expansion of immigrant enterprises in service sectors, and in activities that were previously moving to the developing countries like the garment industry. However, only a small percentage of immigrants are involved in transnational business activities. It is by no means a mass trend. It is nonetheless noteworthy that some of these border-crossing economic transactions take place in the informal sector. For example, Turkish migrants produce jeans in Dutch sweatshops and the products are sold in German markets. Upon discovery of the sweatshops the entrepreneurs are ready to relocate their production (Rath, 2000). 'Willing' workers are a necessary condition for this kind of flexible production. Ethnically-based reciprocity and solidarity form one of the prerequisites for informal production arrangements, juxtaposing ethnic contractors and their workers against outside entrepreneurs (Morokvasic, 1991).

7.3 Political membership: post-national rights

One recent theory of border-crossing membership observes that citizenship has been subject to profound changes since World War Two. According to post-nationalists, its two substantial components – 'collective identity' and citizens' rights – have become increasingly decoupled. Rights formerly tied to belonging in a national community are more and more legitimized in an abstract way and on a global level. One of the sources for the effect of supranational norms has been human rights. Even non-citizen immigrants have been able to assert significant civil and social rights (Soysal, 1994). Basically, the concept of post-national membership starts from the assumption that human rights have become of great importance for the immigrants' legal status, and therefore human rights and citizens' rights have started to converge. The alleged mechanisms that foster this development are international discourses and institutions which induce individual states to comply with supranational norms (Jacobson, 1995). This perspective on political membership enables us to interpret human rights as an effective part of a world culture or world society (Meyer et al., 1997). This claim is definitely novel: until the 1940s the right of citizenship was considered to be a fundamental 'right to have rights'; an insight dating back to the period between the two world wars when stateless persons were unable to turn to an effective supranational authority for support.

The various concepts of what could be called a globalist paradigm are subject to three serious objections. First, the idea of hypermobility does not capture the real-world experience of most international migrants. Only relatively few migrants commute between different places in two or more countries over longer periods of time. The organization and perspective of some households or families, however, is definitely transnational: for example, Chinese business persons from Hong Kong – called 'astronauts'– found a firm in Singapore but settle their families in Los Angeles, New York or Toronto to enhance their children's assets, or as a secure place of refuge in case of political instability (Cohen, 1997: 93). Their mobility should be understood as a consequence of the growing interdependence between the US-American economy and the Pacific economies of Taiwan, Hong Kong, Singapore and China.

Second, the meaning of the term 'hybrid identities' is opaque. It seemingly refers to personal identities, forming combinations of 'in-betweens'. Sometimes, the hybrid is characterized by a cosmopolitan orientation. For example, the 1920s saw elaboration of the concept 'marginal man' to classify those immigrants who did not espouse any integrative tendency; those who were 'rootless' (Park, 1950). However, in the new versions, hybrids are cherished as those who have successfully translated between cultures. This characterization may well apply to intellectuals who 'translate' ideas. One problem, however, is that the cosmopolitan hybrids in the 'third spaces' are thought to be in the vanguard of critics of authoritarian rule and inappropriate discourses.

Yet hybridity does not necessarily lead to resistance against imperialist practices and rule. In short, the inflated diaspora or hybrid perspective is too imprecise to constitute a useful tool for analysis of multiple relations criss-crossing state borders.

Third, apart from the fact that in the foreseeable future there will be no effective supranational institution to guarantee human rights throughout the world, the term 'post-national citizenship' is misleading in real-world contexts such as the European Union. Only citizens of member states are European Union citizens. Thus, not all settled persons are included: for example third-country citizens. Moreover, the European Union is not only a multiple-level system of governance; citizenship is also set on multiple and interactive levels (Marks, 1997: 35; Faist, 1997: 244).

This is just one example in support of the more general conclusion that the development of social rights must be seen in the interplay of various levels of governance within the European Union. Terms such as 'post-national membership' create the false impression of an independent form of emerging citizenship above states. Instead, border-crossing rights within emerging multiple-level governance systems imply a division of labour between supranational, state and sub-state authorities and members (Faist, 2000b). Nevertheless, the unique experience of the European Union suggests that membership can be tied to more than one state or level of governance.

8. Border-crossing expansion of social spaces: syncretist forms of integration

Dense and continuous transnational ties usually evolve out of migratory processes in which border-crossing networks, collectives and organizations regulate the flow of goods, persons and information. Modern mechanisms of mass transport and communication then facilitate ties without propinquity. Transnational ties in these contexts are not usually global but regional. For the various types of transnational spaces to flourish, not only discrimination of immigrants but also the wide latitude of civil, social and political rights must enable immigrants in liberal-democratic immigration states to maintain transnational ties. Types of transnational spaces like diasporas can further encourage the integration of immigrants, as for example among Russian Jews in Germany (Faist, 2000c: chap. 6).

A transnational perspective does not place acculturation, as does the assimilation model, or cultural difference, as does ethnic pluralism, at the centre of the empirical or normative goal. Moreover, hybrid identities are not vested with allegedly progressive capacities, as in the post-modern and post-national interpretations. Rather, the border-crossing expansion of social space explores the intersection between national and transnational ties entertained by immigrants.

8.1 Cultural life: syncretism

Assimilation and ethnic pluralism conceive of culture as territorially confined, based on a common language and relatively static. Cultural learning processes are locally bounded. This is an understanding of culture as *a* culture, a sort of hardware used by a collective. Such cultures may pass through stages of universal modernization: for example, primary and secondary schools act as a sort of informal cultural insurance for nations (Gellner, 1983). For the purpose of analysis of transnational ties and spaces, this understanding must be broadened (Pieterse, 1994: 176-7). The purpose of such an exercise is not primarily to predict the end result. Instead, the aim is to capture the mechanisms of cultural integration more precisely through understanding of culture as human software, akin to a tool kit (Swidler, 1986). This requires examination of concepts of cultural diffusion and evolution. Spatiality and not locality is the point of departure. One must find the structures of symbolic ties and collective representations expressed in private and public images, narratives, institutions and languages (Geertz, 1973: 3-30). This is a useful complement to culture as hardware. And it is especially fruitful for the analysis of immigrant culture. Immigrant groups may undergo rapid changes within one or two generations. In the end, culture as hardware and culture as software may be complementary vantage points. In order to attain a certain degree of stability, dynamic and syncretist elements of culture need limitations as to law and security.

What one observes are combinations of hyphenated identities and self-understandings among immigrants and their children. For example, Islamic organizations in Europe have undergone significant changes which distinguish them from patterns of religion found in the emigration countries. The activities of Islamic organizations in countries like Germany are partly an outgrowth of an ever-increasing re-Islamization of public life in Turkey. For these organizations, Turkish immigrants in Germany used to be primarily of political interest. In the course of time, however, these groups have lost control over the shaping of symbolic ties for their German-based clients. Since the 1950s, Islam has become a forcefully contested current in Turkey, and Islamic groups have tried to gain power in Turkish domestic politics. Since the early 1990s, the Turkish government has departed from the

Kemalist tradition, at times actively fostering a Turkish-Islamic synthesis (Toprak, 1996: 108).

In Germany, the branch of the state-controlled Turkish Directorate of Religious Affairs only took significant action after Islamist organizations such as the Association of the New World View in Europe (*Milli Görüs*) had recruited members and built mosques. The Turkish government had every reason to assume that *Milli Görüs* supported the electoral campaigns of the former Islamic Prosperity Party (*Refah*) in Turkey. While the activities of Islamic organizations in Turkey and Germany may have strengthened Turkish nationalism and Muslim transnational representations, the messages of the organizations involved have contradictory implications. On the one hand, Islamic propaganda emphasises in-group social and symbolic ties and thus segregation from German society. On the other hand, the overwhelming majority of the second and third generations will stay in Germany.

While permanent residence in Germany does not necessarily lead to increased contacts with Germans and vice versa, a one-sided orientation to Turkey gradually changes into a bi- or transnational focus. For example, issues of education and employment are practical questions to be solved in Germany, and so is cultural recognition for all those following the first generation. Even nationalist and religious organizations wooing young Turks who have grown up in Germany deliver a double message: 'Wir, wir, wir sind von hier, sind Einheimische' ('We, we, we are from here, we are indigenous') and 'Wir sind Türken, sind Muslime, sind zivilisiert' ('We are Turks, we are Muslims, we are civilized': cited in Karakao lu–Aydin, 1997: 37).

Islamic organizations in Germany have also realized that in order to work meaningfully with young Turkish adults in Germany, they must have a sustained and legally secured presence in Germany.

This is one of the reasons why the three major Islamic players in Germany have tried to achieve recognition as legally recognized religious organizations. This would elevate their status beyond a simple lawful association to an organization authorized to impose taxes, to have access to television and the other mass media, to instruct Muslim children in German public schools, to cater to inmates of hospitals and prisons, to receive subsidies for their work with the young (to name only a few of the benefits involved). At the same time, the struggle to achieve official recognition has provoked discussion within these organizations about their future direction. Clearly, a Turkey-centred agenda of Islamic revival no longer suffices. Instead, Islamic organizations nowadays grapple with dual citizenship, juvenile crime and social work. In short, in an effort to control young

Muslims' social and symbolic ties in Germany, religious organizations have inadvertently had to take account of syncretist identities and relinquish a one-sided emigration country orientation.

8.2 Economic participation: interstitial entrepreneurship

Like cultural spaces, the border-crossing economic ties of immigrant business are framed by the overall context of a world market. This does not imply, however, that transnational entrepreneurs are identical with 'global players'. Most economic activities are regionally bounded. Numerous relatively privileged migrants, human capital migrants, come from relatively developed countries in the 'South', such as India and Turkey, and concentrate in a few destination countries of the Pacific rim, such as Australia and the United States (Salt, 1997). Others are economic capital migrants who invest abroad, tapping congenial ethnic labour supplies.

For example, Chinese businesspersons from Hong Kong invested in Vancouver in the early 1990s: the reasons given included political stability and easy access to Chinese workers (Wong, 1997: 344-45). Such transnational entrepreneurs do not operate in deterritorialized spaces. On the contrary, their success depends in large part upon establishing solid and dense connections with both emigration and immigration countries. Whether this strategy can contribute to the integration of immigrants into the country of settlement also hinges on the level of discrimination. High levels of rejection hinder entrepreneurs in converting economic capital into social status. Historically, xenophobic tendencies have hampered overall economic growth (Landes, 1998: chaps. 27 and 28). In many cases, we find a progressive development of interstitial entrepreneurship from intra-kinship reciprocity and solidarity, complemented at later stages by partial transnational circuits which include families but also larger groups like ethnic communities.

Three forms of economic transnationalization tend to develop sequentially: first, remittances of migrants from the immigration to the emigration countries in transnational households and kinship groups; second, the inception and growth of immigrant businesses in the immigration countries; and third, transnational production, distribution and sale in economic issue networks and transnational companies (Faist, 2000a: 14-18).

8.3 Political membership: multiple citizenship

Debates on border-crossing memberships in political communities have charted the legal toleration, or even recognition, of citizens' transnational ties in dichotomous manner. As a starting point the canonical approaches use either the individual state or the world level. Thus, the corresponding ideal-typical concepts are national citizenship and post-national membership. However, container space concepts cannot capture the ties of immigrants which extend into several countries. And cosmopolitan approaches are unable to specify the transnational ties with concrete countries. Dual citizenship builds upon social and symbolic ties in transnational spaces. In other words, dual citizenship is an institutionalized correlate of the migrants' life world in transnational spaces. It builds upon solidarity ties among citizens held in trust by sovereign states. The rapid growth of dual citizenship can be interpreted as a reaction of states to the increasing transnational ties of new citizens. It jeopardizes neither the basic targets of state authority and democracy nor the integration of new citizens into political communities. Dual citizenship helps immigrants to acquire citizenship of the immigration country because it reduces the socio-psychological costs of adding another set of loyalties (Jones Correa, 1998). It is one of the instruments with which to enhance the congruence of people settled in a territory with those eligible to vote. In the political sphere, it is not the conclusion of integration but a prerequisite for political participation. The contextual conditions of immigrant life worlds within transnational spaces and relaxed rules of access to citizenship in immigration states are extremely favourable for the expansion of dual citizenship. First, the age of interstitial linkages offers favourable conditions for the emergence of transnational spaces, and for the preservation of continuous and dense ties over time. Examples include diasporas, issue networks and transnational organizations. This is the life-world undercurrent of increased tolerance for multiple citizenship. Second, it does not come as a surprise to find that dual citizenship became an issue of public debate in Europe and North America after the two World Wars and the Cold War. In times of interstate conflicts, the exclusion of outsiders may contribute to a sense of solidarity. Certainly, exclusion and even violence directed at outsiders helps compensate for some of the inevitably hostile feelings of the members of in-groups towards each other (Freud, 1994). This is one possible reason why hot and cold wars constitute a fertile ground for the expansion of national citizenship, as the expansion of universal welfare state principles in the United Kingdom immediately after World War Two suggests.

Conversely, in times of a relative absence of interstate conflicts, the demand for dual citizenship becomes more pressing, and governments are more inclined to tolerate it.

Dual citizenship is usually considered legitimate when the countries involved are democratic systems of one sort or another, or, to be more precise, when the dual citizens can be expected to adhere to democratic principles. Democracies are known not to go to war against each other. A major part of interstate migration, however, traces back to non-OECD countries. For example, about two-thirds of immigrants into the European Union member-states hailed from non-EU countries in the late 1990s. Yet it is not the absence of war but the democratic loyalties of dual citizens that matter. The regimes with which immigration countries tend to wage wars are predominantly authoritarian, and many of their citizens living abroad do not consider them legitimate. Therefore, most Iraqi immigrants in Europe and the Americas, for example, did not side with Saddam Hussein during the First Gulf War in 1990/91. To conclude, it is not the absence of war but the principle of democratic legitimation that forms the moral basis of the political meta-principle 'democracy' which reaches beyond single states and is widely accepted by immigrants. From this point of view, dual citizenship may even be advantageous for the naturalizing country. A potential side-effect may be the exporting of democratic values and ways of thinking into the countries of origin (Spiro, 1997: 1477).

9. Outlook: enriching canonical concepts with an apocryphal model

The concept of border-crossing social expansion can be used to analyse the consequences of particular forms of transnational space arising out of international migration and refugee flows.

Since studies on transnational life-worlds are in their infancy, there is the danger that all four stylized models will be treated as if they are mutually exclusive. As this conceptual overview suggests, the real potential of concepts of transnational membership and participation is to enrich the notions underlying assimilation, ethnic pluralism, and post-nationalism or post-modernism. Even if the unlikely case held true that massive transnationalization eventually turned out to be a only temporary phenomenon – limited mainly to first generation immigrants, exiles and diasporists – its contemporary manifestations suggest that transnational ties should be incorporated into more sophisticated theories of assimilation, ethnic pluralism and post-nationalism, at the very least. But it is equally likely that transnationalization in all walks of life, including capital investment and migration, will prove to be a more enduring structural characteristic of the century that has just started.

Bibliography

Appadurai, A. (1996), *Modernity at Large. Cultural Dimensions of Globalization*, University of Minnesota Press, Minneapolis.
Basch, L., Glick Schiller, N. and Szanton Blanc, C. (1994), *Nations Unbound. Transnational Projects, Postcolonial Predicaments, and Deterritorialized Nation-States*, Gordon and Breach, Langhorne.
Bhabha Homi, K. (ed) (1994), *Nation and Narration*, Routledge, London.
Bhabha Homi, K. (1995), *The Location of Culture*, Routledge, London.
Bonacich, E. (1979), 'The Past, Present, and Future of Split Labor Market Theory', *Research in Race and Ethnic Relations*, vol. 1, AI Press, Greenwich, pp. 17-64.
Breton, R. (1964), 'Institutional Completeness of Ethnic Communities and the Personal Relations of Immigrants', *American Journal of Sociology*, vol. 70, no. 2, pp. 193-205.
Brown, D. (1997), 'Workforce Lessons and Return Migration to the Caribbean: A Case Study of Jamaican Nurses', in P. R. Pessar (ed), *Caribbean Circuits. New Directions in the Study of Caribbean Migration*, Center for Migration Studies, New York, pp. 197-223.
Clifford, J. (1994), 'Diasporas', *Cultural Anthropology*, vol. 9, no. 3, pp. 302-38.
Cohen, R. (1997), *Global Diasporas. An Introduction*, UCL Press, London.
Coleman, J. S. (1990), *Foundations of Social Theory*, The Belknap Press of Harvard University Press, Cambridge.
Durkheim, É. ([1893] 1964), *The Division of Labor in Society,* translated by George Simpson, Macmillan, New York.
Durkheim, É. ([1912] 1965), *The Elementary Forms of Religious Life*, translated by J.W. Swain, The Free Press, New York.
Ekeh, P.P. (1974), *Social Exchange Theory. The Two Traditions*, Harvard University Press, Cambridge.
Engelbrektsson, U. B. (1978), *The Force of Tradition. Turkish Migrants at Home and Abroad*, Acta Universitatis Gothoburgensis, Göteborg.
Esser, H. (1980), *Aspekte der Wanderungssoziologie. Assimilation und*

Integration von Wanderern, ethnischen Gruppen und Minderheiten, Luchterhand, Darmstadt.

Faist, T. (1996), 'The Ethnic Paradox and Immigrant Integration: The Significance of Social and Symbolic Capital in Comparative Perspective', in I. Mucy and W. Olszewskiego (eds), *Dylematy Tozsamosci Europejskich Pod Koniec Drugiego Tysiaclecia*, Univerytet Mikolaja Kopernika, Torún, pp. 151-96.

Faist, T. (1997), 'Migration in Contemporary Europe: European Integration, Economic Liberalization, and Protection', in I. Klausen and L. Tilly (eds), *European Integration in Social and Historical Perspective 1850 to the Present*, Rowman & Littlefield, Boulder, pp. 223-48.

Faist, T. (2000a), *The Volume and Dynamics of International Migration and Transnational Social Spaces*, Oxford University Press, Oxford.

Faist, T. (2000b), *Social Citizenship in the European Union: Residual, Post-National and Nested Membership?*, Institute for Intercultural and International Studies (InIIS), University of Bremen, Working Paper, no. 15, Bremen.

Faist, T. (2000c), *Transstaatliche Räume. Wirtschaft, Politik und Kultur in und zwischen Deutschland und der Türkei*, Transcript, Bielefeld.

Featherman, D., Hauser, L. and Robert, L. (1978), *Opportunity and Change*, Academic Press, New York.

Freud, S. ([1930] 1994), *Das Unbehagen in der Kultur. Und andere kulturtheoretische Schriften*, Fischer, Frankfurt am Main.

Fujita, M. (1998), *The Transnational Activities of Small and Medium-Sized Enterprises*, Kluwer Academic Publishers, Boston.

Furnivall, J.S. (1948), *Colonial Policy and Practice: A Comparative Study of Burma and Netherlands India*, Cambridge University Press, London.

Gans, H.J. (1992), 'Comment: Ethnic Invention and Acculturation: A Bumpy-Line Approach', *Journal of American Ethnic History*, vol. 12, no. 1, pp. 45-52.

Geertz, C. (1973), *The Interpretation of Cultures*, Basic Books, New York.

Gellner, E. (1983), *Nations and Nationalism*, Cornell University Press, Ithaca.

Glazer, N. and Moynihan, P.D. (1963), *Beyond the Melting Pot. The Negroes, Puerto Ricans, Jews, Italians and Irish of New York City*, Harvard University Press, Cambridge.

Gmelch, G. (1980), 'Return Migration', *Annual Review of Anthropology*, vol. 9, pp. 135-59.

Goldstein, E. and Piazza, V. (1996), Naturalization. Dual Citizenship and the Retention of Foreign Citizenship, A Survey, *Interpreter Releases*, no. 517, pp. 61-73.

Gordon, M. (1964), *Assimilation in American Life*, Oxford University Press, New York.

Gouldner, A.W. (1960), 'The Norm of Reciprocity: A Preliminary Statement', *American Sociological Review*, vol. 25, no. 2, pp. 161-78.

Granovetter, M.S. (1979), 'The Theory Gap in Social Network Analysis', in P.W. Holland and L. Stephen (eds), *Perspectives in Social Network Research*, Academic Press, New York, pp. 45-67.

Haas, P.M. (1992), Epistemic Communities and International Policy Coordination, *International Organization*, vol. 46, no. 1, pp. 1-36.

Harvey, D. (1989), *The Condition of Postmodernity*, Blackwell, Oxford.

Hopf, D. (1987), *Herkunft und Schulbesuch ausländischer Kinder. Eine Untersuchung am Beispiel griechischer Schüler*, Max-Planck-Institut für Bildungsforschung, Berlin.

Jacobson, D. (1995), *Rights Across Borders: Immigration and the Decline of Citizenship*, Johns Hopkins University Press, Baltimore.

Jones Correa, M. (1998), *Between Two Nations. The Political Predicament of Latinos in New York City*, Cornell University Press, Ithaca.

Kallen, H. ([1915] 1996), 'Democracy versus the Melting-Pot: A Study of American Nationality', in W. Sollors (ed), *Theories of Ethnicity. A Classical Reader*, Houndmills, Macmillan, pp. 67-92.

Karakao lu–Aydin Y. (1997), 'Ich bin stolz, ein Türke zu sein'. Bedeutung ethnischer Orientierungen für das positive Selbstwertgefühl türkischer Jugendlicher in Deutschland – Ein Essay, in F. Ebert Stiftung (ed), *Identitätsstabilisierend oder konfliktfördernd? Ethnische Orientierungen in Jugendgruppen*, Bonn, pp. 27-38.

Keohane, R.O. and Nye, J.S. (1977), *Power and Interdependence*, Little, Brown, Boston.

Kilic, M. (1994), Deutsch–türkische Doppelstaatsangehörigkeit? *Das Standesamt*, vol. 47, no. 1, pp. 73-78.

Kymlicka, W. (1995), *Multicultural Citizenship. A Liberal Theory of Minority Rights*, Oxford University Press, Oxford.

Landes, D.S. (1998), *The Wealth and Poverty of Nations. Why Some Are So Rich, Why Some So Poor*, Little Brown and Company, London.

Lieberson, S. (1981), *A Piece of the Pie. Blacks and White Immigrants since 1880*, University of California Press, Berkeley.

Marks, G. (1997), 'A Third Lens: Comparing European Integration and State Building', in I. Klausen and L. Tilly (eds), *European Integration in Social and Historical Perspective. From 1850 to the Present*, Rowman & Littlefield, Bouldier, pp. 23-44.

Marshall, T.H. (1964), *Class, Citizenship and Social Development. Essays by T.H. Marshall*, Anchor Books, New York.

Marx, K. and Engels, F. (1972), 'Manifest der kommunistischen Partei 1848', in K.Marx and F. Engels, *Werke*, Bd. 4, Dietz, Berlin (DDR), pp. 461-74.

Meyer, J.W., Boli, J., Thomas, G.M. and Ramirez, Fr.O. (1997), 'World Society and the Nation-State', *American Journal of Sociology*, vol. 103, no. 1, pp. 144-81.

Morokvasic, M. (1991), 'Die Kehrseite der Mode: Migranten als Flexibilisierungsquelle in der Pariser Bekleidungsproduktion. Ein Vergleich mit Berlin', *Prokla*, vol. 21, pp. 264-84.

Park, R.E. ([1928] 1950), 'Human Migration and the Marginal Man', Robert Park, *Race and Culture. Essays in the Sociology of Contemporary Man*, University of Chicago Press, Chicago, pp. 345-56.

Park, R., Burgess, E. and Ernest, W. ([1921] 1969), *Introduction to the Science of Sociology*, University of Chicago Press, Chicago.

Pieterse, J.N. (1994), 'Globalisation as Hybridisation', *International Sociology*, vol. 9, no. 2, pp. 161-84.

Portes, A. (ed) (1995), *The Economic Sociology of Immigration: Essays on Networks, Ethnicity, and Entrepreneurship*, Russell Sage Foundation, New York.

Portes, A. (1996), 'Transnational Communities: Their Emergence and Significance in the Contemporary World System', in R. P. Korzeniewicz and W.C. Smith (eds), *Latin America in the World Economy*, Praeger, Westport, pp. 151-68.

Portes, A., Guarnizo, L.E. and Landolt, P. (1999), 'Introduction, Special Issue: Transnational Communities', *Ethnic and Racial Studies*, vol. 22, no. 2, pp. 217-37.

Rath, J. (ed.) (2000), *Immigrant Businesses: The Economic, Political and Social Environment*, Macmillan Press, Houndmills.

Safran, W. (1991), 'Diasporas in Modern Societies: Myths of Homeland and Return', *Diaspora*, vol.1, no. 1, pp. 83-95.

Salt, J. (1997), *International Movements of the Highly Skilled*, OECD Working Papers, Paris, vol. V, no. 91, International Migration Unit, Occasional Papers No. 3.

Seagrave, S. (1995), *Lords of the Rim. The Invisible Empire of the Overseas*

Chinese, G. P. Putnam's Sons, New York.

Sikkink, K. (1993), 'Human Rights, Principled Issue Networks, and Sovereignty in Latin America', *International Organization*, vol. 47, no. 3, pp. 411-41.

Simmel, G. ([1922] 1955), *Conflict & The Web of Group-Affiliations*, translated by K.H. Wolff and R. Bendix, The Free Press, New York.

Smith, M., Guarnizo, P. and Eduardo, L. (eds) (1998), *Transnationalism From Below*, Transaction Publishers, New Brunswick.

Soysal, Y. (1994), *The Limits of Citizenship. Migrants and Post-National Membership in Europe*, University of Chicago Press, Chicago.

Spiro, P.J. (1997), 'Dual Nationality and the Meaning of Citizenship', *Emory Law Journal*, vol. 46, no. 4, pp. 1411-86.

Stein Barry, N. (1981), 'The Refugee Experience: Defining the Parameters of a Field of Study', *International Migration Review*, vol. 15, no. 1, pp. 320-30.

Swidler, A. (1986), 'Culture in Action: Symbols and Strategies', *American Sociological Review*, vol. 51, pp. 273-88.

Tarrow, S. (1996), 'Fishnets, Internets and Catnets: Globalization and Transnational Collective Action', Instituto Juan March de Estudios e Investigaciones, *Working Paper* 1996/78, Madrid.

Thomas, W.I. and Znaniecki, F. ([1918–1921] 1927), *The Polish Peasant in Europe and America*, 5 Vols, Alfred A. Knopf, New York.

Tilly, C. (1978), *From Mobilization to Revolution*, Englewood Cliffs, Prentice-Hall.

Toprak, B. (1996), 'Civil Society in Turkey', in A. R. Norton (ed), *Civil Society in the Middle East*, E.J. Brill, Leiden, pp. 87-118.

Waldinger, R. (1986/87), 'Changing Ladders and Musical Chairs: Ethnicity and Opportunity in Post-Industrial New York', *Politics and Society*, vol. 15, no. 3, pp. 369-401.

Waltz, K.N. (1979), *Theory of International Politics*, Reading, Addison-Wesley.

Weber, M. ([1924] 1980), *Wirtschaft und Gesellschaft*, 5th edition, J. C. B. Mohr, Tübingen.

Weber, M. ([1918] 1988), 'Der Sozialismus', in *Gesammelte Aufsätze zur Soziologie und Sozialpolitik*, 2nd edition, J.C.B. Mohr, Tübingen, pp. 492-518.

Wellman, B. and Wortley, S. (1990), 'Different Strokes from Different Folks: Community Ties and Social Support', *American Journal of Sociology*, vol. 96, no. 3, pp. 558-88.

White, H., Boorman, S., Breiger, A. and Breiger, R.L. (1976), 'Social Structure from Multiple Networks, I. Blockmodels of Roles and Positions', *American Journal of Sociology*, vol. 81, no. 4, pp. 730-80.

Wihtol de Wenden, C. (1997), 'Kulturvermittlung zwischen Frankreich und Algerien: Eine transnationale Brücke zwischen Immigranten, neuen Akteuren und dem Maghreb', *Soziale Welt*, Sonderband 12, pp. 265-76.

Wong, L.L. (1997), 'Globalization and Transnational Migration: A Study of Recent Chinese Capitalist Migration from the Asian Pacific to Canada', *International Sociology*, vol. 12, no. 3, pp. 329-52.

Zlotnik, H. (1999), 'Trends of International Migration Since 1965: What Existing Data Reveal', *International Migration*, vol. 37, no. 1, pp. 21-61.

PART III:
THE NEW FRONTIERS
OF SOCIOLOGY

11 Some challenges for sociology in the new era

EDWARD A. TIRYAKIAN

Introduction

A century's end and another's beginning is a particularly apposite juncture, a capital 'event' to assess the state of one's discipline. The present juncture is even more apposite given the recognition that we are entering a new millennium (whether as celebrated popularly in 1999/2000 or, for 'purists', in 2000/2001).

The crossing has been a sort of 'liminal period', to adapt the anthropological concept of van Gennep and Victor Turner (Deflem, 1991). On the one hand, it has been attended by the danger of a global series of computer breakdowns (the 'millennium bug') complemented by old eschatological apocalyptic visions privileging the year 2000 as one that would launch the end of the world.[1]

On the other hand, the passage from one millennium to another has also given rise to an unprecedented global celebration, a synchronized mass media event accentuating not merely the religious basis of this jubilation[2] but also the secular reality of what has been termed the 'culture-ideology of consumerism' as a driving force of contemporary capitalism (Sklair, 1995).

What has accentuated the chronological event is its embeddedness in a context of far-reaching and long-term consequences: the coming together of different parts of the world (its 'compression' in time and space as well as in its perception) via interactive networks and flows of people, goods, capital resources, and imageries that have belatedly become recognized in the past two decades as a summary master process: *globalization* (which tends often to be reified, although 'it' is in fact a set of distinct though interrelated

---

1   A secular apocalyptic climate has been part of our world situation for the past half-century or so from an array of terrestrial visions of the end of the world: visions of nuclear warfare, of global warming, and population explosion. The noted historian Eugen Weber concludes his recent overview of apocalypses by stating: 'As we approach another century's ending, now dwarfed by the billennium, preoccupation with end times rises to new heights in a world saturated with them.' (Weber, 1999: 238ff).

2   After all, the year 2000 is the occasion of a Jubilee Year celebrated by one of the world's oldest surviving complex organizations, the Church of Rome.

processes).[3] Crossing the millennium at midnight on January 1, from North to South and East to West, may ultimately be registered as a milestone event in global consciousness, one wherein for the first time in human history truly 'the whole world is watching' (Gitlin, 1980).

The dualism of the event – a mixture of uneasiness if not foreboding and joyful celebration, or what might be termed 'gloom and boom' — is mirrored in a recent issue (October 1999) of *Perspectives*, the newsletter of the Theory Section of the American Sociological Association. Buoyant remarks are made by the chairman of the section that, leaving aside meta-theory (which he sees as dealing with fundamental presuppositions), sociological theory in the form of theoretical research programmes spanning the gamut of levels of analysis from micro- to macro-historical processes 'has in fact undergone an astonishing amount of growth in the last quarter century' (Zelditch, 1999). Alongside this is the more sombre evaluation by another sociologist who views the hiatus in sociology between theory, methodology and substantive knowledge as leading to a Tower of Babel and having as its consequences our failure both to achieve 'the rapid cumulative development of our understanding of society' and to acquire the credibility of other life sciences such as biology (Phillips, 1999).

The present juncture is indeed a critical period for sociology, fundamentally because we are entering a new era; not so much a new chronological era as a new era in the human condition, one which for sociology as a discipline, and for sociological theory as the centre of the 'sociological imagination', demands a rigorous stock-taking and reappraisal of its conceptual framework and boundaries.

The new era to which I refer involves 1. a variety of new social environments which are testing the institutional arrangements and the cultural

---

3   At the end of the twentieth century, 'globalization' (in French, 'mondialisation') became something of a buzzword, but the term is of recent sociological origin. On the basis of modernization analysis and its multidimensional approach to social change, Roland Robertson coined the term in a series of writings that began to appear in the mid-1980s (Robertson and Chirico, 1985; Robertson and Lechner, 1985; Robertson, 1992; for a useful overview see Waters, 1995). Of course, there were non-sociological forerunners to this imaginative conceptualization, notably the vision of presidential aspirant Wendell L. Willkie (1943). Like rationalization, another master process of modernity, globalization has not only had various proponents extolling the benefits of global integration but also its critics. In the latter category are Third World voices who see globalization as yet another form of Westernization/Americanization and, more recently, Western voices who view with dismay the dark side of economic globalization as increasing the inequality between haves and have-nots, environmental degradation, child labour abuses, and slower rates of growth in both industrial and developing countries which result in stagnant wages and growing job insecurity. Among these critics, see Sassen (1998) and Mazur (2000).

codes of long-established societal boundaries as the boundaries of recognized nation-states become more porous, and within nation-states as traditional boundaries in the public sphere dissolve, most patently in the area of gender and sexuality; 2. a transformation of economic life stemming from both the dramatic technological changes of the 'digital age' and from the sweeping deregulation of industry, generating the promise of new abundance while masking increasing job insecurity at every level of the corporate ladder, and 3. globalization which entails, in one respect, greater overall integration, not only in production and consumption patterns but also in global consciousness, for example in the global spread, if not yet general global acceptance, of some formulation of human rights. Growing awareness of various facets of and perspectives on these emergent transformations of the social landscape has started to enter public discourse, for example in calling this era 'late modernity' or the 'second modernity'.[4]

But the new era envisaged here is also characterized by vast new *mappings* of the world, from the depths of the ocean to the celestial heights opened up by the Hubble telescope as a window on a near-infinity of galaxies which increases the possibility that life exists elsewhere; and perhaps of even greater potential significance for sociology, as I will indicate later, the mappings of the human genome and its sequential arrangements. I can only by analogy propose that the new era is akin, in its cognitive transformation, to the 'long sixteenth century' which opened up such vast horizons with the telescope and the microscope side by side with the new mapping of the world by Gerardus Mercator. However, not only is the new era one of cognitive transformations, it is also one in which systematic knowledge is implemented in the technological adaptations of this knowledge to alter basic features of our biosphere.

If this were not enough, there is for sociology another element of the new era, namely the proliferation of the discipline, not only internally to it within and across boundaries of fields and speciality areas, but also across the globe. Regarding the latter, democratization and economic development, singly if not together, tend to favour new centres of sociology in different regions of the world with different experiences of modernization in the past half century. Consequently, the implicit grounding of sociological analysis and interpretation on the mainstream Western experience of modernity – particularly that of the United States – will have to be rethought as part of a

---

4   Giddens has provided an interesting exploration of the adaptation of the subjective self to general conditions of late modernity, including some of the substantial moral issues attending the development of late modernity (1991: 227).

broader 'remapping' of sociology: for example, sociology in countries marked by past colonial experience or by the past authoritarian and/or socialist experience. Such a remapping may stem from the forthcoming twenty-six volumes of the new millennium *Encyclopedia* providing state-of-the-art knowledge on the social and behavioural sciences and their interaction with other life sciences (Smelser and Baltes, 2001); this will undoubtedly be a massive update of both its predecessor of thirty years ago, the *International Encyclopedia of the Social Sciences* (Sills, 1968) and the single volume compendium of sociology brought out by Smelser about a dozen years ago (Smelser, 1988).

Nevertheless, the discipline in all its proliferation and in terms of its political temper has evolved too much for a single voice today to provide an authoritative assessment in the manner of Talcott Parsons some forty years ago, when at the request of the Program Committee of the then American Sociological Society (now the American Sociological Association) he presented a carefully crafted document entitled 'Some Problems Confronting Sociology as a Profession' (Parsons, 1959). This was in its essential features a positive and optimistic appraisal: despite some ideological difficulties facing the profession, sociology, Parsons ventured, had become accepted at research universities and had reached 'what is, perhaps, a first level of maturity as a scientific discipline' (Parsons, 1959: 55). The institutionalization of the discipline was paralleled by the recognition of its autonomy from social philosophy and ancillary social sciences (such as economics), on the one hand, and from applied social remediation or social work on the other. The differentiation and legitimization of sociology in academe resulted in sociology being able to achieve a sustained level of development in both theory and research. Challenges to the profession were, at one level, ideological controversies that could detract from the scientific status of sociology, and at another, the need to maintain interdisciplinary contacts (something which Parsons himself continuously did, not only with other social sciences but with various other disciplines, including biology).

Parsons' assessment provided Smelser with an important legacy. In the introduction to his 1988 edited volume of major sociological fields, Smelser covered the main points of his former mentor's 1959 evaluation, and then indicated some major challenges that he saw facing the profession thirty years later. The unity of the discipline had been shaken by internal conflicts over the 'sociological positivism' of the previous period and, observed Smelser, 'there appears to be no present evidence of an overarching effort at theoretical synthesis of the sort that Parsons sought to effect, and little reason to believe that such an effort is on the horizon' (Smelser, 1988: 12). But Smelser sought to go beyond chaos and cacophony to make a case for sociology in the public sphere. First, to counteract charges of triviality or hostility towards existing traditional institutions and values, sociology had to have spokespersons who adhered to the canons of scientific inquiry and methodological soundness (ibid.: 5). Second, while the ideal for sociology would be the internationalization of its theory and methodology – that is, giving the conduct of its empirical research a universal quality 'crosscutting national and cultural boundaries' (ibid.) – one must recognize ideological limitations to this ideal deriving from national and nationalist traditions. Constraints here stem from the fact that sociological research is mostly funded by national governments prompted to do so by domestic social and political problems.

The closing decade of the twentieth century saw old and grand assessments of theory and its world situation that merit attention, however briefly. These recent sociological visions are links in the sociological tradition that originated with Saint-Simon's premonition of a new industrial order replacing the decadent order of the *ancien régime* and, with the reorganization of society, calling for a new science of society.[5]

1. Three recent sociological visions

A major 'internalist' perspective that has sociological theory itself as its focus is provided by Donald Levine (1995). Sensitive to a feeling of malaise and fragmentation pervasive in sociology (and other social sciences), one that relates to their functional identity in late modernity, Levine makes direct use of 'vision' in seeking to recapture the identity of sociology. One dimension of this vision is the main 'narratives' that sociologists have used in the story-telling of the discipline, with Parsons' *Structure of Social Action* (1937) and Gouldner's *Coming Crisis of Western Sociology* (1970) as polar narratives: the former an evolutionary synthesis, the latter a critical contextual sociology of knowledge narrative.

After arguing in favour of a new eclectic 'dialogical narrative' that would interface competing narratives and draw them into a 'common conversation'

---

5   Saint-Simons's vision was shared by his disciples (in effect, the first school of sociology!), with several of the Saint-Simoniens becoming the builders of the infrastructure of modern Europe and its outreach (such as the Suez Canal). Saint-Simon's acuity even anticipated the transnational European Union as an economic and political reconstruction of European society necessary for economic growth and political stability (Saint-Simon, 1814).

(Levine, 1995: 96), Levine deploys a second vision, tracing images of the 'good society' in various national sociological traditions of the future, from the classical Hellenic to the contemporary American tradition.[6] Yet this provides no solution to an *evolutionary crisis* in the social sciences in general which reflects the fact that in their established forms they 'no longer fulfil the functions of providing orienting frameworks for intellectual communities', (ibid.: 290). Rather than conclude with stoicism, a third vision is invoked: amidst the variety of narratives and national traditions which have produced diagnoses, interpretations and explanations of diverse social phenomena of modernity, unity in diversity is to be found in the *quest for a secular ethic* that stretches back to Dewey and much further back to Aristotle. Levine's study does not give substance to the third vision but suggests that the dialogical approach not only uncovers the indispensable role of non-rational factors in moral life (something buried in the wake of the Enlightenment) but it is itself dialogue as a creative inquiry is a model for ethical life (ibid.: 326). If Levine's vision of sociological visions may seem more formal than substantive, it is of heuristic value in this period of transition to draw attention to the commonality of the sociological enterprise across paradigms (or master narratives) and national traditions; it also points to the inevitability that sociology will face the challenge of moral issues and ethical principles which abound as much in 'late modernity' as in 'early modernity'.[7]

An externalist perspective is presented by the British theorist Martin Albrow. At one level, theorizing initially from a Weberian standpoint, Albrow is keenly aware of the importance of dialogue between sociology and history, of their 'polymorphous relations' (Albrow, 1996a: 2). We cannot accept that the present is the privileged domain of sociological theory (any more than we can take theory to be the monopoly of the social sciences) and that the past is the privileged domain of the narrative accounts of history.

---

6 Levine's discussion of the 'Marxian tradition' alongside the six *national* traditions is incongruous: a case could easily be made for placing Marx in the German tradition, especially within the temporal frame of Levine's discussion.

7 Following a separate path of inquiry, Giddens concludes his study by noting that the emancipatory aspect of late modernity (in his discussion, the capability of adopting freely chosen lifestyles) in turn raises a variety of moral dilemmas (since he does not specify what these are, to suggest one area, the dissolution and decline of the nuclear family as the normative unit of biological and social reproduction is giving rise to a host of dilemmas, moral and legal, regarding rights and responsibilities of marital partners towards one another and their offspring). As to these dilemmas 'No one should underestimate how difficult it will be to deal with these, or even how hard it is to formulate them in ways likely to command widespread consensus. How can we remoralise social life without falling prey to prejudice? If there is no transhistorical ethical principle, how can humanity cope with clashes of 'true believers' without violence?' (Giddens, 1991: 231).

Historians today write narrative accounts that pertain and give meaning to affairs of 'the present' and the immediate past, and they are able to suggest sequential orderings of sets of events that are vital for sociological analysis. The dialogue points to complementarity, not the reduction of one approach to another. Here Albrow enters his own vision of dealing with historical change by means of 'epochal theory', a theoretical perspective on the dynamics of modernity in terms of major epochs of history, with the bulk of the analysis devoted to the nascent epoch, the 'global age' (Albrow, 1996b).

While drawing extensively on the recent literature on globalization, Albrow posits that processes of advanced modernity are those of globality understood economically, politically and culturally as a new macro eco-setting with objective and phenomenological dimensions that transcend the setting of the nation-state which marked the modern age. Boundary-crossing – of ideas, of accommodation between peoples, of capital resources and so forth – of course took place in the modern age (and earlier), but while they were subject to internal integration and regulation by the nation-state, these traditional boundaries no longer hold (ibid.: 146). Albrow's vision of the Global Age is basically an encouraging one, resting as it does on a positive view of individual actions and the global state, the latter not a new Leviathan, nor the United Nations, but the result of voluntary engagements of all those 'who have responded to globality by making the globe the criterion for their active engagement in common purposes' (ibid.: 178).

Given his analysis of emergent globality as new sets of consciousness and social relationships, Albrow calls for a rethinking of our theories of the state which in various (liberal) theories of the nation-state, from Adam Smith to Weber, was implicitly viewed as an impediment or constraint on actors acting out a purpose for the community as a whole.[8] The Weberian tradition, which gives political sociology a central place in examining the institutionalization of power and violence under state authority (the theme of legitimation), has to be given a new formulation. Nation-states, regardless of their ideological presuppositions, can no longer make undisputed claims on individuals; what earlier theories of the nation-state glossed over is that 'the idea of state action is power for the general good and that each person is capable of asserting that' (ibid.: 179). Albrow's political vision is that of the nation-state's diminishing role with increasing global citizenship: the waning

---

8   Albrow does not consider an alternative perspective on the nation-state: not as an unnecessary constraint on individuals but as a necessary facilitator and agent of change, either as the welfare state in Western liberal theories or as the development state in discussions of East Asia economic growth.

of national projects able to provide a sense of civic responsibility is compensated by a sense of responsibility for events in the world that stir global movements and their local initiatives.

Parts of Albrow's analysis may be criticised as inchoate and even overly optimistic. However, it should in the main be viewed as having a dual purpose. First, as a corrective to some of the more pessimistic (even nihilistic) post-modern diagnoses of the end-of-epoch sort (ibid.: 105). Second, as theorizing a new unfolding form of social existence, that of the 'Global Age' which replaces the various features we have come to call the 'Modern Age'. Here, Albrow is inviting us to seek data and evidence in our present setting that are of relevance to 'epochal theory', with a new narrative interpretation replacing the long familiar one that privileged industrial society and the nation-state.

If I understand Albrow correctly, he is sounding a clarion call for sociological theory not to take as its twenty-first century locus the territorial imperatives of the nation-state, and not even globalization as the latest phase of modernity, but to think in terms of large-scale ruptures in the historical process, with the advent of a new epoch replacing at macro and micro levels another epoch. In a sense, then, Albrow is an heir to Saint-Simon's vision of 'organic periods' of societal reorganization following 'crisis periods'.

A second externalist vision is the remarkable three-volume study by Manuel Castells, who seeks, within a broad comparative theoretical frame, to come to grips with salient parameters of large-scale change impacting on the world order (1998). This vision is complementary to Albrow's in two respects. First, it provides much more specific regional data on the transformations of structural change, with the technological revolution centred around information providing the driving force for them (hence the designation of 'The Information Age' as the primary label for our global setting). Second, it pays much closer attention to the dark side of the new age, including the perverse effects of the global economy. Thus, for example, Castells views the juggernaut of the global economy – while it spreads to every part of the world (including colonization of the life world, as Habermas would put it) – as exacerbating uneven development: some segments of humankind and some territories will be discarded as other segments become more valuable.

Those that become economically irrelevant and/or socially excluded may well be subject to two poles of attraction: on the one hand, the global criminal economy, which depends on marginalized consumers and producers, and on the other, fundamentalisms of different kinds which violently reject the values and transnational institutional networks of the information age (Ibid.: 354ff).[9]

Like Albrow, Castells anticipates the declining sovereignty of the nation-state and its replacement by new flexible local and regional arrangements able to develop viable networks with the global economy. This localization of the polity, he adds, is not a new era in participatory democracy, for the people 'are, and will be, increasingly distant from the halls of power, and disaffected from the crumbling institutions of civil society' (ibid.: 358). Castells ends his brilliant sociological exposition on a cautious note. The information age of globalization will neither be a dark age, as its critics fear, nor a new golden age, as its proponents claim; instead, in keeping with the promise of the Enlightenment, there will be an unleashing of 'unprecedented productive capacity by the power of the mind' (ibid.: 359), a kind of 'technological overdevelopment'. But this will take place side by side with 'black holes of informational capitalism' which will hit Fourth World populations particularly hard, for example in Africa and in the American inner cities.

The vision of Castells entails a concluding look at the past, present, and future. While firmly committed to political action and projects as needed for the betterment of society, and while equally hopeful that sociological analysis can provide elements for an informed social action, Castells eschews social theory, or ideology for that matter, as providing the necessary frames for political practice. That is the lesson to be gleaned from the century just past; social theory, if I understand Castells's conclusion correctly, can best serve to specify the frames of the information age which constrain collective creativity and hamper application of the fruits of information technology by trivializing purposive social action. Sociological theory and analysis should be informative in the information age; informative in reconstructing culture from experience, in enhancing the global solidarity of humankind, in inducing corporate heads to assume their social responsibilities (beyond responsibility to stockholders and to securities analysts), and in fostering intergenerational solidarity.

---

9   The resurgence of religion – and of a very militant religion at that, given that it seeks to overthrow the secular state – in several regions of the world, as typified in Afghanistan and Algeria for example, or in milder form in the United States, has provided much material for a reappraisal of sociological theorizing on religion and the trend of modernity (Tiryakian, 1997).

2. Hilbert's legacy

Though of lesser magnitude than a sweeping vision, there is another, different, but perhaps equally appropriate stimulant for sociological theory and reflection at this juncture. One hundred years ago, in celebration of the coming century and the achievements of the one just ending, Paris staged a colossal world fair (The Exposition Universelle Internationale of 1900). The International Mathematical Congress, one of the several scientific and learned bodies to hold their congresses in Paris in 1900, sought out the most eminent and respected mathematician to deliver the plenary address. After due consideration as to whether the honour should go to a French mathematician (the equally eminent Henri Poincaré), the great German mathematician David Hilbert was selected.

What Hilbert presented was 'The Problems of Mathematics', not only a look back at the recent achievements of mathematics but, more significantly, a concise exposition of twenty-three significant research problems for which solutions could be found. This was not only a *tour de force* because it involved a survey of all or nearly all the areas of mathematics at the time; it also proved to be highly heuristic in prodding mathematicians into tackling the problems identified. At least one of Hilbert's problems was solved within a year of his speech, and solving the remainder became a legacy that propelled mathematics into the twentieth century, with each 'solution' becoming a noted event in the profession.[10] I do not pretend to be able to appreciate as a mathematician can either the problems or the solutions, but what warrants attention with regard to this legacy is the important integrative function for the entire discipline performed by specification of the main tasks (or challenges) to be addressed. Let me propose very briefly how we might translate Hilbert's legacy into a directive for sociology.

My thoughts here are grounded on a basic assumption. Barring some global catastrophe in the ecosphere that shatters the global economy and global communication, the processes of globalization will challenge the further internationalization of sociology (as already noted by Albrow and King, 1990). Rather than continuing with the nation-state as the ultimate referent of analysis (or even with sets of nation-states, such as in the world-system perspective), sociological theory will increasingly need to develop on several fronts: the global, the (cross-border) regional, the national, and the

---

10   For a discussion of Hilbert's programme and the severe blow dealt it by Kurt Gödel's theorem, see the article 'mathematics, foundations of' (*Encyclopedia Britannica Online*).

local: all these in the new century will become increasingly interactive as locuses of actors' identities, individual and collective, as well as their purposive actions. Given this assumption (explication of which would call for a separate essay), sociology as a discipline must recognize that its theorizing can no longer privilege the experiences of Western modernity as its core, and in particular, the situation of the United States as the implicit if not explicit context for sociological generalization. 'Voice' must be given to sociological analyses and perspectives from all sociological settings, and these should benefit from the new technologies of the Internet – including the emergent convergent technologies of voice recognition, simultaneous translation, and seamless data transmission – and be in continuous contact and interaction with non-indigenous settings.

To mark this new era, I propose that each national and/or regional sociological society[11] should organize its next annual meeting to answer a dual set of questions: What are the, say, ten most significant empirical problems capable of empirical solution facing sociology in the country? (or region).[12] And, to invoke Parsons' legacy of 1959, a related question to ask would be: What are the major challenges facing the profession in this country? (or region). Finally, as a tacit acknowledgement of Saint-Simon's call for a European parliament, the various national and regional associations of sociology should be invited to send two representatives, one under forty and one over, to the next international congress of sociology to present to the entire body how these challenges appear to members at the 'local' level. Ideally, the occasion for such stock-taking of the entire profession of the sociologist would be the next congress of the International Sociological Association (ISA), at the time of writing scheduled to take place in Brisbane, Australia, in 2002. Of course, it would be presumptuous to specify the procedures and mechanisms that the various sociological bodies should adopt in identifying and specifying the dual set of problems; but hopefully whatever the processes and mechanisms used, including the selection of representatives to the ISA sessions and panels dealing with this assessment, they would be

---

11 Regional' has a double meaning for organizational purposes. In the United States, the American Sociological Association has several regional organizations (e.g., the Southern Sociological Society, the Eastern Sociological Society, etc.), but other countries may not, and instead set up a transnational regional organization together with a national one. For complementary approaches to a new appreciation of regionalism in Europe and East Asia, see Applegate (1999) and Wigen (1999). I am indebted to Josefina Tiryakian for the latter references.

12 To be true to Hilbert's legacy, one should say the twenty-three most significant problems. However, if only ten were identified per major organizational unit, the gains to sociology in the new era would still be considerable.

free of extra-professional political influence and ideology.

In keeping with the above proposal, and the spirit of Hilbert's legacy, let me share with the reader *four* significant interrelated problems, methodological and substantive, which may be capable of 'solutions'.

3. The problem of large-scale 'surprises'

One of the best new voices in sociological theory, Hans Joas, has recently (1999) taken modernization theory to task for its failure to deal with war in its account of modernity. He attributes this to what he sees as faulty assumptions of evolutionary progress, free of violence (intra-state and inter-state). Joas argues that war cannot be detached from the emergence of modernity and that different outcomes of war affect the modernization process in different ways. Hence for Joas there is need to relativize modernization theory (the 'survivor' of development theories after the demise of communism) by viewing the emergence of modernity 'as a result of a contingent historical constellation' (1999: 465) and giving weight to exogenous factors, since 'research on the role of war for social change reveals the impact that international constellations have on the chances for modernization processes' (ibid.: 468).

Of course, I agree with Joas that war is a covert side of modernity and that, without glorifying it (which of course he does not), the influence of war on social change has been neglected by the majority of sociological analyses. This, however, is only a small part of the problem, though it provides ingress to a much broader one: namely that mainstream sociological analysis – and I do not reduce 'mainstream' to 'modernization theory' – has not provided a comprehensive theory of social change, one that would give space to the discontinuities of collective social consciousness that underlie major 'ruptures' or large-scale surprises, not only across very long periods of time but even in the past century, from decade to decade.

To be sure, social scientists have long been fascinated with one kind of rupture in our modern period: revolutions (Goldstone, 1999) and such related topics as internal wars. But that these are unanticipated and unaccounted for in our main conceptual models of social structure, and social change is only part of the story. Hence, for example, if we consider the twentieth century just past, we find a plethora of large-scale surprises confronting us in retrospect. In the Edwardian age, when academic sociology was becoming institutionalized, who or what sociological theory anticipated the rupture of World War One? In the 1920s, the decade of gradual post-war recovery in

Europe, post-imperial reconstruction in Central and East Europe, and economic euphoria in the United States, what economic and sociological theorizing prepared us for the global economic and political disasters of the following decade? Or in the 1950s, when structural-functional analysis was at its zenith (even in the presence of the alternative 'conflict' theory launched by Coser and Dahrendorf), what sociological analysis anticipated the rupture of the 1960s among college students in every part of the world, a political and cultural 'big surprise' that took place in every part of the world? And by the same token, what sociological analysis in the late 1960s foresaw that the 'new left' movement would run out of steam before the end of the 1970s and give rise to a general conservative movement in the very advanced industrial countries that was the locus of the 'new left'? Very much part of the 'surprises' of late modernity have also been the rapid changes in the social consciousness of significant groups of actors, of which the women's movement and the Black Power movement are salient examples. These not only entailed new and bold demands for fuller participation in the public sphere but also, and equally importantly, they entailed change in the individual and collective identities of the activists in these movements.

Yet another set of large-scale surprises to be cited are the enormous socio-political ruptures, the major surprises, that have taken place in Europe in barely one generation, mostly with minimal violence (contrary to what might be expected of drastic change), but also with maximum violence. Despite what one might have forecast in the 1960s, given earlier periods of acute civil strife, Iberian Europe in the 1970s changed with minimal violence from two authoritarian regimes to two democratic ones. But the truly spectacular surprise – the largest-scale surprise of the century – was the overnight implosion of the Soviet Empire, and without the bloodshed that attended the other sudden end-of-empire earlier in the century. Sociologists no less than others, including career sovietologists, simply did not anticipate that a regime so entrenched and seemingly monolithic could collapse within a decade, providing stimuli but no theoretical breakthroughs for a major symposium (Hechter, 1995).[13] If the Soviet case and its consequences can be

---

13 One of the symposium participants proposed that his geopolitical model of empires had accurately predicted the *collapse* of the Soviet empire a decade before its occurrence. While this is a suggestive 'new' approach in sociological theory, not only is the temporal factor problematic (can one say that a 'collapse' involving a time span of 50-200 years is a meaningful prediction?) but also, to avoid historicism, the theory should be applied to comparative cases. For instance, does the United States really contradict the claim that global over-extension beyond the heartland was the root cause of the Soviet downfall? Or, in the case of the British Empire, did it 'collapse' after World War Two because of over-extension beyond the heartland, or did it willingly give up its colonies rather than share welfare state benefits and citizenship with all its fledglings?

viewed as a large-scale 'good surprise' (democratization and the autonomy of nations which were previously satellites with satrap rulers), the past decade witnessed a series of 'bad surprises' with much violence attending the unexpected (in the 1980s) collapse of the multiethnic Yugoslav states that Tito had carefully crafted. Adding a tragic note to the modernity of war (and keeping in mind that World War One was set in motion by the Balkan wars), the dissolution of Yugoslavia was attended not only by the fierce wars of 1994-95 but by the equally fierce intrusion of an 'exogenous factor' in 1999 when the United States, for 'humanitarian reasons', launched NATO's aerial warfare on Serbia, radically altering the premises of NATO action in Europe.

Related to the above is another set of phenomena that appeared in the closing decades of the last century and which constitute anomalies in the general, mainstream sociological understanding of modernity. I refer, on the one hand, to the emergence – in far-flung corners of the world – of ethnic-driven regional nationalisms challenging the authority and legitimacy of the established nation-state, and, complementarily, the emergence of religio-fundamentalist movements seeking voice and dissenting from the secular state. These surprising movements – truly new forces of modernity – were instrumental in the toppling of empires, in driving revolutionary movements, and in forcing existing nation-states to devolve power and authority to ethno-regions. What they entailed methodologically was a challenge against the tacit causal framework of both liberal and Marxist models of modernity which had relegated 'religion' and 'ethno-nationalism' to vestigial status in development models; new sociological voices have since begun a badly-needed theoretical reappraisal (Connor, 1994; Brubaker, 1996; Nairn, 1997; Tiryakian, 1997; Lemert, 1999).

If I have given extended treatment to 'surprises', in the sense of unanticipated ruptures of societal systems, it is for two reasons. First, because it is more likely that the coming decades of the new century hold more large-scale surprises in store, some undoubtedly pleasant, some nasty, in some regions and some countries, than that there will be smooth continuity in the globalization process. In this sense, I can only agree with Joas that there is no historic guarantee of continuous progress, either in political democracy or in economic growth yielding higher standards of living on a global basis.

4. Bringing technology back in

The 'new era' of the twenty-first century will indubitably continue to display the advances in technology and science that have been the distinctive features of 'modernity' (and here we can extend the civilization of modernity back to 'the long sixteenth century' of Gutenberg, Galileo, Bacon and other innovators). These advances will foster important progress which critics of modernization analysis tend to neglect: for example, progress in communications and data transmission as dramatically shown in a 'good surprise', the Internet, which did not exist less than fifteen years ago.

In passing, not only is the continuous acceleration of technological change in the decades to come one of the few certainties that we can count upon, but it will have major consequences on social organization at the national, regional and global levels. Nevertheless, unless I am grossly mistaken, since the 'cultural lag' insight of Ogburn (1950) the main theoretical models of sociology, including models of modernity, have shown scant ability to analyse the impact of technological changes as either endogenous or exogenous factors in social organization.[14] Remedying this shortcoming is certainly one of the major challenges for sociology in the new era.

Technological change (which of course is not a single entity) should be viewed as an independent or intervening variable in the translation and transfiguration of 'nature' to the human condition. And this not only in respect to 'less developed countries', where technology is often seen simplistically or ideologically as a major destabilizer of the equilibrium of traditional society (Shrum and Shenhav, 1995) but also as a key catalyst of change at various levels of society (micro, meso, and macro), and with varying kinds of technology. It requires little theoretical effort for sociologists to grant the 'social construction' of technology, but the real problem is inducing sociologists systematically to link technological change with organizational change at various societal levels.

---

14 For a fuller discussion, but one which reaches the same conclusion as to the present inadequacy of (mainstream) academic sociology in its handling of the interaction between technology and society (and not merely the social construction of technology), see Westrum (1991: 79 ff). I am indebted to Angela O'Rand for this reference.

5. Bringing biology back in

Sociology's theoretical ties with biology are as tenuous as they are old. In the formative decades of sociology in Europe, a good deal of sociological theorizing was prompted by biology; beginning with Comte, who in his philosophy of science acknowledged that the emergence of a science of society was contingent on the science of biological or living phenomena (Simpson, 1969: 60-7). Of the stimuli to sociological imagination based on biological models foremost, of course, was Darwin's *Origin of Species* and its influence on such contrasting theorists as Marx, Gumplowicz and Sumner, not to mention the one perhaps most taken with biology: Herbert Spencer (who popularized Social Darwinism) and his view that society was a complex organism with differentiated structures and functions analogous to those of multicellular organisms. Further stimuli from biology were the studies in experimental physiology by Claude Bernard, whose notion that the internal milieu of the organism gave it stability against the external environment stimulated Durkheim's sociological imagination. The concept of homeostasis derived from Bernard's studies of the functions of digestive organs and popularized by William Cannon in *The Wisdom of the Body* (1932) was a major stimulus for the development of sociological structural-functional analysis by Parsons and Merton in the 1930s, including the significance of the tendency toward equilibrium of social systems.

Parsons, in particular, had a keen and long-standing interest in biology and in medicine. This is evidenced by the lengthy chapter on the social construction of illness in *The Social System*, where he writes:

> (i)t is... of considerable interest that it was in connection with the earlier study of medical practice that the beginnings of the pattern variable scheme were first worked out (1951: 429).

Many of Parsons' last essays pertain to medicine and human biology, which is indicative that even in the final phase of his career he kept abreast of developments in genetic research and of the bearing of modern biological theory on his own attempt to frame a broad theory of human action (1978). The culmination of his life-long theorizing of action theory was the essay 'A Paradigm of the Human Condition', which examines the 'human organic system' and its four sub-systems, including the genetic heritage, as one constitutive interactive component of the action system (ibid.: 382).

The hasty dismissal in the 1970s and 1980s of structural-functional analysis as allegedly fatally flawed because it was 'conservative', and even the more recent rehabilitation of the early *Structure of Social Action* as an exemplar of theory (Barber and Gerhardt, 1999), have prevented sociology from following the overture by Parsons to biological advances. This has reinforced the tendency of sociologists to take a jaundiced view of biological explanations of social behaviour, particularly if they smack of reductionism conducive to racist doctrines of group differences.

In a sense, eschewing biological reductionism in favour of sociological explanations of social phenomena is fundamental to the autonomy of sociology, and it has been a virtue of sociology ever since Durkheim proclaimed the basic methodological principles of sociological causal explanation (1982).

But, as an extension of the discussion of technology, I firmly believe that the incredible strides forward of molecular biology and biotechnology in the decades to come, and certainly the successful completion of the human genome project ahead of schedule at the very start of the new millennium, will have an enormous impact on human society. Genetic therapy, transgenic implants, genetic counselling, genetic mapping are related features of the emergent transformation of the human condition in the new era. It is foolhardy – especially for a layman – to venture to suggest what features of this new revolutionary knowledge and its applications will come into being with popular and government support, and which – perhaps akin to poison gas – may be deemed potentially so lethal as to be excluded from public or corporate use.

However, the challenge that may face sociological theory is that an explanation of social behaviour (and particularly, but by no means solely, pathological and anti-social behaviour) couched in bio-genetic terms may receive important empirical substantiation, with the ultimate challenge being the possibility that culture is involved in the mechanisms of gene activation. Rather than dismissing the hypothesis that social behaviour, including group behaviour, has a biological underpinning as abhorrent or 'unscientific', it might be far more prudent for sociologists to maintain the sustained intellectual awareness of, if not interaction with, microbiological research distinctive of Parsons.[15] This is not to imply that important features of everyday social behaviour do not reflect a 'social construction of reality'; rather that there is a bio-chemical grounding, a set of structures and functions, knowledge of which is exploding and which, if ignored, may well render present sociological explanations antiquated.

---

15 Parsons, it might be noted, had a critical awareness of the claims of E. O. Wilson's 'sociobiology' (Parsons, 1978: 411).

6. Restoring trust

Social scientists, including sociologists, are certainly aware of trust as an unobtrusive but fundamental elementary nexus in social relationships, whether they operate at the micro (face-to-face or interpersonal), meso (institutional) or macro (national and transnational) level (Barber, 1983; Lewis and Weigert, 1985; Fukuyama, 1995; Misztal, 1996; Seligman, 1997). Eisenstadt has aptly summarized a crucial problematic of legitimation in any social order – given 'the ubiquity of fragility, conflicts, and potentialities of change in any setting of social interaction' – as the need for 'the interweaving of power with long-range trust and broad meaning' (Eisenstadt, 1995: 354).

What I see as both problematic and as a challenge for sociology is a corollary of Eisenstadt's observation: what can sociology offer in the way of theory and codification of data that can help restore trust when trust has been negated, and when distrust or mistrust are prevalent among actors? Eisenstadt does not address this question, and if I do it is perhaps because of an uneasy feeling that, today, the normative structures of advanced modernity are characterized more by the *deregulation* of power, trust and ultimate meaning than by their regulation.

While theoretically important, the question is empirically crucial, and at various levels. I have grown aware of the question in recent years as I have worked on problems of national development and national reconstruction in the post-communist world. One feature of communist society – even in its more benign guise during the years before its demise in the Soviet Union and Eastern Europe – was its ubiquitous aspect as a police state dependent on informers who might easily be a fellow tenant in one's apartment building, a colleague at work, the shopkeeper down the street, and so on. At this micro level, then, distrust of any 'other' except for close kin prevailed. At a more macro level, government officials were seen as corrupt and government statistics were distrusted: a general climate of suspicion which hampered cooperative activity beyond a close circle of kin and friends (Andorka, 1993: 330). This is an unfortunate legacy for the post-communist governments, particularly but not solely those in which the new regime officials are recycled ex-communist ones. The carry-over of distrust is equally detrimental to teamwork and investments, both of which are necessary for national development.

A second case of the prevalence of distrust has many empirical instances: situations in which overt and prolonged ethnic violence has taken place both intensively and extensively. There may be a cessation of overt violence, perhaps because of mutual exhaustion, perhaps because of mediation by third parties, but the 'fragility' of the peace is a function of the distrust between self and other. The distrust prevalent in Northern Ireland, Kosovo, Bosnia, Kashmir, Rwanda and Burundi, and in Israel/Palestine concerns perhaps the most publicized trouble areas, but these are by no means the only instances.

Distrust is as likely to occur in long-term democratic societies. At the micro level, long-term relationships between friends and marital partners may be disrupted by a breach of trust by one of the parties.

At the meso level, the trial of a member of a racial or ethnic minority, or her/his treatment by the police authorities, may reveal the profound distrust of the person's reference group in the judicial system; violations of fiduciary trust in the financial and banking world are equally damaging to trust in economic institutions; and lastly, the misconduct of a head of state trapped in a tissue of lies may generate public scorn and distrust of the workings of government.

I will not elaborate further. What I have said should point up the significance of the damage wrought to the social fabric when distrust prevails. Economic rationality – which holds that actors distrustful of each other should 'kiss and make up' because this will reduce their costs and increase their mutual gains – is plausible, but it neglects the fact that distrust is grounded on strong affect and is generated by hurt, revenge, humiliation, and so on.

The remedying of *distrust* will not have a simple or a single solution, for I see 'distrust' as having many situation-specific factors and, like cancer or the AIDS virus, assuming many different forms. Moreover, to extend the analogy, the remedy may well be a 'cocktail of drugs' and multiple forms of treatment. It will require sociology to interact with other (social) sciences in developing the necessary databases – from psychology, biology, history and political science, for instance.

But my own 'vision' – to relate this conclusion to my earlier discussion of visions – is that this integrative effort will crucially help sociology define a meaningful rather than vestigial place for itself in the new era, and in so doing renovate sociological theorizing.

Bibliography

Albrow, M. (1996a), 'On Being Summoned to History and Sociology', *Theory. Newsletter of Theory Section*, International Sociological Association, Spring, pp. 2-5.

Albrow, M. (1996b), *The Global Age*, Stanford University Press, Stanford.

Albrow, M. and King, E. (eds) (1990), *Globalization, Knowledge and Society*, Sage, London.

Andorka, R. (1993), 'The Socialist System and its Collapse in Hungary: An Interpretation in Terms of Modernization Theory', *International Sociology*, vol. 8, no. 3, pp. 317-37.

Applegate, C. (1999), 'A Europe of Regions: Reflections on the Historiography of Sub-National Places in Modern Times', *American Historical Review*, vol. 104, pp. 1157-82.

Barber, B. (1983), *The Logic and Limits of Trust*, Rutgers University Press, New Brunswick.

Barber, B. and Gerhardt, U. (eds) (1999), *Agenda for Sociology: Classic Sources and Current Uses of Talcott Parsons's Work*, Nomos, Baden-Baden.

Brubaker, R. (1996), *Nationalism Reframed. Nationhood and the National Question in the New Europe*, Cambridge University Press, Cambridge.

Cannon, W.B. (1932), *The Wisdom of the Body*, Norton, New York.

Castells, M. (1998), *The Information Age; Economy, Society and Culture*, Blackwell, Oxford.

Connor, W. (1994), *Ethnonationalism: The Quest for Understanding*, Princeton University Press, Princeton.

Deflem, M. (1991), 'Ritual, Anti-Structure, and Religion: A Discussion of Victor Turner's Processual Symbolic Analysis', *Journal for the Scientific Study of Religion*, vol. 30, no. 1, pp. 1-25.

Durkheim, E. ([1895] 1982), *The Rules of Sociological Method*, ed. by S. Lukes, Free Press, New York.

Eisenstadt, S.N. (1995), *Power, Trust and Meaning*, University of Chicago Press, Chicago.

Fukuyama, F. (1995), *Trust. The Social Virtues & The Creation of Prosperity*, Free Press, New York.

Giddens, A. (1991), *Modernity and Self-Identity. Self and Society in the Late Modern Age*, Stanford University Press, Stanford.

Gittlin, T. (1980), *The Whole World is Watching: Mass Media in the Making and Unmasking of the New Left*, University of California Press, Berkeley.

Gouldner, A. (1970), *The Coming Crisis of Western Sociology*, Basic, New York.

Hechter, M. (ed) (1995), 'Symposium on Prediction in the Social Sciences', *American Journal of Sociology*, vol. 100, no. 6, pp. 1520-1626.

Joas, H. (1999), 'The Modernity of War: Modernization Theory and the Problem of Violence', *International Sociology*, vol. 14, no. 4, pp. 457-72.

Lemert, C. (1999), 'The Might Have Been and Could Be of Religion in Social Theory', *Sociological Theory*, vol. 17, no. 3, pp. 240-63.

Levine, D.N. (1995), *Visions of the Sociological Tradition*, University of Chicago Press, Chicago.

Lewis, J.D. and Weigert, A. (1985), 'Trust as a Social Reality', *Social Forces*, vol. 63, no. 4, pp. 967-85.

Mazur, J. (2000), 'Labor's New Internationalism', *Foreign Affairs*, vol. 79, pp. 79-93.

Misztal, B.M. (1996), *Trust in Modern Societies*, Polity Press, Cambridge.

Nairn, T. (1997), *Faces of Nationalism. Janus Revisited*, Verso, London.

Ogburn, W.F. ([1923] 1950), *Social Change*, Viking Press, New York.

Parsons, T. (1937), *The Structure of Social Action*, Macmillan, New York.

Parsons, T. (1951), *The Social System*, Free Press, New York.

Parsons, T. (1959), 'Some Problems Confronting Sociology as a Profession', *American Sociological Review,* vol. 24, no. 4, pp. 547-59.

Parsons, T. (1977), *Social Systems and the Evolution of Action Theory*, Free Press, New York.

Parsons, T. (1978), *Action Theory and the Human Condition*, Free Press, New York.

Phillips, B. (1999), 'Confronting our Tower of Babel'. *Newsletter of Theory Section*, American Sociological Association, no. 21, pp. 2-4.

Robertson, R. (1992), *Globalization*, Sage, London.

Robertson, R. and Chirico, J. (1985), 'Humanity, Globalization, and Worldwide Religious Resurgence: A Theoretical Explanation', *Sociological Analysis*, vol. 46, pp. 219-42.

Robertson, R. and Lechner, F. (1985), 'Modernization, Globalization, and the Problem of Culture in World System Theories', *Theory, Culture and Society,* vol. 2, pp. 103-18.

Saint-Simon, H. (1814), *De la réorganisation de la société europénne*, Egron, Paris.

Sassen, S. (1998), *Globalization and its Discontents*, New Press, New York.

Seligman, A.B. (1997), *The Problem of Trust*, Princeton University Press, Princeton.

Shrum, W. and Shenhav, Y. (1995), 'Science and Technology in Less Developed Countries', in S. Jasanoff, G.E. Markle, J.C. Petersen and T. Pinch (eds), *Handbook of Science and Technology Studies*, Sage,

Thousand Oaks, CA, pp. 627-51.

Sills, D.L. (ed) (1968), *International Encyclopedia of the Social Sciences*, Macmillan & Free Press, New York.

Simpson, G. (1969), *August Comte: Sire of Sociology*, Crowell, New York.

Sklair, L. (1995), *Sociology of the Global System*, Johns Hopkins University Press, Baltimore.

Smelser, N.J. (1988) (ed), *Handbook of Sociology*, Sage, London.

Smelser, N.J. and Baltes, P. (editors-in-chief) (2001), *International Encyclopedia of Social and Behavioral Sciences*, Pergamon/Elsevier, Oxford.

Tiryakian, E.A. (1997), 'The Wild Cards of Modernity', *Dedalus*, vol. 126, pp. 147-81.

Waters, M. (1995), *Globalization*, Routledge, London.

Weber, E.J. (1999), *Apocalypses: Prophecies, Cults, and Millennial Beliefs Through the Ages*, Harvard University Press, Cambridge.

Westrum, R. (1991), *Technologies. The Shaping of People and Things & Society*, Wadsworth, Belmont.

Wigen, K. (1999), 'Culture, Power, and Place: The New Landscapes of East Asian Regionalism', *American Historical Review*, vol. 104, pp. 1183-201.

Willkie, W.L. (1943), *One World*, Simon & Schuster, New York.

Zelditch, M. Jr. (1999), 'Theory Growth in Sociology: Current Status and New Directions', *Perspectives*, no. 21, pp. 1-3.

12 Toward a science of global marginality

ANTHONY J. BLASI

Introduction

We humans often look to the future in those moments when we mark time. We make New Year's resolutions, anticipate the character of coming decades, and write essays such as this one at the turn of centuries. So what can we say about the future of a science such as sociology, given the fact that science by its very nature consists of creating events in which the unknown and hence unexpected can come to light? The more scientifically honest one is, the less one can be a seer. Consequently our discourse about future science, occasioned by the passage from the nineteen-hundreds to the twenty-hundreds, comprises a reflection of what motivates research rather than of what future scientific findings will be, because it is only the motives that are available in the present.

There is a custom in science, honoured more in formal publications than in informal conversation among scientists, of remaining silent on the subject of why a course of inquiry began. The presentation in a typical scientific journal article begins with some references to previous inquiry into something and to some anomaly or problem in the state of the question. The researcher then proposes a method by which the anomaly or problem can be addressed and proceeds to formulate hypotheses and techniques for collecting and analysing data with which the hypotheses can be supported or disconfirmed. But little or nothing is said about why the researcher began the study of the general problem at all. It is almost as if the author does not want to admit that perhaps the topic does not merit the reader's time.

In a parallel development, there is a type of researcher in American social science known as the 'grantsman'. I assume that there is an equivalent type in most nations. The grantsman surveys the kinds of government research that institutes or major foundations are ready to fund, and draws up a corresponding proposal using safe pre-existent techniques, irrespective of whether the grantsman has any real interest in the subject or not. The grantsman is commonly said to be like Willie Sutton, a famous bank robber. Asked why he robbed banks, Sutton said, 'Because that is where the money is'. Why would a grantsman study the grade point averages of sixteen-year-old computer hackers? Because someone wants to spend a lot of money on the matter.[1]

If the grantsman's work is motivated by pragmatism, the passion for a subject that is characteristic of other researchers escapes the parameters of instrumental reason altogether. Max Weber left the selection of what a scholar would study a mystery, so long as the scholar studied it and did not engage in politics or religion in the name of science (Weber, 1918: 129-56). Similarly, many research methodology manuals describe 'the' scientific method of 'testing' hypotheses against empirical data but fail to provide an adequate account of generating hypotheses on the basis of empirical evidence. It was largely by way of reaction against this that people from the symbolic interactionist school of thought abandoned the natural science model and others began to speak of 'grounded theory'. In what follows, I shall follow the example provided by these latter people and begin empirically, albeit with the sociological and other disciplines in mind. I will try to draw out key concepts and a perspective from patterns I find in organized humanity.

1. The empirical situation at the turn of the centuries

It is not possible to proceed without employing some prior principles. In orienting oneself to the situation of societies and the social phenomena within them, one's concepts and values make some phenomena emerge as obvious and important and cause others to be obscure. We combat the limitations imposed by this hermeneutic circumstance through inquiry itself; we use unanticipated findings and anomalies to revise our picture of the world. Consequently our intellectual grasp of the world – of the social world in particular – is not static but rather proceeds in a dialectic with current empirical information.

The scientific experience is thus one of 'dedogmatization' (Gurvitch, 1962: 33–6). What needs to be held in abeyance are not the sensitizing principles with which we begin – concepts and values – but the systems into

---

1   It has become fashionable for funding institutes to encourage 'interdisciplinary team work' with their grants. *Interdisciplinary* is a code word for non-disciplinary; funding institutes do not want to be troubled by researchers who have interests or disciplined thoughts. The underlying assumption is that a perspective yet to be brought to light is in some way superior to one that has undergone scrutiny during the course of a discipline's history. Consequently, it helps grantsmen to be relatively ignorant of their disciplines, if what they want to do is be funded.

which they have come to be fixed.[2] Concepts and values are intrinsic to our orientation to the world; we cannot proceed scientifically without them. However, we need to suspend 'isms' – systems of concatenated and interrelated statements, concepts, and values. At a point in time, such as the turn of a century, when we look to the future, it is important to set aside reified habits of thought that constitute a tyranny of labels, each label representing a past way of thinking and, more unfortunately, a past set of conclusions. One only has to read the sociology of the last turn of the century to see how much of it represents ideological systems that should have been suspended. The sociologists of the time seemed overly enamoured of nationalist categories, which they paralleled with racial conceptions. They felt obliged to ground symbolic and ideational activity in biology, and hence associated social and cultural change with biological evolution. How quaint such notions appear today!

No doubt a hundred years from now someone will examine the writings of today and see them as representative of ideological systems. They will see concatenated schemes of values and concepts as lacking any fit with the human realities of the decade before and the one following the year 2000. I have my own list of ideological phenomena to which I suspect they will be pointing: 1. The rational choice paradigm, which is a distant abstraction that imitates an economic model that has been used in textbooks to explain the supply and demand principle but which itself has no real role in economic research. 2. The reductionist paradigm, which looks for extra-social constants to explain social variations. 3. Mathematical modelling, which would use correspondences in measurements that are too subtle for social actors to observe, and hence are too subtle to explain what the social actors do. 4. Interdisciplinarity, as noted above, which would conduct research without benefit of acknowledged concepts, on the basis of a belief that a funding agency can economize by substituting one large non-disciplinary grant for many smaller disciplinary ones without sacrificing intelligence at the start-up phase of research projects.

But the point of the present discussion is not to develop a critique of present practices but to point to the future.

The principal empirical trend that I suspect will set the agenda for a social

---

2   This statement is subject to easy misinterpretation. I would make a phenomenological distinction between an *a priori* concept or value and an *a posteriori* evocation of a concept or value in the course of apprehending an object. Thus two people can agree on the meaning of a concept while disagreeing about its application to a given object or situation; or they may agree on the merit of a value while disagreeing about which objects embody that value (Blasi, 1988: 31-83).

science in the twenty-first century is the detachment of systems of marginality from their former geographical bases.[3] I say *systems of marginality* rather than *stratification* because the phenomenon in question embraces but goes beyond stratification. *Stratification* referred to rankings, that is, inequalities in class, status, and power (Weber, 1978: 926-40; Weber, 1946: 180-95). If one looked at a geographically limited population – a nation-state, community, tribe – one saw inequalities in material goods, in systems of privilege, and in political resources. However, consider the would-be illegal migrant, captured by the American Border Patrol and returned to Mexico, in debt to loan sharks from whom he has borrowed money to pay smugglers to get him across the border (Samora, Bustamante and Cardenas, 1971). The man's situation is not understandable scientifically in terms of class; many others in his class are not in his situation. It is not a matter of social honorifics or status; the Border Patrol officer could be the son of an illegal migrant worker who was not apprehended a generation ago. Moreover, the intricacies of two nation states' citizenship laws and the political movements behind them do not explain the illegal migration phenomenon; rather, the patterns of migration explain the passage of the laws. There is something broader than stratification in question. The illegal migrant is caught up in the same complex as the Border Patrol officer and the legislator who helps pass citizenship and immigration laws. What is broader than stratification is social structure. C. Wright Mills described social structure in terms of the relationships among the major institutions of a society. In his most famous study at the middle of the twentieth century, he described the dominant placement of the military, the executive branch of the American federal government, and big business in the United States (Wright Mills, 1956). It would no doubt be dogmatic to focus on the same three institutions today, to focus only on institutions deemed dominant, or to focus only on the United States. I would call attention, however, to the relationships among institutions. It is well known that large business enterprises are multinational. There are also important businesses whose clients are other businesses: international law firms, financial services firms, advertising firms, consulting firms, business software firms. Sassen has identified configurations of such firms in 'global cities' – principally New York, London and Tokyo (Sassen, 1991). Consequently, there are at least two institutional patterns of big business: there is the multinational manufacturer and the world city business services centre. The first reflects a detachment from economies that were

---

3   This will represent a supersession of what the dependency version of world system
     theory has described.

national in scope; the second reflects an urban concentration in communications centers.

Education presents us with a comparable situation. It is an institution that once articulated with religion and came to articulate with class divisions in national societies. I suspect that in the coming century the sociology of education will need to focus on a division between an informal transnational system and many formal local systems. The people who participate in the economy of the multinationals and the world city business services economy will have expectations of the schools attended by their children that will not be met by the various public education systems. Private schools with international clienteles and more rigorous standards than can be met by state-sponsored systems will expand. Philanthropic foundations will be concerned with the placement of potentially successful lower-income students into these costly private school settings. The difference between this transnational educational context and the public ones will parallel the lines between those people who participate in the new transnational reality and those who do not. That is why I speak of *marginality* rather than simply of inequality.

2. Opaque oppression in the global order

Marginality can be the setting for what can be termed *opaque oppression*. Traditional oppression was an overt political practice. Individuals and organized groups that held power used the police power of the state to eliminate potential rivals or denied workers or minorities or women the right to organize or to earn compensation sufficient enough to accumulate meaningful resources. Thus the hereditary estate rulers imprisoned activists, many from the rising middle class; and later the owners of industrial firms fired labour organizers and used both public and private police forces to break strikes. Leaders of minority group movements were subject to assassination or arrest. In South Africa there was a system for bureaucratically administering racial inequality. This kind of oppression required a high enough level of punishment and humiliation to intimidate the targeted sectors of the population, but a low enough level to leave the targeted people with the belief that they could escape punishment by acquiescing to their low placement in a system of unequal statuses.

The pattern of traditional visible oppression has come to an end in most parts of the world. The profit system in business led to the accumulation of great resources in the hands of business so that traditional estate rulers lost control over the apparatus of government. However, as the profit system evolved, business leaders resorted to technological efficiencies in production, communications, and transportation; technology in turn requires a skilled workforce. Skilled workers possess the same cultural resources as people in business and government. Consequently, it has become more difficult for people in high positions in business or government to oppress the work force overtly without retribution. The twentieth-century elites ruled directly in government (as in the old Soviet Union) and indirectly (as management or as contributors to political campaigns). The means by which these twentieth-century elites maintained an authoritarian government apparatus ready for use as needed was to persuade the minimally educated public of some menace. The Soviet bureaucracy depended on a myth of an American menace. The American conservative establishment depended on a myth of a Soviet menace. A majority workforce was persuaded to fear some minority. The kinds of oppression that emerged in this pattern were only potentially visible; the courses of action that tended to intimidate people were private rather than public, often technically illegal (though law enforcement personnel were often implicated), and usually not targeted with any strategic effect because the acts of oppression were carried out by freelancers and vigilantes as episodic expressions of lower middle-class frustration rather than as implementations of bureaucratic plans. Oppression came to be democratized into a populism that waxed or waned in expressive rather than instrumental social movement behaviour, over which industrial and governmental elites had no real control. For an era in modern history, business and political elites, fearing such popular mobilization, have become defenders of rights and the opponents of overt oppression.[4]

Entrenched interests still need oppression; however, the oppression needs to be opaque. At this juncture, it is useful to clarify the terms of the discussion. *Oppression* is the stratagem of depriving people with an objective interest in jeopardizing the position of elites of the resources with which to exert power. To be denied the resources of power is to be debilitated, to be made weaker. Oppression can be physical, so that intimidation occurs when an 'example' is made of an upstart by execution, flogging, torture or imprisonment. Oppression can be social, so that intimidation occurs when an upstart is excluded from influential social networks or from gainful employment. Oppression may take the form of majority/minority relationships when it becomes democratized in racist or nationalist populism.

---

4   I think that Marcuse's shrill critique of 'repressive tolerance' missed this development by fixating on an earlier stage (Marcuse, 1970: 81-117).

Oppression becomes *opaque* when culturally prescribed motives for retaining existent elite statuses come to be institutionalized separately from the culturally prescribed motives for changing them. This kind of oppression is opaque because it is impersonal; it is simply an aspect of the differentiation of modern society into separate institutional orders, so that there is little cross-over from business to family, family to education, education to government, government to religion, or religion to medicine. Even the connection between business and government is weakened; businesses are now global, while governments are largely trapped within the parameters of nation states or, at most, regional leagues of nation states.

3. A sociology of marginality

In thinking in terms of pure types, one type would call to mind a monistic society that had no differentiated institutions; oppression in such a society would be interpersonal. In another type, an institution possessing a monopoly on the resources of oppression would become entangled in the affairs of other institutions when the latter threaten the position of elites. A government may interfere with the press, or a corporate conglomerate may buy a news service and reorient it to providing news talk-show entertainment rather than genuine news. Sociology has come to conduct analyses along the lines of this second type because of the period in history in which it emerged as a scientific discipline. In a third type, the differentiation of organized life into distinct institutional orders has gone to such an extreme that the establishment of elites in any one institutional order cannot be affected from a position from within any other institutional order. Conflict increasingly becomes internal conflict: 'in-fighting' that is irrelevant to the shape of the social structure. It is the situation of ultimate institutionalization that may well be most common in the twenty-first century.

   This situation of institutional marginality rests primarily on the marginalization of institutions and only secondarily on the marginalization of persons. Formerly the stranger and the 'marginal man' were individual persons who were marginal to a community (Simmel, 1924: 322-27; Park, 1928: 881-93). In a critique of Park's concept of the 'marginal man', Deegan observed that women, who have been very much *in* their communities, were nevertheless marginal to the formal exercise of power and participation in symbolic life (Deegan, 1994: 55-71). Female marginalization was accomplished by a sexist allocation of roles combined with a marginalization of the family institutional order, in which female roles were concentrated. It is here that I want to return to the theme of the relationship among institutional orders once proposed by C. Wright Mills. Opaque oppression would appear to represent a structured complex of a sharp differentiation of social institutions and an inequality among them.

Elsewhere I have described asymmetrical relationships among institutions, distinguishing between macro institutions and their macro organizations on the one hand, and micro institutions and their micro organizations on the other. The macro organizations are able to make decisions that affect micro organizations as a matter of routine, but micro organizations can rarely bring consequences to bear on the macro organizations. For example, a major corporation can move a production facility from one community to another, leaving the local schools in the abandoned community with a smaller tax base and the local government with a problem of meeting greater demands for social services, leaving local churches with a declining membership, and causing some families to relocate while disrupting the 'breadwinner' roles in the families who stay. The local schools in the community to which the production facility is moved will experience sudden crowding, the local governments will have been manoeuvered into granting major tax abatements, the local churches will be entirely unprepared for a new clientele, and families already in the community will experience a more urban way of life than they were prepared to expect. In-migrating families in the second community will need to adjust to an entirely new social context. While a major corporation can cause all these consequences for local schools, local governments, churches, and families, none of the latter kinds of organization can bring about such consequences for a major corporation. That is what I mean by the *asymmetrical relationship between institutional orders* and the difference between *macro institutions* and *micro institutions, macro organizations* and *micro organizations* (Blasi, 1994: 47-54).

It is my contention that the asymmetrical relationships among sharply differentiated institutional orders, embodied in asymmetrical relationships among organizations, bring about two kinds of marginality – a marginality of persons and a marginality of pursuits. The marginality of persons is a matter of some people being placed in elite positions and upwardly mobile tracks in macro organizations while other people fill positions in micro organizations that can never be really elite. The marginality of pursuits is a matter of the individual person leading a life that is divided between 'serious' pursuits pertinent to a macro institutional order and 'unserious' pursuits pertinent to a micro institutional order.

A sociology of the new marginality would examine the negotiation of boundaries between the various institutional orders (e.g., the industrialization of medicine), the aggregations of resources that make some institutions 'macro', the separate recruitment of people into the macro and micro organizations, the recruitment into upward mobility tracks and non-upward mobility tracks within macro organizations, the socialization of new participants in macro versus micro organizations, and the formation of newly politicized interest groups within the macro/micro structure. Moreover, such a sociology would assess the micro institutional orders as non-routine resources for marginalized persons within macro organizations to achieve personal ends and for marginalized persons outside the macro organizations to achieve collective goals. In short, the routines at work in opaque oppression are likely to engender non-routine reactions that use the social networks and symbolic capital of the micro organizations and institutions. A sociology that is adequately developed for the analysis of such processes should enable people to use such micro-world resources rationally, rather than expressively only or in a self-destructive way.

4. Sociologies of marginal phenomena

As twenty-first century sociologists take up the study of the various differentiated social institutions, the important themes for inquiry can be expected to derive from the relationship between macro and micro institutions. Analyses of such macro institutions as multinational corporations and central governments may play a role that will be comparable to the role that Marx's analysis of the capitalist enterprise played in twentieth-century sociology. The multinational corporation is much larger than the kind of enterprise which Marx had in mind, and its long-term strategies are likely to focus on the impersonal exploitation of the public at large rather than the workforce. Comparative corporate tax rates will pit national governments against each other in a competition of investment incentives. Monopolistic practices, hidden behind international financial transactions in secret banking arrangements, will victimize consumers as well as smaller industrial firms and their employees. The central governments are likely to become sites of confrontation between the multinational corporations and localistic interest groups.

However, it is in the marginal worlds of the micro institutions that the consequences of the emergent macro institutions will be evident. The family has already been under pressure through the course of the twentieth century; it has lost its ability to provide its members with a small community as the economic roles have been removed from family farms and family businesses and located within work places away from the home. The migration of nuclear families to meet economic demands contributed to the decline of the extended family, and the phenomenon of the two-career family threatens even the nuclear family as a viable entity. In addition, the family has lost much of the function of socializing the young; the age-graded school system and the popular culture industry have substituted peer subcultural influences for family-borne traditions. As a secondary consequence of the age-graded school, marriages typically form between partners of roughly the same age, in contrast to former patterns in which males entered marriages with superior cultural and material capital compared to that of their wives. The result is not only a more democratic nuclear family, but a more pluralistic one. Moreover, the prerogatives of being an equal partner in the family are soon claimed by the children. Thus each person has an individual mix of cultural pursuits: the husband may follow the cinema, the wife popular music, the daughter athletics, the son computers. The family soon ceases to be a bearer of singular religious and other cultural patterns, just as it has ceased to be the bearer of craft skills, intellectuality, dress styles, and musical preferences. The consequence is a closer association of the family with purely psychological contents. Given the marginality of the family *vis-à-vis* the macro institutions, the actual psychological content of family life is likely to be filled out by way of contrast to the ways of the corporate and governmental worlds. The sociology of the family is likely to become a contrastive social psychology, a study in the development of personality patterns that run counter to the implicitly normative personality patterns cultivated in office suites. The family may come to be studied as a 'social problem', engendering rebelliousness against the corporate ethos, fomenting individualistic lines of deviance and reinforcing disenchantment with the occupational world.

The sociology of education will need to portray the contrasts between the formal socialization of the cosmopolitan elite and that of the masses. The fascination with students' achievement test scores and the contextual variables that affect them may hopefully end some day. Such studies have some value, but a focus on how schools channel people to or away from the macro structures would appear to be more to the point. Such channelling begins before instruction takes place and before achievement tests are administered. Moreover, what kinds of peer subcultures are encouraged by schools needs to be highlighted. The athletic subculture has been dominant for males outside private elite academies, and the ethos that it has perpetrated appears to be largely dysfunctional. Young males are led into a cult of self-aggrandizement and vanity associated with not particularly useful skills, and a sense of team work which too narrowly encompasses those included in the team. In the late twentieth century, women are demanding and getting equal access to this generally dysfunctional subculture. The sociology of education will need to explore the varieties of ethos that can be cultivated in the school setting and what kinds of activity subtly encourage ethical sensitivities. The fact that schools channel people and the fact that they promote different kinds of ethos are relevant to each another. It would appear that students destined to inhabit the macro institutions will need the cultural resources of the micro institutions in order to develop aspects of their lives apart from the macro organization. Those occupationally destined to inhabit the micro institutions will need resources of empowerment, especially cognitive skills that can overcome the opaqueness of twenty-first century oppression.

Religion will in all probability be another micro institution in the twenty-first century structure. It may persist in part as a custom of worship in assembly, if for no other reason than a sense of value and a sense of supra-individual humanity will continue to be banished from the macro institutions and will require a countervailing communal validation. As a marginal institution, religion has already found allies with other marginal institutions such as the family and the arts.[5] To the extent that schools, especially private schools, shed their authoritarian and bureaucratic quality, they may become successful vehicles of religious culture. However, making religion a curriculum content to be worked on by students, especially as something compulsory, will not be effective, because it would be too similar to the subculture of the macro institutions. Religion thrives at the margin of the macro institutions – not in isolation from the wider world and not as part of the macro institutions. At the margin it can offer a critique of the system of opaque oppression and become energized by the otherwise vague resentment and misgivings that people feel over their encounters with the macro organizations.

A twenty-first century sociology of religion will need to portray and analyse the experiences of marginality that give vigour to the religious impulses that many people have.

Finally, I would point to the arts. There is already evident a tension

---

5   A gravitation of many musicians and graphic artists to religion seems to represent a change from the situation with which Weber was familiar (1978: 607-10).

between commercial art and non-commercial, commercial music and art music,[6] pulp fiction and literature. The commercial variations of the arts are commodities that come from multinational 'media' corporations. The non-commercial variations are sustained by a small interest group in educational, civic, and religious organizations. The corporations supply the small interest group with some materials; the interest group is, for the multinationals, a 'niche market'; however, the multinationals do not really promote the fine arts.

The two art worlds can co-exist, but 'budget cutting' politicians who defund the arts in the schools threaten the very existence of non-commercial variations of the arts. The problem of the arts is analogous to that of religion: shedding the trappings of the macro institution and tapping into people's sense of rebellion and resentment against the ways of the macro organizations.

The arts apparently need to criticise commercial art products; they would thrive in marginality if they did so. Temptations, especially in the world of music, toward 'crossover' phenomena threaten to undermine the artistic critique by blurring the margin between art and commodity.

A twenty-first century sociology of the arts would need to portray and analyse the boundary at which cultural critique can take place.

5. An ethical imperative

It would be facile to assert that, because the effects of the macro institutions will be pervasive, the social sciences should focus exclusively on them. That the macro institutions should be subjected to analysis is clear.

However, for sociology and the other social sciences to give priority to them or even exclusive attention to them would be to share in the warped perspectives, the ideology, of those very macro institutions and their corporate subcultures. Social science itself needs to be part of a countervailing apparatus. It needs be at the service of the micro institutions as well. It needs to identify the margins that demarcate the structure of society. It needs to help empower people to use those margins knowingly and intelligently.

This will entail a thoroughgoing sociology of the micro institutions coupled with a thoroughgoing critique of the macro ones.

---

6   On the impact of this conflict on the music performer's role see Dasilva, Blasi and Dees (1984: 48ff).

Bibliography

Blasi, A.J. (1988), *Moral Conflict and Christian Religion*, Peter Lang, Bern.

Blasi, A.J. (1994), 'Power, Class, Law: The Complementarity of Realpolitik and Soft Sociologies', *Sociologia Internationalis*, vol. 32, pp. 47-54.

Blumer, H. (1969), *Symbolic Interactionism. Perspective and Method*, Prentice-Hall, Englewood Cliffs.

Dasilva, F., Blasi, A. and Dees, D. (1984), *The Sociology of Music*, University of Notre Dame Press, Notre Dame.

Deegan, M.J. (1994), "The Marginal Man' as a Gendered Concept: A Feminist Analysis of Robert E. Park's Epistemology', in R. Gubert and L. Tomasi (eds), *Robert E. Park e la teoria del 'melting pot'/ Robert E. Park and the 'Melting Pot' Theory*, Reverdito Edizioni, Trento, pp. 55-71.

Glaser, B.G. and Strauss, A.L. (1967), *The Discovery of Grounded Theory: Strategies for Qualitative Research*, Aldine de Gruyter, Berlin.

Glaser, B.G. (1992), *Basics of Grounded Theory Analysis. Emergence vs. Forcing*, Sociology Press, Mill Valley.

Gurvitch, G. (1962), *Dialectique et sociologie*, Flammarion, Paris.

Marcuse, H. (1970), 'Repressive Tolerance', in R.P. Wolff, B. Moore Jr. and H. Marcuse (1965), *A Critique of Pure Tolerance*, Beacon Press, Boston.

Marcuse, H. (1970), *A Critique of Pure Tolerance*, Beacon Press, Boston.

Park, R.E. (1928), 'Human Migration and the Marginal Man', *American Journal of Sociology*, vol. 33, no. 6, pp. 881-93.

Samora, J. with Bustamante J.A. and Cardenas G. (1971), *Los Mojados, The Wetback Story*, University of Notre Dame Press, Notre Dame.

Sassen, S. (1991), *The Global City: New York, London, Tokyo*, Princeton University Press, Princeton.

Simmel, G. ([1908] 1924), 'The Sociological Significance of the 'Stranger'', in R.E. Park and E.W. Burgess, *Introduction to the Science of Sociology*, University of Chicago Press, Chicago, pp. 322-27.

Stone, G.P. and Farberman, H.A. (1970) (eds), *Social Psychology through Symbolic Interaction*, Ginn-Blaisdell, Waltham.

Weber, M. ([1918] 1946), 'Wissenschaft als Beruf', published in English translated as 'Science as a vocation', in H.H. Gerth and C. Wright Mills (eds), *From Max Weber: Essays in Sociology*, Oxford University Press, New York, (1946).

Weber, M. (1978), *Economy and Society. An Outline of Interpretive Sociology*, Vol. I, edited by G. Roth and C. Wittich, University of California Press, Berkeley.

Weber, M. (1978), *Economy and Society. An Outline of Interpretive Sociology*, vol. II, ed. by G. Roth and C. Wittich, University of California Press, Berkeley.

Wright Mills, C. (1956), *The Power Elite*, Oxford University Press, New York.

13 New horizons in religious evolution[1]

YVES LAMBERT

Introduction

When the theories of secularization came to the fore in the 1960s and 1970s (Berger, 1967; Dobbelaere, 1981), Western religious development appeared to follow a quasi-linear movement that can be summarized as follows: the more modernity advances, the more interest in religion dwindles, or is simply relegated to the private domain. This is a phenomenon which a previously decisive work accurately described in its title: *The Decline of the Sacred in Industrial Society* (Acquaviva, 1979). It is well known that the developments of the last thirty years have further complicated the pattern. Firstly, towards the end of the 1960s there was the emergence of the NRMs (*New Religious Movements*) in what was one of the most modernized regions of the United States, California, and throughout Christendom the rise and expansion of pentecostal, evangelical and charismatic tendencies. Then in 1978 came the ascension and world-wide influence of Pope John Paul II. Susbsequently, since 1979, and from the Iranian revolution onwards, the importance of religious fundamentalism has become evident, although essentially in the non-Western world. In 1989, the collapse of communism in Eastern Europe gave rise to de-secularization as well as to religious reawakening. Furthermore, the growth of such 'parallel beliefs' as astrology, telepathy, reincarnation, 'spiritism', and the like, is often observed alongside the Christian system of beliefs. Meanwhile, in Europe at least, the erosion of Christianity paradoxically continues and religious relativism is growing more widespread. There are, in fact, four principal religious trends to be observed in current Western religious developments: a decline of Christianity, an internal redefinition of Christianity (see above), an expansion of parallel beliefs and of NRMs, and a shift toward relativism, probabilism, pragmatism, and subjectivism. How are we to explain this decline and revival, breakdown and reconstruction?

There exists a little-known analytical model which can be effectively

---

1   The main part of this paper was first published in *Sociology of Religion* (1999).

employed to compare among contradictory religious evolutions in high modernity. This model, which is a product of comparativism, treats modernity as an axial turning point: that is, as a period involving a general reshaping of symbolic systems, and in particular, of the religious system. This model helps to elucidate the 'post-modernity' debate, account for the aspects of religious losses, redefinitions, conservative reactions, and innovations, identify religious forms characteristic of modernity and high modernity, and distinguish between what is decomposition or recomposition. It is this perspective that the present chapter endeavours to apply to the Western countries. It underlines seven features of modernity: the primacy of reason, science and technology; a craving for individual freedom; the historical emergence of the masses; functional differentiation; economic development; and globalisation. The effects of these factors on religion, as we shall see, have been decline, adaptation, reinterpretation, reaction and innovation. As to redefinition and innovation, the model emphasises an increasing focus on this-life and on humanity, the disassociation of sin and a person's fate after death, the bringing of the divine closer to the human, monism, self-spirituality and parascientificity. Let us begin by considering the notion of 'axial period', and its application to modernity and subsequent analyses of religion (Jaspers, 1954; Bellah, 1976; Kitagawa, 1967; Nakamura, 1986).

1. Modernity as a new axial period

1.1 The concept of 'axial period', modernity and religion

Various historians and philosophers have stressed the key role played by certain periods in history in the development of the techniques, political structures, or world views that came to predominate in following centuries or millennia, before being in their turn questioned, then replaced, or altered and inserted into new systems. 'Man seems to have started again from scratch four times', Karl Jaspers wrote (1945: 37-38): with the Neolithic age, with the earliest civilizations, with the emergence of the great empires, and with modernity. Each of these axial turns produced a general reshaping of the 'symbolic field', to use Pierre Bourdieu's term, and a great religious upheaval which led to disappearances, redefinitions and emergences. Each period eventually gave rise to new religious configurations: respectively, oral agrarian religions, religions of antiquity, religions of salvation (universalist religions), and modern changes. Of the religions of antiquity, only Judaism and Hinduism survived the preceding axial age, albeit greatly changed and preserving typically pre-universalist traits (at least until modernity): a large number of prohibitions, important domestic rites, transmission by descent. We may assume that modernity, too, stands as a major challenge to established religions, as well as being a potential source of religious innovation, especially if it is about to be radicalized and generalized as Giddens argues (1991). Furthermore, the hypothesis of modernity as a new axial turn prompts consideration of very long-term effects, those of civilizations, and enables comparative study and an interpretation which accounts not only for religious decline but also for revivals, mutations and inventions.

The concept of 'axial age' has been used to refer to one particular historical period: the emergence of universalism, philosophy, the great religions, and early science (Jaspers, 1954; Bellah, 1976: 20-50; Eisenstadt, 1986; Hick, 1989: 21-35). This is especially true of the sixth and fifth centuries BC, which were a key stage in the process (Deutero-Isaiah, the era of Pericles, Upanishads, Jain, Buddha, Confucius, Lao-tze) from which Christianity and Islam sprang. This age is considered to be 'axial' because we are still its heirs, particularly through the great religions. However, there is no reason for not considering the Neolithic age, the earliest civilizations, the great empires and modernity as axial ages, since they too saw a general reshaping of collective thought. Therefore, our definition of 'axial age' (or 'axial period') comprises these four ages. At its beginning, an axial age is a kind of cinematic 'fade': it is marked by critical moments of crisis and shifts of thought which lead to a reshaping of the symbolic field which creates a new period of stability. These critical phases vary in duration from, for example, a thousand years for universalism (from the sixth century BC to the rise of Islam) to several millennia for the Neolithic age (from its first emergence to its eventual global expansion and triumph).

Jaspers, while considering modernity to be a new axial period, regarded the turn taken by modernity in the nineteenth century as the harbinger of a probable 'second axial period' (Jaspers, 1954: 38). He hesitated because globalization was not yet a widespread phenomenon when he was writing in 1949, although we may assume that this is the case today. Jaspers identified modernity with four fundamental distinguishing features: modern science and technology, a craving for freedom, the emergence of the masses on the historical stage (nationalism, democracy, socialism, social movements), and globalization. To this list should be added the primacy of reason (a feature that Jaspers implicitly includes in the four features), the development of capitalism, and functional differentiation (the rise of the modern state, and

Parsons' and Luhmann's concept of differentiation among the spheres of activity in society).

This notion of axial age has not been utilized by sociologists in analysis of modernity. However, Szakolczai and Füstös (1996) refer to the 'axial age' and use the concept of 'axial moment' in ways that are relevant to this analysis. They define this notion as follows:

> An axial moment occurs whenever there is a global collapse of the established order of things, including the political system, the social order of everyday life and the system of beliefs – a very rare event – and a major spiritual revival ... Such a period happened in the first centuries (collapse of the Roman republic and rise of Christianity), in the fifth-to-seventh centuries (collapse of the Roman Empire and rise of Islam), in the fifteenth and sixteenth centuries (the waning of the Middle Ages, Renaissance and Protestantism), and finally the two major stages of the dissolution of absolutist politics and the traditional European social order, Enlightenment and socialism.

Thus, what Szakolczai and Füstös choose to define as an axial moment corresponds to key phases in an axial age. For example, the rise of Christianity and Islam are two key phases of the previous axial age (universalism), and the fifteenth-to-sixteenth centuries, the Enlightenment and socialism (or more precisely the rise of industrial society) are the three key phases of modernity. Nonetheless, I believe that it is useful to employ the term 'axial moment' to define such phases within an axial period.

In highly schematic fashion, therefore, we can periodize modernity. It begins with the 'axial moment' of the fifteenth-to-sixteenth centuries, which is not only the beginning of what historians call 'the modern age', but also that of modern science, and of the birth of capitalism and the bourgeoisie. But modernity only becomes a major phenomenon at the end of this period with the Enlightenment and the English and, especially, American and French Revolutions, the birth of scientific method and thought, and the rise of industry (second axial moment). The third 'axial moment' includes the development and triumph of industrial society and of capitalism (nineteenth to mid-twentieth century), first in England and then throughout Europe and North America, the development of socialism, the building of the nation-state, the spread of nationalism and colonialism until its breaking point with the two world wars, and finally, decolonization, globalization and, in the West, the triumph of democracy, of the affluent society, and of the welfare state. Modernity also resulted in the Cold War and the threat of nuclear destruction. The 1960s are often considered to be a turning point: the beginning of the so-called post-industrial, post-Fordist society, information or knowledge society, and the beginning of the moral revolution. Ever since, the tertiary sector has become increasingly dominant; intangible factors of production (information, communication, and knowledge) and new technologies (computers and electronics) have become more important; and the family is becoming less and less traditional. In addition, globalization is complete, the middle class grows increasingly powerful, new problems (unemployment and pollution) and new social movements (feminism, regionalism, ecology, etc.) emerge, and finally, communism has collapsed.

Are we still in the era of modernity or have we entered post-modernity? I share the opinion of Anthony Giddens (1991: 3) that

> rather than entering a period of post-modernism, we are moving into one in which the consequences of modernity are becoming more radicalized and universalized than before.

In fact, that which allegedly defines post-modernity is far from featuring the fundamentally new aspects that characterize an axial turn; but it could constitute a new 'axial moment' (as Szakolczai maintains) explainable in terms of generalized, radicalized and reflexive modernity. The hallmark of post-modernity is the disqualification of 'great narratives': great religions, great ideologies (nationalism, communism, fascism) and the ideology of endless progress. But this only allows us to differentiate ourselves from the prior phase (axial moment) of modernity, and it is partly refuted by new forms of nationalism and by religious fundamentalism. The relativization of science and technology is not new, but it is increasing precisely because the excesses and dangers of the former constitute a dramatically increasing menace (nuclear threat, pollution). One could continue and show that the other features attributed to post-modernity are the logical extension of trends within modernity, like the nuclear threat and pollution : the de-traditionalization of the life-world, the anti-authoritarian revolt, hedonism, new social movements, and above all, individualization. The same also holds for the selective return to certain traditions, once modernity has prevailed over tradition, or for the repeated appeal to local identities, which is a reaction against globalization. Hence I agree with Beckford's criticism (1996: 30-47) of the concept of post-modernity.

Nevertheless, I remain open to the hypothesis that we may be on the brink of some form of post-modernity, or at least of a profoundly new moment in modernity, given that the risk of irreparable pollution and, above all, of nuclear destruction are the most dramatic and the most radical fates imaginable: the very survival of the human species is at stake, which is indeed a fundamentally new phenomenon. Besides, if we consider modernity to be a new axial period, we cannot know where we are in the process, all the more so because modernity involves permanent change – and change at such an accelerated pace that it may not be followed by a phase of stabilization as was formerly the case, and thereby create some kind of permanent turn. In any event, since an axial turn is a cinematic 'fade' where older forms can coexist for centuries with new forms, or survive by adopting new ones, it would be very difficult, while being part of the 'fade', to distinguish the decline of modernity from the birth of post-modernity. At present, we do not have the necessary distance to resolve the matter. In any case, whether we are in post-modernity, late modernity, hyper-modernity or whatever other term one might choose, nothing changes concerning our method of analysis.

1.2 The religious characteristics of the former axial period

Before taking a more detailed look at the religious characteristics of modernity, let us first remind ourselves of those of the preceding axial turn. One can briefly mention the following, in comparison with those of ancient polytheistic religions: an extension to everybody, everywhere (universalism); a major advance in the 'demythologization' of nature; the abandoning of animal sacrifice as the once central rite of agrarian and polytheistic religions; the rejection of the notion of divine affiliation among sovereigns or the aristocracy; the unification and rationalization of religious concepts, either in the form of monotheism or through the Atman-Brahman mode of thought; an emphasis on ethical and spiritual aspects, especially perfect justice for all, either under the judgement of God (monotheism) or according to the logic of karma (karmic religions), with post-mortem destiny dependent on behaviour in this world ; pre-eminence bestowed on other-worldly accomplishment instead of this-worldly success (paradise/hell, rebirth/nirvana), so that the human condition is perceived as an imperfect and provisional state from which one must be saved (hence the expression 'religions of salvation'); greater importance given to inner attitude as opposed to the scrupulous execution of religious rites; formal equality of all individuals under ethical and religious law and before salvation, to which even the sovereign is subservient; the development of theological and philosophical speculation with the emergence of clerics; proselytism as a consequence of universalism and of the call to salvation.

    These characteristics should be set in relation to the general changes with which they are linked: greater mastery over nature in the domains of iron, agriculture, animal power, navigation, urbanization; the growth of populations, towns and trade; the emergence of new social spheres, in particular a middle class and a wave of intellectuals and philosophers who regarded their religious roles as critical; the structuring of states by codes, laws, bureaucracies; the formation of vast empires themselves the source of universalism owing to encounters with distinct religions and the imposition of rules and destinies common to all indigenous populations; the widening distance between extreme social conditions that engendered demands for perfect justice and future compensation; and the closer independence of individuals from primary groups that brought about a more personal form of religiosity.

This turning-point was a radical rupture as regards polytheistic religions, the majority of which were eliminated. Yet some of them survived through adjustment, as in the cases of Judaism, Hinduism, Taoism and the Imperial Chinese religion where certain polytheistic traits have been transferred to new religions (for example, Christian saints performing a functionally analogous role to those of former divinities) and some elements have survived separately ('folklore'). Naturally, continuity has been greatest in the cases of Judaism and Hinduism, which have nevertheless preserved typically pre-universal traits such as the large number of restrictions, the importance of domestic rites, transmission by affiliation. As said, a turning-point is comparable to a cinematic 'fade' where ancient forms long coexist with new ones and interpenetrate with them. Only later can the meaning of these transformations be truly understood: suffice it to imagine what sort of analysis could have been made of religious change in the Roman Empire at the end of the first century AD, with the development of the imperial cult, the co-existence of numerous polytheistic religions, the spread of mystery religions, in particular of 'Mithraism', the onset of Christianity and the predilection for philosophy among the elite. Let us imagine that we are now at such a turning-point in modernity.

By examining the characteristics of religions of salvation and what we know about modernity, we can discern a number of typical challenges. For example, although reason, science and technology have radically demythologized nature and the universe, the religions of salvation had already made great progress in this direction by focusing on and rationalizing ethical and spiritual aspects; a practice which effectively enabled them to adapt to modernity. Likewise with regard to religion, we know that modernity signifies the broad autonomization of social and political life; yet we may also acknowledge that Christianity and Buddhism had achieved this autonomy before they became the instruments for symbolic legitimization of the socio-political order, and were hence able to adapt to the transformation. Another challenge: modernity functioned to re-centre man on earthly purposes; but how were the this-worldly aspects of the religions of salvation reinterpreted, and what was to become of their other-worldly ends, given that modernity could not guarantee immortality or even (nowadays) secure the future? Moreover, when faced with globalization, what happens to the dialectic of universalism present in every major religion when it is directly confronted by other religious or secular universalisms, and the contents of the truth of universalist religions are largely incompatible? (thus placing them in a situation as relativist as that of the polytheistic religions in the Roman Empire). These questions illustrate how the problematic of the axial turn poses problems, while also suggesting that in the face of such challenges, 'axial age' religions, even if they are not lacking in assets, take serious risks which effectively leave them open. Let us examine how comparativists have analysed these situations before briefly summarizing sociological opinion on the subject.

2. Global analyses of the distinguishing religious features of modernity

The purpose of this section is to review the various claims put forward concerning the effects of modernity on religion and the transformations taking place in religion. I shall not attempt to link these analyses systematically, this being the task of the following section. 'I am reasonably sure,' wrote Bellah (1976: 39) that, 'even though we must speak from the midst of it, the modern situation represents a stage of religious development in many ways profoundly different from that of historic religion'. Moreover, as Gordon Melton (1985: 455) remarks,

> during the twentieth century, the West has experienced a phenomenon it has not encountered since the reign of Constantine: the growth of and significant visible presence of a variety of non-Christian and non-orthodox Christian bodies competing for the religious allegiance of the public. This growth of so many religious alternatives is forcing the West into a new situation in which the still dominant Christian religion must share its centuries-old hegemony in a new pluralistic religious environment.

Of course, no new worldly religion or spirituality has spread on a wide scale, and to date the most visible novelty on the modern symbolic landscape has been the growth of secular thought and world-views (science, ideologies, ethics, human rights, and so on). However, also to be observed are fundamental changes in the religious landscape, and we may be in a burgeoning phase of evolution. What do we learn from the global analyses of modernity as a new stage in the religious history of humankind or from those that examine the modernist challenge to religion as a whole?

Jaspers (1954: 278-80) confined himself to some terse but insightful remarks. 'If a transcendent aid does manifest itself', he predicted about completed modernity, 'it can only be to free a man and by virtue of his autonomy', for 'he that feels free lets his beliefs fluctuate regardless of any clearly defined credo ... in accordance with an unfettered faith which escapes any specific definition, which remains unattached while retaining the sense of the absolute and seriousness, along with their strong vitality'. This faith, he adds, 'still has not found any resonance with the masses' and is 'despised by the representatives of the official, dogmatic and doctrinaire creeds'. But 'it is likely, therefore, that Bible religion will revive and undergo modifications'. Hence Jaspers emphasises the will to be free, which fits rather well with contemporary notions of *individualization* but is also an interesting prediction concerning *fundamentalism* and evangelism. Jaspers' beliefs, moreover, are a radical *demythologization*: he believed neither in divine revelations nor in the incarnation and resurrection of Jesus, whom he considered to be only a spiritual genius. But he was convinced that there was an intrinsic transcendent dimension to man constituted especially by the value of life and the need for achievement. Consequently, Jaspers added two further possible characteristics of religion in modernity: new forms of *monism* and *this-worldiness*.

Joseph M. Kitagawa (1967: 61-2) singles out three related distinctive features: *man as the centre*, *this-worldly soteriology* and the *search for freedom* (rather than preservation of order) which closely resemble those of Jaspers. He points out that

> all classical religions tended to take negative attitudes toward phenomenal existence and recognized another realm of reality

which was the most important of them, and that 'in this life, man was thought to be a sojourner or prisoner' yearning for the heaven or nirvana which would release him from suffering, sin, imperfection, finitude.

> A radical change has taken place in this respect in the thinking of modern people, in that, they no longer take seriously the existence of another realm of reality. To be sure, they still use such expressions as paradise, Pure Land, Nirvana and the Kingdom of God. These terms have only symbolic meaning for the modern

mentality (to which) this phenomenal world is the only real order of existence, and life here and now is the centre of the world of meaning.

Thus Kitawaga speaks of 'the single cosmos of the modern man', which he contrasts with the former dualistic cosmos. Religions are compelled 'to find the meaning of human destiny in this world – in culture, society and human personality' in order to fulfil the human vocation (e. g., Gandhi), which entails soteriologies centred on this world.

According to Bellah (1976: 39-44),

> the central feature of the change is the *collapse of the dualism* [my emphasis] that was so crucial to all the historic religions ... There is simply no room for a hierarchic dualistic religious symbol system of the classical historic type. This is not to be interpreted as a return to primitive monism: it is not that a single world has replaced a double one but that an infinitely multiplex one has replaced the simple duplex structure ... 'Behind the 96% of Americans who claim to believe in God', he adds, 'there are many instances of a massive reinterpretation that leaves Tillich, Bultmann and Bonhoeffer far behind' ... The dualistic worldview certainly persists in the mind of many of the devout, but just as surely many others have developed elaborate and often pseudo-scientific rationalization to bring their faith in its experienced validity into some kind of cognitive harmony with the twentieth-century world.

This, he explains, is due to science and individualization, which reduce the distance between the terrestrial and the celestial, the human and the divine, the laity and the clergy.

This resembles Kitagawa's thesis, while the stress on *individualization* reminds one of Jaspers: 'the symbolization of man's relation to the ultimate conditions of his existence,' writes Bellah,

> is no longer the monopoly of any groups explicitly labelled religious ... not only has any obligation of doctrinal orthodoxy been abandoned by the leading edge of modern culture, but every fixed position had become open to question in the process of making sense out of man and his situation ... one might almost be tempted to see in Thomas Paine's 'My mind is my church' or in Thomas Jefferson's 'I am a sect myself' the typical expression of religious organization in the near future.

He adds:

> each individual must work out his own ultimate solutions, and the most the church can do is provide him a favourable environment for doing so, without imposing on him a prefabricated set of answers, knowing that he will have an open and flexible pattern of membership.

Hence we can also speak of *flexibility* and *revisability*. Bellah sees modern man as

a dynamic multidimensional self capable, within limits, of continual self-transformation and capable, again within limits, of remaking the world, including the very symbolic forms with which he deals with it ... with growing awareness that it is *symbolism* and that man in the last analysis is responsible for the choice of his symbolism. In addition, he observes that 'the search for adequate standards of action, which is at the same time a search for personal maturity and social relevance, is in itself the heart of the modern quest for salvation', which refers to *this-worldliness*. Bellah concludes that the view of modern man as secular and non-religious is fundamentally misguided, and that the present situation is actually 'offering unprecedented opportunities for creative innovation in every sphere of human action'.

In analysing 'modern religious attitudes' Hajime Nakamura (1986: 511-60) refers to similar features, but adds to them the *collapse of dualism*. He also deepens the notion of *humanism* and identifies new trends: a movement toward equality, an approach more open to the masses, a *lay tendency* reminiscent of Jaspers' emergence of the masses, and *pluralism*. His analysis encompasses Asia and Japan, providing evidence that some form of modernity has also appeared in the East. He points to the 'denunciation of religious formalism and stress on inner devotion', emphasising pure heart, pure mind, pure faith, the anti-ritualistic and anti-magic, and citing the Reformation but also Hinduism (from Râmânanda, Caitanya, Kabir to Râmakrishna), Sikhism (Nânak) and Zen Buddhism (especially Shinran, once compared to Luther). However, Nakamura also stresses the typically modern *search for authenticity*, which is a further element to be added to the overall picture.

Nakamura discusses *this-worldliness* in terms similar to Kitagawa's, underlining a 'return to this-worldliness', the 'rise in popularity of worldly activity and vocational ethics', and the denial of monasticism not only in Protestantism but also in Hinduism (among the masters already cited and in Tulsî Das), Sikhism, and Buddhism (Suzuki Shôsan shows that to pursue one's vocation is to do as a Buddha does). He follows Kitagawa in his emphasis on the change 'in the evaluation of man ... man conceived as supreme and stress on human love'; whence, he adds, derives a new religious emphasis on 'service to people'. More than any of the other authors, he develops analysis of the 'increased lay tendency of religion' (lay roles, married priests, etc.) and the 'accelerated approach to the masses' (use of vernacular language, service to people, etc.) and the 'heightened movement toward equality of man and anti-discrimination', with its secular as well as religious forms, which we may link with Jaspers' ideas of freedom and emergence of the masses; we again meet the same tendencies in the East. In addition, Nakamura stresses the rise of the idea that each religion is valuable – which is acknowledgement of *pluralism*, a typical global effect of modernity. Interestingly, he shows that all of these changes emphasise the *positive and humanistic aspects of religion*, including the value of the body, at the expense of fear of damnation or asceticism, and that, as a result of the increased value of the human person, there is a new emphasis on religious ethical norms (humanism, Enlightenment, and also Caitanya, Tulsî Dâs, etc.). He adds, however, that all these changes are more pronounced in the West.

Most other general analyses of the relationship between religion and modernity have focused on secularization, emphasising the following features: *demonopolization, privatization, this-worldiness, laicization, decline* in the light of general processes of individualization, rationalization and functional differentiation (Dobbelaere, 1981; Tschannen, 1992). Peter Berger (1967) has emphasised the rise of *secular worldviews, subjectivization* (individualization), and *pluralization*. Danièle Hervieu–Léger (1986) speaks of *deregulation, bricolage, pragmatism, subjectivism*, also stressing (1993: 129-48) that modernity makes secular promises it cannot keep, especially in its present de-utopianised phase which encourages religious restructurings, and especially the development of an emotional community type of religion which values personal experience. Françoise Champion (1993) finds *self primacy, this-worldiness, optimism, alliance with science, love ethics* in the 'mystic-esoterical nebula'. Jean–Paul Willaime (1995) has shown that the fundamental features of modernity (he mentions *systematic reflexivity*, referring to Giddens, *functional differentiation, individualization, rationalization, globalization, pluralism*) may fuel both religious decomposition and recomposition, the latter especially in ultra-modernity because it reasserts the value of traditions, cultures, meaning, and subjectivity. Lester Kurtz (1995) points to: 1. the substitution of religious traditions with rationalism, scientism and individualism; 2. *secularization*; 3. the *revitalization* of traditional forms; 4. the construction of *quasi-religious forms* like civil religion or ideologies; 5. the creation of new forms of religious beliefs and practices through processes of *syncretism*; and he highlights the fact that pluralism can produce religious revitalization as well as relativization. As to post-modern analysts, these have highlighted *self-religion, bricolage, syncretism, pluralism, subjectivism, probabilism, mobility* (Flanagan and Jupp, 1996).

3. A model of the relationships between religion and modernity

What is to be done with so many overlapping concepts? Though probably nothing is missing from the picture, it does not amount to a systematic model of the relationships between religion and modernity. With a view to developing such a model, I shall first analyse the religious effects of each of the distinguishing features of modernity: the primacy of reason; science and technology; the craving for freedom, the emergence of the masses; globalization; the development of the economy; and modern functional differentiation. I shall also take account of their combined effects. This will permit identification of four typical religious effects for each feature of modernity: decline, adaptation or re-interpretation, conservation, and innovation. (Conversely, one should also analyse the influence of religion on the modernizing process, but space precludes such analysis here). The way in which these factors have worked historically may explain the religious situation in each particular country. In the next section, I shall focus on several of the new religious characteristics that have been highlighted: this-worldiness, optionality and self-spirituality, de-hierarchization, para-scientificity, pluralization and relativization, mobility and revisability, loosely organized networks. I shall also include some of the results of the *World Values Survey (WVS)* and of the International Social Survey Programme (ISSP) not so much to test the model as to illustrate it and prepare for the debate on secularization, given that it is primarily a historical model, and that these surveys were not designed to test its sociological relevance. Moreover, the data will clarify what is happening in high modernity. A brief survey follows.

1. The *primacy given to reason* has been an essential factor in modernity, furnishing a robust basis not only for the rapid growth of science but also for individual liberty, the break with tradition, the autonomization of the economy, and the questioning of the legitimacy of both an orderly society and the monarchy. Reason introduced a notion of truth that rivalled religion and tradition. Ernst Troeltsch forcefully emphasised this aspect, following Max Weber. The effect of the ascendancy of reason over religion was and still is considerable and fundamentally ambivalent. While on the one hand reason can be viewed as emanating from God or from a divine order, or at least as not being in contradiction with religion, on the other it can be seen as an effective tool in the war against religion and religious interpretations of the world. Descartes, for example, believed that God created man and endowed him with reason, and that this reason could only lead back to God, albeit solely through a religion purified by reason. For Diderot, by contrast, reason clearly

demonstrated that religion was an invention of man. Weber showed how reason was a factor in the rationalization of religion, while studies on irreligion and the loss of faith illustrate the anti-religious effects due to the influence of atheistic philosophies. We know that neither reason, nor science for that matter, can prove or invalidate the existence of God or of an impersonal divine figure; indeed, arguments can be provided for each, with the consequence that a fundamental ambivalence arises. As a general rule, the more religion has been linked with what reason explicitly questions, the more the use of reason has been opposed to religion; although the opposite is also true in so far as religion has redefined itself in relation to these changes, becoming itself an agent of them: demythologization, human rights, redefinition of the respective domains of religion and science, and so on. In this respect, we may say that France and the United States are diametric opposites.

Sociological data are lacking on the perceived role of reason and the correlation between reason and religion, and no study has yet been conducted on the matter. Dobbelaere and Jagodzinski (1995: 96-101, 210-14) identify the degree of rationalization with the degree of modernization (per-capita GDP, level of education, social structure) and have correlated these elements. The demonstration seems to some extent conclusive: among the ten countries surveyed, the least developed have the highest levels of religiosity – Ireland, followed by Spain and Italy – while the most developed of them have moderate or low levels of religiosity: Germany, followed by France and Sweden. But the relation no longer holds if the analysis takes account of Luxembourg, Switzerland, Austria, Canada and, above all, the United States, which figure among the most developed nations and have the highest levels of religiosity. In any case, and whatever the results might be, we would still be unable to prove much of anything, not only because these indicators are not sufficiently precise with regard to the degree of rationalization, but also because rationalization in itself has a basically ambivalent effect. Consequently, the nature of the relationship should be measured with more precise indicators. The same ambivalence, moreover, holds true for the other factors of modernity, especially science.

2. Obviously *science* may give rise to atheism (scientism, materialism) as well as to reinterpretations (demythologization, critical exegesis), fundamentalist reactions (creationism), or innovations (deism, para-scientific beliefs). From its origins in ancient Greece until the present day, science, in much the same way as reason, has always had a radically ambivalent effect on religion. Archimedes was convinced that the laws of arithmetic revealed the

principles of the divine order of things, and Copernicus marvelled at the laws of creation. As believers in God, Galileo, Newton and Einstein thought that if religious scriptures were at odds with science, they need only be reinterpreted. On the other hand, Democritus thought that the physical world rendered the divine vacuous; and when Napoleon asked the physicist Laplace, 'And where is God in all of this?', Laplace replied, 'My Lord, I have never needed to concern myself with such a hypothesis'. Today, the Big Bang can be considered the last word in explanation of the universe just as easily as it can be considered the hand of God. Finally, Buddhists believe that atomic theory confirms the philosophy of aggregation. From the beginnings of modernity, the main points of confrontation between science and Christianity have without doubt been Galileo's condemnation, Darwinism, Positivism, and Marxism.

Among the religious innovations influenced by science, mention may first be made of the concept of an impersonal God, religious movements such as Christian Science, the Church of Scientology, the New Age, as well as para-science: astrology, telepathy, cosmic energies, waves, extraterrestrials, Near Death Experiences (NDEs), which are all notions perceived as scientific by the majority of their believers. While astrology is in itself not a new domain of knowledge, its present-day interpretation is primarily para-scientific. *Para-scientificity* is a typically modern religious form. Elements borrowed from the human sciences have led to the development of new spiritual movements like Human Potential, Scientology and Transcendental Meditation. There is a belief in the convergence of science ('sheer science', 'new science') and spirituality in Buddhism, in the mystic-esoterical nebula, the gnosis of Princeton, and many New Religious Movements (NRMs) (Champion, 1993). In ultra-modernity, the relativization of science and technology seems able to foster a return to religious traditions, a spread of millenarianisms, and an increase in para-scientific salvationism (Scientology, New Age, extra-terrestrial saviours). But, once again, we lack sufficient data to account for the phenomenon thoroughly.

We cannot speak of science without also mentioning technology. In revolutionizing the conditions and quality of life through the material improvements that they have brought (health, food, housing, transportation, media, leisure), science and technology have contributed to the Copernican revolution that has made worldly happiness the ultimate goal in life, instead of other-worldly salvation. But neither science nor technology has been able to answer the ultimate questions (Where do we come from? Where are we going? What is the meaning of life? Why do we suffer and die?); nor have they been able to eliminate sickness, injustice, misery, unhappiness, and death. Technology may result in a rejection of religion (materialism, for example), in religious adaptation (this-worldliness, humanism, faith-healers), in a conservative reaction (the Amish), or in innovations (UFOs, the Church of Scientology's electrometer), but fundamentalist movements usually adopt modern technology for no other reason than to disseminate their message. The return to a system of beliefs that highlights the importance of this world (this-worldliness) is a consequence of all of the factors of modernity combined.

Despite the lack of sociological data (once again) we can nonetheless gain an indirect idea of science's impact from the 1991 ISSP survey, which asked how respondents perceived the Bible. The following replies were possible: 'The Bible is the actual word of God and it is to be taken literally, word for word'/'The Bible is the inspired word of God but not everything should be taken literally, word for word'/'The Bible is an ancient book of fables, legends, history, and moral precepts recorded by man'/'This does not apply to me'/'Can't choose'. We find that the first two replies – 'actual word'/ 'inspired word'– had rates of 13% and 40% respectively in the Western European sample group of Germany, Great Britain, Ireland, Italy, Denmark, the Netherlands: ranging from the highest in Italy (26%/51%) to the lowest in Great Britain (6% /34%). The rates were 32%/47% in the United States; 10%/ 16% in Russia; 55%/26% in Poland, which was the only country in which the first percentage was higher; and 25%/26% in Israel. With the exception of Poland, the percentage of respondents choosing the reply 'actual word' was higher in older age groups and among those with lower levels of education. In addition, the answer was more frequent among farmers, the working classes, and in the lower middle classes (Lambert, 1998).

Although a less useful indicator, the World Value Survey included a question on the kind of God that the respondent envisaged, with a distinction drawn among 'a personal God' (the 'true' Christian answer), 'a spirit or vital force' (which may be the origin or the architect of the universe, energy, the divine within each creature, cosmic consciousness, etc.), 'I don't really think there is any sort of spirit, God or life force', and 'don't know', 'no reply'. In Western Europe, God was considered by only slightly more respondents to be 'a personal God' (36%) as opposed to 'a spirit or vital force'(34%) (unbelief rate: 11%), in France by 20% and 32% respectively; and in the United States by 69% and 23%, which confirms the difference pointed out above between Europe and the United States (Lambert, 1996). Moreover, 40% of American scientists claim to believe in God. The responses vary mainly according to age: in Europe, the percentage of those choosing 'personal God' decreases from 47% to 28% between the eldest and the youngest generations, but in the United States from 70% to 66%. Similarly, the decrease in the belief that 'God really exists' is 41% to 25%, respectively, in Europe and 67% to 57% in the United States (ISSP). According to a 1994 survey conducted in France, the home of scientism, only 27% of respondents believed in the Judeo-Christian conception of creation (20% in the 18–24 age group), and 49% said that they agreed with the item 'the more science progresses, the more difficult it is to believe in God' (64% in the 18–24 age group), which shows that the problem persists.

3. The primacy of reason has been a factor in the desire for liberty because it allows for individual autonomy in the face of tradition, political power, and religious authority. *Individual consciousness and freedom* may give rise to a rejection of religion, to a more personal religion, to a reaction through the reaffirmation of collective identity, or to (especially in ultra-modernity) bricolages, syncretisms and inventions and parallel beliefs. Mention should also be made of the characteristics highlighted by other authors: the supremacy of man, human love, God's love, the search for authenticity, and, especially in high modernity, pragmatism, subjectivism and self-spirituality. As to be expected, individual choice may give rise to any possibility imaginable *vis-à-vis* religion and the Church, and individualization can be considered the main feature of changes in the value system of high modernity (Ester et al., 1993).

Protestantism was the first widespread religious expression of the desire for liberty and freedom. It brought innovations that were at the time revolutionary: a more personalized faith, the opportunity for the laity to read the Bible in the vernacular (as opposed to a Latin Bible reserved for scholars and members of the clergy), and the possibility of confessing one's sins directly to God. In this new context of denominational plurality and religious wars, freedom of belief was the first important claim laid to individual liberty, and two to three centuries passed before it triumphed. This demand for individual liberty also took the form of economic freedom (freedom of trade and commerce), of general freedom of thought (Enlightenment), and of political liberty (democracy, see below on the emergence of the masses). Freedom of thought also led to deism, natural or civil religion, and offered the option of not believing, which was something even more audacious. The Catholic Church condemned the French Declaration of Human Rights of 1789, and furthermore condemned the freedoms of conscience and speech, as well as the principles of laicity and the separation between Church and State, in the encyclical *Quanta Cura* (1864); while the Syllabus denounced eighty 'modern errors', including the following: 'The Supreme Pontiff can and must reconcile himself with and reach a compromise with progress, liberalism, and modern society'. Insofar as modernity has triumphed in all areas of society, the Catholic Church has finally recognized this evolution while nonetheless remaining critical of it (Vatican II). As we know, the United States has played a pioneering role not only in religious freedom (from the founding of Rhode Island to the First Amendment to the Constitution) but also in the religious pluralism and denominational mobility that are its logical consequences (Melton, 1985). The craving for freedom has conquered new areas, such as sexuality and family life, and in so doing has ignited conflict between permissiveness and traditional ethics and provoked conservative reaction within the Church.

According to the WVS and ISSP surveys, the effects of individualization in late modernity are ambivalent, although rather unfavourable to institutionalized religion. Dobbelaere's variable of a 'Christian worldview' (WVS), which rests on the role attributed to God in the meaning of life, suffering, and death, is negatively correlated, albeit only weakly, with the five criteria of individualization. On the other hand, the variable of 'Christian religiosity', which is based in part on the feeling of being religious, prayer, and the ability to find strength and comfort in religion (which in fact goes far beyond the Christian framework), is negatively correlated with three of these five criteria (they neutralize the effect of age). As regards reincarnation, parallel beliefs, and religious liberalism, positive correlations are obtained, and this would undoubtedly also be the case of everything that gives expression to personal religious responsibility or self-spirituality. Roland Campiche (1992) shows that individualization is also a fundamental tendency of Christian redefinition in Switzerland, although this finding is yet to be confirmed using the same data in the case of European youth (Lambert, 1993; Lambert and Voyé, 1997); and Janssen has confirmed it with a survey on Dutch youth (see below). Especially from the 1960s onwards, with the baby-boom generation, these studies show that church members are increasingly independent in their religious and moral lives (Roof, 1993; Roof et al., 1995). For instance, the 1988-89 Roof sample of 1,400 Americans born between 1946 and 1962 were asked to choose between the following items: 'Going to church/synagogue is a duty and an obligation' and '...is something you do if you feel it meets your needs': 76% opted for the latter, and this choice was echoed by two-thirds of those who considered themselves to be born-again Christians, and also by Catholics (The *National Catholic Reporter*, 8 October 1993).

The present effects of individualization on religious innovation can be illustrated by the spread of religious pluralism, denominational mobility, bricolage and parallel beliefs, which are once again significantly visible in the post-war generations. In the Roof sample, for instance, 33% of respondents were loyal to the religion into which they had been born, 42% had left their church, and 25% had returned after a period of absence. To the extent that parallel beliefs (telepathy, astrology, and the like) are completely free, in that they are not controlled by any institution or orthodoxy, they can be individually defined and may coexist with Christian beliefs. Is it perhaps for this reason that they are more popular with the younger generation than with the older? In the 1991 ISSP Survey, which asked three questions on parallel beliefs, 34% of respondents between the ages of 18 and 29 believed (definitely or rather strongly) that 'good luck charms do bring good luck', as opposed to 22% of those aged 60 or over; 39% and 26% respectively believed that 'fortune tellers can foresee the future'; and 32% and 26% that 'the horoscope affects the course of the future'. One also observes that the NRMs which achieve the most enduring success are those that are not perceived as hostile to the desire for freedom (such as New Age), or which at least claim to develop personal abilities (such as Scientology), while the most rigid and closed 'cults' tend to decline in popularity.

Attitudes to permissiveness can also be illustrated by the WVS. Dobbelaere and Jagodzinski (1995: 218-49) have shown a relationship between 'moral rigidity' (against under-age sex, homosexuality, prostitution, abortion, and extramarital affairs) and Christian religiosity. This is the area in which differences according to church attendance and religious affiliation are most pronounced: for instance, only 18% of those who attend church at least once a week agree with the idea of 'complete sexual freedom', compared to 43% who practically never or never attend church. The corresponding percentages are 4% and 29% for 'marriage is an outdated institution', 13% and 49% for abortion 'when a married couple does not want to have any more children'; while 70% and 47% are in favour of greater respect for authority. The results are similar in the United States or among young adults, although the differences are smaller.

4. The *emergence of the masses on the historical stage* (nationalism, democracy, socialism, communism, fascism, social movements) has also exerted contradictory effects on religion according to the historical role of the Church (i.e., support, neutrality or rejection), as David Martin (1978) has pointed out. Nationalism has not played a major role in the evolution of religion simply because the Church has in general supported nationalistic

claims. Nonetheless, examples such as the Papal State's opposition to the unification of Italy in the nineteenth century, which was one of the main reasons for Italian anti-clericalism, can be cited. Countries like Ireland and Poland, where religion has historically played an important role in preserving and affirming national identity, are found to have the highest rates of religiosity. The main challenges have been raised by changes from monarchical to democratic political systems, and above by all the rise of socialism and communism. In this regard, the United States and France offer interesting points of comparison. In the United States, followers of the Protestant Church have historically been the major force behind the fight for human rights; in France, by contrast, the Catholic Church, especially its internal hierarchy, was monarchist and anti-republican until the end of the nineteenth century. While socialism and communism have never been greatly influential in the United States, they have deeply marked the history of France; and in Europe they have generally been the basis for the opposition between a non-religious or slightly religious left and a rather religious right. This legacy can still be seen today in regard to levels of religiosity, which vary according to social class and political preference. It is to be found throughout Western Europe in the religious differences between the social-democratic and Christian-democratic parties. Finally, late modernity has seen the collapse of communism, religion's worst enemy in the twentieth century. Another consequence of the emergence of the masses has been general de-hierarchization of the relationship between the laity and the clergy, the lay tendency, and the adoption of vernacular languages (from early Protestantism to Vatican II).

The rise of new social movements (counter-culture, feminism, ecology, peace, regionalism) could have renewed the importance, or underlined the failure, of religion according to this schema of support or hostility. Yet this does not seem to have happened. Since churches have not had a great deal at stake in these areas, with some exceptions (abortion, married priests, women in the priesthood), they have not taken any major stand and have given their members the right to choose; and even feminism has found a voice in the churches. These movements have given rise to innovation (counter-cultural movements were one of the main sources of the NRMs in the 1960s and 1970s; ecology inspired spiritual ecology), adaptation (ecology is becoming a significant concern for major religions) and, consequently, reaction (moral majority).

According to the 1990 WVS, when arranged along a left-centre-right political continuum, in Europe 16% of those who attend church at least once a week locate themselves towards the left, compared to 45% of those who either never attend church or only rarely attend; in the United States, the percentages are 9% and 28% respectively. The figures are nearly the same among young adults in the United States, while in the case of young European churchgoers, the rate rises to 28%, which testifies to acceptance of the political left. In addition, when we compare the data collected by the 1981 WVS with those of the 1990 WVS, we find that the differences in church attendance and religious affiliation between the lower and upper classes tend to level out. This points to the fact that the basic principle of social antagonism linked to industrial society is in decline. Membership of a trade union is more common among respondents who do not consider themselves to be regular churchgoers, although this is not the case in the United States. As for the new social movements, one notes very few differences, if any, between regular churchgoers and non-practising or non-religious individuals in terms of approval of and participation in movements such as 'ecology, nature protection', 'non-nuclear energy', 'disarmament', 'human rights', 'women', or 'anti-apartheid'; and this is the case irrespective of age (1990 WVS). This is, of course, with the exception of the most religious individuals, who are less involved in women's movements (or in joining unofficial strikes or occupying buildings and factories, though this is very infrequent), but more involved in human rights organizations.

5. The *development of capitalism* has been a factor in the rise of materialism as well as in reinterpretation, especially as regards this-worldliness. Economics was the first sphere of activity to acquire autonomy, and it contributed to the development of socialism and communism through proletarianization, as I have already discussed. Although in vain, the Catholic Church was long opposed to loans with money-bearing interest. Economics enabled the development of non-religious materialism as well as a religious reinterpretation in terms of this-worldly spirituality, vocational ethics, as illustrated by Weber's celebrated thesis (even though for the Calvinist the aim was salvation). These two aspects can be observed since the very beginning of capitalism (merchant cities and states in the fifteenth-sixteenth centuries) until today. A typical interpretation of the Old Testament sees religious faith as a factor in prosperity, and prosperity as a blessing for the devout (the 'Gospel of prosperity' according to the televangelists). The Catholic Church itself has promoted economic development (Vatican II). Another effect of capitalism especially apparent in high modernity is the shift in the United States towards a market-type religious structure and a consumer-type attitude (Iannaccone, 1992). As for the conservative reactionary effect, we may use

the example of the Amish; instances of innovative effects include televangelists or the spiritual way to make money that the Church of Scientology illustrates. Although more difficult to identify, mention could also be made of the role of spiritual complementation that religion might play in an affluent society, but once again we lack empirical data on these issues. As said, the correlation between per-capita GDP and religiosity is not very conclusive, and the same applies to income level.

6. By *functional differentiation* is meant modern state-building, the differentiation between the public sphere and the private sphere, the Luhmannian autonomization of the spheres of activity. Its first marked effect was to deprive religion of its monopoly over education and culture and to legitimize the socio-political order. It favoured the marginalization of the church and of religion; but in preventing them from legitimizing the dominant order, it also encouraged redefinition of their roles in education, culture, health, social aid and welfare, human rights, peace, and so on, in keeping with the more pluralistic context characteristic of high modernity (Casanova, 1994; Beckford, 1996). It has also produced reactionary effects that seek to maintain or re-establish religion's hold on society (fundamentalist trends). According to Luhmann (1977, 1982), modern society is divided into subsystems, each of which has a specific function and relative independence: politics, economics, science, education, law, art, health, family, and religion. Religion is a subsystem defined by its spiritual function. Among these subsystems, Luhmann also distinguishes between those that are imposed upon or prescribed for all members of society, and which he calls 'professional' – examples being politics, economics, science, education and law – and those that are optional or 'complementary', such as art and, specifically, religion. Finally, he distinguishes between the dual functions of a subsystem, its internal (specific) function and its external function, which he calls performance' to denote its influence on other subsystems on their own terrain.

The WVS and ISSP surveys yield interesting insights into the importance assigned to religion, the performance of religion for individuals, and fundamentalist or secularist attitudes (Lambert, 1998). According to the European Values Survey, religion is accorded less importance than the family, work, leisure or friends, but more importance than politics. And it is within the domains of family, morals and politics (preference for the right) that correlations can be detected, with religion in particular playing a role among the core of practising believers. It is on the 'main issues' that the social role of the church is most welcome (peace, human rights, humanitarianism), and then on ethical questions, though to a lesser extent; and all of this while it is vigorously prevented from involving itself in political life. This demand is greatest in the majority of formerly Eastern European countries, particularly Russia. Furthermore, ISSP surveys show that even in the East (except in Poland), only a small minority agree with the idea of direct religious interference in society – indicated by items such as 'Right and wrong should be based on God's law' and 'We should ban books and films attacking religions'. According to these statistics, we can calculate that approximately 10% of Europeans belong to a 'fundamentalist' pole (which comprises one-third of practising Europeans), and that double that amount belong to a 'secularist' one. Fundamentalists are characterised by their traditionalism, their average age being higher and their level of education lower than those of secularists, with the result that the group has little standing. In the United States, on the other hand, the importance accorded to religion is higher, the expected and actual role of religion is more significant, and fundamentalists are more prominent than secularists.

7. Similarly, *globalization* may bring a radical relativization of religions (in so far as their truths are incompatible) and promote world-wide diffusion and gatherings (missions, NRMs, papal visits, etc.), more pluralist reinterpretations (all religions are acceptable), ecumenism and inter-religious dialogue, fundamentalist reactions, innovations (borrowings, bricolage, syncretism). Each of these effects is growing increasingly acute in the current phase of accelerated globalization (Beyer, 1994), especially among the young. Combined with democracy, globalization facilitates the diffusion of new religions and NRMs or provokes defensive and aggressive reactions (Eastern Orthodoxy).

According to the 1981 European Values Survey, 25% of respondents (17% of 18-29 year olds) thought that there was only one true religion; 53% (56% of 18-29 year olds) said that there were interesting insights in all the great religions; and 14% (19% of 18-29 year olds) said that no religion has any truth to offer. In France, those believing that there was only one true religion dropped from one-half in 1952 to 14% in 1981 (11% of 18-29 years old). In the 1988-89 Roof sample (1993), 48% of baby-boomers agreed that 'All the religions of the world are equally true and good'. At the same time, one observes a shift towards probabilism, especially among young adults: the replies 'probably' (yes or no) were as important as the 'certainly' answers for many beliefs. I shall discuss fundamentalist attitudes in the last section. A good example of syncretism (or bricolage) is the overlapping of the notions of resurrection and reincarnation. In the 1990 WVS, in Europe, about 40% of respondents who believed in resurrection said that they also believed in reincarnation, and vice versa. The rate increased to 50% for young adults. Even the Christian core displays this attitude, although, according to interviews conducted in France, it appears that this group conceives of reincarnation as the resurrection of the body (a one-time reincarnation), while the others prefer to think of it as a multiple resurrection.

We might also consider the interrelations among these factors. For example, by furthering the primacy of reason in the face of a religious monopoly of authority, science was able to create a favourable climate for individual freedom and the emergence of the masses on the historical stage. Science conveys an implicit empiricist pattern that may influence the importance of personal experience in modern religious attitudes (pragmatism, self-spirituality). Science and technology have contributed to the development of the economy (by furnishing the fundamental materials for its expansion), to globalization (by being the most universalized forms of activity), and to functional differentiation (science being one of the differentiatied spheres). In this way they have influenced religion's evolution in each of these areas; the development of the spirit of progress greatly contributing to that of worldly goals. While I could continue to expand on these notions, for lack of space I shall instead turn to some of the new forms of religion typical of modernity and high modernity.

4. Some new religious forms typical of modernity or high modernity

With no claim to exhaustiveness, the following new religious forms can be singled out: 1. this-worldliness, 2. self-spirituality, 3. de-hierarchization and de-dualization, 4. para-scientificity, 5. pluralistic, relativistic, fluctuating, seeking faiths, and 6. loose network-type organizations (indeed, religion without religion). All of these are still more widespread among young people (Tomasi, 1998, 1999).

1. *This-worldiness* (especially as a consequence of science), freedom, emergence of the masses, and capitalism tend to de-legitimize the religions of salvation, as well as reorienting them towards more earthly aims. The importance formerly given to other-worldly salvation has collapsed (Walter, 1996). The notion has even become problematic: for instance, the 'Religious and Moral Pluralism in Europe' research group had to eliminate a question on the idea of salvation because, according to the preliminary tests, it was understood by only one-third of those questioned. During research in a Breton

parish, I observed that Catholicism had been *de facto* reinterpreted as a transcendental humanism directed at earthly fulfilment, while open to an after-life devoid of eternal damnation (Lambert, 1985). This observation can probably be generalized. It seems that the function of the after-life is mainly to free man from the fear of death. New millenarianisms, which propose earthly fulfilment (Jehovah Witnesses, Mormons, Adventists) are growing in popularity. The idea of a covenant between the American people and God expresses a logic similar to that found in the Old Testament, where the fidelity of the chosen people was the guarantee of their prosperity. Televangelists put forward a similar argument by claiming that the expiation of sin and faith in God are infallible ways to ensure heavenly grace and benediction, especially in matters of health, family and employment. A book written by the televangelist Roberts (who could be heard on the Euronews channel in 1998) is significantly entitled *God's Formula for Success and Prosperity*. Many NRMs, notably the most successful of them like Scientology, New Age and Human Potential have mundane purposes; the same applies to parallel beliefs: for instance, telepathy, astrology, or reincarnation (which is usually nothing more than the replaying of the game of life with no idea of karma). Wallis (1984) predicts a better future for world-affirming rather than for world-rejecting NRMs.

An important consequence of this-worldliness is the *disassociation between sin and one's fate after death* (de-soteriologization of guilt), which leads to a relative collapse of the concept of sin (hence to the collapse of the practice of confession in Catholicism), or to a more worldly interpretation: sin distances one from God and prevents one from benefiting from His grace, from being fully happy, from communicating with the deep inner self, from finding earthly peace and harmony, and so on.

2. Besides personal religious autonomy, *pragmatism and subjectivity*, there is *self-spirituality* where the desire for freedom is combined with empiricism in a pluralistic environment. The supreme spiritual authority may be the inner self or some form of 'divine within' (Holy Spirit, divine spark, parcel of the cosmic consciousness), or both. Even if external beliefs, scriptures, norms or authorities are accepted, they must be legitimated through personal experience. In the 1988-89 Roof sample, 31% of baby-boomers agreed that 'People have God within them, so Churches aren't really necessary'. Self-spirituality is important in the mystical, psychological and para-scientific NRMs like Human Potential or the New Age (Champion, 1993; Heelas, 1996), in healing practices, or in many ordinary psychotherapies where the inner self is seen as an infallible source of

guidance; a search for harmony usually follows certain rituals that dampen potentially anarchic consequences, as in the case of New Age (cf. the Findhorn community rites of harmonization). Generally speaking, 'believing without belonging' is expanding, as the last European Values Survey (1999) confirms.

3. It seems more appropriate to speak of *de-hierarchization, de-dualization, bringing nearer the human and the divine*, the layman and the priest, the body and the soul, than of the collapse of dualism emphasised by Bellah, although the feeling of the *unity of the cosmos, holism, monism* is also a part of the picture and is becoming increasingly important. The results are either non-belief, an impersonal God, a more loving and blessing God, indeed a divine Friend, or the adoption of monist beliefs. In Christianity, this bringing of the human closer to the divine can be observed from the birth of Protestantism to present-day Protestantism and Vatican II Catholicism (the use of vernacular language, emphasis on the goodness of God, the friendship of the Lord, instead of omnipotence, sin and hell; the French are now allowed to address God with the familiar 'tu' form rather than with the formal 'vous'); Pentecostalism and the charismatic movement even experience the 'God within' through the descent and active presence of the Holy Spirit. Monism is spreading in the West through esoteric groups, Eastern religions, many NRMs (TM, Divine Light Mission, International Society for Krishna Consciousness, Rajneeshees, which have an Eastern orientation, or New Age, Scientology, Human Potential) and para-scientific beliefs: astrology, telepathy, 'waves', 'energies'. Holism, which is important in therapeutic, mystic, and esoteric groups (Beckford, 1984), is a typical form of de-dualization.

4. Although I have already mentioned *para-scientificity*, some reference should be made to science fiction and phenomena like belief in Near Death Experience. The latter displays several very interesting features: it is not based on a supernatural revelation, nor on a personal illumination reserved to a chosen few, but rather on an experience which is accessible to anyone and everyone and is supposedly verifiable. This belief system is para-scientific and democratic; it is also individualized and unconstrained in that the person is free to choose what s/he believes. It seeks to enchant life by making death into something enchanting (this-worldliness) and there is no conception of guilt, only of responsibility (reviewing one's life). Finally, in so far as it can be grafted on to any other system of religious belief and even on to atheism, it is pluralist and universal in much the same way as human rights are. Appearing in 1969, it quickly spread through the United States and then the world, and its success suggests that it is indicative of high modernity.

5. The pluralism, relativism, probabilism and pragmatism consequent on science, the desire for freedom (personal religious choice), democracy, globalization, and functional differentiation encourage *pluralistic, relativistic, ubiquitous forms of faith* with, in reaction, trends that reassert certainties. Combined with an extreme form of demythologization, they may assume the appearance of a symbolist faith; a faith, for example, that does not believe in the reality of the resurrection of Jesus Christ but maintains that it is nonetheless a necessary symbol to give meaning to life. Combined with mobility, flexibility, and revisability, which are other typically ultra-modern ideas related to freedom, pluralism and accelerated change, they may give rise to what Jaspers calls the 'floating faith' or to what Roof (1993) describes as a 'seeker spirituality': in answer to the question (1988-89 survey) 'Is it good to explore many differing religious teachings and learn from them, or should one stick to a particular faith?', 60% preferred to explore. This notion of mobility is also prevalent among NRMs, as Eileen Barker (1986) observed concerning the Moonies, of whom only one in twenty was still a member two years after joining the movement. Some NRMs are intentionally very loosely organized so that they resemble a spiritual self-service counter, a free resource, as in the New Age and the 'mystic-esoteric nebula' where self-determination is sacred.

6. These very *loosely organized religious or spiritual networks* like psycho-spiritual healing or New Age groups pose an unprecedented sociological problem: can we still speak of the 'religious' with reference to such vague and unstable spiritual forms, especially in the case of an unfocused 'believing without belonging'? The hesitation between describing them as 'religious' or 'spiritual', and the preference of many of their followers for the term 'spiritual', are in themselves indicative of the fluidity of their boundaries. Does this signify a phase of growth or of decomposition in the evolution of religion? The question is an important one, and it also concerns the way in which we interpret the notion of secularization. The answer to it depends on the status and importance of parallel beliefs, self-spirituality, seeker spirituality, and loose networks, bearing in mind that the spread of NRMs is still a very minor phenomenon, with the exception of New Age-type nebula. The problem is best illustrated by the case of Dutch young people (Janssen, 1998), only 39% of whom, according to a 1991 national survey, belong to a religion but 16% can be described as being influenced by New Age or Eastern religions, 18% are doubters, 16% only pray, and a mere 18% are non-believers. Surprisingly, 82% pray at least sometimes, and among non-churchgoers prayer is the most persistent religious element, albeit only in a rather psychological and meditative manner: to gain strength, to accept the

inevitable such as the death of a relative, as a release or as a time to ponder, in keeping with a primarily impersonal conception of the divine. Do these findings point to a stage of religious decomposition, to a minor form of religiosity (a vague backdrop, comforting beliefs), or to the seeds of possible reconfigurations? Are all of the parallel belief systems religious? If we apply the following criteria to define the religious – a super-empirical reality and a symbolic relationship along with it – we must exclude astrology and numerology for instance, but not the beliefs and practices of Dutch young people, except for a few of them (if we are to speak of a religion, we must add the existence of an organization).

Conclusions

In comparing the previous axial turn with the previous axial period, we can reach the following summary conclusions. The least we can say is that we have not observed a religious change of an extent comparable to the emergence of the universalist religions of salvation.

Christianity certainly remains dominant in the West, and so do salvation religions throughout the world. Three-quarters of Europeans and nine-tenths of Americans consider themselves to be Christians. Yet for roughly one-quarter of European Christians, religion is no more than an 'empty shell', a 'cultural' Christianity, while another quarter firmly declare the vigour of their conviction. Is that a little, or is it a lot? This reflects the problem of the glass which is either half-empty or half-full, yet sociologists are appointed not to keep score but simply to try to grasp and understand reality. Nonetheless, sociologists have been amazed by Christianity's ability to adapt to modernity, even if it has done so with much difficulty, especially in the case of Catholicism. To refer back to what was said at the end of the first section, Christianity and Buddhism originally brought about a substantial de-mythologization of nature and strong individualization before they underwent re-mythologization and bureaucratic institutionalization. In addition, those two religions were obliged to adapt to earthly aims. Modernity in a sense boils down to re-mythologization and re-individualization as well as to re-orientation towards this-worldly concerns, not forgetting the beyond, but only hell.

The sociologist can also state that, despite everything, profound change *has* taken place in the religious landscape of some of the most modern countries. Approximately one-quarter of all Europeans and one-tenth of

Americans claim to have no religious beliefs, and this percentage is increasing. Social, political and moral life has assumed great independence from religion, although religion clearly continues to play a significant role, especially among core Christian believers and in some countries, particularly the United States, Ireland and Poland. In this respect, high modernity represents a new configuration characterized by a rather pacifist pluralism in a global democratic context. The previous period was marked by sometimes violent antagonisms due either to the emancipation of society from religious authority or to a desire to eradicate religion from society, as in the case of communism. Certain forms of religion typical of modernity have contributed to a redefinition of society.

To proceed further with this analysis would require updating the questionnaires used by international surveys on religious belief. Besides institutional religion, which is by far the most thoroughly researched, it would be necessary to give closer specification to what one can call the 'religion-resource', the 'spirituality-network' and 'self-spirituality' in order to treat the principal forms of differentiation to be observed among religious attitudes. The expression religion-resource signifies that its centre is not the institution and its authority, but the individual and his/her demands, which may be addressed to one or to several religious resources. The spirituality-network typically corresponds to loosely organized groups and movements like New Age. Here again, the individual is at the centre, and this is also largely the case of autonomous spirituality, which seemingly contents itself with a vague basis that may nevertheless be rich in meaning. Indeed, one must bear in mind that intermediate forms and transitions from one form to another are possible. This simple reference point would enable us to gain better understanding of what is at stake at the dawn of the twenty-first century.

Bibliography

Acquaviva, S.S. (1979), *The Decline of the Sacred in Industrial Society*, Blackwell, Oxford.

Barker, E. (1986), 'Religious Movements: Cult and Anticult since Jonestown', *Annual Review of Sociology*, vol. 12, pp. 329-46.

Beckford, J. (1984), 'Holistic Imagery and Ethics in New Religious and Healing Movements', *Social Compass*, vol. 31, no. 2-3, pp. 259-72.

Beckford, J.A. (1996), 'Postmodernity, high Modernity and New Modernity: Three Concepts in Search of Religion', in K. Flanagan and P.C. Jupp (eds), *Postmodernity, Sociology and Religion*, Macmillan, London, pp. 30-47.

Bellah, R.N. (1976), *Beyond Belief: Essays on Religion in a Post-Traditional World*, Harper & Row, New York.

Berger, P. (1967), *The Sacred Canopy*, Doubleday, New York.

Beyer, P. (1994), *Religion and Globalization*, Sage, London.

Campiche, R. et al. (1992), *Croire en Suisse(s)*, L'Age d'homme, Lausanne.

Casanova, J. (1994), *Public Religion in the Modern World*, The University of Chicago Press, Chicago.

Champion, F. (1993), 'La nébuleuse mystique-ésotérique', in F. Champion and D. Hervieu-Léger (eds), *De l'émotion en religion*, Centurion, Paris, pp. 18-69.

Davie, G. (1996), *Religion in Britain since 1945*, Blackwell, Oxford.

Dobbelaere, K. (1981), 'Secularization: a Multi-Dimensional Concept', *Current Sociology*, vol. 29, no. 2, 1981, pp. 3-153.

Dobbelaere, K. (1995), 'Religion in Europe and North America', in R. de Moor (ed), *Values in Western Societies*, Tilburg University Press, Tilburg, pp. 1-29.

Dobbelaere, K. and Jagodzinski, W. (1995), 'Secularisation and Church Religiosity' (chap. 4), 'Religious Cognitions and Beliefs' (chap. 7), 'Religious and Ethical Pluralism' (chap. 8), in J.W.V. Deth and E. Scarbrough (eds), *The Impact of Values*, Oxford University Press, Oxford.

Eisenstadt, S. (1986), *The Origins and Diversity of Axial Age Civilizations*, State University of New York Press, Albany.

Ester, P., Halman, L. and de Moor, R. (1993), *The Individualizing Society. Value Change in Europe and North America*, Tilburg University Press, Tilburg.

Flanagan, K. and Jupp, P.C. (1996), *Postmodernity, Sociology and Religion*, Macmillan, London.

Giddens, A. (1991), *The Consequences of Modernity*, Polity Press, Cambridge.

Heelas, P. (1996), 'De-Traditionalisation of Religion and Self: The New Age and Postmodernity', in K. Flanagan and P.C. Jupp (eds), *Postmodernity, Sociology and Religion*, MacMillan, London, pp. 64-82.

Hervieu-Léger, D. avec Champion, F. (1986), *Vers un christianisme nouveau?*, Cerf, Paris.

Hervieu-Léger, D. (1993), 'Present-day Emotional Renewals: the end of Secularization or the end of Religion?', in W.H. Swatos (ed), *A Future for Religion? New Paradgms for Social Analysis*, Sage, London, pp. 129-48.

Hick, J. (1989), *An Interpretation of Religion*, Yale University Press, New Haven.

Iannaconne, L.R. (1992), 'Religious Markets and the Economics of Religion', *Social Compass*, vol. 39, no. 1, pp. 123-31.

Janssen, J. (1998), 'The Netherlands as an Experimental Garden of Religiosity. Remnants and Renewals', *Social Compass*, vol. 45, no. 1, pp. 101-13.

Jaspers, K. ([1949] 1954), *Origine et sens de l'histoire*, Paris, Plon.

Kitagawa, J.M. (1967), 'Primitive, Classical, and Modern Religions', in R. Kitagawa (ed), *The History of Religion. Essays on Problems of Understanding*, University of Chicago Press, Chicago, pp. 39-65.

Kurtz, L. (1995), *Gods in the Golbal Village, the World's Religions in a Sociological Perspective*, Pine Forge Press, London.

Lambert, Y. (1985), *Dieu change en Bretagne*, Cerf, Paris.

Lambert, Y. (1993), ''Ages, générations et christianisme', en France et en Europe', *Revue Française de Sociologie*, vol. 24, no. 4, pp. 525-55.

Lambert, Y. (1996), 'Denominational Systems and Religious States in the Countries of Western Europe', *Research in the Social Scientific Study of Religion*, vol. 7, pp. 127-43.

Lambert, Y. (1998), 'The Scope and Limits of Religious Functions According to the European Value and ISSP Surveys', in J. Billiet and R. Laermans (eds), *Secularization and Social Integration. Papers in Honor of Karel Dobbelaere*, University Press, Leuven, pp. 211-2.

Lambert, Y. and Voyé, L. (1997), 'Les croyances des jeunes Européens', in R. Campiche (sous la direction de), *Cultures jeunes et religions en Europe*, Paris, Cerf, pp. 97-166.

Luhmann, N. (1977), *Funktion der Religion*, Suhrkamp, Frankfurt am Main.

Luhmann, N. (1982), *The Differentiation of Society*, Columbia University, New York.

Martin, D.A. (1978), *A General Theory of Secularization*, Blackwell, Oxford.

Melton, J.G. (1985), 'Modern Alternative Religions in the West', in J.R. Hinnels, *A Handbook on Living Religions*, Penguin Books, Harmondworth.

Nakamura, H. (1986), *A Comparative History of Ideas*, Routledge, London.

Roof, W.C. (1993), *A Generation of Seekers*, Harper, San Francisco.

Roof, W.C. et al. (eds) (1995), *The Post-War Generation and Establishment Religion*, Westview Press, San Francisco.

Szakolczai, A. and Füstös, L. (1996), *Value Systems in Axial Moments: a Comparative Analysis of 24 European Countries*, EUI Working Paper no. 96/8, European University Institute, Florence.

Tomasi, L. (a cura di) (1998), *La cultura dei giovani europei alle soglie del 2000. Religione, valori, politica e consumi*, Angeli, Milano.

Tomasi, L. (ed) (1999), *Alternative Religions among European Youth*, Ashgate, Aldershot.

Tschannen, O. (1992), *Les théories de la sécularisation*, Droz, Genève.

Wallis, R. (1984), *Elementary Forms of New Religious Life*, Routledge, London.

Walter, T. (1996), *The Eclipse of Eternity: a Sociology of the Afterlife*, Macmillan, London.

Willaime, J. P. (1995), *Sociologie des religions*, Puf, Paris.

14 Sociology in the twenty-first century: a discipline at the crossroads between senility or regeneration

DIRK KAESLER

Introduction

We have entered the year 2000. The world-system is in turmoil and in crisis. The symbolism of 2000 matches the reality. Sociology, some hundred years ago, set out to help human beings to observe, understand, foresee and solve problems of their societies. Does sociology still serve these aims? And what prospects does sociology have in the twenty-first century, if it has fruitful prospects at all?

It is true that today's sociology has been confronted with new frontiers in scientific-social inquiry resulting from unprecedented developments in the period that we have learned to call 'late modernity' or 'Second Modernity'. The central challenge for our discipline has become whether the intellectual and scholarly enterprise called 'sociology' will be able not only to confront these developments and describe them, but also to contribute to the solution of problems facing the world-system and its inhabitants. Sociology, this intellectual child of the nineteenth century, experienced its maturity during the twentieth. The question for the twenty-first century is whether this mature sociology has the perspective of senility or of a second childhood, a regeneration.

In order to sketch some of my answers to these questions I distinguish the following five questions:

What has become of the nineteenth-century programme of the *sciences morales* in relation to the development of academic *sociology* since the turn to the twentieth century?

Why has academic sociology distanced itself from its cause to contribute to a 'moral improvement' of society?

Should academic sociology reclaim the profile of a modern '*moral science*'? What might be the agenda for sociological intellectuals in the twenty-first century?

Why is the sociological preoccupation with the history of sociology essential for the preservation of the intellectual heritage of sociology?

1. Sociology and the *sciences morales*

Around the year 1850 the international scholarly enterprise called *sciences morales*, *Moralstatistik*, and the like – which meant little more than empirical research into *mores*, the manners of people – was one of the dominant heuristic programmes in the formation of the social sciences. This was the time when the contours of a modern industrialised and capitalist economy and society in most European and North American nations slowly became visible. Understanding the processes behind these changes became one of the major concerns not only of ordinary people but also of politicians and scholars. The success of the natural sciences during the nineteenth century led to the assumption that historical and socio-economic developments are governed by a system of laws.

This system of laws had to be discovered, and the *sciences morales* promised to provide a clear view of it. With the application of quantitative research methods, social science came to be regarded as means to get to grips with the confusing and disturbing developments that changed the entire world. The use of the term *moral* was never very precise, and it varied from author to author. The aim was not to develop new norms or morals but rather to report and systematize observable social developments. The data of *moral statistics* covered all human social behaviour, the term *moral* being used synonymously with 'social'.

The Belgian Adolphe Quételet (1796-1874) is regarded as the first proponent of the analysis of social facts with the help of mathematical methods. According to Quételet, one purpose of science was to develop preventive practical-political measures on the basis of the empirical study of social conditions. The year 1835 saw the publication of the two volumes of his famous *Essai sur l'homme et le développement de ses facultés, ou Essai de Physique sociale*, a compendium of most of his quantitative research on the most diverse kinds of social phenomena.

Quételet did not seek out 'laws' that govern the whole of human societies. He was not so much interested in individual behaviour as in 'typical' human behaviour, and he searched for general patterns behind the latter's fragmentary complexity. He sought to achieve a high level of abstraction which required analysis of great numbers of cases. If there were laws in social reality, he argued, then the mathematical calculation of statistical probabilities on the basis of such great numbers would be feasible.

With hindsight, it can be said that Quételet lost a sense of proportion in his search for social laws: everything that apparently displayed some statistical regularity he treated as a social law; he made no attempt to establish plausible connections between purely statistical phenomena and social reality. Quételet's observation of statistical regularities failed to prove the existence of any laws of human behaviour because he did not have a theoretical framework.

When Auguste Comte (1798-1857) published the six volumes of his *Cours de philosophie positive* in 1830-42 setting out the programme of his *sociologie*, a serious counter-concept to Quételet's concept of *physique sociale* appeared on the scholarly scene. Comte too wanted to research society from a natural scientific point of view, one against all metaphysical speculation and grounded in the ideas of the Enlightenment.

In many European nations a third process blurred the situation even further: the development and gradual institutionalization of official statistics compiled by state agencies. This process, which also occurred at the beginning of the nineteenth century, was important for the formation of academic sociology. Quételet, after his appointment as director of the Belgian Statistical Commission, developed and marketed a model for the organisation of state-controlled statistics. In Germany, for example, various *Statistische Büros* were founded and became the main organizations for the collection and publication of a growing amount of statistical material.

In the case of Germany, it was the founding figure of German sociology, Ferdinand Tönnies (1855-1936), who successfully fought for the pragmatic combination of social statistics and academic sociology. To do so he developed his own concept of *Soziographie* as a version of empirical social research (Tönnies, 1931: 315-27).

For Tönnies, the pure collection of quantitative social facts was nothing but a method to organize data with no analytical or theoretical value. He believed that empirical social research should combine quantitative data with qualitative dimensions, in order to distil 'living cognition', *lebende Erkenntnis*, from the 'cemetery of numbers', which was his expression for state official statistics.

2. Sociology and the moral improvement of society

In order to answer the question why academic sociology has distanced itself from this type of *sciences morales, Soziographie* and statistics, we must look very briefly at the historical path followed by the discipline. A hundred years ago the situation was governed by of one original concept of sociology, regardless of the necessary differentiation within national traditions like those of France, the United States of America, and Germany. As the result of some of the main ideas of the Enlightenment, nineteenth-century sociology was an exciting and orchestrated intellectual enterprise which comprised many different academic disciplines, generations and national traditions. At the centre of this international and cosmopolitan project of 'sociology' we may identify two convictions.

On the one hand there was the belief that science could help human beings to understand and explain their world better. On the other, stood the conviction that academic sociology should contribute to the moral improvement of society, and that preceding discourses on the 'good order' of societies, especially those in the realm of theology and philosophy, could and should be replaced by human reason. God as the source of historical development was to be replaced by the scientific reason of a mankind taking history into its own hands.

It is banal to point out that these ideas were substantially connected to dramatic changes in the societies of Europe and North America, processes generally regarded as the beginning of 'modernity'. The sociological quest for a 'good society' sought to understand these change processes and to devise suitable reactions to them. Regardless of whether such suitable reactions were to be found in secular republican education, in social reforms, or in the formulation of sociology as a critical enterprise for an intellectual understanding of modernity, the basic task of scientific sociology was defined as the identification and diagnosis of those characteristics regarded as determining the 'modern' system of society.

It is part of the intellectual heritage of sociology that the enterprise calling itself 'sociology' began with Auguste Comte, to whom the discipline not only owes its name but also some central ideas still relevant today. What, then, did this French philosopher, the founder of positivism and the enemy of all metaphysics, have in mind with his project of *sociologie*?

First of all it was to adapt the model used by the natural sciences in their exploration of nature to the exploration of society, and of human beings in society. The emphatic belief in science and scholarship characteristic of

Europe after the French Revolution is hard for many of us to understand today, not to mention to share, but it was the origin of Western sociology. Sociology was to research and understand humans scientifically just as physics analysed and understood nature. Comte's programme essentially consisted in the transfer of the model of biology or physics to sociology. In the same way as the natural sciences researched the laws that ruled and determined nature, so sociology was to research the laws of society – that is, how societies functioned. Human societies and humans in societies were – this was the basic belief – as researchable as nature was by biology and physics. This concept of a Comtean *physique sociale* was the starting point of the intellectual project called 'sociology' and it was certainly the origin of its original French version. This model was based on numerous preconditions: orientation to the scientific model of physics, a very special concept of 'laws' linked to that model, and a somewhat restricted answer to the crucial question: What is the purpose of science? Like the natural sciences, which did not pursue research for its own sake but in order to master and control nature, sociology's task was to control and administer society, which meant control over the human beings that formed it.

The task of scientific sociology was thus to predict the behaviour and social action of human beings. Just as physics not only tried to understand nature but also strove to make predictions, so scientific sociology sought to do the same. Not only did the question as to why an apple falls from a tree have to be answered, but scientific research had to discover the laws that govern the apple's falling. If answers are given to this question, this knowledge can be applied to mastering flying objects in general, such as cannon balls, and make them fly in the direction intended and cause certain effects.

This was a relatively simple programme which followed the advice: *voir pour savoir, savoir pour prévoir, prévoir pour prévenir*. First observe what is happening: apples fall from trees, humans form coalitions. Then try to explain what is happening by formulating hypotheses which eventually lead to the formulation of laws. On the basis of these laws try to make predictions of future events: apples will fall because of special conditions, humans will form certain coalitions with a specific degree of probability. Only then does prevention become possible: knowledge of the rules and their probabilities makes it possible to take certain measures, such as placing boxes under the tree so that apples will fall into them, or trying to encourage humans to associate in a way which is in society's interest.

On the basis of these ideas, a concept of social science was formulated which maintained that its task was to master and to manipulate society, following Francis Bacon's motto: *ipsa scientia potestas est*, knowledge itself is power. Auguste Comte's programme incorporated this heritage into the new science of his *sociologie*, the aims of which were to scientifically observe, describe, analyse and predict the life-courses of human beings. If these scholarly efforts generated predictions of unpleasant developments to be prevented, this knowledge should be used rather than intuition. Just as the purpose of physics was to govern nature, so sociology should be the means to govern human society and history.

This programme made no small contribution to fostering human knowledge: it was a radical undertaking which included a hidden assumption of superiority. It entailed that the science which pursued such aims would, in the long run, become not just another discipline but the 'queen of science', or at least of the human sciences. This science would not just offer a modest contribution to the furthering of human wisdom; it would become the science of sciences. This, put extremely briefly, was the programme of sociology only about one hundred years ago. Its traces can still be found in many ways and forms in the sociology of today. There are still numerous sociologists who endorse it and want to implement it, at least in the (very) long run. To be sure, it is not formulated in these crude terms today, but one still encounters the convictions that underpin the programme.

I know – and hope – that such ideas can be found in the minds of (most) of our students. It is for this reason that they have decided to study sociology instead of economics, law or medicine, those various respected disciplines that offer professional qualifications. Sociology is still the intellectual enterprise by which one can learn about human beings and about society without direct practical and professional application outside the reproduction of academic sociology itself. And the ultimate aim of such learning is to help human beings understand themselves as members of societies and comprehend the working of societies and their history, to help them cope with society and not only remain prey to social pressures or so-called historical laws. Still today, sociology attracts people in search of the knowledge and instruments with which to understand society, and to gain the intellectual power that stems from knowledge and then use it actively to change society.

Why, then, is there this recurrent feeling that sociology is in 'crisis'? I believe that one crucial reason for the atmosphere of discontent is the fact that the sociological quest for a 'good society' has been almost totally banned from the scientific agenda of academic sociology. This, I argue, has led to something akin to an intellectual paralysis of sociology. The original belief in science – in former times almost grotesquely strong – has changed into complete subjectivity and the well-known mentality of 'anything goes'.

Of course, first-year students of sociology must learn that scientific sociology is not to be mistaken for social-work, social politics, not to mention socialism. Regardless of the fact that sociology has become an analytical and empirical science, distant from its former sense of moral mission, the old motif of its creation can still be reconstructed. The dream of a 'good society', a human society, the search for an ethical basis of sociological research has always been the 'spirit in the machine' of the social sciences, as Irving Louis Horowitz (1993) has pointed out. This 'spirit' still lingers in some minds, regardless of the 'scientific turn' of academic sociology.

3. Should academic sociology reclaim the profile of a *science morale*?

What, then, might be the task of sociology as a modern 'moral science', as an institutional basis for 'moral awareness'?

Behind this question stands the much more fundamental issue of what kind of sociology is necessary for the twenty-first century. What I have in mind is not only a sociology *of* the twenty-first century but a sociology *for* it. And that notion means a sociology for those human beings who have taken the step into the next century.

Let me briefly mention some inner-sociological prerequisites which I regard as self-evident. The most important of them is putting an end to the paradigmatic separation wrought by the infamous micro- and macro-version of sociological theories, as well as to the split between quantitative and qualitative methods in social research. Since the intermediate theoretical and empirical work of Max Weber, Emile Durkheim, Norbert Elias, Jürgen Habermas, Pierre Bourdieu and Anthony Giddens, such dichotomies should be part of the historical past of proto-sociological concepts. By now the necessity of a self-reflexive sociology should be as obvious as the demand for a sociology sceptical and critical of all forms of domination in whatever domain. Leaving such self-evident requirements for a future sociology aside, I turn to my main concern, which is much more controversial: the return of scientific sociology from a *wert(urteils)freie*, a 'value-judgement-free' enterprise to a *wertbezogene*, a 'value-related' one, to use the well-known Weberian terms (Weber, 1922).

It seems easy to say that sociology should demand a 'good society'. But are there sociological standards for the 'goodness' of a society, for a society orientated towards the improved well–being of humans? Is it really enough for sociology in this respect merely to denounce such a demand as the outcome not of a rational search for scientific truth but of irrational longing, as Theodor W. Adorno wanted us to believe? If, I would argue, sociology as an intellectual and scholarly enterprise dismisses intellectual co-operation in the planning and construction of a 'good society', in the formulation of a programme for a 'good social order', then the inner liquidation of the sociological enterprise that began with such enthusiasm and hope in the nineteenth century is imminent. Sociology will lose its inner legitimization if it ceases to reach out for the 'good life' and terminates cooperation in the creation of an 'utopian realism'. Future sociology, in my opinion, will have to ask questions like the following:

1. What does a 'human' life in society mean?
2. What kind of morals can be sociologically justified?
3. What kind of social conditions will have to be fulfilled to enable humans to lead moral lives?

Comte's enormous ambition to make sociology the paramount science surely must be abandoned at the end of the twentieth century. But the almost total detachment of sociology from philosophy and political philosophy will have to be scrutinized once again. Not in terms of 'going back' but in the sense of reopening systematic discourse with these fields of human wisdom. It may be that historically sociology could only develop by emancipating itself from the traditional moral sciences. But now, after a hundred years of emancipation, it should be possible to think anew about dealing with morals in a moral-free scientific way. I am not talking about a 'sociological turn' of ethical discourse; rather, I refer to the necessity for sociology as a discipline to participate in attempts to find therapies of moral orientation for human beings who have not only lost their orientation but are desperately looking for it.

At the historical beginnings of sociology it was certainly not totally unjustified for its founding fathers, like Emile Durkheim, to seek to construct sociology as a *science morale* in conscious separation from moral philosophy. A programme for the empirical social scientific research of morals can only be questioned if it can be shown that the human beings whose morals are being researched instead require points of orientation, rather than scientific analyses of their moral standards. Durkheim's agenda may have come to an end: humans who have grown insecure in their moral orientations will not be greatly helped by a mystification of morality or the offer of a cult of 'individualism'. These certainly offer no help in the desperate search for moral integration by individuals or society. The moral disorientation of individuals and societies cannot be clarified by social-scientific research into their loss of orientation and destruction. If sociology as a *science morale* is to be resumed, answers must be given to the question of where the moral standards lie. The question of 'standards' of truth, justice and morality, and the perspectives of a 'human society', a 'civil society', will not be substituted by perspectives of pluralistic orientation. There is a plethora of the latter today: perspectives of gender, of race, of classes, of cultures, of religions, of ideological positions. The intellectual-scientific reaction to this fragmentation of our various world-experiences must not be a lapse into a cynical or nihilistic world view; nor must it induce a return to technical fetishism in social research, nor to an otiose game of 'theoretical' debates. The challenge facing sociology is to help and participate in the construction of new forms of value-consensus in a contemporary world of enormous complexity and differentiation.

4. An agenda for sociological intellectuals in the twenty-first century

What I am trying to depict is an agenda for sociology as a sort of testing ground and training camp for intellectuals – sociological *savants* – a sociology which is empirically based, uses the entirety of sociology's theoretical achievements, and supports the development of a socio-political and ethical conscience: intellectuals who do not distance themselves from social reality but accept responsibility by intervening in political debates and conflicts. Of course, such sociological intellectuals would not stand apart from the general political struggle for power; they would instead become crucial participants therein by using their intellectual and rhetorical capabilities to grasp power themselves.

On a common sense model of intellectuals, it is at times of 'crisis' that intellectuals must put forward their critical diagnosis and their enlightening vision for future development. Where, so to speak, are the Marxes, Webers, Durkheims of our times? At the turn of the twenty-first century, we must accept the sobering conclusion that the 'classic' intellectual on the Dreyfus model no longer exists. In distancing ourselves from role-models like Raymond Aron and Jean Paul Sartre, who represented the intellectual as a *spectateur engagé et enragé*, we might be better advised to follow Bourdieu's recommendation of the sociologist who simply follows his/her *métier militant*: an engaged observer and an enraged critic of society; the intellectual as an advocate of the universal who speaks in the name of humankind in the face of the pervasive individual pursuit of particular interests; the intellectual as the protagonist of a general morality who fights with *Zivilcourage* for freedom, tolerance and solidarity; the partisan of the underprivileged who articulates injustice and argues for fairness and tolerance.

The modern sociological intellectual is able to fulfil all these tasks by virtue of a status and social position located in occupations close to the media-informed public: artists and writers, journalists and university professors; but s/he is nevertheless *freischwebend*, in the sense of not belonging to one particular political party or interest group (Mannheim, 1929). Always precarious, the modern sociological intellectual enjoys the independent status granted by the right to freedom of speech in and by the public.

Such a 'plantation' of sociological intellectuals could, in my opinion, only be set up in universities as places for the education of neither technocrats nor ideologues. The old motto of the great German educator Wilhelm von Humboldt, popularised by the German sociologist Helmut Schelsky – *Bildung durch Wissenschaft* (Schelsky, 1960), education by science – may be more than ever important today: we must undertake the necessary interdisciplinary discourse, pursue a multicultural and global orientation, and construct an ecological responsibility.

What I ask for myself and sociology is a greater interest and engagement in public affairs, leaving the protective walls of the ivory-towers of our universities. Intervention by sociologists in the political arena and in media-dominated discourse on values could and should be greatly improved.

I refer to dialogue first of all within sociology itself on the possibility of sociological discourse about values and morals. But also a dialogical co-operation between sociology and the disciplines of the traditional 'value specialists' like political philosophy, comparative religious studies, and theologies. If the co-operation of sociologists in the construction of a rational, non-religious ethics should be the aim of sociology at all, it will not be realized without such dialogue. But with it sociological intellectuals can demonstrate whether or not we have something to offer. The principles of this dialogue will have to be a serious effort to understand each other, the acceptance of differences, a 'politics of acceptance'. It could be the dialogue of the twenty-first century.

5. History of sociology as intellectual heritage of sociology

If one agrees with this vision of future academic sociology as remaining/ becoming an empirical proving ground and training camp for sociological *savants*, using all sociology's theoretical achievements and supporting the development of a socio-political and ethical conscience, it follows that familiarity with the history of sociology is indispensable.

As sociologists conducting research on the history of our discipline, we are well prepared to act as the guardians of the canonical wisdom of more than a hundred years of great intellectual achievements, empirical findings, concepts and theories. We have a duty of honour to the discipline of sociology as long as it remains alive. It depends on ourselves whether academic sociology, this product of the nineteenth century, will survive, and in what form, during the twenty-first.

Bibliography

Comte, A. (1830-1842), 'Cours de philosophie positive', *The Positive Philosophy of Auguste Comte*, 6 vol., Bachelier, Paris. Translated and condensed by H. Martineau (1896), Bell, London.

Durkheim, E. (1893), 'De la division du travail social', *The Division of Labor in Society*, Alcan, Paris. With an introduction by A. Lewis Coser, translated by W.D. Halls, (1984), Free Press, New York.

Horowitz, I.L. (1993), *The Decomposition of Sociology*, Oxford University Press, Oxford.

Mannheim, K. (1929), *Ideologie und Utopie*, Cohen, Bonn.

Mannheim, K. (1936), *Ideology and Utopia: An Introduction to the Sociology of Knowledge*, Brace and Ca., New York.

Quételet, A. (1835), *Sur l'homme et le développement de ses facultés ou Essai de phisique sociale*, vol. 2, Bachelier, Paris. *A Treatise on Man and the Development of his Faculties*, A facsim. Reproduction of the English translated of 1842, with an introduction by S. Diamond, 1969, Scolar's Facsimilies & Reprints, Gainesville.

Schelsky, H. (1960), *Einsamkeit und Freiheit: zur sozialen Idee der deutschen Universität*, Aschendorff, Münster.

Tönnies, F. (1931), *Einführung in die Soziologie*, Ferdinand Enke Verlag, Stuttgart.

Weber, M. (1922), *Gesammelte Aufsätze zur Wissenschaftslehre*, Mohr-Siebeck. Partly in M. Weber, *Selections in Translations*, (1978), ed. by W.G. Runciman, translated by E. Matthews, Cambridge University Press, Cambridge.

15 The idea of alternative discourses

SYED FARID ALATAS

Introduction

To set the stage for this discussion on the problems in the social sciences that have led to calls for alternative discourses, consider the following quotation from the author's introduction to the classic, *The Shi'ite Ethic and the Spirit of Capitalism:*[1]

> Early attempts by the Arabs to make inroads into Europe were relatively unsuccessful. After the subjugation of the North African coast and the conquest of the Iberian Peninsular in the early years of the 8th century AD, further incursions into Europe by Arab-Berber armies appeared to have been checked between Tours and Poitiers by Charles Martel.
>
> By the 16th century, the Ottoman Turks had overrun most of Eastern Europe and their empire extended from northwestern Iran in the east to Budapest in the West. However, both Arab and Ottoman territories throughout Central Asia, the Mediterranean and Eastern Europe came under the threat of Shi'ite heresy which traces its origin to the 14th century.
>
> Contemporaneous with the emergence of the Ottoman Empire in the 14th century was the founding of the Safavi Sufi movement by Sheikh Safi al-Din. His descendant, Ismail (905-930 AH / 1499-1524 AD), a Turkoman from Azarbaijan, was the founder of the Safavi dynasty. In the mid-tenth century, during Ottoman attempts to centralize their control in Eastern Anatolia, Ismail took advantage of the turmoil and attempted to make inroads there. His tribal support came from a number of Turkoman tribes, the Ustajlu, Shamlu, Taqalu, Baharlu, Zulqadar, Qajar and Afshar, collectively known as the *qizilbash* (Turk. red head). What held these tribes together was an *'asabiyyah* (Arabic. *ésprit du corps*) based on the Safavi mystical order to which the *qizilbash* owed allegiance.
>
> So successful were Ismail and his followers in Anatolia, that by the eve of his death the Shi'ites had captured most of Ottoman territories in Europe and controlled Azarbaijan, western Iran, and the Tigris-Euphrates basin. By the reign of Shah Tahmasb I (930 - 984 AH), the Turkic Shi'ite conquerers had extended the rule of Islam to as far as north as the nahr al-rayn (Arabic; the river Rhine[2]). Only the lands to the east of the nahr al-rayn and stretching all the way south into Central Asia and Iran remained under Turkic Shi'ite rule while the

---

1 Muhammad ibn Al-Wabar (1864-1920 AD), the Spanish Arab sociologist, who continued the Khaldunian tradition in theoretical history in Eurasia.
2 Named so after the Arabic, as it was largely Arabic geographical studies which provided detailed systematic accounts of Eurasian climate, ecosystems and natural resources.

regions to the west and south-west of the nahr al-rayn continued to be under Arab Sunni control as in Iberia or were ruled as various Catholic, Lutheran, Orthodox and Jewish principalities as was the case in France, Italy, the Netherlands, and Western Germany. The Turkish Shi'ite domains came to be known as Eastern Eurasia.

We now come to the question that is being posed in this book: Why had modern rational capitalism and the industrial organization of life originated in Eastern Eurasia and not in other parts of Europe or Asia? In other words, why was the spirit of capitalism, the foundation of the capitalistic organization of life, able to fight its way to supremacy against various hostile forces here in Eurasia beginning in the sixteenth century and nowhere else?

The answer undoubtedly has much to do with a certain elective affinity between the spirit of modern capitalism and the Shi'ite ethic. By the fifteenth century, the Shi'ite ethic had presented itself as constituting an ascetic compulsion to be economically successful while at the same time rejecting indulgence in the material world. The wordly asceticism of a number of puritan Shi'ite sects must be contrasted to the warrior ethic of Sunni Islam on the one hand and and the retreatist monasticism of the nahraynian sects on the other, characterising Western Eurasia by an economic traditionalism so inimical to rational capitalist order.

These circumstances present to us the possibility of a sociological theory of the origins of modern rational capitalism. Such a theory requires not only the delineation of the features of the Shi'ite ethic to reveal the affinity with the spirit of capitalism but also an excursus into Nahraynianism and Sunni Islam in order to confirm the absence of such an affinity.

Let us begin with Nahraynianism.

The term nahr al-rayn, from which Nahraynianism, denoting the Catholic, Lutheran, Orthodox and Jewish sects of Western Eurasia, was first applied by the Arabs to the Rhine river in northern Eurasia. Those who lived on either side of the Rhine were referred to as Nahraynians (Arabic. nahrayni). It was only after the arrival of the Turks in the 16th century AD onwards that the term Nahraynianism gained currency in assigning the peoples of Western Eurasia, who did not convert to Shi'ism, their religious identity. Nahraynianism, therefore, was understood by the Turkic Shi'ites to refer to the unconverted natives of Eurasia.

This is not to suggest, however, that there is no naturally occurring entity that can be designated by the term Nahraynianism. This religion consists of Catholic, Lutheran, Orthodox and Jewish sects which all trace their origins to a Europeanised rendition of the faith of Abraham. They profess one God, a personal God, immanent but yet transcendant. They believe in a common set of scriptures, variously known as the Torah, Talmud and Bible. Furthermore, all the sects of Nahraynianism are characterised by their monastic, other-wordly and traditionalistic ethos. This made it impossible for an attitude based on frugality, discipline and systematic work centred on wordly affairs to take root.[3]

---

3   The preceeding sections in italics are ficticious parts of this account of what might have happened had the Turkic Shi'ite tribes actually succeeded in their quest to conquer Ottoman territory.

Who would accept such an account of the religion of Nahraynianism? Who would even accept that there is such an entity as Nahraynianism? What is clear from the above is a number of problems that can be said to beset Eurasian Turkic Shi'ite sociology:

1. The mix of fact and fiction. For example, there is a recognition of the existence of Catholicism, Orthodoxy, Lutheranism and Judaism as well as the Torah, Talmud and Bible but these are not understood according to the self-understanding of these religions.
2. Arabocentrism, that is, the imposition of a category, Nahraynianism, from the outside, that is, by our fictitious Arab and Turkic Shi'ite scholars. This is an imposition which does not accord with the self-description of the Catholics, Lutherans, the Orthodox church and the Jews.
3. There is an attempt to homogenize societes and communities, thereby hiding complexities. Simply stating the commonalities of the Catholics, Lutherans, the Orthodox church and the Jews veils not only the contrary self-understanding but also the variety and heterogeneity of religion in Western Europe.
4. The approach is guilty of textualism in that it attempts to understand the reality of religion in Western Europe in terms of religious texts such as the Torah, Talmud and Bible, assuming that reality corresponds to the text.
5. Stereotyping is rife, as the approach reduces Western European society of the sixteenth century to set characteristics such as traditionalism, monasticism and other-wordly asceticism, when it was quite likely that these characterized only a section of society.

1. Eurocentric social science

We would generally be critical of such social science by pointing to its problematic and sometimes irrelevant aspects, while being conscious of its positive and useful aspects. Such social science seems simple enough to refute and one may wonder whether such bad and irrelevant social science exists in the first place to attract our attention to the problem. As ridiculous as the above fictitious account on *Nahraynianism* may seem, in fact, such irrelevance does exist, but this is in Western European and North American accounts of various parts of Asia and Africa. A case in point is the study of Hinduism, which was named after a river, the Indus river in the Indian subcontinent, a name which was imposed from the outside to encompass a wide variety of beliefs over a vast area of land. The adherents of such beliefs did not always consider themselves as belonging to a single entity that we now know as Hinduism. Yet many textualist and essentialist studies of Hinduism , such as that of Max Weber (1958), subscribe to such constructed myths.

The formative period of the various disciplines of the social sciences and the institutions in which they were taught in much of Asia and Africa was initiated and sustained by colonial scholars and administrators after the eighteenth century, as well as directly and indirectly by other Europeans in vicariously colonised areas.

The introduction of the social sciences in the context of colonial expansion defined the subsequent development of these disciplines during the postcolonial period in a number of ways, leaving the social sciences to be defined by the following characteristics:

1.   *The lack of creativity.* This refers to the inability of social scientists outside the Euroamerican cultural area to generate original theories and methods.

2.   *Mimesis.* This refers to the uncritical adoption or imitation of Western theories and models. Eades provides an example of this, referring to the theorizing of a Chinese anthropologist well-grounded in Sahlins, Firth and Mauss as being largely irrelevant to the Chinese case as a result of the poor ethnography on which the work is based (Eades, 1997: 41-2).

3.   *Textualism*, that is, the assumption that accounts given in, say, religious texts on social structure or other aspects of society actually correspond to what is found in the society in question.

4.   *Essentialism.* This refers to reductionist accounts of a society in terms of certain factors regarded as dominant and overarching, such as caste in India.

5.   The imposition of *categories* and *concepts* from the Euroamerican context that clash with self-understandings.

6.   The absence of *subaltern voices*. For example, Evans notes that in the multitude of materials gathered by Chinese, Vietnamese and Lao ethnographers there is no tradition of recording minority 'voices' (Evans, 1997: 10). If we understand by 'minority' not just ethnic minorities but all other subaltern groups, then we may define such social science as being dominated by an elitist perspective.

All the above are held by many scholars to exist within the context of academic imperialism.

Such problems continue to plague the social sciences. There is an inventory of responses that aim to address these problems. These have emanated from developing societies in Asia, Africa and Latin America and have taken two general forms.

One has been to understand the causes of this state of affairs. These sought to theorise the state of the social sciences and humanities in postcolonial societies and include the theory of Orientalism (Said, 1979, 1990), the theory of mental captivity (Alatas, 1972, 1974), pedagogical theories of modernization (Al-e Ahmad, nd; Freire, 1970; Illich, 1973), the colonial critique of Cesaire (1972), Memmi (1965) and Fanon (1968), and academic dependency theory (Altbach, 1977; Garreau, 1985; Altbach and Selvaratnam, 1989; Alatas, 1995a). Works that address the questions of intellectual imperialism and academic dependency are examples of such theorising on the state of the social sciences.

The other has been to suggest or prescribe one variety or another of alternative discourses to serve as correctives to the type of social sciences that had been introduced during colonial times. The understanding that the social sciences in Asia, Africa and Latin America has been plagued by problems, such as the eight listed above, had led to intellectual reactions among both Western and non-Western scholars. What these reactions have in common is not just the critique of the Eurocentric, imitative, elitist, and irrelevant social sciences that they find in their societies but also the call for alternative discourses. We tend to be familiar with such calls originating in the second half of the twentieth century when in fact they began in the nineteenth century. The calls to decolonize, nationalize, indigenize, sacralize (Islamise or Christianize), universalize, and globalize the social sciences, and for autonomous social science and greater objectivity, are merely more recent manifestations of earlier efforts towards what is seen as more relevant social science.[4]

As noted by Sinha, 'the by now common-place critique of essentialist tendencies in "European"/"Western" orientalist discourses about "other" peoples and places, launched by feminist, post-colonial, post-orientalist and deconstructionist theorists, was in a very serious way already anticipated/ prefaced/embedded in the discourse about "decolonising" the social sciences" (Sinha, 1998: 18). It would be accurate to say that notions of alternative discourses appeared *avant la lettre* in the minds of those who in the nineteenth century came to be critical of Orientalist language and culture studies. While they come under different names, what they have in common is the desire to counter the Eurocentric and Orientalist elements that inform the social sciences. We therefore refer to these discourses as alternatives because they counterpose themselves to what they would each define as mainsteam, that is, largely Euroamerican-oriented discourses.

---

4   For a review of some of these calls see Alatas (1995b).

2. The rise of alternative discourse and its features

As mentioned earlier, the context of academic dependency and mental captivity led to the problematization of a number of issues in the social sciences, such as those of Eurocentrism and orientalism. Eurocentric and orientalist social science was held to lack relevance in one way or another. As a result of awareness of these problems there were various responses in Asia and other parts of the Third World that took the form of pleas for endogenous intellectual creativity (Alatas, 1981), an autonomous social science tradition (Smail, 1961), decolonization of knowledge (Zghlal and Karoui, 1973; Boehmer, 1995; Zawiah, 1994), the globalization of social science (Bell, 1994; Hudson, 1977; Taylor, 1993), the sacralization of knowledge,[5] the indigenization of social sciences (Fahim, 1970; Fahim and Helmer, 1980; Bennagen, 1980; Atal, 1981; Sinha, 1998), and deschooling (Illich, 1973).

The term 'alternative discourses', therefore, is one that we are introducing and which should be understood as a descriptive and collective term referring to that set of discourses that emerged in opposition to what was understood to be mainstream, Euroamerican social science. These discourses have three general characteristics:

1.   they critique the mainstream in terms of theories of the social sciences (for example, the theories of Orientalism, academic dependency, mental captivity, and postcolonial theory referred to above).
2.   They are discourses on the need for alternatives which they all prescribe.
3.   They attempt to restore relevance to the social sciences. For example, proponents of indigenization would seek to discover indigenous notions of self for an indigenized psychology.

Alternative discourses have generally been understood as constituting a revolt against 'intellectual imperialism' as a component of the revolt against politico-economic domination' (Bennagen, 1980: 7). Pertierra recognizes the role of indigenized social sciences as a weapon in neo-colonial struggles as long as the social sciences 'act as the counter-point between the state and society' as opposed to becoming an 'instrument of the state's colonization of civil life' (Pertierra, 1997: 10, 20).

Sinha views the call for indigenization as arising out of the need to 'purge' the social sciences of Eurocentrism and thus register a crucial break from the hegemony of a colonial past ..." (Sinha, 1998: 16).

Alternative discourses are also, implicitly or explicitly, concerned with the analysis of the problems presented by the structure of the world system of

---

5   For a critical discussion on this see Alatas (1995c).

social science, in which the dominant discourse of the core social science powers of the United States, Great Britain and France result in conformity, imitation and lack of originality in the periphery (Kuwayama and van Bremen, 1997: 54-5).

Another feature of alternative discourses is their problematization of the epistemological and methodological underpinnings of the social sciences (Sinha, 1998: 33). This would involve exposing the Eurocentrism and orientalism that undergirds much of the social sciences.

But the aims and objectives of alternative discourses are not to be understood simply in negative terms, in terms of a delinking from metropolitan, neocolonialist control. They are also to be understood in a more positive way, in terms of the contribution of non-Western systems of thought to theories and ideas. Non-Western thought and cultural practices are to be seen as sources of theorizing, while at the same time Western knowledge is not to be rejected *in toto*. Here, there is an explicit claim that theories and concepts can be derived from the historical experiences and cultural practices of the various non-Western cultures, whether culture is defined as co-terminous with the nation-state or otherwise (Enriquez, 1994; Fahim and Helmer, 1980; Lee, 1979, Alatas, 1993).

We can thus formulate a definition of alternative discourses as those discourses which are informed by the various non-Western historical experiences and cultural practices in the same way that the Western social sciences are. Being alternative requires the turn to indigenous philosophies, epistemologies, histories, art and other modes of knowledge, which are all potential sources of social science theories and concepts. Such activities are deemed to decrease intellectual dependence on the core social science powers of the North Atlantic. Nevertheless, most observers and proponents of alternative discourses do not understand this as constituting a rejection of Western social science. For example, Hettne suggests that the solution to academic imperialism is not to do away altogether with Western concepts but to adopt a more realistic understanding of Western social science as reflecting particular geographic and historical contexts (Hettne, 1991: 39).

If we understand alternative discourses in this way, it becomes clear that they are necessary for the universalization of the social sciences, and for the maintenance of internationally recognized standards of scholarship.

It should be obvious, therefore, that alternative discourses refer to good social science. The mainstream social sciences and their critical alternatives, which had since become mainstream, emerged in Western Europe and the United States and were creative, original and responsive to the conditions in which they arose. Apart from the fact that these Western theories were largely Eurocentric in a number of ways, conditions in the West as well as elsewhere today are not comparable to the eighteenth and nineteenth centuries. The newer contexts call for alternatives to the mainstream. What is being defined as alternative is that which is relevant to its surroundings, creative, unimitative and original, non-essentialist, counter-Eurocentric, autonomous from the state, and autonomous from other national or transnational groupings. If alternative discourse is to be understood in this way, it is conceivable that there is a need for alternative discourses in the study of Western societies themselves, to the extent that the problems of lack of originality and creativity afflict the West as well.

It cannot be emphasised enough that such projects stand for the universalization of the social sciences. The search for alternative discourses is a contribution to the universalization of the social sciences to the extent that alternative civilizational voices are added to the ensemble of ideas and works. All, therefore, must be for the project of alternative discourses. What is being advocated here is not a school of thought nor a particular theoretical or metatheoretical perspective, but good social science. Nevertheless, the efforts to create alternative discourses have been plagued by the failure to conceptualize a central phenomenon, that of irrelevance.

3. The failure to extend the sociological approach to the problem of irrelevance

What is clear from the literature of the last forty years is the strong awareness of a lack of fit between Western theory and non-Western realities. Many examples of the irrelevance or non-applicability of Western concepts, theories and assumptions have been noted (Alatas, 1972, 1974, 1995b; Fahim, 1970; Fahim and Helmer, 1980; Parekh, 1992; Pieris, 1969; Singh Uberoi, 1968) and will not be repeated here. Epistemological issues concerning the reliability of truth claims or the origin of knowledge are common to social sciences in both the countries of their origin and in post-colonial societies. But the problem of irrelevance, in the context in which it is being raised here, is not entirely an epistemological one.

On the other hand, sociological approaches concerned with the questions of objectivity or the social basis of knowledge have generally not raised irrelevance as a problem. Objectivity and the social basis on knowledge are universal concerns while the problem of irrelevance is peculiar to the social sciences of some societies.

Therefore, the sociological approach to the question of reliable knowledge must be extended to include political and various other sociological aspects of the cognitive process hitherto not dealt with in the sociology of knowledge. It is necessary first to conceptualize irrelevance by way of presenting a preliminary typology of the phenomenon in order to show the limitations of the sociology of knowledge approach and how this approach may be extended.

A review of the vast literature on the state of the social sciences in various non-Western and postcolonial societies reveals a number of problems said to beset the social sciences in these areas which we may understand as constituting various types of irrelevance. There are a number of theoretical perspectives that address the state of the social sciences in postcolonial societies, such as orientalism (Said, 1979, 1993), academic dependency theory (Altbach, 1977), the theory of mental captivity (Alatas, 1972, 1974), postcolonial theory, and other critiques of the social sciences which note problems in the application and practice of North American and European social science in postcolonial contexts. Each of the problems identified can be understood as illustrating a type of irrelevance, as follows:

1. From the theory of mental captivity we may derive an understanding of irrelevance as typifying social science that is defined by the inability to raise original problems and to devise original methods of problem-solving. This leads to the 'unreality of basic assumptions, misplaced abstraction, ignorance or misinterpretation of data, and an erroneous conception of problems and their significance' in social science (Alatas 1972: 11) and the alienation of the social science enterprise from its surroundings.

2. The theory of mental captivity also discusses redundancy as a problem (ibid.: 12). The uncritical imitation of redundant propositions (that are already known) provides us with yet another aspect of irrelevance: that is, unimportance or triviality.

3. Another aspect of irrelevance is that of unaccordance or disparity as, for example, between assumptions and reality, a point that has been made by all the theories of social science referred to above.

4. Inapplicability, as in the inapplicability of a certain theory, is also an aspect of irrelevance. The theories of Orientalism, Eurocentrism and postcolonial criticism have shown how inapplicable theories are forced unwillingly on to data, which end up in the form of problematic constructions.

5. Irrelevance also connotes sophistry, perversion and mystification. Here

we talk of social science as irrelevant when it mystifies through false and vicious reasoning while being sophistical and appearing as sophisticated. The irrelevance lies in the ability of the social sciences to make attractive truth claims which are illogical, unsound, or groundless.

6. Irrelevance also implies inferiority. Here we refer to inferior, mediocre or shallow social science that gains a respectability in the non-Western outbacks that far outweighs its ideal powers.

7. The irrelevant, servile (alien, other-empowering) commitments of many social scientists to social science agendas originating from without is another type of irrelevance.

The contemporary social sciences also lack relevance in the sense that they are negligent towards the intellectual heritage of non-Western societies. By this I do not mean that the intellectual heritage of these societies (for example, Hindu thought or Islamic philosophy) are not studied. The problem is that they are not regarded as sources of concepts and ideas for the social sciences.

These types of irrelevance, when taken together as a whole, convey the notion of irrelevance as a feature of social science which, as we learn from the theories of Orientalism, academic dependency theory and post-colonial criticism, empowers others and not its practitioners or those on whose behalf they speak. Those who are empowered are colonizers and neo-colonizers, transnational capital, and authoritarian states, whether this comes about through the denigration of natives or the worship of capital. The result is the relegation and confinement of postcolonials to a 'secondary racial, cultural, ontological status' (Said, 1993: 70).

Existing sociological theories of knowledge do not raise the question of irrelevance to begin with and they do not provide a basis for typological and conceptual studies of irrelevance. The sociological approach to the issue of valid knowledge has not thus far raised irrelevance as an issue and as a category in the social sciences, for it is concerned with different issues to do with the social basis of knowledge. All the types of irrelevance listed above (as well as others not yet identified) can be regrouped into four categories of irrelevance derived from four sociological aspects of the cognitive process, thereby extending the sociological approach to a more exhaustive account of the problem of irrelevance:

1. Conceptual irrelevance. The study of the history and logic of concept formation in the social sciences reveals how concepts derived from one cultural language are elevated to the level of universal concepts and comparative dimensions, the application of which veils discrepancies between text and reality (Matthes, 1992). An example would be the use

of concepts from the sociology of religion such as church, sect and even religion itself to talk about Islam. Durkheim was possibly guilty of this. The manner in which he treated magic, for example, was according to the self-understanding of Christianity.[6] Irrelevance types IV and V are found in this category.

2. Value irrelevance. As mentioned earlier, the role of values in prioritizing research according to extra- or non-academic criteria must be taken into account in understanding the establishment and perpetuation of research agendas in the social sciences. An example of this problem comes from Egypt where researchers complain of funds being spent on surveys to find out what people think of the veil, a topic deemed to be of low priority.[7] Often, value commitments not rooted in the immediate surroundings of the researcher prevail. Irrelevance type VIII is found in this category.

3. Mimetic irrelevance. This refers to the uncritical adoption of theories, concepts and methods from external sources, which due to the uncritical and imitative treatment, results in redundance, mystification and mediocrity. Included in this category are irrelevance types II, III, VI and VII.

4. Topical irrelevance. This arises when what is problematic does not stand out but rather remains in the midst of expected familiarity, in the 'field of the unproblematic' (Schutz, 1970: 25). Irrelevance type I comes under this category.

It follows that what must be regarded as relevance is the reversal of all that has been presented above as irrelevance. Relevant social science would then refer to an original, significant (non-redundant), concordant (referring to concordance between assumption and reality), applicable, demystifying, and superior tradition.

Such a social science would be self-empowering to the extent that relevance implies the empowerment of the knowing subject, the practitioners of social science, or those on whose behalf they speak, rather than colonizers and neo-colonizers, transnational capital, and authoritarian states. We may, therefore theorise relevance by way of establishing sociological criteria of relevance. This may be done by putting into reverse the four categories of irrelevance which can be worked out as follows.

1. *Conceptual relevance*. This requires rethinking the universality of concepts and comparative dimensions by, first of all, establishing non-

---

6   Personal communication with Prof. Joachim Matthes, Singapore, September 13, 1997.
7   Personal communication with Dr Ezzat Hegazy, Cairo, June 1997.

dominant cultural languages as sources, and then working to develop truly universal or canopy categories. What would a sociology of religion look like if its concepts were derived from Islam rather than Christianity? The classification of religion may not include Catholicism and Protestantism under the same category of Christianity, because their doctrines and rituals differ too greatly to warrant their inclusion under one religion. Such a sociology of religion would be just as ethnocentric as the Eurocentric sociology of religion that it sets out to correct. The task would be to move beyond such one-sided constructions.

2. *Value relevance.* This refers to the selection of values that we establish as a criterion or standard for the selection of research topics, the drawing up of research agenda, and for policy-making.

3. *Mimetic relevance.* Mimesis can be turned into a virtue in the context of endogenous intellectual creativity which requires self-consciousness of the problem of irrelevance at both the individual and institutional levels.

4. *Topical relevance.* This requires the ability to discover problems, unfamiliarities, in the midst of the familiar or the 'field of the unproblematic'. An example is a Khaldunian theory of the stability of the Syrian state, or a Khaldunian theory of elite circulation in nineteenth-century Sudan.

4. New horizons for Asian sociology

In view of the preceding discussion on alternative discourses and the related problem of irrelevance, it becomes clear that the project of alternative discourses in Asian sociology is equivalent to the task of creating relevant sociology. This in turn requires tackling other problems that relate to the general academic environment as well as the cultural environment in which academic discourse takes place. These are discussed in what follows:

Alternative discourses as relevant social science. Projects to create alternative discourses in the social science, to make social science relevant, can only gain currency and legitimacy if their basis of criticism, the claim of irrelevance, finds a place in the philosophy of the social sciences. Thus far, this claim has tended to remain at the polemical level. The conceptualization of the problem of irrelevance and the systematic elaboration of the concept of relevance has not found its way into debates in the philosophy of social sciences or metaanalysis. As a result, the various calls for alternative discourses, which are founded upon the claim of irrelevance in mainstream social science, run the risk of being dismissed as vague prescriptions without a strong philosophical or theoretical basis.

If irrelevance lacks conceptualization so too does relevance. This is a very basic issue. If a certain problem such as irrelevance is not conceptualised and therefore understood in vague terms, then the solution to the problem, the inculcation of relevance, would of necessity be vague.

The more systematic, cogent and precise we are with respect to the notions of irrelevance and relevance, the more likely the relevance-seeking project is to consolidate into an intellectual movement, no doubt pluralistic in outlook but systematic and thorough in aims and approaches. The four sociological categories of irrelevance and relevance and the eight types of irrelevance enumerated above together constitute an effort to extend the sociological study of the social sciences to include the conceptual problem of irrelevance. This is one way in which problems of Third World social science can become focal concerns of the sociological study of knowledge.

Scholars of previous generations who identified problems of irrelevance are not to be faulted for not attempting such a conceptualization of relevance and irrelevance. The present work is an attempt to extend their concerns with the problem in a more conceptual direction.

Weeding out nativism. The problem of academic imperialism, mental captivity and the uncritical adoption of Western concepts and research agendas had been perceived as having become so pervasive in the social scientific traditions of developing societies that there have beene, from time to time, reactionary calls among critics of Western social science. The result is a high degree of intolerance toward the Western social sciences in terms of theories, methodologies, and the selection of problems. Consider the following viewpoint from a Muslim.

> The fact that concerns us here most is that all the social sciences of the West reflect social orders and have no relationship or relevance to Muslims, and even less to Islam. If we learn and apply Western social sciences, then we are not serious about Islam (Siddiqui, nd: 23).

This attitude can be captured under the notion of Orientalism in reverse or nativism. The idea of Orientalism in reverse was developed by the Syrian philosopher, Sadiq Jalal Al-'Azm. He quotes from the work of a fellow Syrian, Georges Saddikni, on the notion of man (Arabic. *insan*) which runs thus:

> The philosophy of Hobbes is based on his famous saying that 'every man is a wolf unto other men', while, on the contrary, the inner philosophy implicit in the

word insan preaches that "every man is a brother unto other men" (Saddikni, cited in Al-'Azm, 1984: 368).

Al-'Azm then continues with an assessment of the above:

> I submit that this piece of so-called analysis and comparison contains, in a highly condensed form, the entire apparatus of metaphysical abstractions and ideological mystifications so characteristic of Ontological Orientalism and so deftly and justly denounced in Said's book. The only new element is the fact that the Orientalist essentialist ontology has been reversed to favour one specific people of the Orient (Al-'Azm, 1984: 368).

Orientalism in reverse involves an essentialist approach to both Orient and Occident and is, therefore, a form of auto-Orientalism. This can be illustrated by the Japanese case. There is a tradition in Japanese sociology that is defined by *nihonjinron* (theories of Japanese people) which are informed by essentialized views on Japanese society, with the stress on cultural homogeneity and historical continuity. This remains squarely in the tradition of Western scholarship on Japan with the difference that the knowing subjects are Japanese. Hence the term auto-Orientalism as discussed by Lie (1996: 5).

The logical consequence of Orientalism in reverse and auto-Orientalism is nativism. This refers to the trend of going native among Western and local scholars alike in which the native's point of view is elevated to the status of the criterion by which descriptions and analyses are to be judged. This entails a near total rejection of Western knowledge.

Nevertheless, it has to be stressed that the various prescriptions for alternative discourses, particularly in the fields of anthropology, sociology and psychology, are opposed to nativistic approaches to knowledge.

The structure of academic dependency. Obstacles to the emergence of alternative discourses in the social sciences are varied but there are at least two which are universal. One concerns the structure of academic dependency. The structure of academic dependency is illustrated by the relative availability of Euroamerican funding for research, the generally greater prestige attached to publishing in American and British journals, and the higher premium placed on a Western university education, and a number of other indicators. There is also the question of the intellectual dependency on ideas. For example, it will be found that the social sciences in former British colonies are likely to be dominated by Anglo-Saxon theoretical traditions. Such a context presented by the structure of academic dependency is not conducive to the cultivation of alternative discourses.

But what are the possibilities of academic dependency reversal? One practice that would augur well for the emergence of alternative discourses by lessening reliance on European or American standards that may not be appropriate, and at the same time work towards the upgrading of local publication capabilities, is to emphasise the development of local publications such as journals, working papers and monograph series. It also frees academics from being tied to themes and research agendas that are determined by the contents of American and European publications. But this can only work if as much credit is given for locally published works by evaluators, and promotion and tenure committees as it is for American and European publications.

The cultural environment of academic discourse. The other obstacle to the emergence of alternative discourses is related to the intellectual culture in Asia. As far as this is concerned, what is needed is consciousness of the problem of mental captivity and the problems of an uncritically applied social science tradition. This consciousness can be inculcated through publications, seminars, public lectures and teaching in the universities. For example, a more universalistic approach to the teaching of sociological theory would have to raise the question as to whether sociological theory was found in premodern, non-European areas. There is also the matter of teaching the context of the rise of sociological theory which is not only defined by the series of political revolutions in Europe since the eighteenth-century or the industrial revolution, but also by colonization and the emergence of Eurocentrism. This in turn would imply changes in the way sociological theory is taught. For example, there would be more emphasis on Marx and Weber's Orientalist and Eurocentric dimensions.

In other words, even if some inroads are made towards dismantling the structure of academic dependency, in the final analysis what must change is the intellectual culture in Asian societies. This can only be brought about through a process of conscientizing. This in turn can only take place through the various media of intellectual socialization, including the schools, universities and other institutions of higher learning.

Bibliography

Alatas, S.H. (1972), 'The Captive Mind in Development Studies', *International Social Science Journal*, vol. 34, no. 1, pp. 67-87.
Alatas, S.H. (1974), 'The Captive Mind and Creative Development', *International Social Science Journal*, vol. 36, no. 4, pp. 691-9.

Alatas, S.H. (1981), 'Social Aspects of Endogenous Intellectual Creativity: The Problem of Obstacles - Guidelines for Research', in A. Abdel-Malek and A. N. Pandeya (eds), *Intellectual Creativity in Endogenous Culture*, United Nations University, Tokyo.

Alatas, S.F. (1993), 'On the Indigenization of Academic Discourse', *Alternatives*, vol. 18, no. 3, pp. 307-38.

Alatas, S.F. (1995a), *Dependency, Rhetorics and the Transnational Flow of Ideas in the Social Sciences*. Paper presented at the Goethe-Institute International Seminar on Cultural and Social Dimensions of Market Expansion, Labuan, October, pp. 16-7.

Alatas, S.F. (1995b), 'The Theme of 'Relevance' in Third World Human Sciences', *Singapore Journal of Tropical Geography*, vol. 16, no. 2, pp. 123-40.

Alatas, S.F. (1995c), 'The Sacralization of the Social Sciences: A Critique of an Emerging Theme in Academic Discourse', *Archives de Sciences Sociales des Religions*, vol. 91, pp. 1-23.

Al-`Azm, S.J. (1984), 'Orientalism and Orientalism in Reverse', in J. Rothschild (ed), *Forbidden Agendas: Intolerance and Defiance in the Middle East*, Al Saqi Books, London, pp. 349-76.

Al-e Ahmad, J. (nd), *Gharbzadegi (Weststruckness)*, Ravaq Press, Tehran.

Altbach, P.G. (1977), 'Servitude of the Mind? Education, Dependency, and Neocolonialism', *Teachers College Record*, vol. 79, no. 2, pp. 187-204.

Altbach, P.G. and Selvaratnam, V. (eds), (1989) *From Dependence to Autonomy: The Development of Asian Universities*, Kluwer Academic Publishers, Dordrecht.

Atal, Y. (1981), 'The Call for Indigenization', *International Social Science Journal*, vol. 33, no. 1, pp. 189-97.

Bell, M. (1994), 'Images, Myths and Alternative Geographies of the Third World', in G. Derek, M. Ron and G. Smith (eds), *Human Geography: Society, Space and Social Science*, Macmillan, London, pp. 174-99.

Bennagen, P.L. (1980), 'The Asianization of Anthropology', *Asian Studies*, vol. 18, pp. 1-26.

Boehmer, E. (1995), *Colonial and Postcolonial Literature*, Oxford University Press, Oxford.

Cesaire, A. (1972), *Discourse on Colonialism*, Monthly Review, New York.

Eades, J. (1997), *Anthropological Work on China in Japan in Comparative Perspective*. Paper presented at the International Workshop on Indigenous and Indigenized Anthropology in Asia, Leiden, May, pp. 1-3.

Enriquez, V.G. (1994), 'Towards Cross-Cultural Knowledge through Cross-Indigenous Methods and Perspective', in T.B. Obusan and A.R. Enriquez (eds), *Pamamaraan: Indigenous Knowledge and Evolving Research Paradigms*, University of the Philippines, Asian Center, Quezon City, pp. 19-31.

Evans, G. (1997), *Indigenous and Indigenised Anthropology in Asia*. Paper presented at the International Workshop on Indigenous and Indigenized Anthropology in Asia, Leiden, May, pp. 1-3.

Fahim, H. (1970), 'Indigenous Anthropolgy in Non-Western Countries', *Current Anthropology*, vol. 20, no. 2, p. 397.

Fahim, H. and Helmer, K. (1980), 'Indigenous Anthropology in Non-Western Countries: A Further Elaboration', *Current Anthropology*, vol. 21, no. 5, pp. 644-50.

Fanon, F. (1968), *The Wretched of the Earth*, Grove Press, New York.

Freire, P. (1970), *Pedagogy of the Oppressed*, Seabury Press, New York.

Garreau, F.H. (1985), 'The Multinational Version of Social Science with Emphasis upon the Discipline of Sociology', *Current Sociology*, vol. 33, no. 1, pp. 1-169.

Hettne, B. (1991), *The Voice of the Third World: Currents in Development Thinking, Studies on Developing Countries*, no. 134, Institute for World Economics of the Hungarian Academy of Sciences, Budapest.

Hudson, B. (1977), 'The New Geography and the New Imperialism, 1870-1918', *Antipode*, no. 9, pp. 12-19.

Illich, I.D. (1973), *Deschooling Society*, Penguin, Harmondsworth.

Kuwayama, T. and van Bremen, J. (1997), 'Kuwayama-van Bremen Debate: Native Anthropologists – With Special Reference to Japanese Studies Inside and Outside Japan', *Japan Anthropology Workshop Newsletter*, September, pp. 26-27.

Lee Chong, B. (1979), 'Prolegomenon to the Indigenization of Public Administration', *Social Science Journal*, no. 6, pp. 7-26.

Lie, J. (1996), 'Sociology of Contemporary Japan', *Current Sociology*, vol. 44, no. 1, pp. 1-95.

Matthes, J. (1992), 'The Operation Called 'Vergleichen', *Soziale Welt*, no. 8, pp. 75-99.

Memmi, A. (1965), *The Colonizer and the Colonized*, Beacon, Boston.

Parekh, B. (1992), 'The Poverty of Indian Political Theory', *History of Political Thought*, vol. 13, no. 3, pp. 535-60.

Pertierra, R. (1997), *Culture, Social Science and the Conceptualization of the Philippine Nation-State*. Paper presented at the International Workshop on Indigenous and Indigenized Anthropology in Asia, Leiden, May, pp. 1-3.

Pieris, R. 1969, 'The Implantation of Sociology in Asia', *International Social Science Journal*, vol. 21, no. 3, pp. 433-44.

Said, E. (1979), *Orientalism*, Vintage Books, New York.

Said, E. (1990), 'Third World Intellectuals and Metropolitan Culture', *Raritan*, vol. 9, no. 3, pp. 27-50.

Said, E. (1993), *Culture and Imperialism*, Vintage, London.

Schutz, A. (1970), *Reflections on the Problem of Relevance*, Yale University Press, New Haven.

Siddiqui, K. (nd), *The Islamic Movement: A Systems Approach*, Bonyad Be'that, Tehran.

Singh Uberoi, J.P. (1968), 'Science and Swaraj', *Contributions to Indian Sociology*, vol. 2, pp. 119-23.

Sinha, V. (1998), *Socio-Cultural Theory and Colonial Encounters: The Discourse on Indigenizing Anthropology in India*. Manuscript, Department of Sociology, National University of Singapore, Singapore.

Smail, J.R.W. (1961), 'On the Possibility of an Autonomous History of Modern Southeast Asia', *Journal of Southeast Asian History*, vol. 2, no. 2, pp. 73-105.

Taylor, P.J. (1993), 'Full Circle or New Meaning for Global', in R.J. Johnston (ed), *The Challenge for Geography: A Changing World, A Changing Discipline*, Blackwell, Oxford, pp. 181-97.

Weber, M. (1958), *The Religion of India: The Sociology of Hinduism and Buddhism*, H. Gerth and D. Martindale, transl. and eds, The Free Press, New York.

Zawiah, Y. (1994), *Resisting Colonialist Discourse*, Penerbit Universiti Kebangsaan Malaysia, Bangi.

Zghlal, A. and Karoui, H. (1973), 'Decolonization and Social Science Research: the Case of Tunisia', *Middle East Studies Association Bulletin*, vol. 7, no. 3, pp. 11-27.

Index

Contributors

Luigi Tomasi
Visiting Professor of Sociology at the Royal University of Phnom Penh, (academic year 2001-2002), Cambodia. He received his Ph.D. in Philosophy from The Catholic University of Milan and in Sociology from the University of Trento (Italy), where he works. The editor and author of several well-known monographs on the history of American sociological thought, his most recent publication on the subject is *The Tradition of the Chicago School of Sociology* (1998).

Raymond Boudon
Professor at the University of Paris, Sorbonne (France). He is a member of the Institut de France (Académie des Sciences morales et politiques), of the British Academy, of the Academia Europea, and of the American Academy of Arts and Sciences. His publications include: *Le juste et le vrai: études sur l'objectivité des valeurs et de la connaissance* (1995); *Études sur le sociologues classiques* (1998); *Le sens des valleurs* (1999).

Michel Wieviorka
Professor at the École des Hautes Études en Sciences Sociales (France) and Director of the Centre d'analyse et d'intervention sociologiques. He has published *The Making of Terrorism* (1993); *The Arena of Racism* (1995), and with Alain Touraine *The Working-Class Movement* (1987) in English, and some twenty books in French. He is also the founder and editor of the monthly journal *Le Monde des Débats*.

Shmuel N. Eisenstadt
Professor Emeritus at The Hebrew University of Jerusalem (Israel). He has written extensively on the themes of social theory and religion. Among his books are: *European Civilization in a Comparative Perspective: a Study in the Relations between Culture and Social Structure* (1987); *Comparative Social Problems* (1966); *Fundamentalism, Sectarianism and Revolution* (1999).

Nico Stehr
Senior Research Associate in the Sustainable Research Development Institute of the University of British Columbia (Canada). During the academic year 1999-2000 he was professor at the Mercador-Universität (Germany). His current research interests are reflected in his books *Practical Knowledge* (1992); *Knowledge Societies* (1994); *Governing Modern Societies* (with Richard V. Ericson, 2000).

Volker Meja
Professor of Sociology at the Memorial University of Newfoundland (Canada). His recent books include *Knowledge and Politics: The Sociology of Knowledge* (1990); *Karl Mannheim and the Crisis of Liberalism: The Secret of These New Times* (1995); *Sociology of Knowledge* (1999).

Pierpaolo Donati
Professor of Sociology at the University of Bologna (Italy) and Director of the Centro Interdisciplinare di Ricerca Sociale. His publications include *La società civile* (1997); *Verso una nuova cittadinanza della famiglia in Europa: problemi e prospettive di politica sociale* (1994); *La teoria relazionale della società* (1991).

Ulrich Beck
Professor of Sociology at the Ludwig Maximilian University, Munich (Germany) and at the London School of Economics, London (Great Britain). His publications include *Risikogesellschaft. Auf dem weg in eine andere Moderne* (1986); *Individualisierung und Integration: neue Konfliktlinien und neuer Integrations modus?* (1997); *Was is Globalisierung? Irrtumer des Globalismus-Antworten auf Globalisierung* (1997).

Zdzisław Krasnodębski
He taught sociology and philosophy at the University of Warsaw (Poland). Since 1995 he is Professor of Eastern European Cultural History at the University of Bremen (Germany).His main publications are: *Understanding of Human Behaviour* (1986); *The Decline of the Idea of Progress* (1991); *The Postmodern Cultural Dilemmas* (1996); *Max Weber* (in Polish).

Talis Tisenkopfs
Head of the Department of Sociology at the University of Latvia (Latvia) and project director of the Institute of Philosophy and Sociology at the same university. Editor in-chief of the annual *Latvia Human Development*. His recent publications are *Latvia Human Development Reports* (1998, 1999, 2000); *National, State and Regime in Latvia* (2000).

Steven Grosby
Associate Professor of Philosophy and Religion at Clemson University (USA). He is the author of *Biblical Idea of Nationality: Ancient and Modern* (2000) and the translator and editor of Hans Freyer, *Theory of Objective Mind: an Introduction to the Philosophy of Culture* (1998). He has also edited two volumes of selected writings by Edward A. Shils, *The Calling of Education* (1997) and *The Virtue of Civility* (1997).

Thomas Faist
Lecturer at the Institute for International Studies (inIIS) at the University of Bremen (Germany). His recent books include *Social Citizenship for Whom? Young Turks in Germany and Mexican Americans in the United States* (1995); *Migration, Immobility and Development. Multidisciplinary Perspective* (1997); *The Volume and Dynamics of International Migration and Transnational Social Spaces* (2000).

Edward A. Tiryakian
Professor of Sociology at Duke University (USA). He has published extensively in the areas of modernization and the comparative aspects of development and national identity in Asia and Europe. His publications include *New Nationalism of the Development West, Toward   Explanation* (1985); *Theoretical Sociology Perspectives and Development* (1970); *The Global Crisis: Sociological Analysis and Responses* (1984).

Anthony J. Blasi
Professor of Sociology at the Tennessee State University (USA) and 2000-2001 President of the Association for the Sociology of Religion. His recent books are *A Sociological of Johannine Christianity* (1996); *Religion and Seniors' Mental Health* (1999). At present he is co-editing a handbook on early Christianity and the social sciences and writing a history of the Notre Dame University programme.

Yves Lambert
Research Director of the Group for Sociology of Religion and Laicity (CNRS-EPHE) (France). He has studied the evolution of a Breton parish from 1900 until the present day. He has carried out a large-scale survey on French rural youth and analyses for the European Values Surveys (1981, 1990, 1999). He is now preparing a book on the comparative sociology of religions. His main publications are *Dieu change en Bretagne* (1985); *The Scope and Limits of Religious Functions According to the European Values and ISSP Surveys* (1998).

Dirk Kaesler
Professor of Sociology at Philipps-Universität, Marburg (Germany) and President of the Research Committee on the History of Sociology in the International Sociological Association (ISA). Among the publications are *Max Weber. Eine Einfuhrung in Leben, Werk und Wirkung* (1995); *Soziologie als Berufung. Bausteine einer selbstbewuBten Soziologie* (1997); *Klasssiker der Soziologie* (1999).

Syed Farid Alatas
Lecturer in sociology at the National University of Singapore (Singapore). He has contributed articles to a number of scholarly journals and in 1997 published the book *Democracy and Authoritarianism in The Rise of the Post-Colonial State in Indonesia and Malaysia.*